T0247815

FREE AND EQUAL

FREE AND EQUAL

A MANIFESTO FOR A JUST SOCIETY

Daniel Chandler

Alfred A. Knopf

New York | 2024

THIS IS A BORZOI BOOK
PUBLISHED BY ALFRED A. KNOPF

www.aaknopf.com

Knopf, Borzoi Books, and the colophon are registered trademarks of
Penguin Random House LLC.

Library of Congress Cataloging-in-Publication Data
Names: Chandler, Daniel (Economist), author.
Title: Free and equal : a manifesto for a just society /
Daniel Chandler.
Description: London ; New York : Allen Lane, 2023. |
Includes bibliographical references and index. |
Identifiers: LCCN 2023027089 (print) | LCCN 2023027090 (ebook) |
ISBN 9780593801680 (hardcover) | ISBN 9780593801697 (ebook)
Subjects: LCSH: Rawls, John, 1921–2002. | Equality. | Democracy.
Classification: LCC JC575 .C475 2023 (print) | LCC JC575 (ebook) |
DDC 320.01/1—dc23/eng/20230812
LC record available at https://lccn.loc.gov/2023027089
LC ebook record available at https://lccn.loc.gov/2023027090

Jacket design by John Gall

Manufactured in the United States of America
1st Printing

For Martha, Charlie and Irie

Coco, Eloise and Max

Ira, Peggy and Dash

CONTENTS

PREFACE TO THE AMERICAN EDITION

As the world's oldest continuous democracy, America has much to be proud of. Its founding ideal—of a self-governing community of free and equal citizens—was revolutionary in its time, and, however imperfectly achieved, has inspired advocates for freedom and democracy around the world ever since.

And yet today, the world finds itself looking to America for all the wrong reasons. Although many rich democracies face common challenges—cultural polarization, loss of trust in politics, inequality, ecological crisis—on nearly every dimension these problems are at their most extreme in America. Indeed, the recent history of the United States is a cautionary tale of the dangers of unbridled capitalism and its capacity to corrupt democracy, stunt opportunity, and sow social discord and unrest.

A huge amount has been written about the nature and causes of these problems, and we now have an increasingly sophisticated diagnosis of our current ills. What has been missing—and what I hope this book can provide—is a coherent vision of what a better, fairer society would look like.

This isn't just a question of new policies, important though that is. We need a new philosophy—a vision of the common good that builds on, rather than rejects, the core values of liberal democracy, and which can inspire people to transform their societies for the better. But while politicians like Ronald Reagan and Margaret Thatcher—the architects of "neoliberalism"—could look to thinkers like Milton Friedman and Friedrich Hayek, to whom can we look for fresh inspiration today?

The premise of this book is that the ideas we need lie in the work of arguably America's greatest ever political philosopher: John Rawls.

Rawls is the towering figure of twentieth-century political thought—someone who is routinely compared to the most important thinkers in the Western tradition, from Plato to John Locke, Adam Smith, and John Stuart Mill. What makes his ideas so vital right now is that they are fundamentally hopeful and constructive, providing us with what Rawls calls a "realistic utopia"—an achievable vision of the best that a democratic society can be. They are both a vital antidote to widespread cynicism and an unparalleled resource for developing a unifying and transformative progressive politics.

Rawls's philosophy is also fundamentally easy to grasp and surprisingly practical. At its heart is the idea that society should be fair, and that to work out what that means we should imagine how we would organise society if we didn't know our position within it—whether we would be Black or white, gay or straight, rich or poor—as if behind a "veil of ignorance."

If we imagined society in this way, he argued, we would choose two simple but powerful principles, to do with freedom and equality respectively. As we shall see, these principles offer us a toolkit for navigating the most important issues that animate our public discourse, from questions about free speech and the role of money in politics to debates about racial and gender inequality, the climate crisis and the future of capitalism.

While Rawls was writing in the 1970s, his ideas are more relevant today than ever. At a time when individual freedom and democracy are under attack from the right, and where basic liberal values are regarded with suspicion on parts of the left, they offer a much-needed affirmation of a free, tolerant, and democratic society, where people with different beliefs about religion and morality live together in a spirit of mutual respect, and where we agree to resolve our differences peacefully through the ballot box.

Crucially, they also show us how we can combine freedom and democracy with true economic justice. As we shall see, Rawls's ideas point towards a new economic paradigm—one in which we harness the benefits of markets for all, right down to the least well off, and secure for each and every citizen not just the opportunity to pursue their dreams but also the essential conditions for dignity and self-respect.

These ideas offer the basis for the kind of galvanising and broad-based vision that has been missing from progressive politics for a generation. They represent a unifying alternative to divisive forms of "identity politics," combining the deep respect for different ways of living which is the key to transcending the culture wars with an economic agenda that would address the long-neglected concerns of lower-income voters, not simply for higher incomes, but for a sense of independence, meaning, and social recognition.

Rawls's philosophy, then, provides the moral foundations for reimaging liberal democracy in America and beyond. But philosophy alone is not enough. If we want to change society we must combine abstract principles with a practical agenda for reform. While Rawls said relatively little about such questions, in my capacity as both an economist and philosopher, they are at the heart of this book. In the process of writing it, I have looked around the world for the most promising examples of how we could do things differently—from new forms of participatory democracy in Brazil to experiments with a universal basic income around the world and the German model of co-management, in which workers share power with owners. There is no shortage of ideas about how we could improve our societies. What is missing is the political will to make change happen.

At a moment of deep social division and even crisis, it might seem naïve to turn to philosophy. But as Rawls argued, it's precisely in moments like this, "when our shared political understandings . . . break down," that we need philosophy the most. The questions that divide American society most deeply today—about the scope and limits of individual freedom, and the economic obligations we have towards our fellow citizens and future generations—are fundamentally moral ones. The task of philosophy is, as Rawls put it, to "focus on deeply disputed questions and to see whether, despite appearances, some underlying basis of philosophical and moral agreement can be uncovered." While we're unlikely to agree on everything, we can at least hope to narrow our differences "so that social cooperation on a footing of mutual respect among citizens can still be maintained."[1]

Like other democratic societies, America has faced periods of impasse before, when it has been divided at the deepest level—the Civil War, the Great Depression, struggles over civil rights in the 1960s. The immediate resolution to these conflicts came from mass political action, not philosophy; and it is through democratic politics that we must strive to find a peaceful way out of the challenges we face today. But as in those periods, the challenge facing progressives in America and beyond is not simply to win votes but to change minds: to forge a new consensus about our guiding values, how to interpret them, and how to make them a reality.

FREE AND EQUAL

Introduction

What would a fair society look like?

Most of us—and by "us" I mean citizens of the world's rich democracies—would agree that the societies we live in are far from fair. Although we don't all agree on exactly *what* is unfair about them, many of us would point to a familiar list of problems: a political system dominated by the rich; the profound influence that class, race and gender continue to have on people's opportunities; the enormously unequal distribution of money, power and social prestige; and a rapidly unfolding climate and ecological catastrophe that threatens the ecosystems on which we and future generations depend.

These problems lie at the root of a growing sense of discontent with liberal democracy as we know it. Across the world, trust in politicians and satisfaction with democracy is at a historic low, and politics is increasingly volatile. This discontent has given rise to an authoritarian populism that now poses the most serious threat to liberal democratic values since the Second World War. From Donald Trump in the U.S.A. to Marine Le Pen in France, and from Jair Bolsonaro in Brazil to Narendra Modi in India, right-wing populists have assumed increasingly prominent roles in national politics and seem determined to roll back basic freedoms and undermine the democratic process. In the wake of Russia's brutal invasion of

Ukraine in February 2022, and with the rise of an increasingly autocratic and assertive China on the global stage, the future of liberal democracy is deeply uncertain.

It's all too easy to decry the state of politics and society today, and there is no shortage of commentary about how and why we have reached this point. What is much harder to find is a coherent vision of what a better, fairer society would look like. Our public debate is divided between an established political class that seems broadly content with the status quo, and more radical critics on both the left and right who appear to want to overthrow it altogether. In this book, I will argue that liberal democracy *is* worth defending, but that we cannot maintain the status quo, and nor should we want to. Rather, we need to recover a sense of the transformative potential of liberal and democratic ideals, and use them to articulate a vision of a better society that people will stand up and fight for.

This kind of vision is sorely lacking. Since the 1980s and the rise of "neoliberalism"—an outlook characterized by an almost religious faith in markets and an overriding focus on economic growth— our political discourse has become increasingly narrow and technocratic. This period stands out for its distinct lack of idealism and imagination, as questions about our values and ideals as a society, and how we can realize them, have been pushed to the sidelines. We have, in the words of the philosopher Roberto Unger, been living under a "dictatorship of no alternatives."[1] This is not a problem only for those of us who think our societies stand in need of far-reaching reform. It is this moral and ideological vacuum at the heart of our politics that has made space for the rise of illiberal, anti-democratic populism.[2]

Of course, debate hasn't stopped entirely, but there is a sense in which the broad outlines of our political and economic institutions have taken on an air of inevitability, and it has become increasingly difficult to think or talk about big ideas that would really change our societies for the better. In the absence of a clear alternative, moments of crisis—moments, historically, that have so often been powerful catalysts of progress—have largely come and gone. Almost fifteen years since the 2008 financial crisis laid bare the excesses of market fundamentalism, what stands out is just how little has changed; and while the Covid pandemic has shone a spotlight on the deadly human cost of entrenched social inequality and underfunded public services, talk of "building back better" seems all too likely to come to nothing. The result is a paradoxical sense of stasis—paradoxical because there is a real appetite for change; and, for better or worse, some kind of change seems all but inevitable.

There have been some promising signs of intellectual renewal. The growing sense of crisis across the world's liberal democracies has created space for fresh thinking, and we are starting to see a shift from diagnosis to solutions, with increasing interest in some pretty radical ideas, from citizens' assemblies to a universal basic income. What is missing, however, is an underlying ethical or ideological framework that can bring often rather disparate policy proposals into a coherent whole. This will be impossible to achieve unless we go back to first principles and reflect on some unavoidably moral and philosophical questions about what is just and what is fair, and about what it means to live together as free and equal citizens in a democratic society. In light of the urgent problems we face—poverty and inequality, war, an ecological crisis—it's tempting to dismiss this as an intellectual indulgence. But it is nothing of the sort: it is an essential starting point for developing a truly transformative politics. After all, without a clear idea of where we want to get to, how can we know that we are on the right course? And how can we muster the energy to do the difficult political work that is needed to get there? At stake is more than just the next election—it is the chance to shape a public philosophy for the post-neoliberal age.

In taking up this challenge, we are immediately confronted by an apparent lack of intellectual reference points. Most people would struggle to name a major recent thinker who could rival the likes of Friedrich Hayek or Milton Friedman—the pioneers of neoliberalism whose ideas underpinned the politics of Margaret Thatcher and Ronald Reagan in the 1980s and continue to shape our public debate.[3] Indeed, you would be forgiven for thinking that the past few decades have been a rather sterile period for political thought, and that we need to start again from scratch. And yet this could not be further from the truth. The optimistic message of this book is that the ideas we need are hiding in plain sight, in the work of the twentieth century's greatest political philosopher, John Rawls.

Although many people haven't heard of Rawls, his ideas revolutionized political philosophy, and he is perhaps the only thinker of the past hundred years whose place in the canon of Western political thought is universally accepted, alongside the likes of Plato, Thomas Hobbes, Adam Smith and Karl Marx. This reputation rests above all on his book *A Theory of Justice*, whose publication in 1971 marked a watershed moment in the history of political ideas. Rawls set out to develop a picture of the best that a democratic society could be—a "realistic utopia," as he put it.[4] In doing so, he achieved what many had thought to be impossible, or even a contradiction in terms: whereas politics and philosophy had long been divided between a classical liberal tradition that prized individual freedoms above all else, and a socialist tradition that was often willing to sacrifice these freedoms in the name of equality, Rawls articulated a philosophy that was committed to both freedom *and* equality at the deepest level.[5] His ideas define a humane and egalitarian liberalism— a much-needed alternative to the harsh neoliberalism that dominates our political discourse. In his work, we have an unparalleled, and as yet untapped, intellectual resource for responding to the crises we face today.

So who was Rawls, and where did his ideas come from? John Rawls— "Jack" to his friends—was born into a moderately affluent middle-class household in Baltimore, Maryland, on 21 February 1921, the second of five sons. His mother, Anna Abele Rawls, was an accomplished and politically active woman, and an early chapter president of the newly founded League of Women Voters in Baltimore.[6] His father, William Lee Rawls, was a highly respected and successful lawyer. Rawls's early childhood was marked by the tragic deaths of two of his younger brothers, Bobby and Tommy, one of whom died after contracting diphtheria from him, an experience that left him with a deep appreciation of the role of luck in shaping our lives.[7] Despite his comfortable upbringing, as an adult Rawls recalled how his sense of injustice had been awakened by his mother's struggle for women's rights, and by a growing awareness of poverty and racism as he made friends with other, less privileged children, sometimes to the disapproval of his parents.[8]

Rawls excelled at school, and in 1939 he enrolled at Princeton

University, where he tried his hand at subjects including chemistry, music, maths and even art history before deciding to major in philosophy. At Princeton, he developed a strong interest in theology and ethics, planning to attend divinity school and become a priest in the Episcopal Church. But these plans were interrupted by the Second World War. After graduating in 1943, Rawls enrolled as a private in the infantry, where he trained as a radio signaller before being deployed to New Guinea, the Philippines and finally Japan. The young Rawls experienced the violence and inhumanity of war first-hand: his division was involved in intense combat (he was awarded a Bronze Star for dangerous work behind enemy lines), and he passed through the remains of Hiroshima shortly after it was devastated by an American atomic bomb in August 1945.

Rawls's experiences as a soldier and his growing awareness of the atrocities of the Holocaust provoked a profound crisis of faith, leading him to abandon his Christian beliefs and ambitions. In 1946, he returned to Princeton as a graduate student in philosophy, motivated by a new set of questions which would come to shape his life's work. In the face of the bloodshed and cruelty of the war, Rawls found himself asking whether human life on Earth was really redeemable. If God cannot be the basis for our faith in the possibility of a just society, then what can be? What, exactly, does justice require of us? And is a just society realistically achievable?

Rawls devoted the rest of his life to answering these questions. He spent twenty years developing his ideas before publishing *A Theory of Justice* in 1971, at the age of fifty.[9] The reception was unprecedented for a densely argued work of philosophy spanning 600 pages.[10] It was reviewed not just in academic publications but in mainstream newspapers such as the *New York Times*, where it was described as a "peerless contribution to political theory" and listed as one of the five most significant books of the year.[11] The book's historical importance was instantly recognized, and it was widely lauded as a work the likes of which had not been seen since John Stuart Mill, or even Immanuel Kant.[12] This assessment has stood the test of time: nearly forty years later, the philosopher G. A. Cohen wrote that there are "at most two books in the history of Western political philosophy [that] have a claim to be regarded as greater than *A Theory of Justice*: Plato's *Republic* and Hobbes's *Leviathan*."[13] Rawls spent the rest of his life defending, refining and, in some cases, amending the body of ideas he set out in *A Theory of Justice*, including writing a second major book, *Political Liberalism*, published in 1993, just under a decade before his death at the age of eighty-one.

Tributes mourned the passing not simply of an intellectual giant but of a much-loved husband and father of four, and a person of singular moral character. The picture that emerges of Rawls from his friends, colleagues and former students is of a quiet, private man who spent most of his time at work or with family and close friends; a dedicated and conscientious teacher who encouraged female philosophers in a male-dominated field; and, despite his achievements, an individual of remarkable humility. Reflecting on Rawls's "legendary" modesty and kindness, the philosopher Michael Sandel recalled receiving a phone call during his first days as a young assistant professor at Harvard in the early 1980s. "A hesitant voice on the other end said: 'This is John Rawls, R-A-W-L-S.' It was as if God himself had called to invite me to lunch, and spelled his name just in case I didn't know who he was."[14]

It's almost impossible to overstate Rawls's influence within academia. Before Rawls, political philosophy, at least in the Anglo-American tradition, was more concerned with linguistic analysis of concepts than with substantive questions about how we should organize society—so much so that the respected historian of political thought Peter Laslett had famously declared in 1956 that "For the moment, anyway, political philosophy is dead."[15] After the publication of *A Theory of Justice*, no one could make such a claim. Rawls's work provided a model of constructive and systematic political thinking which inspired a new generation, leading to "an outpouring of philosophical literature on social, political, and economic justice unmatched in the history of thought."[16] He shaped this literature in a profound way—defining both the questions that were asked and how people went about answering them. Of course, as with any great thinker, his ideas were fiercely contested, but as Robert Nozick, one of Rawls's leading contemporaries (and critics) put it in 1974, "Political philosophers now must either work within Rawls's theory, or explain why not." To a large extent, the same continues to be true today.[17]

And yet, Rawls's ideas have had little impact on real politics. Beyond those who have studied philosophy, there is little awareness of his work: in the words of Rawls's former student Samuel Freeman—a distinguished philosopher in his own right—Rawls's influence outside academia has been "nil."[18] While some "third way" thinkers flirted with his ideas in the 1980s, this largely came to nothing, and there was little evidence of his idealism or economic radicalism in the politics of Bill Clinton or Tony Blair in the 1990s and 2000s.[19] Since then, Rawls has been largely overlooked within mainstream political debate.[20] In fact, it's hard to think of any other political thinker where there is such a large gap between their influence within the academy and in society at large.

How can we explain this puzzling fact? First, there is Rawls's personality. Rawls disliked public speaking, in part because he suffered from a stammer that developed as a boy after the death of his younger brothers. In contrast to some of his better-known contemporaries, he had little interest in playing the role of "public intellectual." He almost never gave interviews; he routinely declined public awards and invitations; and he rarely commented in public on topical political issues.[21]

Rawls's lack of purchase on real politics also reflects the abstract nature of his work. Rawls was a philosopher's philosopher. He was interested in asking the deepest, most fundamental questions. What is justice? What is the nature of democratic legitimacy? How can we balance the demands of freedom and equality? Although his aim was to develop principles that could help us determine how to organize society, he said relatively little about what this might look like in practice, believing that was a job best left to social scientists.[22]

Finally, there is the wider political context in which Rawls was writing. One of the ironies of Rawls's legacy is that just as his ideas were coming to dominate political philosophy, politics was moving in the opposite direction with the rise of Reagan and Thatcher. Rawls's strongly egalitarian liberalism seemed oddly out of step with the times. In the period since, his potential as the basis for a new political direction has been obscured by misunderstandings that have led some to dismiss his ideas as little more than a nostalgic defence of post-war America.[23]

Looked at another way, though, the gap between Rawls's unrivalled stature within philosophy and his lack of public impact may not be as strange as it seems. It often takes a generation or two before truly great thinkers filter through into popular consciousness: although Adam Smith was writing in the second half of the eighteenth century, it wasn't until the nineteenth century that his writing really shaped an emerging classical liberal politics; and while Marx was influential as a writer in the nineteenth century, his ideas had their greatest impact in the communist revolutions and societies of the twentieth century.[24] Now, for the first time since the publication of A Theory of Justice more than half a century ago, there is an urgent need and appetite for systematic political thinking on a scale that only a philosopher like Rawls can provide—and his ideas are uniquely suited to the challenges we face today.

For all the richness and complexity of Rawls's writings, at the heart of his theory of justice is a strikingly simple and powerful idea: that society should be fair. If we want to know what this would look like, he argued, we should ask ourselves what kind of world we would choose to live in if we didn't know who we would be within it—rich or poor, Christian or Muslim, gay or straight. Rawls proposed that we could use this thought experiment, which he called the "original position," to identify a clear set of principles that could guide us in designing our major social and political institutions. If we chose our principles in this way, he argued, as if behind a "veil of ignorance," they would be fair, in the same way that someone might cut a cake more fairly if they didn't know which piece they would end up getting.

Rawls argued that we would select two fundamental principles, concerned with freedom and equality respectively, alongside a further principle of "intergenerational" justice and sustainability. First, we would choose to protect our most important personal and political liberties, including freedom of conscience, speech and association, as well as equal voting rights and opportunities to influence the political process more broadly. After all, if we didn't know who we would end up being in society, we wouldn't want to risk being persecuted for our religious beliefs or sexual preferences, or being denied the right to vote because of our gender or the colour of our skin.

This first principle—the "basic liberties principle"—is what makes Rawls's theory distinctively liberal, and it provides the basis for designing a democratic constitution and political system. His second principle, which has two interlocking parts, provides a framework for thinking about our social and economic structures, and it is this principle that gives his theory its distinctively egalitarian flavour. All of us, he argued, would want to live in a society where everyone has a fair chance to succeed in life, irrespective of their class, race or gender. This notion—which Rawls referred to as "fair equality of opportunity"—isn't just about preventing discrimination, but about giving everyone a truly equal chance to develop and employ their talents and abilities. At the same time, Rawls argued that we would permit inequalities only where they ultimately benefit everyone—say, by encouraging innovation and growth—and that we would organize our economy so as to maximize the life chances of the least well off: something he called the "difference principle." If those who have the least could accept that society is fair, he argued, then surely those who have more could do so too.

Alongside these two principles we would recognize our obligations towards future generations by adopting the "just savings principle," according to which we have an overriding duty to maintain the material wealth and vital ecosystems on which society depends. Whatever we do to increase prosperity and raise the living standards of the least well off must be consistent with this basic commitment to social and environmental stewardship.

I imagine this brief summary will have raised as many questions as it answers. Why is the "original position" the right way to think about fairness? Would we really choose these principles over all the other alternatives? Which freedoms should be counted as "basic liberties"? How exactly can inequality benefit everyone?

In the first part of this book we will unpack Rawls's key philosophical ideas, and respond to various criticisms and misunderstandings of them. But my aim is not merely to describe or explain these concepts; rather, it is to use and apply them. So, in the second part of this book, we will pick up where Rawls left off, looking at how far our actual societies fall short of his inspiring ideal and, crucially, developing a bold, practical agenda that would make it a reality. In doing so, we will see how Rawls's theory can help us not just to defend but to reimagine liberalism—both as a set of values and as a way of organizing society.

Why is liberalism worth defending?

In recent years, "liberal" has become a term of abuse on both left and right. In the popular imagination, liberalism is almost synonymous with the mainstream political establishment; and, for many people, criticizing it has become something of a catch-all for expressing discontent with the state of society today. Among the various criticisms, two main lines of attack stand out. The first—what we might call the "egalitarian" critique—associates liberal ideas with an overriding commitment to free-market capitalism. The problem with liberalism, on this view, is that it leads to economic structures that are the source of so many of the problems we face—poverty, inequality, insecurity, the climate crisis. A second line of attack, more common on the right, though evident across the political spectrum, is the belief that liberalism is grounded in an individualistic conception of human nature that fails to recognize the importance of family, community and religion in our lives. On this view—often referred to as the "communitarian" critique—liberal ideas are held at least partly responsible for problems ranging from rampant consumerism to family breakdown, and for a wider sense of social and spiritual alienation.

These criticisms deserve to be taken seriously. They highlight real issues, and they are not entirely wrong in pointing the finger at something called "liberalism." But liberalism is not a single set of ideas or policies, it is a broad and evolving intellectual and political tradition—something its critics often fail to recognize. Such strictures are best understood as criticisms not of liberalism per se, but of neoliberalism.[25]

Rawls's philosophy defines a vastly more attractive liberalism which can respond to these concerns. As we shall see, he provides one of the most searching critiques of capitalism developed by any liberal thinker, and a powerful argument for a more humane, equal and sustainable society. And far from celebrating selfish individualism, it is cooperation and reciprocity that are the cornerstones of Rawls's theory—a theory which recognizes the vital role that family, community and religion play in most of our lives.

Contrary to what most people think, it is the egalitarian liberalism of Rawls and the generation of philosophers who have developed and refined his ideas which represent the mainstream of liberal political philosophy today.[26] Indeed, it is surprisingly hard to find a serious philosophical defence of the kind of individualism or market fundamentalism that so many people have come to associate with liberalism. That this is not more widely recognized reflects, at least in part, a failure on the part of contemporary philosophers—including Rawls—to communicate more widely and to engage directly with the pressing political issues of the day.

Such engagement is essential, because reinventing liberalism as an intellectual tradition is not an end in itself but the first step in developing a truly progressive politics that can bring about a better society. In using the term "progressive" here, I don't want to suggest that this book is addressed to a specific political party or grouping: part of what is so appealing about Rawls's ideas is that they transcend, or at least blur, some of the familiar dividing lines within our societies. Engaging with his thinking is an opportunity for each of us—whomever we vote for, and whether we tend to identify as liberals, conservatives, socialists, greens, or none of the above—to take a fresh look at our views about politics and society.

Having said that, the ideas in this book will feel most familiar to those on the broadly "progressive" or "left" wing of the political spectrum. In part, this is because Rawls's principles invite us to change our most basic political and economic institutions—how we organise the democratic process, the role of government and markets in society—sometimes in rather fundamental ways. In this sense, they represent an alternative to the strong deference to tradition that is one of the defining features of "conservative" political thought. They are also "progressive" in the sense that they embrace a strong commitment to a diverse, tolerant and substantially more equal society.

And yet, although emphatically egalitarian, Rawls's theory also represents an alternative to the socialist tradition. This is not to disparage socialism, at least not in its democratic form.[27] There is a long history of fruitful dialogue between egalitarian liberals and democratic socialists—indeed, these two traditions have much in common; and in recent years self-described "socialists"—those inspired by the likes of Jeremy Corbyn in the UK, or Bernie Sanders and Alexandria Ocasio-Cortez in the U.S.A.—have been an important source of dynamism within the wider progressive family. But socialist politics still has a tendency towards statism and a somewhat dogmatic hostility to markets and private enterprise; and although today's socialists often have a strong sense of what they are *against*—inequality, poverty, capitalism—it's less obvious what exactly they are *for*, or what the long-term goal is towards which socialism can lead.[28] The result is a politics that lacks a deeper sense of coherence. This is not simply an intellectual problem—it is a real obstacle to electoral success. One of the principal criticisms of the Labour Party's "socialist" manifesto under Jeremy Corbyn's leadership in the 2019 UK general election was that although it was full of individually popular policies, such as increasing taxes on high earners and nationalizing the railways, it read more like a wish list than a cohesive programme for a better society.

While Rawls's ideas can bring greater coherence and ambition to progressive politics, they also show us how we can bridge some of the social and cultural divides in our societies. A common criticism of progressive politics today is that it has become a form of "identity politics," by which I mean that it aims to advance the interests of specific groups—women, Black people, the disabled, the LGBTQ+ community—*instead* of an inclusive idea of the common good. Such disapproval is often overblown: campaigns like "Black Lives Matter" are not about privileging the interests of one group over another but about securing for Black and other minorities the rights and opportunities that the rest of us take for granted. If anything, it is the rise of white nationalism on the right that represents identity politics in its truest and most dangerous form. In any case, Rawls's principles represent a unifying alternative to identity politics of any kind. This doesn't mean abandoning the struggle for, say, racial justice or gay rights; and there is nothing wrong with disadvantaged groups organizing themselves to fight for their rights—indeed, this has often been a vital source of progress. Rather, it means being clearer that these struggles are part of a wider project of realizing universal values. At the same time, Rawls's ideas show us how we can overcome the false choice between protecting the rights of specific groups and developing an economic agenda that would benefit them all. Any meaningful progressive politics must do both.

One of the most striking trends in recent decades has been the way in which politics has increasingly come to be shaped by differences in personal values and culture—like the divide between what the writer David Goodhart has memorably referred to as "anywheres" and "somewheres."[29] Mainstream progressive parties have come to be dominated by people with a more "culturally liberal" outlook—often younger, more educated, less religious and living in cities—and have struggled to connect with citizens of a more "traditional" or "conservative" sensibility—often older, less educated, more religious and living in small towns or the countryside. Perhaps more than any other liberal thinker, Rawls explicitly sought to appeal to people with very different moral and religious beliefs, and his philosophy can help us to reach across these fault lines.

Rawls's ideas also provide the basis for a progressive politics that is genuinely transformative. As we shall see, each of his principles has far-reaching, real-world implications: his basic liberties principle calls for radical reforms to how we fund political parties and the media, and to engage citizens more directly in the democratic process; while his second principle, in combination with his commitment to sustainability through the just savings principle, provides the basis for a fundamental reshaping of our economic institutions. Indeed, it is in this last arena where we really see the profound implications of his ideas. Our first priority must be to avert ecological and climate breakdown while there is still time, and to bring about the transition to a truly sustainable society—a transformation that will change almost every aspect of how we live, and which is a precondition for the survival not just of liberal democracy but of humanity itself. At the same time, we must embrace an economic agenda that will not only tackle discrimination and achieve equality of opportunity, but also address inequality at its source, hand real power to workers and ensure that everyone has the opportunity for meaningful and dignified work.

Over the course of this book, we will assemble a comprehensive programme that would reinvigorate our democracy and transform our economy. The aim, in the end, is to use Rawls's theory to construct a "realistic utopia": to describe a set of institutions that are the best we can hope for, given what we know about human nature and the constraints of the natural world. In doing so, I hope to dispel the pessimism that is holding back our societies, as if our hands are tied by rigid economic laws and large-scale reform is doomed to failure. As we shall see, such pessimism simply isn't warranted: there are plenty of exciting and workable ideas about how we could do things differently, and we will use Rawls's principles as a framework for bringing the most promising proposals into one place, drawing on lessons from history, evidence from the social sciences (including my own discipline, economics), and inspiring examples from around the world. This will take us well beyond Rawls's own brief and often tentative remarks about the practical implications of his ideas; in some cases, we will even have to depart from what Rawls himself wrote. After all, his comments are not the final word—how could they be? The problems we face, and our understanding of the world, are always changing and evolving, and in applying his principles we should always strive to rely on the best available information. While no institution is perfect, and we cannot know for sure how new policies will work until we try them, the case for change is overwhelming. Ultimately, the real obstacles to reform are political not practical.

It's important to state at the outset that Rawls's principles, and the proposals put forward in this book, are simply a contribution to democratic deliberation—a set of arguments to be discussed and debated. This might seem obvious, but a common reaction to Rawls, and to political philosophy more broadly, is that they are somehow an "elitist" attempt to pre-empt democratic debate. Why should we accept one philosopher's opinion as the basis for organizing society? Shouldn't we leave these matters to the people? Given the dismissive attitude that political elites often take towards the views of "ordinary" citizens, these concerns are entirely reasonable. But, in a democratic society, the arguments proffered by political philosophers are just that—arguments; and the audience for them is not an all-powerful state but citizens at large. Although I will propose specific reforms, my aim is not to draw up a fixed blueprint but to demonstrate the power and flexibility of Rawls's theory for helping us to think more clearly about how we can build a better society. These ideas are not an alternative to democratic debate, but an integral part of it; and whether they have any influence depends solely on their capacity to persuade enough citizens that they are worth pursuing: nothing more, nothing less.

What are the chances that these lofty ideals will have a meaningful impact on real politics? How can we overcome the inevitable resistance from entrenched elites whose hold on political power and economic resources would be challenged by them? I will come back to these questions in the Conclusion. But we must remember that what is politically achievable is not predetermined—it depends on what people believe in and are willing to fight for. My aim in this book is to sketch a vision of what a fair society could look like, and to persuade you that this is both morally desirable and practically feasible. But bringing this about will require determination and a commitment to action—to changing minds, to winning elections and to experimenting with new policies and institutions.

I often find myself coming back to a particular quote which, I think, captures what is so unique and inspiring about Rawls's ideas. It comes from the philosopher Thomas Nagel's review of *A Theory of Justice* in 1973. "The outlook expressed by this book is not characteristic of its age," Nagel wrote, "for it is neither pessimistic nor alienated nor angry nor sentimental nor utopian. Instead it conveys something that today may seem incredible: a hopeful affirmation of human possibilities."[30] We need this kind of outlook today more than ever. My hope is that this book brings that same spirit to the problems we face today; and that, in doing so, it leaves you with a renewed confidence in the possibility of a better society—and the energy to go out and make it a reality.

Part ONE

1

What's Fair?

Justice is the first virtue of social institutions, as truth is of systems of thought. A theory however elegant and economical must be rejected or revised if it is untrue; likewise laws and institutions no matter how efficient and well-arranged must be reformed or abolished if they are unjust.

John Rawls, *A Theory of Justice*[1]

We tend to take for granted the way in which society is organized: political and economic institutions change slowly, and they can take on an air of naturalness or inevitability. But we must not be fooled by this illusion. There is no natural or neutral way to organize society— our democracy and economy are the products of human choices, and it is within our power to change them. Together, these structures comprise a social system which, in Rawls's words, "is not an unchangeable order beyond human control but a pattern of human action."[2]

Our societies require a range of institutions in order to function: they require political structures, such as parliaments and elections, which we can use to make collective decisions; a legal system, including courts and a judiciary, which can enforce these decisions; economic institutions, such as markets and property rights, which facilitate production and trade; and social structures, such as the family, which help to sustain our society and pass on our shared culture from one generation to the next. These institutions—what Rawls referred to as the "basic structure" of society—influence our lives in profound and unavoidable ways. They determine our rights and obligations as citizens, and the opportunities open to us through education and work; and, through their impact on culture, they even shape our values, dreams and aspirations, and hence the kinds of people we are and want to be.

In a democracy, we share a collective moral responsibility for how we design the basic structure of our society, and the impact it has on each of our lives. For Rawls, this is what justice is all about, and he devoted his life to identifying a clear set of principles that could guide us in designing these institutions. His starting point was the idea that society should be fair—this is why he called his theory "justice as fairness." His life's work was, in effect, an attempt to unpack this fundamental idea; to think through what it would mean to live together on terms that everyone could accept as fair. As we saw in the Introduction, Rawls proposed a powerful and intuitive thought experiment, which he called the "original position," in order to answer this question. If we want to know what a fair society would look like, he argued, we should ask ourselves how we would choose to organize it if we didn't know what our individual circumstances would be, as if behind a "veil of ignorance."

Rawls argued that we would select two overarching principles of justice, relating to freedom and equality respectively, alongside a further principle of intergenerational justice and sustainability. As we shall see over the course of this book, these principles provide a remarkably clear and powerful framework for thinking our way through many of the most challenging issues facing our societies today, from questions about free speech and the role of money in politics, to those concerning poverty, inequality and the climate and ecological crisis; and in the second part of this book, we will adopt these principles as the basis for developing a practical agenda to change our society for the better.

But before we take up these real-life challenges, we need to look in a bit more detail at the principles themselves. Although just over 100 words in total, they are the essence of Rawls's theory, and contain within them an enormously rich set of ideas.

Rawls's Two Principles of Justice

FIRST PRINCIPLE: Each person has an equal claim to a fully adequate scheme of equal basic rights and liberties, which scheme is compatible with the same scheme for all; and in this scheme the equal political liberties, and only those liberties, are to be guaranteed their fair value.

SECOND PRINCIPLE: Social and economic inequalities are to satisfy two conditions: first, they are to be attached to positions and offices open to all under conditions of fair equality of opportunity; and second, they are to be to the greatest benefit of the least advantaged members of society, consistent with the just savings principle.[3]

At first sight, the principles are rather dense: it's not obvious what they mean, or why they are so distinctive, and the aim of this chapter is to explain this. But one thing is readily apparent: they are designed to answer the specifically political question of how we should organize our most important social institutions, rather than any wider moral questions about what makes life worthwhile, or what we owe our friends and family. This focus on *social* justice—the justice of institutions, as opposed to the justice of individual actions—set Rawls apart from many thinkers in the liberal tradition, so much so that one prominent philosopher referred to this aspect of his theory as "the coming of age of liberal political philosophy."[4]

Rawls also distinguished between "domestic justice"—which is the focus of his theory—and both "local" and "global justice."[5] While domestic justice, and hence Rawls's principles, are concerned with how we should organize the basic structure of society—the core institutions without which it couldn't function—they are not meant to tell us how we should organize the internal life of the various associations that operate *within* the basic structure, such as families, churches or sports teams.[6] These are matters of "local justice." Of course, Rawls's principles set some limits on how these associations can operate—churches cannot punish heretics beyond expelling them, and parents cannot deprive their children of medical help or a decent education. But within these broad limits, private associations should be free to organize themselves as they see fit.

Neither are his principles designed to answer questions about "global justice"—justice between, rather than within, countries—such as what obligations rich countries have to poorer ones, or whether one country can intervene in another to protect human rights. In the context of enormous global inequalities, climate change and even war, these are undoubtedly pressing issues, with hugely important practical implications, from how we structure the global trading system to how much money we should spend on international aid and how we should share the costs of phasing out fossil fuels and adapting to a warmer planet. But the relationship between countries differs significantly from the relationship between citizens within a country, and working out the details of these obligations calls for a different set of principles.[7] Following Rawls, we will focus on domestic justice—on how we should design the basic institutions of an individual country—since it is disagreement about this question which underpins the crisis of faith in liberal democracy today, and which must be the starting point for the political and social renewal we so urgently need.[8]

FREEDOM

The foundation of any liberal democracy is a commitment to protecting certain fundamental rights and freedoms. This idea is accepted today across the political spectrum: it is the driving force behind the modern human rights movement, and many countries enshrine a set of fundamental rights in a written constitution. And yet, although there is general agreement that everyone is entitled to certain basic freedoms, there is disagreement about which ones. Should gay people have the right to marry? Should women have the right to an abortion? And what should we do when our most basic freedoms come into conflict with one another? Should, for example, freedom of expression give religious believers the right to refuse to serve gay customers?

Rawls's first principle—the basic liberties principle—can help us answer these difficult questions. Let's start by looking at which freedoms Rawls considered to be truly "basic liberties" (in this discussion, I will use "liberties," "rights" and "freedoms" interchangeably). We can group them into three loose categories: personal, political and procedural.[9] The personal liberties include freedom of conscience, thought and expression, freedom of association, and the rights that are needed to ensure our individual freedom and bodily integrity—including freedom from violence and coercion, freedom of movement, free choice of occupation, the right to a private family life, freedom of choice in questions of sexuality and reproduction, and the right to own personal property like clothing and housing. These freedoms create a protected space in which we can think freely and pursue our own idea of how we want to live our lives—what religion we want to follow, if any; whom we want to be in a relationship with, and whether we want to start a family; what kind of work we want to do, and how we spend our time outside work. They reflect a deep commitment to the liberal ideal of a society in which people with different moral and religious values can live side by side, and where we agree not to use the power of the state to impose our beliefs on anyone else. At a time of rising intolerance and growing "culture wars," this commitment is more important than ever.

Next come the political liberties, which encompass all the rights and freedoms that underpin the democratic process. These include not just the right to vote and to stand for office, but also wide-ranging freedoms of political speech and association, including the right to scrutinize and criticize the government and to form political parties and campaign groups. Crucially, Rawls's first principle does not seek only to guarantee our formal equal political rights but also to create a political system in which we have substantively equal opportunities to exercise those rights and to influence collective decision-making, irrespective of wealth, race, gender and so on. This is what Rawls meant when he said that the equal political liberties "are to be guaranteed their fair value."[10] In most advanced democracies, rich individuals and powerful corporations have come to exert an outsized influence over the democratic process, in large part through making donations to political parties and their ownership of the news media. This tendency for democracy to degenerate into plutocracy—government by the wealthy—concerned Rawls deeply, and he argued that the failure to address this was one of the most serious problems with our societies.[11] As we shall see in Chapter 5, achieving political equality in this sense will require far-reaching reforms to democracy as we know it, starting with an entirely new system for funding political parties and the news media.

The personal and political liberties are the core substantive freedoms protected by the basic liberties principle, and they correspond to the liberal and democratic aspects of the familiar term "liberal democracy." Alongside them are what we might call "procedural liberties," or the rights and liberties associated with the rule of law. At the most basic level, "the rule of law" means that the state should act in accordance only with laws that have been approved through a legitimate political process. Moreover, everyone should be subject to the same laws, which should be administered in a regular and impartial manner. In practical terms, the procedural liberties under-pin vital protections like freedom from arbitrary arrest and the right to a fair trial. These freedoms are a precondition for enjoying all the other basic liberties: after all, without the rule of law, democracy would be meaningless since the state could act with impunity, and none of our personal liberties would be secure.

But what exactly does it mean for a liberty to be "basic"? Basic liberties, as Rawls conceived them, are both "fundamental" and "inalienable." They are "fundamental" in the sense that a basic liberty can be limited only in order to protect another basic liberty. To take a relatively uncontroversial example, we can limit free speech where this is necessary to prevent violence, and hence protect our basic right to physical safety and bodily integrity. But it would be wrong for the state to limit our basic freedoms simply in order to satisfy the moral or religious views of the majority. So, for example, it would be wrong to ban gay relationships simply because some people—or even most people—think homosexuality is a sin. Similarly, the state cannot limit the freedom of a religious minority simply because this would satisfy the beliefs of the majority. No matter how much we might disagree with our fellow citizens about personal morality and religion, the basic liberties principle calls on us to respect each per-son's freedom to live according to their own beliefs. The only limit on this freedom is the freedom of others to do the same.

The protection of basic liberties covered by Rawls's first principle also takes strict precedence over the pursuit of economic justice, which is the focus of his second principle (in this sense, the order in which he listed his principles really matters).[12] So, for example, the state cannot take children away from their parents, even if doing so would promote equality of opportunity; and neither can it bypass the democratic process, or disenfranchise particular groups of vot-ers, even if doing so would lead to faster economic growth and make it easier to address poverty. In other words, we can immediately reject the kinds of arguments that authoritarian communists have sometimes made to justify the denial of basic personal and political freedoms, and which continue to be made in present-day China and elsewhere. And, of course, it isn't only those on the hard left who are or have been willing to subordinate basic freedoms to economics—the same is true of authoritarian neoliberals such as General Augusto Pinochet, who oversaw a brutal free-market regime in Chile in the 1970s and 1980s.

The basic liberties are also "inalienable," meaning we cannot voluntarily give them up, or "alienate" ourselves from them.[13] In other words, in a society organized according to this principle we would not be able to sell ourselves into slavery or sell our right to vote, even if we wanted to. For Rawls, the role of the state is not, as some libertarians believe, simply to enforce voluntary contracts; rather, it is to maintain the conditions that are the basis for our freedom and equality as citizens, and to permit slavery would go against this most basic commitment.

Rawls's account of which liberties are "basic" has a number of distinctive features that distinguish his theory from other liberal thinkers, with important practical implications.

First, as we have seen, he argued that both personal and political—or liberal and democratic—freedoms are "basic" and so deserve special protection. We often talk about these freedoms as if they are inseparable—hence the term "liberal democracy." But this hasn't always been the case, and in giving both types of freedom equal weight Rawls sought to transcend an important philosophical divide.[14] On one side of this divide is a school of thought often associated with the eighteenth-century philosopher Jean-Jacques Rousseau, but with roots going back to classical Athens. It argues that political or democratic freedoms, or what the philosopher Benjamin Constant referred to in an influential essay in 1819 as the "liberties of the ancients," are the most important. On this view, personal freedoms like those of religion and conscience are, at best, instrumentally important because they help to promote a healthy democratic culture. The problem with this way of thinking is that it has a dangerous tendency towards illiberalism, or the "tyranny of the majority": when the will of a democratic majority clashes with the personal freedoms of a minority, the former takes priority. This is the idea that self-professed "illiberal democrats" like Hungary's Prime Minister, Viktor Orbán, appeal to when they argue that in a mainly conservative and Christian country there is nothing wrong with laws that discriminate against gay people.

A second school of thought, more closely associated with thinkers like John Locke and with the modern liberal tradition, instead regards the personal freedoms—the "liberties of the moderns"—as the most important. Its proponents tend to value democratic freedoms mainly as a means to securing our personal freedoms and economic prosperity more widely, rather than as intrinsically valuable in their own right. But this way of thinking can lead to distinctly undemocratic conclusions: until the early twentieth century, many self-described "liberals" were opposed to universal suffrage on the grounds that it posed a threat to freedom (though they were often more concerned with protecting the property rights of the rich than with freedom of conscience and expression).[15] In a more modern context, we can see similar notions at play when neoliberals have used international institutions like the World Bank and the International Monetary Fund to impose a particular idea of economic freedom on crisis-stricken developing countries.[16] In rich countries, meanwhile, the tendency to hand over ever more power to unelected regulatory agencies and central banks sometimes displays a similar disregard for the importance of democratic oversight.[17]

The basic liberties principle, by contrast, says that political and personal freedoms are equally important and neither has an automatic priority over the other. For Rawls, these freedoms are "co-original"—they share a common source in an underlying ideal of citizens as both free and equal. Free citizens must be able to choose how they want to live, and equal citizens must have the same power to shape the law as everyone else. Both types of freedom have inherent value, in addition to their instrumental value in protecting one another.[18] In this sense, Rawls's theory is a true theory of liberal democracy.

Perhaps the most striking and consequential feature of Rawls's list of basic liberties is that it includes only a very limited set of economic freedoms—namely, freedom of occupational choice and the right to own personal property, which Rawls defined rather narrowly to include, for example, a right to own personal possessions and to have control over one's living space. In other words, Rawls rejected the notion, associated with many followers of the classical liberal tradition, that freedom of exchange is on a par with, or should even take priority over, personal freedom or political equality. Various thinkers have offered their reasons as to why economic freedoms should have this privileged status, and we will look at some of these arguments in Chapter 3. But whatever the justification, the practical implication is always the same: if wide-ranging economic freedoms are given such a strong priority, this severely limits what the state can do to address poverty or inequality, or even to regulate markets in order to promote economic growth. It is this strong precedence given to economic freedoms that explains the association between (classical) liberalism and laissez-faire economics, and it is this way of thinking that has prevented us from addressing many of the failings of contemporary capitalism. Rawls, however, rejected this approach, arguing that questions about taxation and property should depend on how we can best promote the idea of economic justice defined by his second principle.

What justifies Rawls's claim that personal and political freedoms are basic, but most economic freedoms are not? The answer brings us to perhaps the most original aspect of Rawls's first principle: not its assertion that some liberties are more important than others, but how it gives us a framework for determining which liberties are "basic" and for handling the conflicts that inevitably arise between them.[19]

In expanding on his first principle, Rawls explained that the basic liberties are those rights and freedoms that we need in order to live freely and to play our part in society.[20] As citizens, he argued, we need two essential moral "powers" or "capacities." First, the "capacity for a conception of the good"—in other words, the ability to reflect on and pursue our own idea of how we want to live. Second, the "capacity for a sense of justice"—the ability to form our own view about how we should organize society, and to cooperate with others on fair terms. Having these capabilities is what makes us free and equal citizens, and they are a precondition for the existence of a democratic society.[21]

The basic liberties are the freedoms we must have if we are to develop and exercise these capacities. The political liberties guarantee our freedom to discuss moral and political questions, to criticize the government and to take part in public life, without which it would be impossible to cultivate or act according to a sense of what is fair—our "capacity for a sense of justice." At the same time, we need the personal freedoms of thought, speech, conscience and association in order to define and pursue the kind of life we want to lead—our "capacity for a conception of the good." These personal freedoms give us space to follow our own path and they are the foundation of a rich social and cultural world in which we can explore different ideas about how to live beyond those we were brought up with.[22]

Being clear about the underlying purpose of our basic freedoms helps us to think about their limits. The basic liberties principle does not protect every instance of an abstract right like free speech: speech is protected as a basic liberty only where it is essential for us in developing and exercising our moral capacities. So, for example, we should give the strongest possible protection to speech about political, moral and religious questions, since that is integral to developing our sense of what is fair and how to live. But some forms of speech, such as commercial advertising, play no meaningful role in enabling us to develop or exercise these capacities. While true basic liberties can be limited only in order to protect other basic liberties, freedoms like commercial speech can be limited, Rawls argued, for a wider set of "public reasons," such as promoting public health or economic efficiency.[23]

Keeping in mind the underlying purpose of our basic freedoms also provides a way to resolve the conflicts that inevitably arise between them. When faced with such a conflict, we should seek to prioritize them according to their importance for living freely and for cultivating our two moral capacities. At the heart of this approach is a recognition that no basic liberty is absolute: in principle, we can limit any of them if doing so is necessary to maintain a "fully adequate" set for everyone. As we shall see in Chapters 4 and 5, this flexibility is an important corrective to the absolutism about rights that is common in contemporary political debate, as if one basic freedom must always take complete precedence over everything else.[24] We can see this, for example, in the way in which the U.S. Supreme Court has repeatedly struck down laws to limit political donations on the basis that these are protected forms of speech, and that freedom of speech has an almost absolute priority over the claims of democratic political equality; or in the notion that freedom of religious belief should always trump the rights of the LGBTQ+ community, which has been used to justify wide-ranging exemptions for religious believers from anti-discrimination laws.

Of course, the idea of "striking a balance" raises its own difficulties. We cannot simply look at Rawls's first principle and read off a definitive solution to any given clash of rights. Resolving them inevitably involves a degree of judgement about the relative importance of different freedoms, and there may be a range of reasonable solutions. This flexibility is not a bug or a flaw, it is a valuable and intentional feature of Rawls's approach: rather than seeking to answer every question in advance, it recognizes that democratic debate about the precise scope of our basic freedoms is often justified, and provides a coherent framework for conducting this debate.

We are now in a position to understand why Rawls's first principle only includes a limited set of economic freedoms, like the right to hold personal property. We have a basic right to own housing and personal possessions like clothing, books and computers, because otherwise it would be impossible to live freely and to express ourselves. To see how vital these liberties are, we only have to imagine what it would be like to live in a society where the state, or indeed other citizens, could come into one's home at will, or tell us what to wear or read.[25] The same is true of freedom of occupational choice: for many of us, what we do for a living is an important part of our identity, and being free to decide what job to do is an integral part of living our life according to our own beliefs. But most of the economic freedoms prized by classical liberals—being free from taxation, being able to run a business without regulation, and so on—do not pass this test. We simply don't need these rights in any absolute sense in order to live freely or engage in democratic debate.

This way of thinking explains Rawls's approach to the question of who should own the "means of production"—firms, machinery, raw materials and so on—which historically has been at the heart of the debate between socialism and capitalism. While we have a basic right to own personal property, this does not imply that companies or natural resources should necessarily be privately owned. Rawls was clear that the basic liberties principle is compatible both with private ownership and with "liberal socialism," where firms are ultimately owned by workers or by the state. This is not to say that we can leave issues around ownership and workplace democracy unresolved—indeed, they are at the heart of the economic agenda that we will develop later in the book; only that the basic liberties principle alone cannot provide us with an answer. That requires a broader ideal of economic justice, which brings us to Rawls's second principle.

EQUALITY

While the basic liberties principle gives us a template for protecting our most important freedoms and designing a democratic political system, Rawls's second principle can help us think about how we should organize our core social and economic institutions: the structure of the education system, the role of markets, the size of government, the nature of property rights and so on. In combination with the just savings principle, which we will return to shortly, it provides us with an ideal of economic justice that is both liberal and egalitarian, while recognizing the limits of our finite planet—a truly systematic alternative to the neoliberalism that continues to dominate economic thinking and which serves to justify the ecological destruction and inequality that blight our societies today.[26]

As we have seen, Rawls's second principle has two distinct parts. First is "fair equality of opportunity": the idea that social positions—not just jobs, but places at university, public offices (such as being a judge) and so on—should be open to all on the basis of their skills and abilities, and that everyone should have an equal chance to develop their talents in the first place. The second part is the "difference principle": the idea that inequalities in society are justified only if they benefit everyone, and specifically that we should organize our economy so as to maximize the life chances of the "least advantaged."

Before saying more about the different aspects of this principle individually, it's important to see how they relate to one another. To do so, it helps to imagine a society in which people hold different positions—for example, cleaners, teachers, architects—each of which comes with different rewards: some are more highly paid or have more power, while others offer greater scope for gaining social recognition or developing a sense of accomplishment. Fair equality of opportunity is about making sure that each of us has an equal chance to compete for any of these roles regardless of where we are born or who our parents are. The difference principle, by contrast, is about making sure that the rewards attached to those positions are fair. In other words, even if we all had a fair shot at becoming an architect, this wouldn't necessarily make it fair that architects earn so much more than cleaners. Whether this disparity is justified ultimately depends on whether it helps to promote the interests of the least advantaged—by encouraging people to undertake the long training needed to become an architect, say, and to apply their skills to building things that people value, such as houses, shops and offices.

We can also illustrate the relationship between fair equality of opportunity and the difference principle using the analogy of a competition or race. Equality of opportunity is often described as giving everyone a fair start in the "race" of life. But equality of opportunity has nothing to say about the prizes at the other end. Should the race be one in which "winner takes all," as is increasingly the case in our societies today? Or should everyone get the same reward for taking part? Or somewhere in between? If equality of opportunity is about having an equal start, then the difference principle is about making sure that the prizes are fair. By combining these two elements, Rawls's second principle rejects the false dichotomy between equality of opportunity and equality of outcome that characterizes so much debate about economic justice. And yet, while the two parts of Rawls's second principle have to be understood together, each also has transformative implications of its own.

FAIR EQUALITY OF OPPORTUNITY

Equality of opportunity is, of course, a familiar concept—it is one of the guiding principles of economic policy in most modern liberal democracies. But while most of us would agree that equality of opportunity is something we should be aiming for, this apparent consensus masks deep divisions over what it actually means and what it would take to realize in practice.

We can distinguish two distinct interpretations of this principle that sit behind our political debate. The first, which Rawls referred to as "formal" equality of opportunity, is the idea that jobs and other positions should go to the most qualified candidate, irrespective of irrelevant characteristics like class, race or gender. Formal equality of opportunity is, in effect, a principle of non-discrimination. At a minimum, it requires laws that make outright discrimination illegal, and it also calls for policies which would help to overcome unconscious bias and prejudices that put some groups—women, certain ethnic minorities, LGBTQ+ people—at an unfair disadvantage.

Formal equality of opportunity is a basic requirement of equal citizenship, and a precondition for any fair society. To be denied access to a job or a place at university simply on the basis of your gender or the colour of your skin is to be denied one's basic dignity and equality as a citizen. But formal equality of opportunity on its own is not enough. The problem is that making sure that jobs and other positions go to the most skilled candidates doesn't count for much if some people don't have a chance to develop those skills in the first place. We know, for example, that children who are born into richer and more educated families tend to go to the best schools and have more opportunities to develop valuable social and cultural skills at home. These unequal starting points have huge effects on people's lives. In countries like the UK and U.S.A., for example, someone whose parents earn £10,000 more than their friend's parents will, on average, go on to earn £5,000 more than their friend.[27] This relationship is even worse for certain ethnic minority groups:

in America, Black children born to low-income parents have just a 2.5 per cent chance of ending up in the richest fifth of households as adults, whereas white children born into families with the same income are four times more likely to reach that level.[28]

By contrast, Rawls advocated for "fair" equality of opportunity, where everyone would have an equal chance to develop their natural skills and abilities, irrespective of class, race or gender. In such a society, people with the same natural talents and motivations would have the same general prospects—the same chances of going to university, or of getting a certain job, and so on—regardless of their origins.[29] As the philosopher R. H. Tawney put it, true equality of opportunity "depends not only upon an open road but upon an equal start."[30]

As we shall see in Chapter 6, realizing this ideal requires much more than the absence of overt discrimination. At the very least, we need to overhaul our education system so that children have the same opportunities irrespective of parental income. And while discussion about equality of opportunity tends to focus on the education system, this principle actually has much wider implications. If we want to give every child an equal start, then we also need to reduce poverty and inequality directly, since there is a limit to how far the education system can make up for the different opportunities that children have at home. Measures to reduce poverty and inequality must also sit alongside a much greater effort to overcome the specific structures and norms that perpetuate racial and gender inequalities, from the impact of pervasive—and often unconscious—racial bias, to the way in which women are widely expected to do the bulk of child-rearing in society. Equality of opportunity also has implications for healthcare: we have a responsibility as a society to make sure that everyone can achieve a decent level of health, since we need to be in good health in order to apply for a course of study or a job.[31] Finally, we also need to look beyond purely economic opportunities, and make sure that people from all walks of life have a fair chance to participate in social and cultural life more generally.[32]

The case for fair equality of opportunity rests in part on its benefits for economic efficiency and growth, in the sense that we can all gain from living in a society where everyone has the same chance to develop their skills and abilities, and to compete for different jobs. A whole host of studies attest to the economic benefits that would come from addressing racial and gender inequalities and providing equal opportunities to children from poor backgrounds: one recent paper by economists at the London School of Economics estimated that eliminating gender differences in employment would increase productivity by 32 per cent on average.[33] And yet the tendency to focus on economic efficiency misses the most important point. The case for equality of opportunity ultimately rests on a more fundamental moral commitment: it is simply unfair that random circumstances of birth over which we have absolutely no control—such as class, race and gender—should have such a profound influence over our lives. This means we should pursue equality of opportunity, for example by investing in education for disadvantaged children or promoting more equal representation for women and ethnic minorities on company boards, whether or not such initiatives will increase economic growth. That it is so rare to hear this argument is symptomatic of the impoverishment of our public discourse, where economic efficiency has become the default way of justifying policy.

Political discussions of equality of opportunity are also frequently derailed by critics who like to point out the absurd implications of taking the idea of an "equal start" to its logical conclusion. In particular, families inevitably have a huge influence over children's development and subsequent life chances, not just because of differences in financial resources, but through the subtle transmission of skills, attitudes, interests and culture. We know, for example, that activities such as reading to children can improve their performance at school. Does a commitment to fair equality of opportunity mean we should prevent some parents from reading to their children at night? Or force all parents to do so?

Of course not. This disturbing conclusion follows from thinking about equality of opportunity in isolation: if this was the only thing we cared about, then it might be better to abolish the family and raise children in some kind of institutional setting where we could ensure that every child was treated exactly the same. But part of the value of Rawls's theory is that it cannot be reduced to a single principle, and we should always think of his principles in the round. His first principle, which includes the right to a private family life, clearly limits what the state can do to promote equality of opportunity. Parents should be free to share their personal interests with their children, to help them with their homework and to introduce them to their friends and contacts, even if this means that some children have advantages that others don't. These wide-ranging parental freedoms are basic liberties because without them it would be impossible for parents and children to form the intimate relationships that play such an important role in most people's lives, and which are so vital for children's development.[34] But respecting parental rights does not mean giving up on equality of opportunity. As we shall explore in Chapter 6, the state can and should limit the opportunities that wealthy parents have to buy unfair advantages for their children; and we can use the education system to help compensate for inequalities that arise at home.

Fair equality of opportunity is an intuitively attractive principle. But does it go far enough?

Let's imagine a society with perfectly fair equality of opportunity. The state would do everything that it could to eliminate discrimination and give all children an equal chance to develop their talents; but beyond this, the distribution of income would be left to the market, meaning some people would end up with more money and social status than others, reflecting a combination of differences in talent, the choices they make and, of course, luck. Such a society could be called a "fair" meritocracy. At first sight, this looks rather appealing; it would certainly be an improvement on the status quo, and something like this has come to be accepted as the guiding idea of economic policy in many liberal democracies. As the philosopher Michael Sandel has argued, "At the level of principle at least, and political rhetoric, meritocracy has won the day," with mainstream politicians on both the left and right claiming that their policies will create a truly level playing field. Inasmuch as there is still some criticism, "the complaint is usually not about the ideal but about our failure to live up to it."[35]

On closer inspection, however, even a fair meritocracy is not as attractive as it might seem. For a vivid depiction of what is wrong with the meritocratic ideal, we need look no further than the writings of the sociologist Michael Young, whose satirical book *The Rise of the Meritocracy*, published in 1958, popularized the term.[36] Young described a fictional society where success and influence depended strictly on merit, defined as "intelligence plus effort." While the term "meritocracy" has since acquired positive connotations, Young was frank that he was describing a dystopia rather than a utopia—a highly unequal society, where the old aristocracy of wealth and social class had merely been replaced by an aristocracy of "merit." In such a society, those at the bottom would be condemned to suffer the double indignity not only of being poor but of being looked down on and held entirely responsible for their lowly status. After all, from the perspective of a meritocracy, they have exactly what they deserve. In what feels like an increasingly prescient warning, Young portrayed a society riven by social conflict and on the brink of violent rebellion.[37] Rawls read Young's book and echoed many of his concerns, warning that in a meritocracy a privileged elite would pull away from the rest, and that, in such a society, it would be impossible for the least well off to maintain their self-respect.[38] The rhetoric of meritocracy is generating the same dynamics today: as Sandel argues, the "hubris" of society's educated elites, combined with the "humiliation" of those who have been left behind, has created a dangerous, even explosive, cocktail of discontent.[39]

A fair meritocracy, then, although it would be preferable to the status quo, could still be extremely unequal. Is this something we should be worried about? To a committed meritocrat, inequality isn't necessarily a problem: the basic premise of a meritocracy is that if we create a level playing field, the outcome will be fair even if it is very unequal, because people will get what they deserve. There is something attractive about this notion—it seems to fit with everyday notions of individual responsibility. But, as Rawls argued, the underlying moral idea—that in a meritocracy people get what they deserve—is fundamentally flawed. After all, we can only really deserve something if we are responsible for it in some way: someone who wins the lottery might be entitled to keep their winnings, but no one thinks they "deserve" them in any deep moral sense. And yet we are no more responsible for the talents we are born with than we are for our class, race or gender—they are the outcome of a "natural lottery" over which we have no control.[40] If we are bothered by the influence of class, race or gender on life chances, then we should also be bothered by the influence of differences in natural ability. As Rawls said, "From a moral standpoint the two seem equally arbitrary."[41]

What about effort? In a meritocracy, success depends on effort as well as natural talents. Even the most talented sportsperson or musician has to train and practise in order to succeed, and the same is true for almost any other area of life—no one becomes a doctor or an engineer without a lot of hard work. Common sense suggests that people should be rewarded for their effort. But, as Rawls pointed out, it's not at all clear we can take full credit for that, either. The effort we put in as adults depends in part on character traits that we develop as children, such as perseverance and the capacity to defer gratification. And whether we develop these traits in turn depends largely on the opportunities and encouragement we receive as children at home and in school, circumstances that we can hardly be held responsible for.[42] This is not to say that we can never be held responsible for what we do, but simply that the distinction between what we can and can't be held responsible for—and consequently between what we do or don't "deserve"—is not as simple as it might seem.[43]

In any case, even if we believed that people should be rewarded in proportion to their effort, this still wouldn't justify the inequalities that are generated by markets. How much effort we put in does have some impact on how much we earn—other things being equal, people who study hard or work longer hours tend to get paid more. But the differences in earnings that we see in a market economy are not simply the product of differences in effort, but reflect the way in which the forces of supply and demand shape the economic value of different people's talents. Data scientists are paid so much more than nurses not because they work harder, but because of the enormous demand for the skills that data scientists have relative to supply. And, of course, the forces of supply and demand that shape how much we earn depend on further factors that are completely beyond our individual control: on what other people want to buy, on how technologies make some skills more valuable than others, and on whether the talents we possess are common or rare in the population as a whole.

Where does this leave us? It might seem as if the only alternative to a society with perfect equality of opportunity would be one with perfect equality of outcome. After all, if we don't really "deserve" the differences that follow from our natural talents or efforts, then maybe it would be better if everyone had the same income and wealth. But Rawls rejected this notion. He argued that we should encourage people to develop and apply their talents, and to gain from them financially and otherwise—but only if in doing so they also benefit those who are less fortunate, whether directly through the services they provide, or indirectly via the taxes they pay. In this way, rather than lamenting the fact that some people are born with more economically valuable abilities than others, we can harness the incredible diversity of human skills and interests in a way that benefits everyone.[44] This thought lies behind the most distinctive aspect of Rawls's vision, and the concept which completes his theory of justice: the difference principle.

THE DIFFERENCE PRINCIPLE

The basic liberties principle and fair equality of opportunity are, at least on some level, reasonably familiar liberal ideas, though in Rawls's hands they take on new meaning. But the difference principle—the notion that social and economic inequalities can be justified only if they ultimately benefit everyone, and, specifically, that they should be "to the greatest benefit of the least advantaged members of society"—is striking and highly original in its own right, and has transformed subsequent debates about economic justice. It is this principle which makes Rawls's theory an unmistakably egalitarian one, and which has the most far-reaching practical implications for how we should organize our economic institutions.[45]

While the difference principle is concerned with the fortunes of the "least advantaged," it is not simply about alleviating poverty.[46] Rawls also endorsed a separate "basic needs principle"—the idea that, as a society, we have a fundamental obligation to make sure that everyone has access to the minimum level of resources they need not simply in order to survive but in order to exercise their basic freedoms and to participate in the life of society. These include material resources like food, shelter and housing, but also a basic level of education and training.[47] Although it doesn't explicitly appear in his two principles, Rawls argued that we could think about this commitment to meeting basic needs as part of, or even taking priority over, the basic liberties principle—after all, there is little point in having freedom of religion or the right to vote if you don't have somewhere to live or enough food to eat.[48] And yet, while meeting basic needs is vital, for Rawls economic justice is about much more than basic needs. It is about making sure the overall distribution of resources in society is fair.

This brings us back to the difference principle. The difference principle is, in effect, a strongly egalitarian ideal of "shared prosperity." Terms like "shared prosperity" are often used so vaguely that it's hard to know exactly what they mean (who is against shared prosperity?). The difference principle moves us beyond this loose rhetoric by defining a precise criterion for thinking about just how widely shared prosperity should be. The core idea is that we should organize our economy in such a way that the living standards of the least well off will be higher than they would be under any other economic system, within the limits of ecological sustainability as defined by the just savings principle, which we will return to shortly.[49] For Rawls, the difference principle was ultimately grounded in a spirit of reciprocity, or even "fraternity": that we should only want some people to have more than others if this also benefits those who have less.[50] It provides a framework for thinking about the design of our economic system as a whole—not just the level of taxes and benefits, but the role of markets, the power relations between owners and workers, and the balance between public and private ownership.

So how exactly can inequality benefit everyone? The basic logic of the difference principle is familiar: inequality creates incentives which in turn can encourage economic dynamism and growth, and this is something we can all gain from, right down to the least well off. So, for example, we can all be better off in a society where doctors are paid more than hairdressers, because this can help to make sure that enough people are willing to undertake the arduous medical training, not to mention putting up with the long nights and emotional demands of the job. More generally, as new technologies emerge and as people's tastes change, higher wages can help to direct people towards the sectors of the economy where there is high demand—whether that be for more care workers in an ageing society, or for software developers in the age of the internet. In a society where people are free to choose their job, we cannot force anyone to do useful work—rather, we have to rely on incentives to encourage people to do one job rather than another.* The same basic process encourages the success of the most productive firms, while inefficient ones, or those producing things that people no longer want, tend to decline. And, of course, the possibility of making money can be an important spur to innovation and entrepreneurialism, encouraging people to create new products and companies which, in turn, are the key drivers of long-term economic growth.

We can see the logic of the difference principle most clearly if we compare it to a perfectly equal society, where everyone has the same income regardless of what they do or how hard they work. There would be no financial incentive to go to medical school, or to take the risk of developing a new product or starting a new business, or even to work at all, since everyone would get the same income regardless. Financial rewards obviously aren't everything—many, if not most, people would still "work" because they wanted to help others and contribute to society, or because it gave them a sense of meaning and an outlet for their creativity. But both economic theory and historical experience suggest that a perfectly equal society would be much poorer than the societies that we live in today. In other words, by allowing for a degree of inequality, we can make *everyone* better off.

The difference principle, then, provides an alternative to the idea of equality at any cost that is sometimes associated with extreme forms of communism or socialism.[51] But it also provides an alternative to the idea that we should simply maximize economic growth without considering how the benefits are distributed—something which is often associated with liberalism, or at least with neoliberalism, and which continues to have a strong influence over economic policy today. To use the "pie" analogy much loved by economists,

---

* This doesn't mean we should rely exclusively on markets. Market wages for care work, for example, are often much too low to attract enough people into this vital sector. In these kinds of cases, the state can and should try to increase the rewards associated with certain jobs.

the difference principle calls on us not to maximize the overall size of the economic pie, nor to rigidly insist that everyone should have a perfectly equal slice—but to make the size of the slice that goes to the least well off as big as possible.

Why should we care so much about the position of the poorest in society? We will come back to this question in the next chapter. But the simple answer is that we are trying to organize society in a way that everyone can accept as fair regardless of their particular circumstances. In light of this aim, it makes sense to focus on those who have the least, since they will generally have the most reason to object to their position. The difference principle is the economic principle most likely to secure their willing support: in a society organized according to this principle, while the least well off would have less than others, they would know that society has done everything it can to improve their prospects, and that in any other society they would have even less. And if those who have the least in society can endorse our economic system, surely those who have more can do so too. As Rawls put it, in such a society, "The least advantaged are not, if all goes well, the unfortunate and unlucky—objects of our charity and compassion, much less our pity—but those to whom reciprocity is owed as a matter of political justice."[52]

When Rawls talks about the "least advantaged" in relation to the difference principle, he is referring to the least advantaged *workers*, namely those with the lowest earnings potential, whose skills are least in demand. There is some ambiguity about how we should define this group—the closest approximation is probably to think about the class of minimum-wage workers, though Rawls suggested that, as a rule of thumb, we could also think about the bottom half of the income distribution.[53] It is crucial to note here, too, that the difference principle is concerned with inequalities between people who are able to play a full part in economic life. It is not designed to help us think about how we should support those who cannot work as a result of disability or ill-health—a vitally important matter, but one that raises specific issues that the difference principle is simply not designed to answer.[54]

It is also important to note that the difference principle is concerned with maximizing the life chances (or "lifetime expectations") of the least advantaged, rather than with maximizing the income of whoever happens to be poorest at a given point in time.[55] In other words, our aim should be to make sure that the lowest earners have the best possible opportunities for earnings and employment over their lifetime—but it is up to every individual to take advantage of those opportunities. The actual income and wealth that people end up with will depend, in part, on the choices they make: whether they decide to study, how hard they work, and so on. This is important from a moral perspective because it leaves plenty of room for individual choice and responsibility: as Rawls put it, "What a person is entitled to depends on what he does."[56] In particular, it means that those who choose not to work cannot expect the state to top up their incomes, at least not above what is necessary in order to meet their basic needs. In this way, the difference principle helps to maintain a healthy connection between contribution and reward, reflecting the underlying idea of economic justice as a form of reciprocity, where each of us makes a fair contribution to the work of society in return for a fair share of the benefits.

The focus on life chances also has practical advantages. Critics of the difference principle have sometimes suggested that it would require constant interference to divert funds to the least well off, conjuring dystopian images of excessive government control.[57] But this misconstrues the point. The difference principle is concerned with the structural inequalities that affect the life prospects of different social groups—those that result from the way we organize our social and economic institutions—rather than inequalities that inevitably arise as people make choices and go about their lives.[58] It requires no more interference than any conventional system of government funded by taxation.

While the difference principle provides an elegant framework for balancing equality with efficiency, it's not immediately apparent what its practical implications are. In particular, there is no simple answer to the question of how much inequality we should tolerate as a society. This depends on a whole range of complicated empirical questions, including how important financial incentives are in motivating people to work. If people are mainly motivated by how much money they can make, the difference principle could justify an economy with low taxes and hence a rather high level of inequality, on the basis that this would promote economic growth which would benefit the least well off.* But, as we shall see in Chapter 7, people's motivations to work are about much more than money, and there is little doubt that in most, if not all, countries inequality is well beyond the level that could reasonably be justified as being in the interests of the least well off. Indeed, in very unequal countries, such as the U.S.A. and UK, higher taxes and less inequality could actually *increase* economic growth.

Whatever the optimal level of taxes and inequality, the difference principle is not a justification for laissez-faire economics. There is nothing about how markets work in theory or in practice that guarantees that the benefits of economic growth will be widely shared, let alone that they will maximize the living standards of the least well off. We have seen this very starkly in recent decades: in Western Europe and North America, the top 1 per cent of earners captured 28 per cent of the total increase in pretax incomes between 1980 and 2016, more than three times as much as the *entire* bottom half.[59] The difference principle calls for a proactive role for the state in bringing about widely shared prosperity, not only through taxes and transfers, but through how we organize our economic institutions in the round, from the education system to the distribution of ownership and the balance of power between workers and owners.

Those who oppose greater economic equality sometimes argue that inequality is a brute fact of life—an inevitable consequence of natural differences between people—and that denying it is like refusing to accept the inevitability of death. But the difference principle does not deny that some people will be born with more economically "valuable" talents than others. As Rawls put it, these are "natural facts," and so they are neither just nor unjust. What *is* just or unjust is how we as a society choose to respond to those facts.[60] In an aristocratic society, our status and prospects in life depend on whether we are born into the right class; in a meritocratic society, they depend on whether we are born with the right talents.

---

* Even so, inequality would still be limited to a level that is compatible with meaningful political equality (as guaranteed by Rawls's first principle) and fair equality of opportunity.

The difference principle offers an alternative vision of society—one grounded in reciprocity, in which we harness our natural differences for the good of all.

Beyond Income and Wealth

By asking us to prioritize the life chances of the least well off, the difference principle already offers an important challenge to prevailing ideas about economic justice on both left and right. But the difference principle is not only an argument for more equality, it is also the basis for a much broader and more humane perspective on the kinds of inequality that matter. This second aspect has sometimes been overlooked, but it represents an even deeper shift in how we typically think about our economy, with far-reaching practical consequences. There is a tendency in both politics and academia for debates about inequality to focus on money—on inequalities of income and, to a lesser extent, wealth. And, of course, these inequalities matter enormously: they determine who is able to share in the material prosperity of society, and who has access to everything from food and housing to holidays and culture. But the discontent with our economic system today is about much more than unequal access to financial resources. Indeed, the almost exclusive focus on income and wealth overlooks some of the most important inequalities in our societies: it reflects a narrowly materialistic view of human nature and fails to appreciate the extent to which people want to be in charge of their own lives, to engage in meaningful work, and to develop relationships—at work and elsewhere—which support a sense of dignity and self-respect.

The difference principle offers a much-needed corrective to this blinkered perspective. It is concerned with the distribution not just of income and wealth, but of economic power and control, and of opportunities for self-respect.[61] For Rawls, these three broad categories represented vital "primary goods"—goods that everyone has reason to value, whatever their beliefs about personal morality and what makes life worthwhile.

We are used to thinking about income and wealth, but how should we understand and measure economic power and control and opportunities for self-respect? Let's look first at the former, or what Rawls called the "powers and prerogatives of offices and positions of authority and responsibility."[62] Just as some jobs or positions come with more income, others come with more power and responsibility—indeed, these things often go hand in hand. And in most countries control over how firms are run is concentrated almost exclusively in the hands of owners or shareholders and the managers who work on their behalf, while most ordinary employees have very little say.

This concentration of power in the hands of owners and managers is so familiar that we tend to take it for granted, and questions about where such powers should lie have been largely ignored by liberal philosophers, at least in recent decades. This in turn has provided a convenient intellectual context for a concerted and largely successful effort to undermine trade unions, historically the most important source of worker power. The difference principle puts the issue of economic power and control squarely back on the agenda. It reminds us that there is nothing natural about the power that owners have over workers today, and that this disparity needs to be justified rather than simply assumed. This doesn't mean we should abolish workplace hierarchies altogether: a degree of hierarchy is essential for any large or complex organization to function effectively, and without it economic activity would probably grind to a halt. And yet, while some hierarchy is necessary, there is plenty of scope to vary the balance of power between owners, managers and ordinary employees, from trade unions, through co-management between workers and owners, all the way to worker cooperatives. From the perspective of the difference principle, workplace hierarchies are justified only if they have compensating benefits for the least advantaged, say, by increasing productivity and leading to higher wages. As we shall see, thinking about economic justice in this way provides a powerful rationale for much greater democracy at work.

Self-respect—the third primary good covered by the difference principle, alongside financial resources, and economic power and control—is even harder to measure, and to think about politically. Self-respect is a subjective state of mind, and depends in part on a person's character and relationships—things that are largely outside the scope of politics.[63] But whether people feel a sense of self-respect is also influenced by objective features of our social and economic institutions, including the availability and nature of paid work. These features of our social institutions—what Rawls referred to as the "social bases of self-respect"—are part of the basic structure of society for which we all share a common moral responsibility. Indeed, he repeatedly stated that the "social bases of self-respect" were the most important primary goods, since "without [self-respect] nothing may seem worth doing."[64]

Rawls defined self-respect as having confidence that your goals in life are worthwhile, and in your ability to achieve them.[65] Moreover, he argued that most people will only feel their life is worthwhile if they have opportunities to develop and apply their skills and capacities in interesting and complex ways. He called this the "Aristotelian principle," noting that activities which failed to satisfy this principle were "likely to seem dull and flat," and that unless we organized society with this idea in mind, people's "vitality and zest will fail as their life becomes a tiresome routine."[66] Of course, there are lots of activities that can be "meaningful" in this way, from playing a sport or learning a musical instrument, to raising children or taking an active part in a local or religious community. But when it comes to thinking about justice and public policy, paid work has a special importance, both because of the sheer quantity of time that most of us spend working, and because it is one of the most important ways in which we contribute to society and satisfy the ideal of reciprocity that underpins the difference principle.[67]

Alongside opportunities to develop and apply our skills and creativity, self-respect also depends on social recognition. As Rawls argued, without the recognition of our peers it is hard to maintain a strong sense that our goals in life are worthwhile, and "when we feel that our plans are of little value, we cannot pursue them with pleasure or take delight in their execution."[68] To some extent, this is about being seen and treated as an equal by society as a whole. This is one reason why every citizen is entitled to an equal set of basic liberties, since it's hard to see how anyone could maintain a sense of self-respect in a society that denied them the right to vote because of their gender or the colour of their skin. But, for the most part, social recognition comes from the smaller communities and associations that we are part of, from family and colleagues to synagogues and temples. We don't need everyone to recognize the value of our way of life—in a diverse society, where people have such different moral and religious beliefs, that is all but impossible. What matters is that each of us can find a community of some sort that shares our values and from which we can derive a sense of confidence in our plans and goals.[69] The basic liberties are important here because they provide the conditions in which a multitude of groups, associations and communities can flourish. But again, paid work has a special role to play, since our colleagues can be an important source of community in their own right, and it is often through work that our talents and contributions are recognized by our peers.

Most people need opportunities for meaningful work and social recognition in order to feel that their goals in life are worthwhile. But, for Rawls, self-respect also depends on having confidence in our ability to achieve those goals—in other words, on having a sense of agency or independence. This also points us towards the importance of paid work, as well as towards the limitations of redistribution and the modern welfare state. Being unemployed and dependent on the state for income can undermine one's sense of agency, especially given the intrusive systems of assessment and conditionality that exist in most means-tested benefit systems, and the stigma and suspicion that are often directed at those who are unable to work. By contrast, having decent opportunities for paid work can be a vital source of the agency and independence that are so essential for self-respect.

Expanding our understanding of inequality in this way provides a much richer viewpoint for thinking about how we should organize our society and economy. But it also creates new complications. In particular, it means that we have to consider what to do if and when we face a conflict between these different primary goods: income and wealth, power and control, and the social bases of self-respect. For example, the received wisdom among economists has often been that concentrating power in the hands of owners makes firms more productive, which in turn leads to higher wages, and consequently that there is a fundamental trade-off between higher incomes and greater democracy at work. As we shall see in Chapter 8, this view is not supported by the evidence: we can have more workplace democracy without undermining economic dynamism and growth. But even if it were true that concentrating power in the hands of owners is good for economic growth, we have to balance this against the loss of control for employees, which in turn can lead to poorer working conditions and less interesting jobs. How should we balance these goals? Is it more important to increase wages or to empower workers and ensure broad access to meaningful work? There is no simple formula for resolving these issues, and Rawls argued that in attempting to do so we should ask ourselves what the least well off would prefer.[70]

Thinking about inequality in this way points us towards the need for a genuinely transformative economic agenda. It is not enough simply to increase taxes and transfers or to strengthen the welfare state as we know it. Indeed, as we shall see, Rawls explicitly stated that "welfare state capitalism" could never fully achieve his principles of justice.[71] Rather, we need to reimagine our economic model in a more fundamental way—embracing a more universal approach to meeting basic needs, developing a comprehensive agenda to increase earnings and share society's wealth, and putting meaningful power in the hands of ordinary workers.

SUSTAINABILITY AND INTERGENERATIONAL JUSTICE

The difference principle represents a paradigm shift in how we think about our economy, displacing the narrow focus on maximizing growth which has dominated economic policy for decades. But Rawls's theory also demands that we take seriously the environmental and ecological limits on growth which our societies continue to ignore, with increasingly devastating consequences. Living within these limits is an essential part of respecting the obligations we have towards future generations (not to mention those we have to other countries).

Rawls proposed the just savings principle to address the question of justice between generations, or "intergenerational justice," and in doing so provided the first systematic account of this topic.[72] The essence of this principle is that we should treat future generations as we would have had previous generations treat us.[73] As the name of the principle suggests, Rawls's main concern was to help us think about savings, or the accumulation of material wealth. He argued that we have a fundamental duty "to make possible the conditions needed to establish and to preserve a just basic structure over time"; conditions which include not just physical assets, such as buildings and machinery, but technology, culture and critical aspects of the natural world.[74] On this basis, he claimed that very poor countries have a moral obligation to save a certain amount of their income in order to promote investment and economic growth, at least up to a point where they can guarantee every citizen's basic needs and liberties.[75] But most countries—and certainly all of the world's rich democracies today—have already far surpassed this level.[76] While these countries can continue to save and pursue economic growth, they are not morally required to do so, and the just savings principle is perfectly compatible with a "stationary economy" where growth has stopped entirely.[77] The main implication of this principle for such countries is that they should not leave future generations poorer as a result of their actions.[78]

While Rawls was focused on society's material wealth, the most urgent issues of intergenerational justice today involve society's "natural wealth," including the clean air, stable climate and healthy ecosystems that we all depend on.[79] We have an obligation to maintain this natural wealth, which is the basis for life and an important source of human well-being, for future generations too. Looked at this way, the just savings principle in effect implies a commitment to what has come to be known as "sustainable development," typically defined as "development that meets the needs of the present without compromising the ability of future generations to meet their own needs."[80] At the very least, we have to maintain the capacity of the environment to provide the critical "ecosystem services" our societies need in order to survive and flourish, including water, air, energy and fresh food, the absorption of waste, and access to nature for culture and recreation; and beyond this, there should be a broad presumption not to deplete finite resources that are difficult to replace.[81] Whatever we do to increase prosperity and raise the life chances of the least well off has to be consistent with this commitment to sustainability.

As we shall see in Chapter 7, our societies are dangerously failing to live up to this commitment: the world is facing the prospect of catastrophic and irreversible ecological and environmental breakdown, driven by the elimination of wild spaces and natural habitats and our unsustainable consumption of fossil fuels and other nonrenewable resources. Addressing this crisis, and bringing about a transition to a sustainable economic model, is the most urgent and important policy priority of our times, and this effort will determine the context within which all the other reforms we will discuss in this book must take place.

Rawls's principles may at first seem familiar or even obvious, but they have profound transformative potential. Together, they provide a unified and comprehensive framework for reimagining society, moving us beyond vague platitudes about freedom, equality and sustainability and towards a precise interpretation of which freedoms deserve special protection, what kind of equality we should be aiming for, and the nature of our obligations towards future generations. In the second half of this book, we will look at how our societies currently measure up against these principles, and develop a bold but achievable programme to remake our political and economic institutions so that they realize Rawls's powerful vision. But before we do that, we first need to look more closely at the justifications for—and critiques of—Rawls's argument. How can we be sure that he is right?

2

A New Social Contract

There is obviously no consensus that Rawls's principles are the correct way to think about what a fair society would look like—if there were, I wouldn't have written this book. Some people will find them intuitive or attractive in their own right, while others will be more sceptical. Most of us probably endorse something like the basic liberties principle, though we may disagree about the details; while Rawls's strong commitment to equality, via the difference principle, is evidently at odds with the prevailing wisdom in most liberal democracies today. And there are plenty of other accounts of how we should organize society, put forward by socialists, classical liberals, libertarians, conservatives and more; indeed, Rawls developed his theory partly in response to the failings of these alternatives. So why should we prefer his vision?

To answer this question, and to put Rawls's principles on a more secure footing, we first need to delve a bit deeper into his philosophy. Most of his writing was devoted to justifying his principles—explaining why we should accept them and how they could provide the basis for a new political consensus. The power of Rawls's underlying argument helps explain why his ideas have achieved such a privileged position among philosophers, and should help persuade us that they are worth pursuing.

As we have already discussed, Rawls's starting point is the idea that society should be fair, in the sense that it should be organized according to principles that all citizens can accept. But how can we identify such principles?

In a modern society, where citizens hold different views about personal morality and religion, there is no external standard that we can appeal to. We cannot, for example, look to divine law or the word of God, since there is no religious authority or sacred text that we can all agree on; nor is there some objective natural law that is simply apparent to everyone.[1] Rawls referred to this as the "fact of reasonable pluralism"—the fact that citizens have different beliefs about religion, morality and the best way to live. This is not a temporary feature of society, or something that will disappear as a result of scientific progress. Rather, it is an inevitable consequence of the free use of human reason in the face of genuinely difficult questions.[2] In light of this, the only way to identify fair terms for living together is to look for principles that we can agree to among ourselves.

The idea that society should be organized according to laws or principles that citizens could willingly agree to has a long history in liberal and democratic political thought. Rawls referred to it as the "central thesis" of liberalism, and it is at the heart of the "social contract" tradition associated with many of the most important thinkers in the modern history of Western philosophy, including Hobbes, Locke, Rousseau and Kant. Despite this impressive lineage, this tradition had largely fallen into disrepute when Rawls was developing his theory in the 1950s and 1960s.[3] Political philosophy at that time (inasmuch as it existed at all) was dominated by utilitarianism: the idea that we should organize our social and political institutions in whatever way will maximize social "utility" or "welfare," typically defined as "happiness" or "subjective well-being."[4] Although utilitarianism had plenty of critics, they had, in Rawls's words, "failed . . . to construct a workable and systematic moral conception to oppose it." As a result, philosophers were largely left to choose between a rigorous but, to many, unattractive utilitarianism, and what Rawls called "intuitionism"—a looser approach which sought to balance the demands of multiple values, such as utility, freedom and equality, in a rather ad hoc way.[5] Rawls's aim—and historic achievement— was not merely to critique utilitarianism, but to develop an equally systematic alternative. He did so by breathing new life into the notion of a social contract, explaining and revising it in important ways, and with such success that it has become the dominant mode of thinking about justice among philosophers today.

The key consideration for any social contract theory, including Rawls's, is to specify how citizens are to reach an agreement about basic political principles or institutions. At first sight, it might seem like we don't need to rely on philosophy at all: could we not, say, convene a constitutional convention where we thrash out an agreement on basic political principles, once and for all?[6] In a large modern society with millions or even billions of citizens, this would obviously be a huge practical and logistical challenge; although with the advent of modern information technologies, something like this may well be technically possible. The fundamental problem with such an approach is not practical but moral: if real citizens were to try to reach an agreement of this kind, the outcome would be disproportionately influenced by those who hold the most power and resources. We could face a situation in which billionaires were able to use their wealth to bribe other citizens to choose principles that would benefit the wealthy; or where a dominant religious group— whether that be Christians in America, or Hindus in India—could secure agreement to principles that would privilege their beliefs over those of other faiths through sheer force of numbers.

In other words, even if we were able to come together in person and agree to basic political principles, there is no reason to think this would be fair. A fair agreement can only be reached under fair conditions, and the point of Rawls's "original position" thought experiment, which we touched on earlier, is to define an ideally fair hypothetical situation in which we can imagine citizens coming to such an agreement. In contrast to real life, where people with more resources or social status would be able to influence the outcome, the original position asks us to envisage the contract that citizens would enter into if everyone had the same degree of influence and was unaware of their particular circumstances—how much money they had, their race, gender or sexuality, even their religious beliefs and wider goals in life—as if behind a "veil of ignorance."[7]

The "veil of ignorance" encapsulates the intuitive idea that just because something is good for us individually doesn't mean it is fair. Suppose we meet a banker who opposes a high rate of tax on top incomes simply because this would make them worse off. Even if they were right that they would be materially worse off with higher taxes, most of us would agree that this has nothing to do with justice or fairness.[8] In the original position, the fact that we don't know our own skills or social position, or even our religious and moral beliefs, means that we cannot tailor our choice of principles simply to benefit ourselves. Of course, even if we agree that we should approach these kinds of issues impartially, this isn't always easy to do: our ideas about politics and justice tend to be shaped by our own interests and experiences in ways that we are not fully aware of. The "veil of ignorance" helps us to overcome this by restricting the reasons we are able to offer for and against different principles, preventing us from arguing for certain ones in terms of our own individual interest, and forcing us to justify them from an impartial perspective. Crucially, this doesn't rely just on our own self-discipline: Rawls's thought experiment isn't simply an exercise we do in isolation, but a framework for collective debate. Even if we can't see our own blind spots and end up arguing for principles that serve our particular interests, we can rely on other people to point this out.

Although the parties in Rawls's thought experiment aren't aware of their own characteristics or interests, they know they have certain fundamental interests that all citizens share. First, they know that they have an overriding interest in being able to develop and use the two moral capacities that we discussed in the previous chapter—the "capacity for a conception of the good" and "the capacity for a sense of justice." In other words, they value being able to reflect on and deliberate about how to live and what a just society would look like, and they recognize the advantages of living in a society where others can do the same. Second, they know that they have some concrete idea of the kind of life they want to lead: they have dreams and ambitions, relationships and commitments, which are important to them; they just don't know their precise nature—whether, for example, they want to prioritize professional success, personal relationships or spiritual growth. The parties' aim in choosing principles is to secure the most favourable conditions for advancing these interests: for developing and exercising their moral powers, and for pursuing their goals in life, whatever those might be.[9]

Crucially, the parties know that whatever their conception of the good life, they will benefit from having more of the all-purpose resources that Rawls called "primary goods." Rawls highlighted five key ones: basic rights and liberties; free and fair access to social and economic opportunities; plus the three that we discussed in the previous chapter: income and wealth; economic power and control; and the social bases of self-respect. This helps to make the choice that the parties face more tangible—in effect, when it comes to choosing between different principles, they think about which would provide them with the most primary goods.[10]

The parties also have some general knowledge about the world, so that they can make an informed choice about how different principles would play out in practice.[11] First, they recognize "the fact of reasonable pluralism"—that citizens have different ideas about religion, personal morality and how to live. They also know widely accepted facts and theories from the natural and social sciences, such as how societies have to operate within certain physical and ecological limits, and about the role that incentives play in a well-functioning market economy. And they are aware of the broad material circumstances in which they are making this decision—specifically, that they live in a world characterized by "moderate scarcity," where there are enough resources to meet everyone's basic needs, but not so much that everyone can have as much as they want; and where social cooperation is necessary for all to have a decent standard of living. (After all, in a world of true abundance, we wouldn't have much need for a theory of justice, at least not when it comes to the distribution of material resources.) This knowledge means the parties can think through the implications of alternative principles and how they might work in practice.

In Rawls's thought experiment, each party simply wants to find the principles that would be best for them individually. This is sometimes misinterpreted as implying that people are fundamentally self-interested. But although we imagine the parties in the original position choosing principles that would help them to advance their own goals, there is nothing to say that these will be purely selfish. After all, in real life we don't just care about ourselves, we care about our friends and family, and even about the well-being of people we don't know. More importantly, the whole construction of the original position reflects a deep commitment to taking other people's interests and perspectives into account. If we thought people were essentially selfish, there would be no point in undertaking this thought experiment. Far from embodying selfishness, the original position expresses a profoundly empathetic perspective. As Rawls put it in the final sentence of *A Theory of Justice*, "Purity of heart, if one could attain it, would be to see clearly and to act with grace and self-command from this point of view."[12]

Since the parties in the original position are, by construction, identical—they have the same basic interests and knowledge, and so are bound to want the same things—what is best for one person will be best for everyone. In effect, this turns the question of reaching a collective agreement into one of individual choice. As we shall see, this has some important benefits: in particular, it allows us to draw on the methods of "rational choice theory"—the branch of philosophy that studies what it means to be rational in different contexts—which in turn means we can obtain a more precise answer about which principles we would choose or agree to. But using the language of a social contract or agreement, rather than of individual choice, helps to remind us that the parties are choosing principles for society as a whole. It also points to an important condition on the choice they make. When we enter into a contract, we agree to be bound by it. In the same way, when the parties agree to principles in the original position they have to do so "in good faith," taking into account whether or not they could honestly abide by their agreement no matter where they end up in society.[13]

Why should we—real-life citizens—be interested in the principles that this rather abstract situation would produce? Some critics of Rawls's thought experiment, and indeed of the wider social contract tradition, have argued that hypothetical agreements cannot generate binding obligations. After all, in the real world, contracts have legal force only if we have *actually* agreed to them. But this line of thinking misses the point. The original position is not a legal device, it is a thought experiment, and the reasons we should abide by the "agreement" reached in the original position are moral, not legal. Unlike laws which give us *external* reasons to do something, namely the threat of punishment, it provides us with *internal* reasons to support certain principles: it takes moral ideas that on some level we already endorse and shows us what their implications are. Indeed, the force of this thought experiment comes precisely from the fact that its various features—all of the assumptions about what the parties know and what their interests are—embody ideas about justice and fairness that most of us believe in here and now: that, in a democratic society, political power should be exercised on the basis of principles that everyone can accept as fair; that when it comes to justifying laws, everyone's interests should count equally; that simply because a principle benefits me or you doesn't make it fair or just; and so on. In this sense, the original position is, as Rawls put it, a device for "public reflection and self-clarification."[14] It can help each of us, as individuals, to work out what we really think; and, crucially, it can help us to reach—or at least move closer to—a consensus about what we are aiming for as a society.

The original position, then, is really a tool for working out the implications of certain fundamental moral ideas that most of us are already committed to, whatever our politics. Does this mean that it merely reflects back to us our existing beliefs, with all their prejudices and shortcomings? The short answer is "no": anyone who fully engages with this thought experiment is likely to find themselves reconsidering at least some of their preconceptions. But the question does point towards some deep issues about the nature of moral theory. One way of thinking is that moral theory is a search for an objective truth that exists prior to and independently of the specific moral convictions we hold here and now. But Rawls rejected this notion. Instead, he sought to discover the "most reasonable" moral principles—those that are consistent with our strongest and most reliable beliefs, or what he called our "considered convictions of justice."

Rawls proposed a distinctive approach for doing this—the method of "reflective equilibrium."[15] In thinking about justice, he argued, we should begin by identifying the beliefs that we are most confident about, and which we think any reasonable theory of justice should be able to accommodate, such as the idea that slavery is wrong, or that no one should suffer extreme poverty. We should then try to identify the general principles that underpin these positions, such as the principle that all citizens are entitled to certain basic freedoms, which would prohibit slavery, or that everyone should be able to meet their basic needs, which would rule out extreme poverty. If we find that there is a mismatch between these general principles and our convictions in particular cases—for example, if our conception of freedom prevents us from levying taxes, but this implies leaving unemployed people to starve—then we either have to revise our general principles, or change our view about the specific case in question.

For Rawls, this process of reflection and deliberation is the essence of moral theory. Rather than seeking an objective moral truth which is prior to and independent of our moral reasoning, our aim is to discover the most reasonable conception of justice by reaching a state of "reflective equilibrium," when our convictions about what is just in specific cases fit with our commitments to general principles. Of course, we might never reach a state of perfect equilibrium, and new problems and questions might lead us to change our minds (Rawls continued to revise and refine his own ideas about justice throughout his life). But the concept of reflective equilibrium helps to make sense of this exercise and gives us something to aim for. It calls on us to approach moral and political questions with an open mind, and to be willing to reconsider both particular cases and general principles. While this process of reflection starts with the convictions we already have, we don't just end up where we started. As Rawls shows, it can lead us towards new and unfamiliar ideas, such as the difference principle.

THE CHOICE OF "JUSTICE AS FAIRNESS"

But the question remains: why would the parties in the original position choose Rawls's two principles over all other possible alternatives?

The original position is, in effect, a tool for testing and comparing different principles in a systematic way, thinking through their implications from a variety of perspectives. While it might not be immediately obvious which principles we (or, to be precise, the imagined parties in the thought experiment) would choose— there are bound to be arguments for and against each one—in the end we have to come to a judgement about what would be best on balance.[16] In theory, we could compare every pair of conceivable principles that we can think of in order to decide which one we prefer. But, for Rawls, the most important comparison was between "justice as fairness"—the name he used to refer collectively to his own principles—and the utilitarianism that dominated political philosophy at the time.

The comparison is important not only because it mattered to Rawls. The basic logic of utilitarianism—that society should aim to maximize "utility," typically interpreted as well-being—has an obvious appeal; and, like Rawls's theory, it offers a way of grounding political principles in common reason rather than in religion or the authority of tradition, features which have made it attractive to many liberal and Enlightenment thinkers including David Hume and John Stuart Mill. Moreover, it continues to play an important role in public policy, especially via its influence on economics, a discipline that has, at times, uncritically accepted utilitarian ideas, such as cost–benefit analysis, where the decision whether or not to pursue a given policy is based on weighing its pros and cons, typically quantified in monetary terms.

How can we show that the parties in Rawls's thought experiment would choose his principles over utilitarianism? At first sight, in the special conditions of the original position, utilitarianism might appear to be the more rational choice. One of the central tenets of rational choice theory is that when we are faced with options whose outcome is uncertain, we should choose the one with the best outcome on average; or, to use the technical term, the option that would maximize our "expected" (or average) utility. To take a very simple example, suppose you want to drive from Manchester to London on a given day, and there are two different routes. You don't know how long each option will take since it depends on the traffic on a given day. In order to choose a route you would want to work out how long each takes on average, and how bad it would be if, for example, you were to get stuck in traffic—and then choose the option that would be best on average, all things considered. Since the parties in the original position are choosing principles under conditions of almost total uncertainty about how those principles will affect them, it seems as if it would be rational to want to organize society in whatever way tends to maximize people's well-being on average—in other words, to choose the principle of "average utility."

Why, then, did Rawls reject utilitarianism in favour of his two principles? Rawls argued that, while maximizing expected utility is a rational way to make decisions in most cases, it would be irrational to do so in the special conditions of the original position.[17] After all, the decision we are making in the original position is no ordinary one—we are deciding on the principles that will determine our life chances once and for all. In other words, the stakes are incredibly high. The problem with the principle of average utility is that although it would, by definition, lead to the best outcome on average, it leaves open the possibility of some truly intolerable scenarios. In particular, it offers no guarantee that our basic rights and freedoms—like freedom of speech or religion, or even democratic government—would be respected. Of course, it is possible that respecting these freedoms would tend to promote the welfare of society overall, and many utilitarians have made this kind of argument. But if we could improve social welfare by violating these freedoms—for example, if we could increase economic growth by replacing democratic government with a dictatorship of experts; or if we could increase the happiness of a large Christian majority by discriminating against Muslims or by banning gay relationships— then, from the perspective of utilitarianism, we should do so.

Rawls argued that in this special kind of situation—when we are faced with a choice between two uncertain options, one of which could turn out to be truly intolerable—we should follow a different decision-making strategy, known as "the maximin rule." To be precise, rather than choosing the option that is best on average (maximizing expected utility), we should compare the worst outcome under each option, and then choose the option where the worst outcome is as good as possible (in other words, we should "maximize the minimum"—hence "maxi-min"). To see how this might work, let's return to our driving analogy. Suppose now that you are driving from Manchester to London because you need urgent medical care that can only be provided in the capital, and if you get stuck in traffic there is a real risk of permanent injury or even death. And suppose, further, that one route is faster on average, but has a risk of very long delays; yet on the other route you are all but guaranteed to arrive on time. In this case, it would be rational to choose the route that would definitely get you there on time, even in a worst case scenario, rather than the one that would be fastest on average.

Coming back to the choice in the original position, the maximin strategy clearly favours Rawls's principles over utilitarianism. After all, if we choose utilitarianism, then, although we know that we will be better off on average, we also know that there is a risk of being violently persecuted for our religious beliefs, or prevented from living with the people we love. By contrast, we know that if we choose Rawls's two principles then even the worst-case scenario will be perfectly tolerable, since our basic liberties will be protected and, thanks to the second principle, we will also have a decent share of economic resources. The same reasoning would lead us to reject any set of principles where we might be denied our basic rights: we would reject the imposition of religious laws, since we would never want to risk being in a persecuted minority; and we would reject extreme forms of libertarianism where economic freedom is prioritized over democracy, or where we might be left to starve.

In short, Rawls argued that the parties would choose his principles instead of utilitarianism because it would be irrational for them to gamble with their basic liberties when they could select an alternative which would protect them. This argument is not, as some critics have suggested, based on a general psychological assumption that people are very risk averse.[18] Rather, it reflects the extremely high stakes of the choice that the parties face in the original position: when, and only when, the stakes are this high, it is rational to play it safe.[19] In this context, to choose utilitarianism would be like playing Russian roulette. As Rawls put it, anyone who thinks we would all be willing to gamble with our religious freedom or freedom of sexuality fails to grasp what it really means to have religious beliefs or to be in love.[20] We also have to remember that the parties in the original position are required to choose principles "in good faith"—principles they could live by, whatever their actual beliefs or social position. But who could honestly agree to abide by laws that deprived them of their basic freedoms? If we found ourselves in such a society we would surely do everything we could to escape, or even to undermine, its laws.

So far, we have focused on why the parties in the original position would want to protect their basic liberties by choosing Rawls's first principle. But what about his other principles: fair equality of opportunity, the difference principle, and the just savings principle? While most people agree that we should protect certain basic rights and freedoms, there is a much wider range of viewpoints about how we should distribute economic opportunities and resources, and about our obligations to future generations, and so understanding this part of the argument is even more vital.

The first thing to note is that the parties in the original position would want to guarantee that they would be able to meet their basic needs—for food, shelter, housing and so on. Rawls's maximin argument comes into play here again: just as rational parties would want to play it safe rather than take a gamble on being in a persecuted religious minority, they would want to guard against the possibility of being truly destitute. This is why, as we touched on in Chapter 1, Rawls argued that a commitment to meeting basic needs was on a par with, or should even take priority over, the basic liberties principle.

Since the parties don't know their class, race or gender, they would also want to make sure they had the same opportunities in life irrespective of these factors—in other words, they would choose the principle of fair equality of opportunity. They would recognize that this is an important social basis of self-respect, since it's hard, if not impossible, to hold one's head high in society if you are denied equal opportunities simply because of some unchosen or arbitrary trait. Moreover, they would see that we could all benefit from living in a society where everyone had the opportunity to develop their skills and capacities, and jobs were filled by the people most qualified to do them.[21]

The parties would also select the just savings principle, according to which they would agree to treat future generations as they would have wanted previous generations to treat them. They would want to ensure that each generation contributes its fair share towards establishing and preserving just and democratic institutions, by accumulating and maintaining the natural and social resources on which society depends. Above all, they would recognize their obligation to maintain the stable climate and vital ecosystems that are the basis for human civilization. No one would want to take a chance on being born into a generation suffering the consequences of ecological and climate breakdown.[22]

Still, why would the parties choose the difference principle? A common mistake is to think that the case for the difference principle rests on the same maximin argument that Rawls used to defend the basic liberties principle. It's easy to see where this comes from: after all, maximin is the idea that we should choose the option where the worst outcome is as good as possible, and this sounds suspiciously like the difference principle, which tells us to maximize the prospects of the least well off.[23] But this superficial similarity is misleading. As we have discussed, the maximin rule is only rational when we are faced with a choice where the worst-case scenario is truly intolerable. But in any society that offers protections for fundamental freedoms and a decent social minimum so that people can meet their basic needs, this is no longer the case.

Since the parties in the original position don't know their own talents and abilities—whether they are physically strong or academically gifted—or even what kinds of aptitudes are valued in their society, they might first consider an equal division of resources. But they would quickly see that they could do better by allowing for a degree of inequality in income and wealth, as well as power and authority: higher wages could provide incentives that would increase economic output, while hierarchies would allow us to create large firms and organizations, and so benefit from economies of scale. In doing so, they could increase the overall wealth of society in such a way that *everyone* would be better off.

While the parties would reject perfect equality, this still doesn't quite settle matters in favour of the difference principle. After all, we can make everyone better off than they would be in a perfectly equal society without going as far as *maximizing* the life chances of the least well off. Indeed, advocates for neoliberalism and trickle-down economics could (and often do) argue that even in our hugely unequal societies the poor are better off than they would have been in a strictly equal one. From the perspective of the original position, in which the parties have no idea whether they will be rich or poor, the most plausible alternative to the difference principle is another kind of utilitarianism—what Rawls called "restricted utilitarianism."[24] Restricted utilitarianism accepts that we need to protect basic liberties, provide a social minimum, and guarantee fair equality of opportunity; but beyond these "restrictions," the aim is simply to maximize the average level of welfare in society. In this way, the parties could protect their most fundamental freedoms while ensuring that, by definition, they would be better off on average than under any alternative. This is surely the most attractive kind of utilitarianism, and something like this could be the basis for a familiar liberal politics where the state protects basic freedoms and then seeks to maximize economic growth.*

Why would the parties in the original position prefer the difference principle to this kind of utilitarianism? Rawls's argument rests on the idea that the difference principle is most likely to secure not just the grudging acceptance but the willing support of the least well off. Although a society organized according to restricted utilitarianism would ensure that everyone's basic needs are met, it could still lead to a situation where the least well off are required to make sacrifices simply in order to benefit those who already have more, just as those on the lowest incomes have frequently been forced to accept more insecurity and lower wages in the name of promoting economic growth. Rawls worried that in such a society the least well off would come to resent their position, and feel that its institutions had been designed to benefit other people without taking their own needs or interests into account—a worry that has been borne out all too plainly in recent years. Rawls also argued that the difference principle would provide a more transparent basis for public debate, since primary goods like income and wealth are objectively measurable, while "utility" is not.

In contrast to the argument for the basic liberties principle, which is pretty decisive, the case for the difference principle is more finely balanced. Rawls argued that, in the end, we should

---

* Though even here, if we were really committed to maximizing average welfare, then we would also want to put in place measures to ensure a reasonably equal distribution of income, since in general people with lower incomes will benefit more from a given amount of money than the rich.

prefer the difference principle because it embodies an ideal of reciprocity. For Rawls, a just society is one in which we can "face one another openly," in the sense that we can offer a justification to one another for the way society is organized, including to the least well off. Restricted utilitarianism, by contrast, appeals not to reciprocity but to an improbable degree of altruism or selflessness: it permits a situation in which we ask the poorest in society to make sacrifices so that other people who are already richer than they are can have even more.[25] For Rawls, the importance of reciprocity in justifying the difference principle is pragmatic as well as moral. He argued that by appealing to reciprocity rather than altruism, the difference principle was grounded in a more realistic account of human psychology, and so more likely to secure the ongoing support of real-life citizens; a position that, as we shall see in the next chapter, is strongly supported by the latest research in moral psychology, and which has deep roots in human evolution.[26]

The original position thought experiment provides a powerful argument for supporting Rawls's principles, and a compelling demonstration of how they can be justified to all. In doing so, it puts the burden on those who reject them to explain why, and to propose something better. Even so, some people find the whole exercise too abstract, or think the parties would choose differently, and it's important to remember that this is simply one of a wider set of arguments for Rawls's vision of "justice as fairness." As we saw in Chapter 1, we can also argue for his principles more directly, by showing how successfully they address difficult questions about basic freedoms, and how they combine a belief in equality of opportunity and individual responsibility with reciprocity and widely shared prosperity. Our support should also depend on a careful consideration of whether and how we could put them into practice, which is the focus of the second part of this book. In the end, the case for Rawls's principles depends on taking *all* of these arguments in the round.

POLITICAL LIBERALISM

Even if we can see how the parties in the original position arrive at Rawls's principles, why should we have any confidence that real-life citizens would accept them? As we have already discussed, the "fact of reasonable pluralism" means that citizens will always disagree about a whole range of moral, spiritual and metaphysical questions. But if consensus on these issues is impossible, why should we expect anything different when it comes to politics?

In thinking this through, Rawls distinguished two ways in which citizens might come to accept broadly liberal principles and institutions. First, they might do so for purely strategic reasons, leading to what Rawls called a "modus vivendi"—a practical compromise (literally, "a manner of living"). In a modus vivendi, citizens respect basic rights because they recognize that no single group is powerful enough to dominate the others, and the alternative of civil unrest or even war would be worse for everyone. Rawls often referred to the reluctant acceptance of a degree of religious tolerance after the European Wars of Religion in the sixteenth and seventeenth centuries as an example of a modus vivendi; and, historically, advances in individual freedom have often been grounded in compromises of this sort.[27]

But Rawls wanted to show that something more than a modus vivendi is possible—that citizens with different personal beliefs can endorse shared political principles for *moral* rather than strategic reasons. He described this ideal as an "overlapping consensus": a society in which a wide range of people—Christians and Hindus, atheists and humanists—could come to an agreement about basic political principles.[28] This is desirable because those freedoms will always be vulnerable in a society where citizens support them only for strategic reasons—after all, each group would simply be waiting for an opportunity to force its views on everyone else. But an overlapping consensus is also desirable in its own right, since, for Rawls, the guiding idea of justice is that we should organize society according to principles that everyone accepts because they are fair, and not simply because they don't have the strength of numbers to do better. As Rawls put it, we should aim for a society that is not only stable—in the sense that it has widespread support and can sustain itself over time—but "stable for the right reasons."[29]

In his second major book, *Political Liberalism*, Rawls set out to demonstrate that citizens committed to a range of different personal moral and religious beliefs could nonetheless come to endorse shared values for organizing their society. The key to his argument was to emphasize three distinctively "political" features of his principles.[30]

First, they are narrow in scope, in the sense that they address only "political" questions about the basic structure of society. They do not try to answer questions about individual morality or the best way to live—for example, they neither deny nor confirm the existence of God or the truth of traditional religious beliefs. Whereas we have to make a collective decision about our fundamental freedoms, the nature of the political system and the structure of the economy—after all, there can only be one set of laws—it is neither necessary nor obviously desirable to reach a collective agreement about which god to worship, or about which are the most important human virtues.

Second, the principles are "political" in the sense that they are independent or "free-standing" from any of the wider moral or philosophical systems of belief that citizens might hold—what Rawls referred to as "comprehensive moral doctrines." These are sets of values which, as the name suggests, try to answer most, if not all, moral questions: about what makes life worth living, how to treat friends and family, what virtues we should celebrate and cultivate, and so on. Religions are the most obvious example of a comprehensive doctrine, though secular philosophies like utilitarianism or humanism can play a similar role.[31] If we want to find a way of justifying principles to *everyone*, then we cannot derive those principles from such a doctrine, since there is none that everyone shares. While Rawls's principles are not derived from any particular world view, they are nonetheless compatible with a wide range of moral and religious perspectives—they can, for example, be endorsed by people of any religion as long as they believe in freedom of religious expression; and we can think of them as a module that can fit into the wider belief systems that citizens hold.[32]

Finally, Rawls's principles are "political" in the sense that they draw on familiar ideas in society's "public political culture." In a democratic society, there are certain ideas that are part of our common heritage and which are often found, either implicitly or explicitly, in important texts like Magna Carta, the preamble to the American Constitution, or the Universal Declaration of Human Rights, and in the ways in which these have been interpreted over time. In the absence of a common religion, these ideas provide us with a source of genuinely shared values from which we can try to derive political principles that everyone can support. Rawls highlighted the idea of society as a "fair system of cooperation" and the idea of citizens as "free and equal," which we have already touched on, as the building blocks of his entire philosophy.[33] He argued that these notions were part of the "common sense" of democratic life and would be familiar to citizens irrespective of their wider religious and moral beliefs.[34] Of course, they aren't the only ideas in our public political culture, and they can be interpreted in a variety of ways, but they provide a reasonable starting point for identifying principles that can win over a wide range of citizens.[35]

Any concept of justice that hopes to win broad support in the real world has to be political in these three ways: to be narrow in scope; to be free-standing of any comprehensive moral doctrine; and to be grounded in widely shared ideas drawn from the public political culture. The original position ensures that Rawls's principles possess these features.[36]

The claim that political principles should be justified independently of any comprehensive doctrine, and without reference to a conception of personal morality or virtue, puts Rawls on one side of a significant dividing line within Western philosophy. In fact, from classical Greece through to the present day, many, if not most, philosophers have taken a different approach. The assumption has often been that before we start to think about our rights as citizens, and about how we should design our political institutions, we must first answer the more fundamental question of what a good life looks like. In Aristotle's words, "Before we can [investigate] the nature of an ideal constitution . . . it is necessary for us first to determine the nature of the most desirable way of life. As long as that is obscure, the nature of the ideal constitution must also remain obscure."[37] Once we have an answer to this question, we can design a system of rights and institutions that will encourage people to live a good and virtuous life.

But this approach gets things the wrong way around.[38] The basic problem is that people will always disagree about "the most desirable way of life." Aristotle may have hoped that we could use philosophy to settle this once and for all, but more than 2,000 years later, we are no closer to reaching a consensus. Indeed, compared to most societies in human history, modern liberal democracies contain an unprecedented diversity of ideas about how we should live our lives. If we design our laws to promote only one of them—for example, one derived from Christian scripture—then how can we hope to justify this to citizens who hold different beliefs?

More worryingly, thinking about politics as the pursuit of a particular conception of the good life can open the door to intolerance and even oppression. Indeed, this perspective often sits behind the so-called "culture wars," and the rise of ethnic and religious nationalism. Of course, many people in all of the major faiths support freedom of religion and other basic liberties; and contemporary philosophers like Michael Sandel have argued that engaging directly with questions about virtue and "the good" can help to strengthen popular support for liberal institutions, by connecting them with people's deeper moral convictions. But if we accept the basic premise that we should design our society around just one such doctrine—even a broadly liberal one—then this makes it much harder to object to Christian fundamentalists who want to outlaw homosexuality or to white nationalists who want to discriminate against Black people. Of course, we can try to persuade them that their specific beliefs are wrong—that there is nothing wrong with being gay, and nothing inherently superior about white people. But if we accept that politics is about promoting a particular vision of how to live, then we cannot object to their general aim of using the power of the state to promote their own beliefs.[39]

In philosophical circles, Rawls's approach is described as asserting the "priority of the right over the good." On this view, our rights define a framework within which we can each pursue our beliefs about how to live; in contrast to the alternative, where we start with a particular conception of the good, and design rights in order to promote it. Rawls's approach provides a powerful philosophical foundation for individual freedom and pluralism and a bulwark against religious and ethnic authoritarianism. At the same time, it is also the basis for a critique of a certain kind of liberalism. For some, liberalism is not simply a set of political principles, but a comprehensive ideal of how to live—the ideal of individual autonomy. From this perspective, what we might call "comprehensive" (as opposed to "political") liberalism, a good life is one in which we freely, or autonomously, choose our goals through an active process of rational reflection, rather than based on an unquestioning acceptance of the religious or moral values of our immediate family or community.

There is nothing wrong with this idea—indeed, there is something very attractive about this way of thinking. The problem arises if we make "autonomy" the basis for justifying our fundamental rights and freedoms. If we argue that we should support freedoms *because* they are the most likely to lead people to live "autonomous" lives, then our support for liberal institutions will depend on an ideal of autonomy that many citizens reject.[40] For many religious believers, living in accordance with God's law is the essence of a good life, rather than individual autonomy; and hence to say that basic freedoms promote autonomy may not count for very much with them. This may sound like a rather academic debate, but it has important real-world implications. Critics often accuse liberals of being committed to an excessively secular and rationalistic moral outlook that many people don't share; and some liberals encourage these kinds of criticisms by adopting a dismissive attitude towards religion (the kind associated with the evolutionary biologist Richard Dawkins, who famously argued that believing in God is an irrational "delusion").[41] Rawls's theory shows us how we can detach our support for liberal political institutions from "liberal" ideas about how to live. In doing so, it offers us the basis for a more inclusive politics which can reach across the cultural and religious lines that are increasingly dividing our societies.

Part of the appeal of Rawls's theory—and indeed of liberalism more broadly—is that it expresses a certain kind of neutrality with respect to different ways of living. But this neutrality is not absolute. As critics sometimes point out, liberal institutions are far from "neutral," in the sense that some ways of living are more likely to flourish under them than others. To take an obvious example, people who believe the state should enforce Sharia, or any other religious law, will never be able to realize their ideals fully in a liberal society (though they will be free to live according to those rules on a voluntary basis). Moreover, it seems likely that in a society where boys and girls are entitled to a fully equal education, fewer people will end up endorsing views that deny the moral and civic equality of women.

To say that liberalism isn't neutral in this absolute sense is not a criticism—it is a statement of the obvious. No set of political principles or institutions could be truly neutral in this way. Rawls argued that we should strive not for neutrality of effect—which is impossible—but neutrality of aim or intent.[42] In other words, while any society will inevitably end up shaping its citizens' beliefs and favouring some ways of living over others, what matters is that our institutions do not actively set out to promote a particular way of life.

By scrupulously avoiding controversial moral or religious doctrines, Rawls shifted the weight of justifying his principles to the intuitive ideas that he identified in the public political culture, above all the ideas that society should be fair, and that citizens should be free and equal. The fact that these ideas, at least on some level, are shared by people across the political spectrum and with a wide range of personal beliefs, should give us hope that Rawls's principles can gain wide support and fulfil their role as a shared basis for resolving contentious political questions.[43]

Of course, there is some dispute about how widely shared these ideas really are, and the rise of authoritarian and avowedly anti-liberal political movements in recent years is a reminder that we cannot take support for even the most basic liberal values for granted. But there is little doubt that they have deep roots in the political culture of most Western democracies; and, as the philosopher and economist Amartya Sen has highlighted, ideas of individual freedom and toleration can be found in the traditions of Arabic, Indian, Chinese and other cultures too.[44] For all the criticism of "liberalism" today, these ideas continue to define the boundaries (however vague) of legitimate democratic debate: it is the fact that racist or authoritarian views are incompatible with any reasonable interpretation of fairness, freedom and equality that rightly sets them outside the boundaries of acceptable political discourse.

There will always be those who reject the basic conception of citizens as free and equal, or who think of society not as a system of cooperation but as a competition between groups striving for domination. In a sense, Rawls's theory has little to say to such people. This is not an oversight, but a pragmatic acknowledgement that there are limits to what we can achieve through the power of reason. If we want to persuade others, then we always need to find some common starting point—there is no use in trying to convince someone that an independent judiciary will help promote freedom if they reject the notion of freedom altogether. Put another way, every argument has to begin somewhere, from some shared premise, and any argument for a liberal or democratic society will face a similar difficulty. The persuasive power of Rawls's theory lies in the fact that it starts with ideas that so many of us share.

PUBLIC REASON AND THE DUTY OF CIVILITY

Rawls's principles are meant to help us work out how we should design our most important social institutions rather than to guide our behaviour as individuals. But they sit alongside an ideal of citizenship, or of how we should treat one another in our capacity as citizens. At a time when our politics is increasingly polarized and intolerant, and when many people seem to have lost faith in the possibility of reasoned debate, we need this more than ever.

The essence of Rawls's ideal of citizenship is a moral duty—the "duty of civility"—to engage in politics in a certain way.[45] This is partly about *how* we express ourselves and respond to others. We should approach political debate with a certain attitude—with an open mind and a spirit of compromise, a willingness to listen to views we disagree with and to take those views in good faith; and we should try to abide by the rules of logic and evidence, appealing wherever we can to accepted facts rather than disputed theories. These attitudes, or "political virtues," are a vital precondition for a healthy and respectful democratic debate. But civility, for Rawls, is also about *what* views we express in the first place. When it comes to important political questions, we should appeal to "public reasons"—to political values that we sincerely think all our fellow citizens can accept, such as Rawls's principles of justice—rather than to moral and religious beliefs that some of them inevitably won't share. Moreover, in order to count as "political," these values or principles must share the three features that we discussed in the previous section: they must be narrow in scope—concerned only with how we organize the basic structure of society; independent of any single comprehensive moral doctrine; and derived from ideas in our public political culture.[46]

This approach is particularly relevant when it comes to issues such as gay rights, abortion, stem-cell research, school prayers and so on, which touch on controversial moral and religious questions. If we take the idea of public reason seriously, then these debates about, say, abortion, should be concerned with how to balance various political values with one another, such as the rights of women to control their bodies, the importance of gender equality, and the rights of unborn children as future citizens.[47] In conducting these debates, we should try to leave religious ideas about the moral status of the foetus or the respective roles of men and women in society at the door, not because we don't believe in them—many people clearly do—but because we recognize that these are beliefs that we cannot expect all our fellow citizens to share. As we shall see in more detail in Chapter 4, this provides us with a distinctive way to approach these kinds of issues, one which can help us to reach a broader consensus and diffuse the so-called "culture wars."

The idea of public reason might initially sound quite restrictive. Surely we should be free to speak our minds using whatever arguments seem most compelling to us? After all, what is the point of having freedom of conscience, thought and speech if we can't use them?

First of all, the duty of civility, including the requirement to use public reasons, is a strictly *moral* duty, not a legal one. We cannot and should not use the law to enforce it—doing so would violate our basic freedom of expression which is protected by the first principle of justice.

Second, this duty does not limit citizens to using only Rawls's principles. We have a moral duty to appeal to the political principles that we sincerely believe are the "most reasonable" basis for cooperation between free and equal citizens—in other words, the principles that our fellow citizens are most likely to accept as fair.[48] While Rawls devoted his life to defending his own theory of "justice as fairness," he recognized that there was room for disagreement, at least within certain limits. He argued that we could think of his principles as part of a family of reasonable political principles, all of which would give special precedence to a set of basic liberties, and a guarantee that everyone would be able to meet their basic needs.[49] We can think of this family of principles, with their protections for basic rights and a decent social minimum, as defining the boundaries of acceptable political debate—or of public reason—in a democratic society; drawing a line between, say, those who are opposed to race-based affirmative action because they think it is unfair, and outright racists who reject the basic equality of certain groups.[50]

Third, the duty of civility is only meant to apply in the "public political forum." This is most relevant to political candidates and elected representatives, as well as judges and government officials. For the rest of us, this duty comes into play most obviously when we are deciding whom to vote for. Rather than thinking about who would advance our own economic interests or religious views, we should choose the candidate who is most likely to promote whatever we think are the most reasonable political values and policies.[51]

To be clear, the idea of public reason does not apply to civil society or what Rawls called the "background culture." In the background culture—in books and journals, in churches and mosques, in community groups and voluntary clubs, and of course at home and with friends—we should feel free to make whatever arguments we like. This is where we can thrash out whether God exists and the meaning of life. The fact that debates like these take place in the background culture does not diminish their importance—for many of us, they are the ones we are most passionate about, and the basic liberties are there precisely to make sure that we can discuss them freely. But, as far as possible, we should keep them separate from questions of what the law should be. This doesn't mean that politics will become technocratic and stripped of moral content—far from it. It simply means that our political conversation will be concerned with political values like fairness, equality and freedom, rather than religious ones like sin or faith.

Fourth, the idea of public reason applies in its strictest form only when we are debating constitutional essentials and matters of basic justice, namely our fundamental rights and freedoms and the structure of our social and political system. Many day-to-day political questions—such as how much public money we should devote to parks and green spaces, or to culture and the arts—are clearly not of this type. Even in these cases, though, we should try to appeal to public reasons where we can. We might argue, for example, that we should invest more in national parks because access to nature is vital for mental health, and something everyone can benefit from.

Finally, the idea of public reason doesn't preclude people from appealing to religious or other non-public reasons altogether. Rawls argued that citizens could appeal to such reasons even in the public political forum, subject to the "proviso" that their positions were also supported by genuinely public ones in due course, as Martin Luther King did by invoking God's will in support of civil rights—rights which were also justified on the basis of fundamentally political values like civic freedom and equality.[52]

It goes without saying that political debate today falls far short of the ideal set out by Rawls's duty of civility and his notion of public reason. For Rawls, a civil and respectful public culture is a vital public asset—something that is built up gradually through constant practice, but which can all too easily be lost. We have run down our stocks of civility to dangerously low levels, and building a more inclusive and respectful public debate is one of the central challenges facing democratic societies today.

Rawls devoted his life to justifying his theory of "justice as fairness" in a way that could appeal to people whatever their religious or philosophical outlook on life. The strength of his argument should give us confidence that his principles can form the basis for a broad political consensus. And yet, as you would expect for a thinker of Rawls's significance, his theory has also been criticized from a variety of directions. The last step before we think about putting Rawls's principles into practice is to understand and respond to these criticisms.

3

Rawls and His Critics

Rawls's ideas have probably been the subject of more academic discussion over the past fifty years than those of any other political thinker, inspiring hundreds of books and thousands of articles. While many have sought to explain, develop and refine his theory, others have been more critical. On the right, classical liberals and libertarians have attacked Rawls for his strong commitment to equality and his willingness to intervene in markets. On the left, socialists have often dismissed him as yet another liberal apologist for private property and capitalism. Rawls's communitarian critics, meanwhile, have argued that his theory fails to take seriously the importance of family, religion and community. Finally, "realist" critics have argued that thinking about what a perfectly just society would look like is a naive and idealistic distraction, which does little to help us address urgent challenges like poverty and discrimination.

While these criticisms have mostly come from academics, they have obvious counterparts in mainstream political debates about liberalism, and if we are to lay the foundations for a transformative politics grounded in Rawls's ideas then we need to address them head on. As we shall see, doing so ultimately serves to bring out the remarkable depth and resilience of Rawls's thought, and the way it cuts across conventional philosophical and political dividing lines.

FREEDOM: THE CRITIQUE FROM THE RIGHT

One of the most distinctive features of Rawls's liberalism is his strong commitment to equality through the difference principle, the idea that we should organize our economy so as to maximize the prospects of the least advantaged. As we've seen, this is a far cry from popular understandings of liberalism today, which have been shaped by thinkers like Friedrich Hayek and Milton Friedman, who in turn drew inspiration from a longer tradition going back to Adam Smith and John Locke. One of the defining features of this "classical" liberalism is the idea that individuals have a basic right to free exchange and to do what they like with their property and that, for the most part, the state should not interfere with these economic freedoms.[1] This way of thinking provided the intellectual underpinnings for the rise of neo-liberalism in the 1980s, which in turn profoundly reshaped popular ideas about the role of the state, and helped to foster a sense of irreconcilable conflict between the values of freedom and equality. These ideas continue to shape our politics today, where policies whose aim is to promote equality, such as progressive taxes or public spending on social services, are frequently criticized from the right as a threat to "freedom," or as being a form of "socialism" and so, by implication, authoritarianism.

Perhaps the clearest articulation of this way of thinking, and the one aimed most directly at Rawls, comes from the philosopher Robert Nozick, one of Rawls's contemporaries at Harvard. Although Nozick lavished praise on *A Theory of Justice*, describing it as an "undeniably great advance over utilitarianism," he also set out a wide-ranging and influential critique, pointing to a number of "deep-lying inadequacies in Rawls's theory."[2] Moreover, he developed an alternative theory of justice which put property rights front and centre, and which justified a radically different vision of society to what Rawls had in mind. Although less well known than Hayek and Friedman, Nozick is widely recognized as the most important philosophical proponent of right-wing liberalism, or "libertarianism," in the twentieth century, and his ideas have been an inspiration to many on the right.[3]

At the heart of Nozick's theory is the idea that we have a natural and absolute right to do whatever we like with ourselves and with our property, as long as we respect the right of others to do the same. The role of the state, he argued, is to protect these rights: only a "minimal state, limited to the narrow functions of protection against force, theft, fraud, enforcement of contracts, and so on, is justified," and "any more extensive state will violate persons' rights not to be forced to do certain things, and is unjustified."[4] Nozick referred to this as the "night-watchman state," and insisted that the state could tax citizens only to pay for public goods that are necessary for protecting property, such as a police force, an army, and a basic legal and bureaucratic infrastructure for enforcing contracts. He opposed anti-discrimination laws on the basis that employers should be free to hire whomever they like, and claimed that forcing the rich to pay taxes in order to fund equal educational opportunities or alleviate poverty was "on a par with forced labor."[5]

Nozick did not simply argue that Rawls's difference principle was too egalitarian, he rejected the whole idea that justice is about trying to bring about a fairer or more equal distribution of resources. For Nozick, justice isn't about fairness or equality, but about protecting property rights. As long as the distribution of resources in society is the result of voluntary transactions that respect people's rights, it is just, even if it is extremely unequal; and the state has no right to interfere to promote an egalitarian agenda that some citizens don't share. From this perspective, the justification for market inequalities is not that markets are fair or efficient, but simply that they are the outcome of transactions that people have a right to make. If citizens want to promote equality of opportunity or address poverty, then they must do so on a voluntary basis.

Nozick's views are pretty extreme: they put him on the far-right branch of the liberal family tree, and it's hard to find anyone in politics today who takes such a hard line about the absolute priority of property rights.[6] Most liberals accept a bigger role for the state, including maintaining free and competitive markets (say, by breaking up monopolies), providing certain public goods like healthcare and education, and ensuring a basic safety net. But many right-leaning liberals share with Nozick the notion that economic freedoms deserve a special kind of protection, and that the state should interfere with them only in order to promote a very limited set of goals; and this idea sits behind much of the opposition we see today to policies that seek to alleviate poverty or promote equality.[7]

But why should economic freedoms take such precedence over addressing poverty or inequality? One answer—which Nozick championed, but which built on the ideas of John Locke—rests on the notion that property rights are "natural rights." Nozick argued that we have a natural and absolute right to "self-ownership"—to do what we like with our bodies—and that since the things we make are in some sense an extension of ourselves, we should be free to buy and sell those things without regulation or taxation. But why should this far-reaching conception of self-ownership take priority over, say, our interests in avoiding starvation, or in freedom from discrimination? To assert that property rights are "natural," as Nozick does, simply dodges the question.

Nozick is surely correct that if we have a right to anything, we have a nearly absolute right to control our own bodies, and the intuitive appeal of his theory rests on the idea that some economic freedoms really do seem to be prerequisites for living a free life. But economic freedom is not "all or nothing," and the choice is not between giving it absolute priority in all its forms and abandoning it entirely. As we have seen, one of Rawls's most important contributions was to distinguish the economic freedoms that are truly essential from those that are not. Freedom of occupational choice and a right to own personal property are basic liberties because, just like freedom of speech and religion, they really are necessary for us to develop our moral capacities as citizens and to pursue our goals in life. But we don't need absolute freedom to accumulate wealth without limit, or to hire people on whatever terms we like, in order to think and live freely.

Nozick's "natural rights" theory has been widely criticized, including by other thinkers on the right.[8] But appealing to innate property rights isn't the only line that those on the right take to defend market inequalities and to attack thinkers like Rawls who want to promote equality. We have already encountered one such argument in Chapter 1: the meritocratic idea that as long as people have equal opportunities and a fair start in life they deserve whatever they earn in a free and competitive market. From this perspective, taxes that promote equality are unfair because they end up taking money from people who deserve it and redistributing it to those who don't; and while we might want to have some kind of basic safety net in place, any further effort to promote equality would be unfair and unjust.[9]

This meritocratic way of thinking is deeply embedded in our public culture. But as we saw in Chapter 1, on closer inspection it quickly starts to fall apart. In particular, the idea that we deserve our market earnings rests on the belief that they are down to our own effort and hard work, and to some extent they are. But they are also—perhaps mostly—the product of luck: of being born with particular talents into a society where those talents happen to be in relatively high (or low) demand. This insight isn't unique to Rawls: Nozick, Friedman and Hayek all rejected the meritocratic ideal, and Hayek argued that people's market incomes bore "little relation to anything we can call moral merit or deserts."[10] Of course, in a fair society it is important that people's incomes reflect their choices and there is a connection between contribution and reward, but the difference principle achieves this without leading to the extreme view that we morally deserve our market incomes in full.

A third argument against equality, also deployed by those on the right, is that taxes and other policies needed to achieve it will undermine economic efficiency and growth. This often rests on the utilitarian logic that low taxes and a minimal state will tend to maximize economic growth, which in turn will maximize overall social "utility," or welfare.[11] As we saw in the previous chapter, utilitarianism is not a very secure foundation on which to build an argument for basic rights—economic or otherwise—since they can always be sacrificed if doing so will increase social welfare overall. And in any case, it's far from clear that this way of thinking can really justify low taxes or laissez-faire capitalism. In fact, the very same utilitarian logic has also been used to make the case for large-scale redistribution, on the basis that the same amount of money will usually bring about more happiness or "utility" in the hands of someone who is poor than someone who is rich.

This brings us to the so-called "slippery slope" argument that those on the right sometimes make against thinkers like Rawls, a line of attack which the economist Thomas Piketty has described as "the classic argument of conservatives throughout history."[12] This is perhaps most closely associated with Hayek, who warned in his hugely popular book *The Road to Serfdom*, published towards the end of the Second World War, that public ownership, economic planning and the modern welfare state would inevitably lead to the kind of authoritarianism seen under the Nazi Party or in the Soviet Union. He later made similar arguments against the kinds of ideas advocated by Rawls, arguing that "any attempt" to achieve fair equality of opportunity was "apt to produce a nightmare," since it would create an inexorable demand to eliminate remaining handicaps "until government literally controlled every circumstance which could affect any person's well-being."[13] The same logic is still at play today when conservatives claim that policies to address poverty or provide free healthcare will somehow lead to "socialism."

While Hayek had good reason to fear the rise of totalitarianism, nearly eighty years later his thesis has not been borne out by events. The recent history of advanced democracies has shown that there is no inexorable tendency for progressive taxes, or policies designed to achieve equality of opportunity, to lead us down the slippery slope to totalitarianism.[14] Conversely, even a very strong commitment to economic freedom is no guarantee that our personal and political liberties will be respected: as we touched on in Chapter 1, some of the worst violations of these basic rights have been perpetrated by regimes committed to laissez-faire economics, such as General Pinochet's brutal dictatorship in Chile, which itself was influenced by Friedman and other right-wing liberals. The threat to basic freedoms from the rise of authoritarian populism today surely owes more to our failure seriously to pursue fairness and equality than any lack of respect for economic liberty.

OWNERSHIP: THE CRITIQUE FROM THE (SOCIALIST) LEFT

Rawls's egalitarian liberalism obviously puts him at odds with many thinkers on the right. And yet his theory has often been regarded with scepticism on the left too, especially by those who look to the socialist and Marxist traditions for inspiration.

Some of this scepticism reflects common misunderstandings of Rawls's ideas, which are often glossed as a justification for contemporary inequalities, or even a "philosophical version of . . . 'trickle-down' theory."[15] The socialist writer Paul Mason captured the general feeling among many on the left when he described Rawls's approach as "a form of political bean counting—asking, how do we inflict neo-liberalism in the least unjust way?"[16] It should already be apparent from the previous two chapters that Rawls was far from an apologist for trickle-down economics or the status quo. Although the difference principle shares with trickle-down the idea that inequalities can, under certain conditions, work to everyone's advantage, the similarities end there. Advocates for trickle-down have typically justified tax cuts for the rich on the basis that some of the benefits will make their way to those at the bottom. But the difference principle is radically more egalitarian, calling on us to organize our economy so as to *maximize* the life chances of the least well off. And while trickle-down's proponents have generally assumed that the benefits of economic growth will automatically find their way to the poorest in society, Rawls was under no such illusions.

Even among those who recognize Rawls's strong commitment to equality, it is often assumed that his ideas simply justify a more generous welfare state, with little to say about questions of work and production. While his early writings were not entirely clear on this point, in his later work Rawls explicitly rejected "welfare state capitalism," arguing that we cannot create a fair economy through redistribution alone. As we have seen, the difference principle is concerned not just with income and wealth, but with inequalities of economic power and control and of opportunities for self-respect; and this broad perspective, in turn, points towards the limitations of the welfare state, putting questions about meaningful work and workplace democracy squarely on the agenda. If there is a criticism to be made here, it is that Rawls said so little about what this would all look like in practice. But as we shall see, when his ideas are properly understood, they provide the basis for a truly transformative economic agenda.

Critics on the left have also pointed to Rawls's relative silence about race, gender and disability, arguing that this points to a deeper flaw in his theory, and indeed with liberalism more widely.[17] On disability, Rawls was clear that the difference principle was designed to address the question of how we should distribute resources between people who can play a "normal and fully cooperating" role in society, including through work, and so it was never meant to address the question of justice for the severely disabled. This is a real gap in Rawls's theory, and while other scholars have addressed this vital question, it is beyond the scope of this book to revise and extend his ideas in this way.[18] However, when it comes to the basic rights of disabled citizens, and to questions of race and gender, Rawls's theory already provides a powerful framework. The basic liberties principle calls on us to make good on the longoverdue liberal promise of civic and political equality for all citizens irrespective of disability, race and gender, or indeed any other arbitrary characteristic; while fair equality of opportunity demands that we do whatever it takes as a society to address ongoing forms of discrimination, as well as the historic legacy of gender inequality and racial exploitation.

While much of the scepticism towards Rawls on the left is grounded in misunderstanding or in frustration at a lack of practical detail, there are also real differences, especially between Rawls and his socialist critics—though not on the issues you might first imagine.[19] One might expect socialists to argue for a more equal distribution of resources than the difference principle. But it's not clear there is much room to the "left" of the difference principle in this sense.[20] Of course, we can imagine more egalitarian principles which would prioritize greater or even perfect equality even if this meant lowering the absolute living standards of the least well off. But few socialists advocate for such thoroughgoing equality of outcome.[21] Alternatively, one might think that socialists would be critical of Rawls's support for a broadly market-based economy, since replacing markets with a planned economy was a key feature of twentieth-century socialism in the Soviet Union and (until the 1980s) in China. But today, most socialists recognize that markets have important advantages over planning, and when they criticize markets they are usually not objecting to the existence of markets per se, but to the naive faith that some liberals have in their "perfect" efficiency, and the widespread disregard for the poverty and inequality that exist in most market economies. Here, Rawls and socialists are on the same page—Rawls also recognises that markets are far from perfectly efficient; and the difference principle offers a strongly egalitarian alternative to the market distribution of income and wealth.

The real disagreement between Rawls and his socialist critics is about the role of private ownership. For many socialists, private ownership of the means of production is both the defining feature of capitalism and the reason why capitalism is unjust; while the abolition of this type of private property is the non-negotiable core of socialism in practice.* By contrast, Rawls adopted a more pragmatic approach. He rejected the idea that private ownership of firms and raw materials was inherently unjust and argued that the problem with capitalism as we know it is not the existence of private property, but the fact that ownership is so heavily concentrated in the hands of a wealthy elite. Rawls argued that one way to address this would be to abolish private property altogether and embrace some kind of liberal or market socialism, but he spent more time exploring the advantages of what he called "property owning democracy"—a society where property is privately owned but widely, if not quite equally, distributed. When socialists criticize Rawls, they generally have this idea in mind.

For many socialists, then, the fundamental problem is that Rawls's theory allows for the continued existence of private property, and hence "poses no threat to capitalist relations of production."[22] But what, exactly, is so bad about private ownership? Some socialists agree with Rawls that there is nothing inherently wrong with private property, but argue that in practice it will be impossible to create a truly fair society as long as it exists. Private property, they claim, is incompatible with democracy, because in any private-property economy some people will inevitably come to own large amounts of wealth, or to control large firms, giving them outsized influence over the political process. If this really was inevitable, it would provide a strong argument for socialism on Rawls's own terms, given his commitment to political equality as a basic liberty.[23] And in light of the enormous wealth and political influence of billionaires like Elon Musk and Mark Zuckerberg, we should obviously take this criticism seriously. But as we shall see in Chapter 5, we can protect democracy without abolishing private property: first, by using the tax system to reduce inequalities of income and wealth directly; and second,

---

* Since most socialists have no problem with people owning *personal* property, such as clothing or even housing, I will use the term "private property" to refer to private ownership of the means of production.

through measures that would insulate the political process from wider economic inequality, such as replacing large private donations to political parties with a carefully designed system of public funding.

For some socialists, however, the problem with private property is more fundamental. To understand this way of thinking, it's helpful to look back to Marx. For Marx, private ownership is inherently unjust because it leads to the exploitation of workers by "capitalists" (those who own the means of production, or "capital"). People often use the term "exploitation" as shorthand for whatever is unfair about work under capitalism, such as poverty wages, endemic insecurity and degrading working conditions. But for Marx, and for orthodox socialists, "exploitation" has a more specific meaning: workers are exploited because some of the value of what they produce is appropriated by capitalists in the form of profits.[24] If workers could choose freely whether to work for themselves or sell their labour, this might not be such a problem. But since most workers don't own the technology or equipment that they need to be productive in a modern economy, they have little choice but to sell their labour to capitalists. The conventional socialist solution to this form of exploitation is to "socialize" the means of production—to transfer ownership to workers or the state so that the value which would otherwise have gone to capitalists can be shared among workers or with society as a whole.[25]

There is no question that work under capitalism as we know it is deeply unjust. But it's far from certain that the Marxist theory of exploitation—that capitalism is unjust because workers receive less than the full value of what they produce—is the best way to think about what is wrong with capitalism or what a fair economy would look like.[26] As the philosopher Will Kymlicka has argued, this theory is "both too weak and too strong."[27] It is "too weak" in the sense that even if we eliminated exploitation, our economy would still be unfair. A society where all firms are owned by workers or by the state, and where workers are paid exactly the value of what they contribute to production, would eliminate exploitation as it is defined by Marx. But this would do nothing to address the unequal opportunities that different workers have to develop their skills; and neither would it address the inequalities that inevitably arise in a market economy between, say, low-skilled shop assistants and high-skilled lawyers. While it made sense for Marx to focus on the gaps between owners and workers as distinct classes in the nineteenth century, today the line between owners and workers is less marked, and most of the rise in inequality in recent decades has been driven by increasingly unequal wages between different kinds of workers.[28] Marx's theory has little to say about this issue.

The Marxist theory of exploitation is also "too strong" in the sense that it condemns activities that appear to be unproblematic. In particular, it implies that it is always wrong to profit from hiring someone else, since this necessarily involves expropriating part of their labour, which is why we need to abolish private ownership. But is it *inherently* unjust to hire someone else and make a profit from doing so? What about people who have built up savings from work and invested them in stocks and shares, and hence benefit from profits indirectly? And does it really make sense to say that highly paid executives and professionals are being unfairly exploited even when they wield significant bargaining power? The force of Marx's argument rests on the assumption that workers have to sell their labour or starve, but the existence of the welfare state means that for most people this is no longer true.

The orthodox notion of exploitation also runs into trouble when it comes to thinking about justice for those who are unable to do conventional paid work, such as severely disabled people, carers (most of whom are women) and the involuntarily unemployed.[29] For Marxists, the wage relationship is inherently unjust because workers are forced to give up some of the value of what they produce to someone else. But by this logic, isn't it also a kind of exploitation to tax workers to help carers and the unemployed? After all, this involves transferring some of the value of what workers produce to people who have played no direct part in its production. As the socialist philosopher G. A. Cohen pointed out, the Marxist theory of exploitation appears to be underpinned by an idea of self-ownership—that we have a natural right to the value of what we produce—rather similar to that held by people like Robert Nozick, and with many of the same unpalatable implications.[30] Of course, most socialists do care about inequalities between high- and low-paid workers, and, historically, socialists have been among the most important advocates of support for the unemployed and for carers.[31] The point is not that socialism and libertarianism are the same—clearly they are not—but simply that, on closer inspection, the orthodox socialist idea of exploitation seems worryingly incomplete as an account of what is unjust about capitalism, and, taken seriously, leads to conclusions that even most socialists would reject.

These problems have led some "revisionist" socialist thinkers, such as Cohen and John Roemer, to develop new theories about what justice and fairness mean for socialists. These thinkers have tended to conceive of socialism as an ethical commitment to equality, and to argue for a more pragmatic approach to ownership. Rather than condemn private property outright, they have focused, for example, on the fact that what is owned is so unequally distributed, or on the ways in which property has been acquired through force and coercion.[32] There is more to say about these ideas than we can cover here, but what stands out is the degree to which they resemble Rawls's outlook.

Some socialists point to a different problem with private ownership, namely that it leads to "alienation." Whereas exploitation is concerned with the way in which private ownership leads to an unfair distribution of income, alienation is concerned with how work in a capitalist economy can stunt our potential for flourishing as human beings. There are various different accounts of alienation, and why private ownership leads to it. Some emphasize the commodification of labour as its source: the fact that we work to survive rather than as an end in itself. Others emphasize the fact that so much work is dull and repetitive, providing few if any opportunities for enjoyment or intrinsic satisfaction.[33] For socialists, the way to bring an end to alienation, and to guarantee meaningful work for all, is to abolish private ownership and put workers (or the state) in charge.

The socialist idea of alienation focuses on questions about the nature and organization of work which liberals have all too often

ignored.[34] But one of the great strengths of Rawls's theory is precisely that it can address these concerns. It does so via the importance it attaches to inequalities of economic power and control and,
crucially, to the opportunities that work provides for individual
achievement, social recognition, and ultimately self-respect.[35] Rawls
argued that in a society organized according to his principles "the
narrowing and demeaning features of the division [of labour] should
be largely overcome," and that everyone would have fair opportunities for meaningful work.[36] In later chapters we will see how this can
be achieved in practice.

Rawls's idea of self-respect provides the basis for a distinctively
liberal account of how we can overcome "alienation," at least in the
context of work. Like Marx, Rawls recognized that we have a special responsibility as a society to make sure that citizens have fair
opportunities for self-realization through work. But whereas Marxists have sometimes fetishized a certain kind of "non-alienated," self-
directed work as if this is the only way to lead a meaningful life, for
Rawls and other liberals work is just one source of meaning among
others. Our responsibility as a society to guarantee the availability
of meaningful work is grounded in a pragmatic recognition that
some kind of work is more or less necessary for most of us, and that
since this typically takes up so much of our time it is bound to shape
our lives in profound ways. In practical terms, as we shall see, we
can ensure these opportunities not by abolishing private ownership
altogether but by ensuring that all workers can leave bad employers
without falling into poverty, and through new forms of workplace
democracy.

COMMUNITY: THE COMMUNITARIAN CRITIQUE

One of the most persistent criticisms of liberalism, and of Rawls's
theory, is that they rest on an unattractive and frankly unrealistic
conception of people as fundamentally selfish and individualistic,
and that this in turn is the source of a wider indifference or even
hostility towards "community" of various kinds—family, local community, religion, the nation and so on. This communitarian critique,
as it is often loosely referred to, has become a familiar reference
point among those on both the left and the right who argue that

there is something rotten at the heart of the liberal ideal. And this is not simply a philosophical debate about human nature: communitarians argue that the liberal elevation of personal choice has given rise to an excessively individualistic culture which is responsible, at least in part, for social problems ranging from the decline of civic and religious associations to an epidemic of loneliness. These criticisms have also served to foster the sense that liberalism can only ever appeal to people with a "cosmopolitan" or "secular" outlook, and has little to offer those more closely tied to a particular place or religion.[37]

As we touched on in the Introduction, this critique makes the most sense when it is directed towards neoliberalism, whose proponents have often championed crude individualism and the pursuit of self-interest, with little concern for the consequences this might have for family or community life. By contrast, Rawls's liberalism is grounded in an ideal of reciprocity rather than self-interest, and takes very seriously the importance of family, religion and other forms of community.

And yet Rawls's ideas have been a focal point for the communitarian critique of liberalism.[38] Critics tend to focus on the original position thought experiment, which appears to encapsulate everything that communitarians think is wrong with liberalism. For a start, the parties in the original position are represented as self-interested, in the sense that they choose the principles for organizing society that would be best for *them*. Moreover, they appear to be a pale imitation of real-life human beings, detached from the values and social commitments that make us who we are. The philosopher Michael Sandel has famously claimed that Rawls's theory rests on a psychologically incoherent conception of the "unencumbered self," according to which people simply "choose" their values as if from a menu; while the political scientist Francis Fukuyama has accused Rawls of "the absolutization of autonomy, and the elevation of choice over all other human goods."[39] A closely related criticism is that Rawls failed to recognize that our values and beliefs are shaped by our social context, and that many of us have commitments that we simply cannot imagine ourselves without—that are "constitutive" of who we are—such as the sense of duty we feel towards our family, or our religious beliefs. For Rawls's communitarian critics, the fact that his theory, and by extension much of contemporary liberal philosophy, was built on such obviously shaky foundations is reason to call the whole project into question.*

These criticisms raise important, if rather abstract, issues, and are no doubt well made against some kinds of liberalism. But they make little sense directed at Rawls. This is not a question of subtle interpretation—Rawls's communitarian critics often attribute to him positions that he explicitly rejected.[40] The source of this confusion is a tendency to (mis)interpret the description of the parties in the original position as an account of human psychology or of the metaphysical nature of the self. Rawls was aware that his thought experiment might give rise to these sorts of misunderstandings, and he did his best to pre-empt them, stating explicitly that the original position was not an account of human psychology but a "purely hypothetical situation" designed with the specific aim of helping us to identify basic political principles for a diverse and democratic society.[41] As we have seen, the description of the parties in the original position is not grounded in empirical claims about human psychology but in moral claims about the kinds of reasons that are relevant when it comes to selecting such principles. Rawls compared the original position to acting or role play, explaining that "when . . . we simulate being in the original position, our reasoning no more commits us to a particular metaphysical doctrine about the nature of the self than our acting a part in a play, say of Macbeth or Lady Macbeth, commits us to thinking that we are really a king or queen engaged in a desperate struggle for political power."[42]

In fact, properly understood, the original position embodies

---

* Rawls's theory is also criticized on the grounds that attempting to identify universal principles fails to respect the diversity of values across different societies. In fact, Rawls's universalism is already qualified since, as we saw in Chapter 2, his principles are explicitly developed from ideas found in the public culture of modern democracies. Nonetheless, they do identify basic rights and freedoms that *all* citizens in such societies are entitled to. But this is a strength rather than a weakness of his theory. Would we really want to allow religious communities to punish people for being gay, or to prevent girls from going to school? This seems to be where the critique of universalism leads, but few are willing to accept those implications.

almost the opposite of what its critics claim. Far from being grounded in the idea that people are inherently egotistic, it assumes that people are motivated by a desire to live with others on terms that are both mutually beneficial and fair. It asks us to put ourselves in other people's shoes and to consider other people's points of view, and then to choose principles that will be acceptable to everyone. The fact that the parties choose the principles that are best for them individually is just an analytical device to help work out this difficult problem.[43] And although the parties in the original position imagine themselves to be without knowledge of their actual values and commitments, Rawls was well aware that, in real life, these will be shaped by our social context. Indeed, he took this to be so obvious that he called it a "truism": "the social system," he wrote, "shapes the wants and aspirations that its citizens come to have. It determines in part the sort of persons they want to be as well as the sort of person they are."[44]

Similarly, Rawls explicitly recognized that we have "constitutive" commitments which are so fundamental that we cannot imagine actually giving them up, noting that citizens "may have, and often do have . . . affections, devotions, and loyalties that they believe they would not, indeed could and should not, stand apart from and evaluate objectively."[45] The fact that the parties in the original position are ignorant of their particular values and relationships doesn't mean these don't matter, or that real-life citizens could easily abandon them—quite the opposite. The point of this thought experiment is to remind us that *everyone* has deep and non-negotiable commitments, and that, just as we would never want to live in a society that would force us to reject our religion or our loved ones, we should respect the fact that others will want the same for themselves.

What about the idea that Rawls and other liberals elevate choice over all other human goods? The basic liberties principle does protect our freedom to choose whom we want to spend our time with or what religion we want to follow, even where this goes against the norms and beliefs of our family or community. But this isn't grounded in the belief that people should choose their values as if from a shopping list. What matters isn't choosing itself but having the *freedom* to choose—to change our religion, or leave our community—if we need or want to.[46]

Far from ignoring communitarian concerns, Rawls devoted a lengthy section in *A Theory of Justice* to explaining how, in a society organized according to his principles, "the values of community are not only essential but realizable."[47] The basic liberties—freedoms of speech, conscience and association—guarantee our freedom to create communities of all kinds; while the difference principle would provide us with a fair share of the resources we need to take part in family and communal life.[48] At the same time, these principles protect us from the excesses of community: they ensure, for example, not only that gay people are free to leave a family or religious community that rejects them, but that they would have the resources to support themselves.

It seems clear that, at least at a philosophical level, there is no deep conflict between Rawls's principles and the value of community. But some communitarians worry that even if this is the case in theory, in practice liberal institutions tend to have harmful effects.[49]

For those on the left, the problem lies with the economic policies often advocated by liberals—a single-minded focus on economic growth; the embrace of unregulated markets; the tolerance of high levels of poverty, insecurity and inequality. There is surely no question that our existing economic structures undermine community in various ways. Economic growth has been pursued with little attention to the implications for local economies—the decline of the "high street" being an obvious contemporary example. Endemic poverty and insecurity make family life almost impossible, and leave many people with little time to get involved with their local community or religious groups. High levels of inequality, meanwhile, are leading to an increasingly fragmented society in which rich and poor live in different areas, go to different schools and work in different places.

But these criticisms do not apply to Rawls's egalitarian liberalism. A society organized around the difference principle would be a society in which no one had to choose between meeting their basic needs and spending time with their family, going to their temple, church or mosque, or joining a football team or community group. Moreover, since inequalities of class, race and gender would be drastically reduced, citizens would have similar life experiences, which in turn would help to sustain a sense of community at both the local and national levels.

While communitarians on the left often point to the way in which inequality has undermined community, those on the right tend to emphasize almost the opposite, highlighting the threat posed by the pursuit of equality and the welfare state. The basic story here is roughly as follows: before the advent of the modern welfare state, people had to rely on family, neighbours or colleagues in times of need and hardship—in raising children, through sickness and unemployment, and of course in old age, and they often created voluntary associations such as trade unions and mutual and friendly societies in order to meet these challenges. Today, the state fulfils many of these functions, providing benefits for the sick, unemployed and elderly, and delivering public services including education and healthcare; and this in turn has weakened family ties and made various forms of community association superfluous—or so critics claim.

However, it's not at all clear that the welfare state is responsible for the problems of family and community breakdown—poverty, inequality and insecurity seem to be more likely culprits. And even if the welfare state has weakened the role of family or community as a form of mutual aid, we would have to balance this against its very important advantages in making sure that everyone—and not just those who are lucky enough to have a supportive family or community network—can meet their basic needs. Moreover, there is nothing about Rawls's principles that requires a bureaucratic, centralized state to deliver public services, and there are many good reasons for a more decentralized and community-oriented approach—by putting more control in the hands of local government, say, and using charities and non-profit organizations. The lesson to take from the right's critique is not that we should abandon the welfare state or dismantle public services, but that we need to think more carefully and creatively about how we design them.

The idea that liberal institutions inevitably undermine community simply doesn't stand up to scrutiny, at least not when we consider Rawls's inclusive and egalitarian liberalism. And although the state should steer clear of promoting one kind of community over another, such as an official religion or a particular idea of the nuclear family, there is scope for it to play a proactive role. We could, for example, support spiritual organizations, charities, sports clubs and so on through subsidized spaces or tax breaks; and we can invest public money in local infrastructure like libraries, parks and high streets in order to foster a healthy sense of local community.[50]

REALISM: THE CRITIQUE OF "IDEAL THEORY"

There is a final critique to address, which in some ways cuts the deepest. The problem, for some, is not so much that Rawls came to the wrong answer, but that in trying to work out principles for a perfectly just society he was asking the wrong question.

One version of this criticism comes from so-called "realists," who argue that Rawls's theory is just too abstract, too detached from history, psychology and the messy realities of democratic politics, to be of any use. According to the philosopher Raymond Geuss, rather than following Rawls and asking what an ideally just society would look like, political philosophers should focus on understanding and critiquing the institutions and power relations in the societies we *actually* live in. In doing so, they should take their lead from Lenin's famous question, "Who whom?"—or, as Geuss elaborates, "Who does what to whom for whose benefit?" For Geuss, Rawls's obsession with dreaming up distant utopias was at best naive, and at worst a deliberate ploy to distract us from addressing the inequalities and injustices in the societies in which we live.[51]

It's easy to see how Rawls's theory might appear naive. After all, he envisages a society where citizens abide by the rules of public reason, supporting policies that they sincerely think are fair and just, rather than ones which advance their own self-interest. But we have to remember that this is an ideal—something for us to aspire to—and not a description of political reality. While Rawls thought that moral notions of justice and fairness can and do play a role in shaping people's political beliefs and actions, he never claimed that these were the only, or even the most important, source of their motivation; and he was clear that when it comes to designing political institutions, we have to do so on the basis of a realistic account of human psychology, taking people as they are and not as we would like them to be.

It is, however, true that Rawls never provided a detailed account of how politics actually works, or how we could build a political movement capable of putting his ideas into practice. Those looking to him for an analysis of how powerful elites obstruct change and maintain their hold on power, or to gain a better understanding of the structures that maintain racial inequalities over time, are bound to be disappointed, since these simply aren't questions he was trying to answer.[52] Similarly, he never set out a theory of political change, nor did he try to identify a political "agent" that could be the vehicle for social transformation in the way that socialists have typically looked to the "working class." A lot of the criticism aimed at Rawls is simply frustration that he didn't try to address these important issues. But this was not the product of naivety or lack of interest, but because he recognized that what we should be aiming for as a society and how we can get there are two separate questions; and that, while political philosophy is critical for answering the former, it is at best secondary for the latter. Rather than rejecting Rawls's ideas, we need to combine them with a realistic theory of change and with a political strategy tailored to our circumstances here and now.

Some realist critics appear to go further and suggest that people are fundamentally self-interested, and that moral ideas play no role whatsoever in shaping people's behaviour, especially when it comes to politics. This bleak and one-dimensional view of human nature, popularized by economists as *Homo economicus*, has come to shape thinking across the political spectrum. On the right, it has been used to justify an almost total reliance on markets, on the basis that they harness self-interest for the common good, and to disparage egalitarian ideals as hopelessly utopian. While on parts of the left, especially among Marxists, a similar point of view sits behind the idea that politics is simply a battle for one class to advance its interests over another.

If it were true that people's political behaviour is purely self-interested, there really would be little practical value in thinking about what a fair or just society would look like. But this is just as unrealistic as the claim that morality is the only thing that matters. Otherwise, it would be hard to make sense of why politicians spend so much time appealing to moral values like freedom, equality and individual responsibility.[53] Similarly, the idea that people are fundamentally selfish is hard to square with the fact that so many rich people support welfare policies that they are extremely unlikely to benefit from. We don't have to rely on casual observation to reject this way of thinking: social scientists and psychologists have established beyond doubt that moral ideas play a critical role in driving people's political behaviour.[54] Moreover, the evidence increasingly supports the basic "realism" of Rawls's emphasis on reciprocity—the willingness to cooperate and share with others who are similarly disposed, even at some personal cost—as a fundamental norm of social behaviour, as opposed to either self-interest or altruism. Experiments conducted by psychologists consistently find that people are willing to share even when they could have more by acting selfishly, and that they make personal sacrifices in order to uphold certain norms of reciprocity (usually by "punishing" those who they think have acted unfairly). Anthropologists, meanwhile, have found evidence of reciprocity in the form of sharing food and other resources beyond the immediate family in all societies going back to the advent of *Homo sapiens*. Indeed, it is increasingly apparent that our capacity for cooperation and reciprocity has deep roots in our evolution as a species, and is more or less hardwired into our psychology.[55]

There is nothing unrealistic, then, in thinking that moral ideas can and do shape political behaviour, even if this is only part of the story; and Rawls's emphasis on reciprocity appears to fit well with the latest science. But even among thinkers who accept an important practical role for moral and political philosophy, some have rejected Rawls's approach. One of the most powerful articulations of this view comes from Amartya Sen, the Nobel Prize–winning economist and philosopher, and a former colleague of Rawls's at Harvard.[56]

While he warmly recognizes Rawls's fundamental contribution to political philosophy, Sen insists in his 2009 book *The Idea of Justice* that Rawls has largely taken the discipline in the wrong direction.[57]

Sen's starting point is that political philosophy should offer us practical guidance about how we can address injustices in our societies. In particular, a theory of justice should help us to compare and ultimately decide between the different policy choices that we are actually faced with here and now. The problem with Rawls's theory, according to Sen, is that it is "transcendental," in the sense that it develops a detailed picture of a perfectly just society, rather than being "comparative," in which case it would help us compare and choose between different policies and institutions. While imagining a perfectly just society might be an interesting philosophical exercise, Sen argues, it is largely irrelevant in practice: just as we don't need to know that Everest is the highest mountain in the world to work out whether Mont Blanc is higher than Mount Kilimanjaro, we don't need to know what an ideally just society would look like to know that society would be more just if we could reduce torture, poverty or illiteracy. For Sen, political philosophy should be less concerned with asking what "spotless justice" would look like than with the more modest, useful and fundamentally comparative question, "How would justice be advanced?"[58]

There is much to admire in Sen's critique, including his sense of urgency in wanting to address real-life injustices, and his belief that political philosophy can and should help us in this task. And Sen is right that while there has been a burgeoning of academic political philosophy in recent decades, much of it inspired by Rawls, most of it has been rather abstract, and too little attention has been paid to the actual challenges that are the mainstay of public debate, from tackling discrimination to addressing poverty and illiteracy. But as we shall see in Part II of this book, Rawls's principles provide a powerful tool for carrying out precisely the kind of work that Sen wants to do.

In responding to Sen's critique more directly, it's helpful to look at how Rawls understood the relationship between his principles and the practical task of social reform. Rawls described his own work as an exercise in "ideal theory," the aim of which is to work out "what a perfectly just society would be like."[59] This is not about constructing a best-of-all-possible-worlds Panglossian fantasy, but about identifying principles and institutions that are the best we can hope for given the facts about human psychology and the material world we live in. Having a coherent idea of what a perfectly just society would look like can itself be a powerful source of motivation, offering a sense of hope and a corrective to the cynicism that pervades our political discourse. But if this was all Rawls's theory could offer, it would have limited practical value, since there is little chance of becoming such a society in one giant leap. For Rawls, however, "ideal theory" was always a precursor to "non-ideal theory": whereas the former defines the goal, the latter "asks how this long-term goal might be achieved, or worked towards, usually in gradual steps."[60] We need ideal theory because without a clear target to work towards, however remote, we are always in danger of merely tweaking the edges of existing institutions or, worse, of moving in the wrong direction altogether.[61] But Sen is wrong to suggest that ideal theory only gives us such a target; it also gives us a set of values with which to choose between different policies by comparing how far they would move us towards this destination.[62] So, for example, Rawls's basic liberties principle calls on us to prioritize protecting basic freedoms over economic growth; while the difference principle says that we should adopt economic policies that will advance the interests of the least well off, even if they don't go as far as maximizing their life chances.

Still, one might wonder whether we really need a complex philosophical theory of justice such as Rawls's to make progress in addressing the world's most serious injustices, like poverty and famine. These issues are so urgent that engaging in philosophical reflection about precisely why poverty is unjust can feel like a self-indulgent luxury. In the case of famine, where almost everyone agrees that something needs to be done, there may be little value in further philosophical reflection. But this kind of consensus is rather rare. We are often unsure, both as individuals and as a society, not just about which policy would be most effective in achieving a given goal, but about what our goals should be in the first place; about how much inequality we should tolerate, and how we should balance equality against freedom and economic efficiency. These moral disagreements are as much an obstacle to creating a better, fairer society as are practical disagreements about which policies would be most effective, and we need a theory like Rawls's to help us resolve them.

In the end, the only way to see whether Rawls's principles can help us with the real problems and choices we face today is to put them to the test. In the rest of this book, we will do just that.

Part TWO

4

Freedom

●────────●

Our societies fall well short of Rawls's inspiring vision of a truly fair society. But how can we change our core political and economic institutions in order to make it a reality? While some countries have further to go than others, this isn't about tackling the shortcomings of any particular nation; it's about defining a realistic long-term goal that all democratic societies can work towards. Different countries will have different priorities, but the fundamental challenges facing liberal democracies around the world—the structure of the political system, the role of markets, the design of the welfare state, and so on—are essentially the same.*

We will start, as Rawls does, with the basic liberties principle, and its commitment to wide-ranging personal freedoms (we will look at political freedoms and the democratic process in the next chapter). These freedoms are the liberal core of Rawls's theory, and the foundation on which everything else is built. They are the basis for our most important legal rights, and for a society in which we can live our lives freely, and according to our own beliefs, without

---

* The policy ideas developed in the rest of this book take for granted the existence of a well-functioning state and bureaucratic infrastructure, and countries that lack these basic institutions will inevitably need to focus on putting them in place first.

unwanted interference from either the state or our fellow citizens—a society where we can express ourselves and speak our minds, where we can love whomever we like, follow the religion of our choosing, decide what kind of job we want to do and how we spend the precious time we have on Earth.

We are probably closer to achieving this aspect of Rawls's ideal than any other. It is no exaggeration to say that citizens in today's rich liberal democracies enjoy more wide-ranging personal freedoms than has been true of almost any society in history. The principles of freedom of speech, conscience and religious belief are very widely recognized; and over the past fifty years or so we have seen enormous progress in extending the sphere of basic personal freedoms to include sexual and reproductive rights, with most democratic countries now respecting women's right to have an abortion, and the rights of LGBTQ+ people to live freely and as equals.

And yet, despite this progress, these liberties are under threat. The rise of right-wing populism has given an increasingly prominent voice to ethnic nationalists and religious fundamentalists who are intent on removing some of our most intimate freedoms, and who often reject the ideal of a tolerant and pluralistic society altogether. According to the Economist Intelligence Unit's global "Democracy Index," civil liberties such as freedom of speech and religion have been in decline since at least 2008, and the speed with which they are declining appears to be getting faster.[1] A number of Eastern European countries, including Poland, Hungary and Russia, have introduced laws that discriminate against the LGBTQ+ community, for example.[2] And we have also seen a disturbing willingness to target the religious freedom of Muslim citizens, to the extent that in 2009 a Swiss referendum approved a constitutional amendment banning the construction of minarets (a tower typically built into or next to mosques).[3] The U.S. Supreme Court's decision in June 2022 to overturn *Roe v. Wade* (1973), and with it the constitutional right to an abortion that has existed in America for nearly fifty years, marks a watershed moment in this anti-liberal backlash, and shows that even long-established freedoms can no longer be taken for granted. In the wake of this ruling, Republican-controlled states have introduced near-total bans on abortion, even in cases of rape and incest, and there is now a very real possibility that other basic liberties will come under attack, from the relatively recent right to gay marriage to more established rights like access to contraception.[4]

Fortunately, in most liberal democracies there is strong public support for extensive individual freedoms. Although anti-liberal voices have recently become more outspoken, surveys generally find that a large and growing majority of the population are in favour of gay rights and religious liberty: the proportion of people who say that society should tolerate homosexuality increased from 51 per cent in 2002 to 72 per cent in 2019 in the U.S.A., from 74 per cent to 86 per cent in the UK over the same period, and is as high as 94 per cent in Sweden; while large majorities across all regions of the world think that people should be able to practise their religion freely.[5] Similarly, most people are broadly comfortable with ethnic and religious diversity: a 2021 study of seventeen advanced economies, including the U.S.A., UK, France, Germany and Australia, found that 76 per cent of people thought their societies were better off with people from a range of ethnic and religious backgrounds, and in most of these countries this number was increasing.[6] But even among the majority who accept that citizens should generally be free to live their lives according to their own beliefs, there continues to be a great deal of controversy about what this means in practice and how we should handle certain "hard cases" where different basic freedoms come into conflict with one another, such as in debates about the limits of free speech, and the conflict between religious freedom and LGBTQ+ rights.

These kinds of questions have become an increasingly central part of our political debate in recent years. Politicians and commentators, especially on the right, have cynically exploited disagreements about sexuality, abortion and ethnicity to foster a sense of irreconcilable cultural division within our societies. What's more, there is a worrying tendency on all sides to approach these matters in a rather absolutist way, leaving little room for compromise. The result is a growing sense of scepticism about whether the liberal ideal of a truly tolerant and pluralistic society is either coherent or achievable.

If we want to realize this ideal, we need to confront these debates head on and find a way to build a broader consensus about the scope of our most fundamental basic freedoms. In this context, Rawls's ideas are needed more urgently than ever, and can help us find common ground even where there appears to be none. And it is only once we are confident of what our basic liberties should be that we can start to think about how to design a constitution and legal system that will protect them in practice.

BEYOND THE "CULTURE WARS"

Some of our core personal freedoms have become the focal point of the so-called "culture wars." Questions about sexuality and abortion, religious freedom and free speech play a central role in these debates, which are often framed as a battle between "progressives" committed to a secular and individualistic morality and conservatives committed to a more "traditional" religious outlook, with each side threatening to impose its world view on the other. The prominent American conservative Pat Buchanan famously captured this way of thinking at the Republican National Convention in 1992, when he described the "culture wars" as a "war for the soul of America," and today this kind of rhetoric has become increasingly common.

These disagreements often seem intractable, and framed in this way they probably are. Rawls's theory offers a way to reframe them and defuse the sense of irreconcilable conflict. We must begin by rejecting the conception of politics that sits behind the "culture wars": that politics is a battle for moral supremacy, or a struggle for one group to impose its own idea of how to live on everyone else. As we saw in Chapter 2, Rawls's distinctively "political" liberalism offers an alternative—a society where people with different moral and religious outlooks respect one another's right to live according to their own beliefs, and where we agree not to use the power of the state to impose our views on others. For many of us, it may seem obvious that a commitment to reproductive rights and sexual freedoms is consistent with this—after all, no one is being forced to have an abortion or to be gay. And yet conservative critics of "liberal" rights and freedoms sometimes argue that asking them to support gay rights is like asking them to approve of gay relationships, and hence to abandon their beliefs. We can and should reject this. But doing so means making the case for our personal freedoms in a particular way, one that calls on progressives to recognize the legitimacy of moral and religious views with which they may deeply disagree.

To see how this might work, let's take the debate about LGBTQ+ rights, and specifically the rights of gay people to have intimate relationships.[7] One way we can argue for these rights is to engage directly with the moral question at hand, namely whether homosexuality is morally right or wrong. In other words, we can argue that gay people should be free to form intimate relationships because there is nothing wrong with being gay and same-sex relationships are as valid as any other. At first sight, this appears to be the natural, even obvious approach—after all, it reflects what many progressives believe, myself included (indeed, as a gay man, this belief is particularly close to my heart).

But the problem with this argument is that it depends on a moral belief that some citizens won't share, in this case, the idea that there is nothing wrong with being gay. In doing so, it makes the mistake of engaging with religious critics of gay equality on their own terrain, and turns this into a debate about who has the right moral view, as if resolving this would allow us to impose that view on everyone else. But just as it would be wrong for conservatives to limit gay rights on the basis of their religious beliefs, it would be wrong for us to justify such rights by appealing to moral precepts that many of our fellow citizens cannot accept. No matter how strongly we believe that gay relationships are worthy of equal respect, and even if we struggle to understand those who believe that homosexuality is a sin, we have to recognize that for some people this is part of their faith and no reasoned argument will persuade them otherwise.

This doesn't mean giving up on gay rights—not at all. It means adopting a different approach. In particular, we should put the debate about the morality of homosexuality to one side, and focus instead on the specifically political principle that whom we love or choose to have sex with is something that should be left to individuals rather than being controlled by society on the basis of the moral beliefs of its members.[8] We don't need to get involved in a debate about whether or not homosexuality is a sin in order to establish the fundamental importance of equal rights for gay citizens. In a liberal society, people should be free to come to their own conclusion about this sort of question, and we should try to justify our laws in a way that can appeal to citizens with a wide range of moral and religious views.

We can apply the same approach to a whole range of issues, from abortion to religious freedom. In the case of abortion, this means bypassing the question of whether abortion is right or wrong according to the doctrine of any religious authority, and focusing instead on whether it should be legal. The answer depends on weighing up certain political values, like the rights of women to control their bodies, the importance of gender equality, and the rights of unborn children as future citizens. This doesn't lead towards an immediate solution, but it rules out the most extreme positions. As Rawls argued, any reasonable attempt to balance these values will recognize women's rights to bodily autonomy in the early stages of pregnancy, justifying a right to abortion within a given window of time; while, beyond a certain point, the rights of unborn children should take precedence, though where exactly this point lies is a difficult question.[9]

At the heart of this approach is a commitment to resolving our disagreements by appealing to public reasons (political values that our fellow citizens can share) rather than to our personal moral or religious beliefs. This is not just the right thing to do, it is a precondition for healing our divided societies, and a pragmatic way to build the widest possible support for our most essential liberties. It makes it clear that social conservatives can be (political) liberals too—that it is perfectly consistent to believe that homosexuality is a sin, or that abortion is morally wrong, while at the same time recognizing that this is not a legitimate basis for coercive restrictions on sexual or reproductive freedoms. In this way, we can make an argument for vital individual rights that most citizens can accept.

Of course, to say that social and religious conservatives *can* support freedoms ranging from gay rights to abortion is not to say they will. But it's worth remembering that the same fundamental idea underpins widespread support for religious liberty. Most of us, including most religious believers, recognize that we can and should support freedom of religious expression, even if we think other people's beliefs are misguided or false. As Rawls noted, the Catholic Church adopted such a position in its Declaration on Religious Freedom in 1965; and similar stances can be found in other major religions, from Buddhism to Islam.[10] The case for other liberal freedoms simply extends this principle to a wider range of issues.

We can see this way of thinking at work in the significant number of social conservatives who support gay rights despite believing that homosexuality is a sin.[11] In America today, while 30 per cent of people continue to think that gay and lesbian relationships are morally wrong, only 18 per cent think that such relationships should be illegal.[12] In the UK, surveys in the early 2010s found that 35 per cent of people thought gay relationships were sometimes or always wrong, but just 18 per cent disagreed with the idea that the law should treat gay people the same as everyone else, and only 5 per cent disagreed with the idea that gay people "should be free to live their own life as they wish."[13]

Although the politically liberal argument won't persuade everyone, it is the most promising basis for achieving a wide consensus about our basic rights and freedoms. Adopting this approach doesn't mean we have to stop debating moral issues around sexuality or abortion altogether. Those of us who believe that there is nothing wrong with being gay can still try to persuade our fellow citizens to adopt a more tolerant and accepting attitude, and to explain the hugely damaging psychological impact that parents can have on their children by rejecting or repressing their sexuality or gender identity. But when it comes to questions about our most elemental freedoms, we should avoid arguments about personal morality and sin and focus on our fundamental right to live according to our own beliefs. These debates will still be difficult and arouse intense feelings, but they won't have the same existential character that they have today—and that is something all of us should welcome.

STRIKING A BALANCE: HOW TO DEAL WITH HARD CASES

The first step in trying to build support for core liberal freedoms, then, is to argue for them in as inclusive a way as possible. But even if we do this, we still face a host of challenging situations where different basic freedoms come into conflict with one another. Fortunately, Rawls formulated his basic liberties principle precisely with these kinds of hard cases in mind.

To help us think about these issues, it's worth distinguishing between "vertical" and "horizontal" applications of our basic rights and liberties.[14] Vertical applications are concerned with protecting our basic freedoms from the undue interference of the state. They include the right to criticize the government without fear of arrest, to have an abortion, and to have intimate relationships with whomever we please irrespective of their race or sex. Historically, the struggle for freedom has often focused on winning these kinds of rights. But as most democratic countries have come to recognize wide-ranging vertical rights, there has been a shift of focus towards horizontal ones. These are concerned with protecting people's basic freedoms from infringements from their fellow citizens, or from non-state actors, such as firms or religious organizations. In other words, they are about what to do when one person's right to exercise their basic freedoms interferes with another's right to do the same. So, for example, should people be allowed to exercise their right to protest directly outside abortion clinics, or does this unduly interfere with women's rights to have an abortion? Should parents be able to exercise their parental freedoms in order to withdraw their children from classes about other religions or about LGBTQ+ issues, or should children's rights to a comprehensive education take priority?

Let's stay with the theme of LGBTQ+ rights. As LGBTQ+ people have won vertical rights—the freedoms to have sex and form relationships and, increasingly, the right to get married—the debate has shifted towards horizontal rights, and specifically what this all means for individuals and organizations who are opposed to gay relationships for religious reasons. In particular, does the liberal commitment to freedom of religious expression give believers the right to discriminate against gay customers on religious grounds? This has been the subject of a number of high-profile court cases in both the U.S.A. and the UK, including a famous pair revolving around whether or not Christian cake-shop owners could refuse to serve gay customers who wanted to purchase cakes to celebrate their getting married.[15]

At first sight, there is something funny about so much attention being paid to "gay cakes." But these patisseries raise important issues which continue to be the source of heated political and legal controversy. Some conservatives claim that anti-discrimination laws could bring about "the end of religious freedom" itself. Whereas progressives have argued that religious exemptions to these laws are the thin end of a dangerous wedge which would in effect establish a "right to discriminate," undoing decades of progress.[16] This debate, and others like it, is fuelled by the tendency to assert the absolute priority of one set of freedoms over another in a way that leaves no room for compromise. So, for example, some conservatives have argued that freedom of religious expression should have near-total priority over rights to equal treatment and non-discrimination. Meanwhile, some progressives appear to take the opposite stance, namely that whenever there is a clash between the rights of disadvantaged minorities and religious freedom, the former should always have precedence.

This tendency can lead to rather extreme conclusions. If religious people were granted blanket exemptions from anti-discrimination laws, this would seriously undermine the basic civic equality of LGBTQ+ citizens and their ability to participate fully in society. Just imagine what it would be like to live in a society where you could be lawfully turned away from a shop or job simply for being gay. What's more, the same reasoning could be used to justify other forms of discrimination—for a Christian baker to refuse to serve Muslim customers, or for white hotel owners to refuse to accept Black guests. At the same time, the other extreme—that anti-discrimination laws should always take priority, with no exemptions on religious grounds whatsoever—also seems problematic. No one seriously thinks churches should be forced to hire priests irrespective of their religious orientation, as would normally be required by anti-discrimination laws; and even if we think the Catholic Church's position that only men can be ordained is morally indefensible, this is ultimately a question for Catholics to resolve among themselves.

Most of us, then, probably accept the need to strike a balance here, and in most countries the law does try to do this, allowing limited exemptions from anti-discrimination laws on religious grounds. But then why does it feel like there is so little room for compromise? For some progressives, the fact that social conservatives are using basically liberal arguments to justify blatantly illiberal positions is proof that liberalism is fundamentally flawed and incoherent. Part of the problem is the feeling that there is no principled way to go about striking a balance, which in turn encourages each side to push their particular interests as far as they can go, rather than seeking out a compromise which seems reasonable to everyone.[17]

The value of Rawls's theory is that it gives us a coherent framework for balancing our basic freedoms. As we saw in Chapter 1, no individual basic liberty has an absolute priority over any other: we always have to think about the basic liberties as a whole. When faced with a conflict between two basic freedoms, we should prioritize them in terms of their relative importance for developing our "moral capacities"—the ability to reflect on questions about justice and the good life—and for enabling us to live according to our own beliefs.

To see how this might work, let's return to the debate about whether religious people should be exempt from anti-discrimination laws. The starting point is simply to recognize that this involves a genuine clash of important freedoms, and that any solution will involve careful calibration. Progressives should resist the temptation to dismiss claims about religious freedom as simply a bad-faith attempt to use liberal principles for illiberal ends (even if this is sometimes the case); and religious conservatives need to accept that while religious expression is a truly fundamental freedom, it is still just one basic freedom among others.

As we've seen, there are some instances where religious organizations should be exempt from anti-discrimination laws: in general, they should be free to hire clergy and to set their own terms of membership in line with their religious beliefs, at least when they are operating in private non-commercial contexts. Freedom of religious expression should take priority here because it would be hard for religious organizations or communities to exist at all without it. But these exemptions should not normally extend to public or commercial settings. Being free to choose whom to employ as a priest is clearly vital for the existence of a flourishing religious community, whereas the freedom for religious individuals to decide whom to employ or which customers to serve in these contexts is not. In these situations, the freedom for LGBTQ+ citizens to walk into a shop or apply for a job without fear of discrimination should take priority, since this is an essential precondition for their civic equality and self-respect. If this means that some of us feel we cannot pursue certain careers—such as running a cake shop—because of our faith, then so be it; each of us has to take responsibility for the consequences of our beliefs.

There is more to say about which organizations should be granted limited exemptions from anti-discrimination laws and when, and other scholars have developed more fine-grained answers to these questions.[18] My aim here is not to offer a definitive resolution to this complex issue, but to illustrate how Rawls's framework can guide us towards a position which takes both sides seriously. While a degree of judgement will always be involved, this isn't a weakness of his theory, but simply reflects the limits of how far any set of abstract principles can take us. We can, however, bring them to bear productively on other debates about our basic rights and freedoms, including one of the most important and controversial: freedom of speech.

FREE SPEECH

Over the past three decades, the rise of the internet and the growth of social media have led to an explosion of "speech" in all its varied forms. In most democratic countries, there is more speech, and speech is more free, than at any time in human history. There is much to celebrate here: the internet has given all of us access to an unimaginably vast amount of information, and created new opportunities for marginalized voices to make themselves heard. But there is also an all-too-familiar dark side, including the growth of anonymous online hate and abuse and the spread of misinformation, which is threatening the very possibility of reasonable democratic debate.

These issues have put a spotlight on difficult questions about where, if at all, we should draw the limits of free speech. There is growing pressure for the state to introduce or expand so-called "hate speech" laws, and to regulate offensive or misleading information on social media; and among progressives there is a growing concern that the liberal commitment to free speech makes it difficult, if not impossible, to protect the rights of certain minorities, and an increasing sense of scepticism about whether this commitment is worth defending at all.

Rawls's basic liberties principle can steer us through this fraught debate, showing us how we can combine a strong commitment to free speech with a more proactive role for the state in criticizing hateful and anti-democratic ideas, and in fostering a truly inclusive and tolerant society. As we have seen, free speech—at least when it comes to political, moral and scientific questions—is a basic liberty. It enjoys this status because being free to speak our own minds and to hear a wide range of views about these questions is essential for developing and exercising our capacity to think about how we want to live and how society should be organized. The basic liberties principle allows the state to regulate the time, place and manner of speech in a reasonable way: we can, for example, limit the length of speeches given in Parliament so that everyone gets a chance to be heard; or prevent noisy political protests from taking place in residential neighbourhoods at night. It also allows us to regulate other forms of speech, such as commercial advertising, which have little relation to our ability to develop and exercise our moral capacities if there are good public reasons for doing so, like preventing fraud or promoting public health. But when it comes to political, moral and scientific questions, this principle sets a high bar for any legal restrictions on speech.

Since freedom of speech is a basic liberty, the state can ban protected forms of speech only if doing so is necessary to protect another basic freedom.[19] So, for example, we can limit speech in order to protect individuals from physical violence, or to protect democracy itself in the face of a violent political rebellion (a possibility which, since the storming of the U.S. Capitol by supporters of Donald Trump seeking to overturn the 2020 presidential election, no longer seems far-fetched). The state can also intervene to prevent people from threatening or harassing specific individuals, both in person and online, even where there is no immediate threat of physical violence. No one should have to tolerate such abuse, and banning it does not undermine our basic right to free speech since we can always express the substance of our political and moral views without resorting to threats and harassment. As we shall see, we can also restrict private political advertising and donations, in order to protect our fundamental entitlement to meaningful political equality.

Things are more complicated in the case of misinformation.

Whereas political and moral speech are protected as basic liberties, this protection does not necessarily extend in full to false or misleading speech since, like fraud and libel, this has little value in developing and exercising our capacities as citizens. This means that, at least in principle, the state can limit false information even where this does not pose a direct threat to other basic liberties, as long as this serves an important public purpose, like the need for shared facts in facilitating democratic debate. At the same time, just because the state can limit certain kinds of misinformation—say, by requiring platforms to remove demonstrably "fake news"—doesn't mean it should do so, since we also have to consider the risk that an incumbent government could abuse these powers to advance a partisan agenda. Given these risks, we should first exhaust other ways of promoting informed public debate, including voluntary self-regulation and public funding for trusted sources of information, topics we will come back to in the next chapter.

Let's return to whether and how the state can limit speech in order to prevent violence. While people generally support this idea, putting it into practice raises difficult questions, like how close does the connection have to be between speech and potential violence to justify an outright ban? Rawls endorsed the so-called "Brandenburg test" that has been at the heart of American constitutional law since a landmark Supreme Court ruling in 1969.[20] According to this test, the state should intervene only where speech is intended and likely to lead to imminent violence. This approach recognizes that context matters—whether we should step in to prevent people from spouting violent ideas depends on whether there is anyone listening and whether anyone is likely to act as a result. It also requires a pretty direct causal connection between speech and potential acts of physical violence, and in doing so guards against the possibility that the state will abuse its powers to stifle legitimate debate. But there is room for disagreement about when speech meets these criteria, and even whether they are too strict. As the free-speech advocate Timothy Garton Ash has argued, assessing whether violence is likely or imminent has become considerably more complex in an age where incendiary words and images can travel so easily across space and time; and we know from painful historical experience that even where the threat is not strictly imminent, a slow drip of dehumanizing abuse can ultimately lead to violence, as it did during the Rwandan genocide of 1994.[21]

While, at least in some cases, the basic liberties principle justifies a ban on "dangerous speech" (speech that can lead to violence), it does not support the more expansive legal restrictions on offensive, insulting and degrading speech which are common in many democracies under the rubric of hate speech laws.[22] So, for example, while we can prevent neo-Nazis from harassing or threatening people in the street, or directly inciting violence, we cannot impose a blanket ban that would prevent them from posting their hateful views on the internet. Similarly, while we can break up violent anti-democratic protests, we cannot outlaw authoritarian and anti-democratic political speech altogether.[23]

In this respect at least, Rawls's position closely resembles the American legal system, where free speech has a very strong protection under the First Amendment of the U.S. Constitution. But it is at odds with the UK and most other European countries, as well as Canada, India and Australia, all of which have adopted laws that ban so-called "hate speech." While the details differ from one country to the next, these laws typically involve an outright prohibition on speech that is insulting or degrading towards individuals or groups on the basis of generic characteristics such as race, religion or sexuality, irrespective of whether there is any direct threat of harassment or violence.[24] There is an active debate in some countries about expanding the scope of these kinds of laws: in the UK, the Law Commission—an independent statutory body charged with recommending changes to the law—recently proposed extending the legal definition of hate speech to include speech that is likely to stir up hostility on the basis of sex or gender.[25] While this debate is driven by valid concerns about racist, homophobic and misogynistic abuse, in seeking to prevent insult and offence more broadly, many hate speech laws already go beyond what can be justified by the basic liberties principle. From this perspective we should, if anything, be moving in the opposite direction—trimming back these laws so that they focus more directly on preventing threats, harassment and violence.

For many progressives, this might seem counter-intuitive. After all, hate speech laws generally seek to prohibit views that are contrary to the basic values of any decent society, and to advance goals that all of us should share, like promoting a culture of tolerance and mutual respect, and protecting the dignity and safety of oppressed minorities. But rejecting wide-ranging hate speech laws does not mean abandoning these goals or turning a blind eye towards the wider harms created by hateful and anti-democratic speech; and it certainly should not be interpreted as expressing indifference towards, let alone approval of, those views. Rather, it means that as far as possible we should try to address these harms without restricting speech itself.

In part, the responsibility for combating hateful and anti-democratic views rests with each of us as individual citizens: we can and should do what we can to oppose these ideas and to persuade others to oppose them. But the state should also join the fight. As the philosopher Corey Brettschneider has argued, although the state should refrain from using its "coercive" powers to limit speech except in the most exceptional circumstances, it can and should make full use of its "expressive" powers to criticize views that reject the equal status of minorities or the idea of democratic government, and to promote the basic liberal and democratic values of toleration and mutual respect.[26]

What would this look like in practice? Politicians, judges and public officials should explicitly condemn the racist views expressed by groups like the Ku Klux Klan in the U.S.A., or the English Defence League in the UK; and they should strongly criticize groups that are opposed to democratic politics, whether they be revolutionary communists or authoritarian nationalists. More broadly, the state can and should actively promote certain core political values. As we shall see, the education system has a critical role to play here, but the state can also use public holidays, awards and monuments to celebrate our fundamental equality as citizens and to combat hate and prejudice in society—as is the case with Martin Luther King Day in America, for example—and it can employ its spending power to express these values, including withholding tax breaks or funding from organizations that express hateful and anti-democratic views.

There are limits to this strategy, and we have to be careful that, in taking on a more active role, the state does not stifle free debate.[27]

And yet, some free-speech advocates reject the idea that the state should take a stance on these issues at all, arguing that it should remain strictly neutral.[28] But the state cannot and need not be neutral about whether citizens should be treated as equals, or whether the political system should be democratic. When the state protects hateful and anti-democratic views, it does so not because it is neutral, but because it is committed to the fundamental principle that citizens should be able to express their own minds and to hear a wide range of opinions, even those which are opposed to liberal and democratic values.

Even so, sceptics might worry that criticizing hate speech won't be as effective as banning it. But the evidence does not obviously support this view: there is no correlation between strict hate speech laws and lower levels of prejudice and abuse, and coercive restrictions on racist or anti-democratic speech can backfire.[29] After the Netherlands prosecuted the far-right populist politician Geert Wilders in 2016 for inciting discrimination against people of Moroccan descent, his "Party for Freedom" climbed in the polls and went on to win the second-largest number of seats in the Dutch House of Representatives in the March 2017 general election.[30] We also have to take into account the very real possibility that hate speech laws will be abused, as they often have been, usually in ways that strengthen powerful majorities.[31] And in the end, even if we could show that such laws would be a more "effective" way to reduce the prevalence of hateful and anti-democratic speech, the intrinsic importance of free expression means this should always be a last resort.

Civility and "Cancel Culture"

The controversy over free speech today is not only about what the state can and cannot do, but about how we as citizens—both individually and collectively—should respond to views we disagree with or find offensive. There is growing concern about a breakdown of "civility": that political debate has become more angry and fractious, especially as it plays out on Twitter and other social media platforms; and that people are increasingly unwilling to listen or talk to people they disagree with. These sentiments are often expressed as criticisms of "cancel culture," a term typically used by those who worry—not without reason—that the boundaries of acceptable political discourse have become too narrow, and that there is a growing tendency to try to "cancel" people whose views lie outside them.

These are important concerns. As we saw in Chapter 2, Rawls argued that we each have a duty to respond to our fellow citizens with courtesy and politeness, a willingness to listen and a spirit of compromise—even in the face of views we profoundly disagree with. This is a noble aspiration, and a degree of civility in this sense is necessary in any healthy democracy. But calls for civility today sometimes focus exclusively on tone or style, rather than the content of our public conversation—as if those who respond angrily to outright racists are at fault, rather than those who express these hateful views in the first place. This in turn has led some people to question whether civility is really something we should be aiming for. Surely there are some opinions—like the views of neo-Nazis, or those who advocate political violence—that we should completely reject and which don't deserve to be treated with respect?

The problem here is not with the notion of civility itself, but with a narrow conception of what it entails. For Rawls, the "duty of civility" is not only, or even mainly, about style. It is also about substance: when it comes to politics, we should do our best to ensure that the positions we advocate lie within the boundaries of public reason—in other words, that we can justify them by appealing to political values that our fellow citizens can accept.[32] While these limits may be fuzzy, at the very least they require that we recognise the civic equality of all citizens irrespective of class, race, gender and so on, and that we agree not to impose our personal moral or religious ideals on others. This notion can help us answer the question at the heart of the "cancel culture" debate, namely what are the limits of acceptable political opinion in a diverse, modern democracy? As we have seen, there is space within the realm of public reason for a debate about how to balance the rights of gay citizens with freedom of religious expression—but there is no room for those who deny the right of gay people to have intimate relationships. Similarly, there is room for disagreement about whether we can use positive discrimination to address racial inequalities (a topic we will return to in Chapter 6)—but we should utterly reject those who deny the civic equality of Black citizens. In this way, the idea of public reason resists the tendency to restrict political debate unduly, while recognizing that there are lines that no reasonable citizens ought to cross, even if they cannot be enforced by law.

Of all the issues that have become embroiled in recent debates about "cancel culture," transgender rights have proven to be one of the most divisive. Opponents of transgender women having the right to access certain "women-only" spaces, such as public toilets, prisons or women's refuges, frequently claim that their views are wrongly being stifled. Advocates for these rights often argue that their opponents' views are "transphobic" and, just like xenophobic or homophobic views, lie beyond the pale of reasonable democratic discourse.

How can Rawls's notions of civility and public reason help us here? At the simplest level, they would encourage a more respectful and emotionally intelligent conversation—there is no excuse for the mocking or outright offensive language that has become so common, or for belittling the significance of, say, the use of pronouns. It would also shift the focus from rather philosophical debates about the relationship between sex and gender and what it really means to be a "woman" (or a "man"), and towards practical discussions about how we can address the urgent challenges faced by transgender citizens, including widespread harassment and discrimination, and shockingly high rates of violence, mental-health issues and suicide.[33] There is clearly a legitimate debate to be had about the relationship between sex and gender, and people with "gender critical" views that some transgender people find offensive should nonetheless be free to express them. But for the most part there is no need for the state to take a stand on this question, and we don't have to reach a consensus about it in order to improve transgender people's lives.

So, for example, whether transgender women should be housed in women-only prisons should depend not on an abstract debate about how to define the term "woman," but on an evidence-based assessment of how best to protect the safety of all inmates. And yet, although concerns about personal safety are clearly "public reasons," they must be supported with credible evidence, and in practice the supposed "threat" posed by transgender women has frequently been exaggerated.[34] We should draw the line at those who twist the facts in order to demonize transgender citizens, or who deny their equal right to live freely and without discrimination. While we should still aspire to respond to our fellow citizens respectfully, such people have already broken the duty of civility in a fundamental way.

We also have to remember that our moral duty to act with civility rests on the assumption that our basic rights and personal safety will be protected, and that we have fair opportunities to influence and participate in political debate. For many disadvantaged minorities, these conditions have not been met: Black and transgender citizens are often fighting for their most basic rights—and, in some cases, their lives—and in many societies poor and marginalized voices are systematically excluded from the democratic process. In this environment, it may be too much to ask for civility in its fullest sense, and it's no wonder that some people feel the need to "shout." If we want greater civility in our public life, then we also need to redouble our efforts to secure basic freedoms for *everyone*, and to transform our democratic structures.

THE CONSTITUTION AND THE JUDICIARY

By far the most important institutional mechanism for securing our basic freedoms is to enshrine them in a constitution. The purpose of a constitution is partly symbolic or educational: it serves as a public statement of fundamental values that are shared across party political lines, and in doing so inevitably shapes the political culture.[35] And, of course, a constitution also plays a legal role, setting out in law the structure of the democratic process and the relationship between the different branches of government, as well as our most important individual rights and freedoms. This legal function is typically enforced by an independent judiciary with the power to strike down, or at least call into question, any laws that go against the constitution. Of course, no constitution can guarantee that our basic freedoms will be protected, and if a determined majority of citizens want to undermine them, they will usually find a way to do so. But a well-designed constitution can slow the pace of change when fundamental liberties are under threat, creating time for public reflection and for people to rally in their defence.

Today, most democratic countries have adopted the constitutional model, with a written constitution enforced by an independent judiciary (as we shall see in more detail below, the UK is a rare exception in lacking a written or "codified" constitution). And yet the legitimacy of this model is increasingly being called into question. Critics argue that it is undemocratic because it removes power from elected representatives and hands it over to unelected judges.* One of the most vocal recent critics of this model is the Hungarian Prime Minister Viktor Orbán, who describes himself as an "illiberal democrat." He has railed against the role of the European courts in protecting rights for gay people and for women, and attacked the power and independence of the Hungarian judiciary, including by stacking the Constitutional Court with allies and limiting its jurisdiction.[36] And such scepticism about the role of the courts is increasingly widespread. While the basic role of the Supreme Court is widely accepted in America, the long-term politicization of the process for nominating justices, and the willingness of the newly conservative-dominated court to overturn long-established precedents such as *Roe v. Wade*, have seriously undermined its legitimacy.[37] In the UK, as in many other European countries, there have long been rumblings of discontent, mostly from those on the right, about how human rights legislation has prevented Parliament from passing laws on controversial topics like prisoner voting rights and the treatment of migrants.[38] A number of high-profile clashes between the UK government and the UK Supreme Court in relation to the Brexit process have created an unprecedented level of hostility towards the judiciary, with the front page of the *Daily Mail* newspaper accusing certain judges of being "Enemies of the People."[39] At the time of writing, the governing Conservative Party has embarked on reforms that would weaken the scope of human rights protections and limit the power of the courts in holding the government to account.[40]

It is tempting to dismiss populist criticisms of the courts as purely

---

* Most of this criticism is focused on "legislative judicial review," which gives the courts a say over which laws can be passed or enforced. This is different from ordinary judicial review, whereby the courts ensure that the state only acts on the basis of laws that have been democratically approved, and that those laws are properly applied. The latter is integral to the rule of law, and a precondition for meaningful democracy.

cynical. After all, while politicians like Orbán invoke the language of democracy to justify their assaults on the judiciary, they often simultaneously attack basic democratic norms and institutions.[41] And yet, while these criticisms are sometimes made in bad faith, it would be a mistake to dismiss them out of hand. After all, they point to a real tension between the "liberal" commitment to wide-ranging personal freedoms, and the "democratic" commitment to majority rule.

In this context, it is more important than ever to understand why constitutional courts are a legitimate part of a democratic society and what their role should be. As we saw in Chapter 1, one of the distinctive features of Rawls's first principle is that it includes both personal *and* political freedoms. While Rawls's support for equal political rights leads quite naturally to majority rule as the central mechanism for democratic decision-making in the elected legisla-ture, we have to remember that no basic liberty is absolute, and there is no automatic priority for political over personal freedoms, or vice versa. As such, we can use a constitution to limit the scope of major-ity rule if doing so would help to protect our basic liberties overall.[42]

It is helpful here to distinguish between two cases where we might want to do this. First, we might want to protect democracy itself, by enshrining constitutional protections that would prevent an elected government from passing laws that would unduly restrict the freedom of the press or deny certain groups the right to vote. Most people accept that these kinds of restrictions on majority rule are perfectly legitimate. Second, and more controversially, we might want the constitution to protect our basic personal freedoms, including those relating to sexuality and reproductive rights. Critics argue that these kinds of protections constrain the democratic pro-cess, and on one level they are right. But we also have to remember that in a democratic society, the constitution is itself an expression of popular sovereignty and should ultimately be created (and be amendable) through a democratic process, albeit one that is more demanding than a simple majority vote in the legislature. Instead of thinking about the constitution as an external constraint on democ-racy, it makes more sense to think about it as establishing different levels of democratic decision-making: ordinary democratic politics, which is subject to majority rule; and constitutional politics, which touches on our most basic freedoms and which requires something more.[43]

Rawls's first principle helps explain the legitimacy of constitutional limits to majority rule. But it also sets limits on the scope of the constitution and the role of the judiciary. While right-wing critics of the courts have tended to argue that they should have less power, some progressives have argued that they should have more, and that the constitution should not only enshrine our commitment to basic freedoms, but to social and economic justice more widely. While there is a legitimate role for the courts in making sure that citizens can meet their basic needs, and in preventing discrimination, Rawls argued that we should not rely on them to enforce fair equality of opportunity or the difference principle in full.[44] In part, this simply follows from the notion that since majority rule is a basic liberty, we can limit it only to protect another equally basic freedom. But there are also pragmatic reasons for restricting the courts' remit in this way. Courts are well positioned to determine whether our personal and political freedoms have been violated. But they generally lack the expertise to determine whether we have done enough to achieve equal opportunities in education or to maximize the prospects of the least advantaged; and for the most part these questions are best resolved through the ordinary democratic process.[45]

How to Design a Resilient Constitution

How can we be sure that a constitution will actually protect our basic freedoms? Some critics have claimed that, in practice, constitutional mechanisms often do more harm than good—that they are vulnerable to excessive politicization and to being captured by vested interests, as they arguably have been in America today. But the balance of evidence suggests that if a constitution is designed properly, it can offer meaningful safeguards for basic freedoms.[46] Moreover, the proliferation of constitutional democracies over the twentieth century means we can now draw on a large body of evidence about how to make this model work.

First, constitutions should be written down, and ideally "codified" into a single document. The UK is one of a handful of democracies, alongside Israel, New Zealand, Sweden and (arguably) Canada, without a codified constitution, relying instead on a sprawling body of "constitutionally relevant" statutes accumulated over the past 800 years, making it "the longest and, arguably, the most complex constitution in the world."[47] This complexity makes it difficult for the constitution to serve its "educational" role as a charter of fundamental political values. Even more worrying is that key aspects of the UK's "constitution" are either entirely unwritten or have never been formalized into law. For example, there is nothing in the UK's constitution which sets out how the Prime Minister should be chosen, or what their powers are, and there is precious little detail about the role and structure of the legislature, meaning the country's democracy ultimately relies on respect for established conventions (a system that the constitutional historian Peter Hennessy has referred to as the "good chaps" theory of government). This leaves the UK more vulnerable to politicians, or indeed judges, who are willing to defy convention in order to advance their own agenda, as Prime Minister Boris Johnson did in 2019 when he attempted to suspend (or "prorogue") Parliament in order to "get Brexit done."[48] Although the UK's uncodified model survived this test, it's not at all clear it could withstand a more serious challenge from someone like Donald Trump. While every democracy has to rely on unwritten norms to some degree, a codified constitution would help guard against these dangers.[49]

Second, constitutions should be hard—but not impossible—to change. For a constitution to provide meaningful protection for our most essential liberties, it should not be subject to revision through a simple majority vote of the legislature. This highlights another problem with the UK model, where the most important legal protections for basic rights and freedoms are set out in the Human Rights Act which could, in principle, be overturned by a majority vote in Parliament. At the other end of the spectrum, some countries, including Germany, have so-called "entrenchment" clauses which put certain basic principles beyond revision altogether.[50] This may be appropriate for protecting the most fundamental aspects of a constitution, like equality before the law and the democratic nature of government. But every constitution also needs a process for clarifying and updating its contents, so that the people retain ultimate control, and in order to address new or unforeseen issues. The American

Constitution is famously difficult to change: an amendment must first be proposed by a two-thirds vote of both Houses of Congress, or, if two thirds of the states request one, by a convention called for that purpose; and then ratified by three quarters of the state legislatures.[51] A more promising model used in some Nordic countries is to adopt a lower threshold for approving any changes while extending the process over time. In Finland, the legislature can propose an amendment by a simple majority which then has to be approved by a supermajority of two thirds after the next general election. In Denmark, constitutional amendments must be passed twice by a simple majority, with a general election in between, followed by a popular referendum with support from at least 50 per cent of those voting and 40 per cent of those eligible to vote. These mechanisms create space for considered democratic scrutiny and ensure that any changes have substantial and sustained public support.[52]

Finally, and perhaps most importantly, an effective constitution depends on a judiciary which is reasonably independent of the political process.* The U.S.A. provides a salutary warning of the dangers of excessive politicization. The appointment of Supreme Court and other federal judges is thoroughly political: candidates are nominated by the president and then approved (or not) by the Senate, meaning that the entire process is dominated by politicians.[53] Recent confirmations have seen the Senate vote almost entirely along party lines, with each side refusing to back nominations made by the other; and Supreme Court judges are increasingly ruling on key cases in largely predictable partisan blocks.[54]

Fortunately, the U.S.A. is something of an outlier in this respect. The international evidence suggests that the most effective way to protect judicial independence is to combine an appointment process for judges which is largely insulated from politics with constitutional protections against their removal from office.[55] Almost two thirds of

---

* The judiciary should not be totally independent of the political process, since its legitimacy depends on there being some mechanism for the people to hold judges to account. It also depends on putting in place measures to ensure that the judiciary—which in many countries has typically been dominated by affluent white men—is broadly representative of the wider population.

countries with a constitution have "judicial councils" which exercise independent control over the appointment, promotion and removal of judges and over the budget for courts. In the UK, for example, an independent commission recommends nominees for the Supreme Court to the Secretary of State for Justice for their approval. The process has, in the short period since the Supreme Court was established in 2009, been largely free of overt political interference.

In the U.S. context, where the politicization of the judiciary has reached crisis point, introducing a judicial council for the Supreme Court would require an amendment to the constitution. But there is room for improvement within the existing constitutional settlement. For a start, the U.S.A. could introduce fixed-term rather than lifetime appointments to the Supreme Court, to avoid the perverse situation in which judges try to time their retirement to ensure a successor with a similar political outlook, and presidents seek to appoint ever younger justices.[56] Other ways to depoliticize the Supreme Court might include reinstating supermajority requirements for nominating judges (which was the norm until 2013); introducing a "Supreme Court Panel," whereby the court would shift from nine permanent justices to a rotating roster of all the judges from the federal Courts of Appeal; or even selecting Supreme Court justices at random from a wider pool of Appeal Court judges.[57]

SHARED VALUES AND CIVIC EDUCATION

No matter how well we design our constitutional structures, in the end a liberal democracy can survive and flourish only if its citizens share certain basic political values and if they are willing to defend the institutions that realize them when they come under attack, as they increasingly have in recent years. Success also depends on citizens who themselves embody these values in the way they behave and interact with one another—who are reasonable and tolerant, who approach politics with a sense of fairness and a spirit of compromise, and who are willing to appeal to public reasons when it comes to important political questions.

The rise of authoritarian political movements over the past decade has served as an urgent reminder that we cannot take any of this for granted. Although the vast majority of people in both

Europe and North America support representative democracy, around 40 per cent think that a "technocracy" (rule by unelected experts) would also be a good form of government, while around one in six in America, the UK, France and Italy say the same about military rule.[58] And while nearly everyone in these regions says that freedom of religion and speech are important, only 57 per cent of Europeans think it is *very* important that people can practise their religion freely, while about 75 per cent say the same about freedom of speech.[59] Worryingly, support for liberal democratic values appears to be weaker among younger generations with no direct memory of the authoritarianism of the twentieth century. Whereas about two thirds of older Americans (born in the 1930s and 1940s) think it is extremely important to live in a democracy, this falls to less than one third among millennials (born since the 1980s).[60]

How can we restore faith in basic liberal values, and foster the kinds of attitudes or "political virtues" that are the lifeblood of any healthy democracy? For Rawls, this is part of the wider issue of "stability," or whether a society can generate enough support to sustain itself over time. In the end, the most important sources of stability in a democracy are the benefits that citizens experience from living in it: the freedom to pursue their own goals, the opportunity to participate in politics as equals, and access to a fair share of resources.[61] From this perspective, our first response to waning enthusiasm for liberal democracy should be to acknowledge the shortcomings of our existing institutions—the ways in which the rich are able to dominate the political process; the poverty, inequality and insecurity generated by modern capitalism—and transform them so that they are genuinely worthy of people's allegiance.

At the same time, as we have already touched on in the discussion of free speech, the state can and should use its "expressive" powers to foster support for liberal and democratic values and attitudes, including through monuments and public holidays celebrating historic individuals or events, and through public honours like damehoods and knighthoods in the UK, the Legion of Honour in France and the system of presidential and other medals in the U.S.A. But perhaps the most important way the state can promote these values and virtues is through the education system.

Liberal and democratic thinkers have long recognized the vital civic role played by the education system: this was first popularized in France in the late eighteenth century, and was one of the reasons why figures like George Washington and James Madison supported the development of a public education system in the U.S.A.[62] Rawls, too, insisted that the education system should "encourage the political virtues" such as reasonableness and mutual respect in order to prepare citizens to be "fully cooperating members of society."[63]

While the importance of civic education has long been recognized in principle, it has increasingly been neglected in practice. In most countries today, the overwhelming focus of the education system is on preparing citizens for economic life.[64] This is, of course, one of the most important functions of any education system and an essential part of providing all children with genuinely equal opportunities—but it has increasingly pushed civic education to the sidelines. In America, the bipartisan Common Core State Standards Initiative, which sets out overarching aims for the public schools system, states that education must prepare all students for "the global economic workplace," but makes little reference to equipping them to participate in civic life.[65] Just nine U.S. states require a full year of civic education, and only eight have a stand-alone assessment in civics; while federal government spending per pupil on civic education is less than one tenth of 1 per cent of the spending on "STEM" subjects (science, technology, engineering and mathematics).[66] In the UK, despite attempts in the early 2000s to strengthen the civic aspect of education, a cross-party report in 2017 concluded that the "current state of citizenship education is poor."[67] A European Commission report on civic education found that nearly half of EU countries failed to incorporate civic education into teacher training, and that more than a third had no guidance on how to assess students in relation to civics.[68]

In order for our education system to fulfil its civic function, we must transform it.[69] At the very least, this means making every young person aware of their rights and freedoms, of how the political system works, and about the diversity of religious, moral and political beliefs in society. But civic education is about more than knowledge, it is also about developing certain skills and capacities. Citizens need the analytical skills that are essential for developing their own views about what is right and wrong with society, and how we could improve it. They need communication skills so they can express themselves lucidly and persuasively. And, of course, they need the social and relational skills that are vital for organizing with others in order to bring about change. Finally, we need to cultivate a commitment to basic liberal values, and nurture attitudes and character traits that reflect them.

Dedicated civic education classes have a vital role to play. Beyond imparting knowledge about the variety of ways in which citizens can participate in politics, these should actively cultivate political capacities by, for example, encouraging respectful debate about controversial social and political issues and through "mock elections." Children should also engage in "service learning" which takes them out of the classroom to learn directly about issues such as social exclusion and racial inequality. There is a strong case for a form of compulsory national citizens service too. Just as we can legitimately compel young people to take part in education for the sake of developing their capacity for work, we can do the same in the name of developing their capacity for citizenship and to foster a sense of community which cuts across class, racial and religious lines.*

We also need to reshape the education system much more comprehensively. The development of critical thinking skills, for example, is something that should inform how we teach every subject. And certain subjects are especially important in preparing citizens for civic life. As the philosopher Danielle Allen has powerfully argued, we should strengthen the role of the humanities and social sciences—literature, philosophy, history, sociology, economics and so on—since they are crucial in developing our political capabilities, and people who study these subjects appear to be more civic-minded and more likely to be politically active.[70] And yet, in recent

---

* Critics of this wide-ranging ideal of civic education argue that it strays into territory that should be left to parents. Some religious parents have argued, for example, that they should be able to take their children out of classes where they would learn about other religions or LGBTQ+ relationships. While parents should be free to share their religious and moral beliefs with their children, in these cases children's interests in having access to a fully comprehensive education should take priority, since this is essential for them to develop their moral capacities and play a full role as citizens.

years, the focus of education policy in most countries has been on promoting STEM subjects, often at the expense of the humanities.

We must also look again at how we organize the school system. A key part of equipping young people for life in a modern democracy is encouraging them to develop respect and tolerance for different political beliefs and ways of living. To some extent, we can "teach" these attitudes; but there is now a large body of research demonstrating that direct social contact, at least under the right conditions, is perhaps the most effective way to promote these attitudes.[71] A recent study of schools in England, for example, found that children in more ethnically diverse schools were far more likely to have positive feelings towards, and make friends with, children from other ethnicities.[72] School admissions policies should be designed to encourage a mix of children from a diverse range of backgrounds.

SHARED IDENTITY AND LIBERAL PATRIOTISM

The cultivation of shared political values is essential for any liberal democracy to flourish. But are they enough by themselves? Or is an emotional sense of belonging also essential, as many people believe? If they are right, then how can we foster a truly inclusive sense of shared national identity?

The resurgence of illiberal nationalism as a potent political force has given these kinds of questions a new urgency. Around the world, authoritarian leaders from Donald Trump in America to Narendra Modi in India have increasingly sought to foster narrow notions of ethnic or religious national identity. But liberals and progressives are divided about how to respond. A common reaction is to spurn all forms of national identity. After all, nationalism has all too often been a force for exclusion and persecution—an ideology used to justify the subjugation of one country by another, as in the case of empire; or the repression of minority groups within countries, as with slavery and segregation in the U.S.A., and the Nazi Holocaust. Anyone with even a basic awareness of history should have a healthy scepticism about the dangers of nationalism.

But we should think twice before we reject the idea of shared national identity outright. First, as a matter of basic political realism, we have to accept that for many people this is an important part of who they are, and the natural human tendency to form groups means this is unlikely to change any time soon.[73] The instinctive hostility that some progressives have towards any expression of national identity unnecessarily alienates people for whom it matters, and leaves a vacuum that has been filled by exclusionary forms of nationalism. Second, and on a more positive note, a sense of shared national identity can be an important source of social solidarity, something that can motivate people to look beyond their personal interests and recognize that they are part of something bigger. Indeed, people are more likely to support egalitarian social and economic institutions if they feel a sense of community with their fellow citizens.[74] This is all the more vital in our increasingly diverse democracies, since it encourages us to look not only beyond our individual self-interest, but also beyond the interests of any religious or ethnic groups to which we might belong.

Rather than reject the idea of national identity altogether, we should try to harness it in the service of social justice by fostering a truly inclusive "liberal" patriotism.[75] This would have to be grounded in aspects of a particular country that, at least in principle, everyone can celebrate, which immediately rules out ethnicity or religion as its basis. Instead, it would have at its heart a commitment to political values like freedom, toleration, equality and democracy, and to the genuinely shared project of building a society that can put these values into practice. This would be a project with a history we can all identify with, a future we can make together, and whose achievement we can take pleasure and pride in.[76]

Such a vision of inclusive national identity might strike some people as naive. Our political discourse today is dominated by a pervasive sense of ethnic and religious division, and the rise of exclusionary forms of nationalism would suggest that popular manifestations of national identity are moving in the wrong direction. But, in reality, almost the opposite is true. A study of the U.S.A., France, Germany and the UK between 2016 and 2020—a period of divisive debates about race, which followed an unprecedented refugee crisis in Europe—found that national identity had become *more* rather than less inclusive. In all these countries, there was a significant decline in the share of people who thought that a particular birthplace or religion was essential for belonging to the national community, and these views are now firmly in the minority.[77]

Nevertheless, one might still wonder whether it is really possible to build a meaningful sense of shared identity around distinctively political values and institutions. Can these really play the same role as religion or ethnicity have in the past? At least on a personal level, it seems clear that endorsing liberal political values can be an important part of who we are. As Rawls put it, "our commitment to treat other citizens as equals, and therefore to respect their freedom of religion, say, may be just as elemental a part of our identity as our affirming a particular religion and fulfilling its practices."[78] And history suggests that political values can and have helped to build meaningful shared identities. The U.S.A. is the most celebrated example of a country where liberal and democratic political values (roughly, those embodied in the constitution) have fostered a sense of patriotic identity.[79] Of course, the U.S. Constitution in its original form was deeply flawed, allowing Black people to be enslaved and women to be relegated to second-class status; and an inclusive, political American identity has always coexisted with the exclusionary, nativist tendencies that are on the rise again today.[80] But, for many Americans, the political ideals set out in the constitution, and the core institutions that realize them, however imperfectly—Congress, the Supreme Court and so on—are among the defining features of what it is to be American. A similar story can be told about other democratic countries, whether it is the importance of republican political values in shaping French identity, or the pride that many British people take in the provision of universal public healthcare through the National Health Service.

Even if it is true that political values fail to arouse quite the same strength of feeling as ethnic or religious ties, this would not be a reason to reject inclusive patriotism. All political ideologies face challenges in winning and maintaining the support of citizens, and ethno or religious nationalism both tend to alienate and radicalize minorities. In the end, the stability of a liberal society depends on the substantive benefits experienced by its citizens, and this is something we should celebrate. While exclusionary nationalists all too often rely on sowing social discord to win popular support, we must focus our energy on making tangible improvements to people's lives.

Immigration

The idea of a political community naturally raises the question of how we should control membership of that community, and hence the thorny topic of immigration. A substantial increase in the overall scale of immigration into many rich democracies in recent decades has thrust this issue into the political spotlight. In the UK, the foreign-born population increased from about 5.3 million in 2004 to almost 9.5 million in 2019, and opposition to immigration was one of the driving forces behind Brexit. In Europe the 2015 refugee crisis, itself driven by conflict and persecution in countries including Syria, Afghanistan and Iraq, saw more than 5 million people reach European shores.[81] Across Europe, America and elsewhere, the far right has amplified anxieties about the scale of immigration, blaming new arrivals for a whole host of social and economic problems and promoting explicitly racist narratives about a "great replacement" of white, Christian populations. The left, by contrast, has tended to downplay or even dismiss popular concerns as grounded in racial prejudice.

What would a fair immigration policy look like? Some progressives insist that justice requires "open borders," or the abolition of all controls on immigration. This position is often grounded in a strand of liberal thinking known as "cosmopolitanism," which holds that we should treat all people equally irrespective of where they live, and that from a moral point of view borders are an entirely arbitrary construct which we would be better off without. There is no question that we have moral obligations to people in other countries simply by virtue of our common humanity, and these should shape immigration policy—at the very least, we should welcome refugees fleeing persecution or extreme deprivation. But just as we have special duties towards our family members, the obligations we have to our fellow citizens are different and typically stronger than those we have to people in other countries.[82] The source of these obligations is not common ethnicity or religion, but the fact that we share political power with our fellow citizens, and this needs to be wielded in a way that can be justified to every member of the community. Even if national borders have no deep moral significance—many are the product of historical happenstance and global power politics—they nonetheless serve a legitimate purpose, since some kind of territorial boundary is essential for any political community to exist.[83]

While calls for stricter immigration policies are sometimes motivated by racist notions of "purity," there are legitimate reasons why citizens might want to limit the number of people moving to their country. Increased immigration has often been justified on the grounds that it tends to boost economic growth. But the benefits have often been felt by richer citizens, while those on lower incomes have sometimes lost out. In the UK, for example, migration from the EU between 1993 and 2017 is estimated to have led to a nearly 5 per cent reduction in wages for the lowest earners, while the highest earners saw their wages increase by more than 4 per cent.[84] And although in most cases immigrants to rich countries have contributed more in taxes than they receive in the form of benefits and social spending, a wider lack of investment means that increased immigration has often put additional pressure on public services and exacerbated housing shortages.[85] From the perspective of the difference principle, immigration policy should be guided not simply by the potential benefits for aggregate economic growth, but above all by the degree to which it can improve the life prospects of the least well off within a given country.

We also need to recognize that high levels of immigration can make it more difficult to create a stable sense of political community and national identity, especially if new arrivals come from countries with very different cultures and political traditions. In a liberal society immigrants, like everyone else, should be free to live according to their own beliefs, within the limits of the law. We cannot force immigrants to "assimilate" into the mainstream culture, and it is possible that new immigrant communities may lead rather separate lives to those of their fellow citizens. But we can—and indeed should—encourage immigrants to participate in social and political life, so that they can mix with their fellow citizens in schools, at work and in their local community, and, in doing so, absorb the core political values of liberal democracy. So, for example, we should help new immigrants to learn the dominant language and make it easy for them to access education and to work. Similarly, there is a place for citizenship tests and ceremonies which celebrate certain core political values, such as a commitment to democracy and individual freedom.

Doing more to foster shared values and civic bonds is a crucial step towards protecting not only personal but also political freedoms from the incursions of authoritarian populists. These political liberties are, of course, at the heart of Rawls's basic liberties principle too, which affirms our fundamental right to take part in and influence collective decision-making on genuinely equal terms. Living up to this demanding ideal will require a wholesale transformation of democracy as we know it.

5

Democracy

•────────•

The twentieth century witnessed the triumph of democracy. In 1900, there were just twelve democratic countries. Today there are 118, nearly two thirds of the total.[1] The idea that democracy is the only legitimate form of government is now so widespread that authoritarian populists such as Donald Trump and Victor Orbán who are perfectly willing to denounce "liberalism" all claim allegiance to democratic principles, even as they undermine them in practice; and countries that no one would consider to be democratic, like Russia or Belarus, often spend significant sums in maintaining a veneer of legitimacy by staging "elections."[2]

If democracy is so popular, then what is there to worry about? As we have seen, widespread support for democracy in principle sits alongside a troubling openness to non-democratic alternatives. There is also enormous discontent with democracy as we know it: a recent study found that whereas two thirds of citizens in "developed democracies" felt satisfied with democracy in the 1990s, today a majority are dissatisfied.[3] In part, this reflects discontent with the *results* of our existing political systems—their failure to address poverty, inequality, climate change and so on. But people are also dissatisfied with the democratic process itself: a survey of thirty-four democracies found that fewer than one third of citizens felt that their elected representatives cared about what people like them thought, and about half disagreed with the idea that the state is run for the benefit of the people.[4] There is widespread frustration, too, at a lack of opportunities for most citizens to influence the democratic process: across the OECD group of rich democracies, just one third of people feel they have a say in what government does.[5] In many rich democracies, a majority of citizens think their political system needs major changes or to be completely reformed.[6]

This dissatisfaction is contributing to a growing sense of democratic crisis. Donald Trump's baseless attempts to overturn the 2020 U.S. presidential election have brought trust in democracy to an all-time low, and the 2024 election may yet test America's democratic institutions to their limit. His actions have already emboldened leaders in Mexico, Brazil, Peru and Myanmar to question unfavourable results.[7] These worrying developments merely accentuate a widely documented trend towards democratic erosion and decline: according to the think tank Freedom House, for each of the past fifteen years there have been more countries whose democratic institutions are deteriorating than those where they are improving—with 2020 the worst year yet on record.[8]

Given the very real threats to democracy today, it's tempting to go on the defensive, and there is no question that our first priority must be to protect our most basic democratic institutions, including freedom of the press, the integrity of elections and the independence of the judiciary. But we must also recognize that democracy as we know it isn't working, and that people are right to be dissatisfied. As we will see over the course of this chapter, the rich really do dominate the political process, and our existing institutions make little effort to engage ordinary citizens in collective decision-making. These problems are not simply the result of democracy's inherent limitations, nor can we put them down to "bad actors" or corrupt individuals—they are entirely predictable consequences of the way in which we have chosen to organise the political process. If we want to restore faith in democracy, we need to redesign it from the bottom up.

In taking up this task, we first need to know what we want from our political system. In thinking about this, we often tend to jump directly to certain familiar institutions, such as free and fair elections, universal suffrage, and freedom of the press. But we need to go deeper: we need a guiding principle that we can use to identify what is wrong with our existing political structures, and how we should change them. For Rawls, political equality is that principle. A fundamental commitment to this principle is what distinguishes a democracy from monarchy, oligarchy, aristocracy, and other forms of government in which a minority calls the shots; and it is Rawls's commitment to this principle that makes his theory an unmistakably democratic one.[9]

A democracy, then, is a political system grounded in political equality.* But what exactly does this mean?[10] At the very least, "political equality" means having certain basic rights—what Rawls referred to as "the equal political liberties"—including the equal right to vote, freedom of speech, freedom of the press and freedom of association (the right to organize into political parties, campaign groups and so on). These rights ensure that each of us is free to participate in the democratic process—to vote, to speak our minds, to organize with others. Without these rights, political equality would be impossible, and any society worthy of being called a "democracy" will protect them.

But, as we saw in Chapter 1, political equality is not just about having equal rights: for Rawls, it is about having substantively equal opportunities to exercise those rights. After all, as we know all too well, even with these basic rights in place, the rich can easily come to dominate politics. This is why Rawls's first principle is committed not just to equal political liberties, but to their "fair value."[11] Of course, some people will always have more *actual* influence than others, whether because they have devoted their life to politics or because they can captivate an audience with their rhetorical powers. What matters, however, is that everyone has the same *opportunity* to influence and participate in the democratic process, irrespective

---

* Political equality is the first priority for any democratic political system, but it is obviously not the only thing that matters. We should also design our political institutions to promote rational, timely and evidence-based decisions, and to encourage reasonable, respectful and meaningful deliberation. Ultimately, we want a system which tends to produce policies that are fair and just, and which is likely to protect our basic freedoms as a whole.

of how much money they have, or indeed their race, gender or sexuality.[12]

Designing a system that achieves this ideal is at least as complex as the task of designing a fair and efficient economy. But we can begin by breaking down the idea of political equality into three key components.[13] First, and most obviously, this requires "voting equality": all adult citizens should have the right to vote, all votes should have equal weight, and citizens should have regular and frequent opportunities to exercise this right. We cannot be political equals if some of us are denied the chance to vote or if some votes count for more than others.

Although voting equality tends to take centre stage in most discussions about democracy, political equality demands much more than this. After all, by the time voting happens, most of the action has already taken place. Voting is ultimately a decision-making procedure—a way of taking a measure of citizens' views and preferences at a given point in time. But these views are not static, and democracy is not simply a process of aggregating fixed preferences. Democracy is also an ongoing process of collective deliberation and debate through which we work out what we think about important political questions and through which we try to persuade others.[14]

If we are serious about political equality, then everyone must have a reasonably equal opportunity to take part in this wider process of democratic deliberation. For this to happen, everyone must have an effective opportunity to learn about what they are being asked to vote on—whether candidates (as in an election) or policies (as in a referendum)—and the likely consequences. This "enlightened understanding," as the democratic theorist Robert Dahl called it, forms the second core component of political equality. If some people are better informed about the options facing them, then they are better positioned to achieve the results they desire. Although formal rights such as freedom of speech and association are essential, enlightened understanding also depends on every citizen having had a decent education, and on the actual existence of reliable sources of information which allow them to find out about those standing for office, the implications of different policies, and what other people think about these matters.

The third component of political equality is "effective participation."[15] Every citizen must have an equal opportunity, beyond simply voting, to make their positions known and to persuade others of their views. If some citizens are denied these chances while others are able to dominate the debate, real political equality will always elude us. Freedom of speech and association is essential once again, but this kind of political engagement ultimately depends on people having fair opportunities to exercise these rights—to speak and write, and to organize with others.

As we shall see, in a large-scale modern democracy, both enlightened understanding and effective participation depend on a range of intermediary institutions, the most important of which are political parties and the news media. These are, to borrow a phrase from the political scientist Jan-Werner Müller, the "critical infrastructure" without which democracy is all but impossible to imagine.[16] If we are committed to political equality, then we need to think much more carefully and imaginatively about how these institutions work, and how to prevent them from being dominated by a wealthy elite.*

TODAY'S DEMOCRATIC REALITY

Sadly, political equality remains a long way from our reality today. This is difficult to measure—data is scarce and often hard to compare across countries, and there are few widely accepted metrics, at least compared to economic equality. These challenges are complicated further by the fact that we typically measure outcomes rather than opportunities—we see how much people are actually involved in or influence politics, rather than the chances they have to do so.[17] Nonetheless, the fact that ethnic minorities and people on low incomes are typically much less likely to vote, or to engage in politics in other ways, strongly suggests that they face unequal

---

* Rawls's principle of political equality, and hence this chapter, is concerned with the formal political process, or, to be more precise, with how we make decisions that are enforced using the coercive power of the state. As we shall see in Chapter 8, Rawls's second principle also justifies much greater democracy within the workplace. Other organizations and associations, from charities to religious or campaigning groups, may also want to operate along similar lines, but for the most part that is up to them.

opportunities to participate in the first place. After all, there is little reason to think that these groups are inherently less interested in politics than anyone else.[18]

One good measure of political equality is how responsive government decisions are to the views of rich or poor citizens. (We could do the same for other groups, such as men versus women or majority versus minority ethnic groups, but most research to date has focused on income.) In a society where everyone has roughly equal opportunities to take part in and influence the political process, we would expect to see a weak relationship between how much money people have and the decisions made by the government. But in reality the preferences of rich citizens appear to have a much greater influence on government policy than those of average and poorer voters.

Most studies of this issue have focused on America, where data is widely available, and where concerns about the role of money in politics are most acute. In a seminal study published in 2014, the political scientists Martin Gilens and Benjamin Page collated data on 1,779 proposed changes to U.S. federal government policy between 1981 and 2002, spanning economic policy, social services, healthcare and foreign policy.[19] In each case, they looked at the relationship between the decisions actually taken and the views of three different groups, as measured in surveys: "average" citizens—those with median levels of income; "rich" citizens—those in the ninetieth percentile; and "interest and advocacy groups," such as business associations, trade unions and charities. Their results are deeply troubling. They found that once we take into account the views of rich citizens and interest groups, the preferences of average citizens had almost no impact on which policies were adopted. When the rich wanted something different to the average American, they almost always got their way.[20] Interest groups had somewhat less influence than the rich, but still much more than average citizens, with business-oriented interest groups such as the U.S. Chamber of Commerce wielding about twice as much influence as mass-membership groups such as trade unions. A host of other studies have confirmed the same basic finding that the rich exert an outsized influence in American politics.[21] These inequalities in turn have created a wedge between what most Americans want and what they actually get, holding back popular policies to address climate change, invest in schools, provide more affordable healthcare and levy more progressive taxes.[22]

In some ways, America is the country where we would most expect this result, since it is both more unequal than most other rich democracies and has some of the world's weakest regulation of lobbying and political donations. But similar research in other countries has reached much the same conclusion. In a study looking at thirty countries, including most of the established democracies of Western Europe and the English-speaking world, the political scientist Larry Bartels found that "governments' responsiveness to citizens' preferences was highly skewed in favour of affluent citizens," and since rich citizens were generally less supportive of the welfare state, this tended to lower combined spending on pensions, health, education and unemployment benefits significantly.[23] It's worth noting too that, if anything, these kinds of studies underestimate the degree to which money shapes politics in many contemporary democracies: although they look at how politicians respond to the views expressed by different groups in surveys, they cannot account for the ways in which the wealthy are able to shape these views in the first place, through their influence on political parties, advocacy organizations and the media.

THE CASE FOR ELECTORAL DEMOCRACY

It's tempting to blame the endemic failure to achieve meaningful political equality on electoral democracy itself. Critics of this model argue that elections are inherently flawed and that representative democracy is a betrayal of "true," or "direct," democracy, where citizens themselves vote for policies, rather than electing representatives to do this on their behalf.[24]

At first sight, these critics appear to have a point: after all, in an electoral democracy, a small group of representatives has more political influence than everyone else. But our aim is not to ensure that everyone has perfectly equal influence—after all, some people will always be more interested in politics than others—but that they have broadly equal *opportunities* for influence. And the electoral model, at least when it is working well, has some decisive advantages as a mechanism for achieving this. In an ideal representative democracy, everyone would have an equal right to vote as well as roughly equal opportunities to stand for office and to participate in democratic debate more widely. In such a system, elected representatives would generally reflect the views and preferences of the wider population, and the need to get re-elected would provide a mechanism for citizens to hold their representatives to account. Of course, actual representative democracies are far from ideal.[25] Nonetheless, if designed well, elections offer a tried and tested method for achieving political equality in a society with millions, or hundreds of millions, of citizens.

What about direct democracy? This model has a long pedigree going back to the earliest "democracy" that developed in Athens around the fifth century B.C., where most decisions were taken by an assembly in which all (male) citizens were entitled to attend, speak and vote.[26] It has an obvious appeal as a way of achieving political equality, since everyone could participate and we wouldn't have to worry about the difficulties of holding elected representatives to account.[27] But it also has serious drawbacks, especially when operating at scale. In practice, in any democratic assembly, some people inevitably tend to become very involved, while most people take a back seat (even in ancient Athens, historians estimate that as few as 1,000 out of a citizen body of around 30,000 were actively engaged in the assembly, while an even smaller group of around twenty "professional" politicians initiated most policy).[28] What this means is that, even in a direct democracy, a small group of fully participating members become de facto representatives. But, in contrast to the electoral model, there is no mechanism to ensure that they are in any way representative of the wider population. Moreover, as the scale of the community increases, the direct model simply ceases to be a feasible way to make decisions with any semblance of political equality. To give each of Athens' 30,000 citizens just ten minutes to speak would have taken more than a year, even if the assembly met for twelve hours per day every single day. As we shall see, while direct democracy has a role to play at the local level, it is simply not feasible at the national level in a large modern society.*

The earliest democracies, including Athens, often combined direct or "assembly" democracy with the use of random lotteries to select citizens for public duties.[29] This method had all but disappeared from democratic discourse and practice, but the growing discontent with the electoral model has prompted a recent surge of interest.[30] Random selection has some real advantages: it offers a more scalable alternative to elections than direct democracy, and appears to offer a foolproof way of achieving political equality, since by definition every citizen has the same chance of being selected. But it is not an attractive wholesale alternative to elections either. The fundamental problem is that, on its own, random selection would leave most people with no way of participating in the formal process of decision-making. Having a final say over political decisions, even if only indirectly through one's elected representatives, is valuable in its own right; and there is a danger that if most people don't have any direct opportunity to get involved in politics, they will simply disengage, leading to a decline in the quality and vibrancy of political debate.[31]

Part of the appeal of these alternatives is that—at a time when trust in the political class is so low—they would do away with the need for political parties and professional politicians altogether. But we should not be so quick to dismiss these elements of the electoral model. As in other areas of life, so in politics, there are important benefits from a division of labour. By creating a specific role for political parties, electoral systems are more likely to foster both technical expertise about particular policy areas and, perhaps more importantly, a distinctly "political" kind of expertise—the ability to articulate and argue for different ideas about the kind of society

---

* In principle, modern communication technology means that a form of direct democracy based on online referendums may well be technically feasible. But such a system would leave little if any room for political parties which, as we shall see below, perform a vital role. While referendums surely have a place, no one seriously thinks we could or should run a modern government on the basis of referendums alone.

we want to live in, and to mobilize people to bring about change. We have to remember that democratic politics is not simply about representing a fixed set of interests or characteristics; rather, it is a dynamic process in which people put forward different visions of how we can fix the problems facing society. Political parties and politicians play a critical role in this, and it's hard to imagine a healthy and vibrant democracy without them.[32]

Despite its limitations, then, the representative model has some decisive advantages over alternative systems which justify its central role in any large-scale modern democracy. This doesn't mean we should dismiss these alternatives altogether: while we should stick with elections as the central mechanism for achieving mass political equality, we can and should augment them with an expanded role for direct democracy at the local level, and with random selection at the national level. An increase in direct participation would help breathe new life into the democratic process, and we will look at how we can do this later in the chapter. But first we need to think about how we can improve the electoral system itself.

Making Elections Work Better

Making elections work better should be at the heart of any serious programme of democratic renewal, and this must begin with the design of the voting system itself. There are two main models. The UK, U.S.A., Canada and India are among the 28 per cent of countries that currently elect representatives to their national legislature using "first past the post." Under this system, a country is divided into geographical constituencies with a single representative, and in each constituency the candidate with the most votes wins. The major alternative to first past the post is "proportional representation," where citizens vote for a political party rather than an individual candidate, and each party receives a share of elected positions in proportion to their overall vote share. Nearly 40 per cent of countries use this system, including the majority of European countries and of "established" democracies around the world.[33]

From the perspective of political equality, proportional representation has some conspicuous advantages.[34] The key one is that it tends to create a better match between elected representatives and

the views of the population as a whole. The most obvious reason
for this is that, under proportional representation, votes translate
directly into seats, and in this sense every vote counts equally, irrespective of where that vote is cast: if 10 per cent of the population
favour a particular party, it will have 10 per cent of the seats in the
legislature. By contrast, under first past the post, the share of seats
for a given party depends not just on how many votes they win, but
on where those votes are located. To take a hypothetical example,
suppose 10 per cent of the population support a party whose votes
are evenly spread across each constituency, meaning they get 10 per
cent of the votes in each area. In a proportional system, this party
would win 10 per cent of the seats, but under first past the post they
would get none. For those voters, it is as if their votes simply don't
count. This is not a purely theoretical possibility: in the 2015 general
election, the UK Independence Party won 13 per cent of the national
vote, but secured only one seat out of a total of 650.[35]

Critics sometimes worry that by making it easier for small parties
to win seats, proportional representation will encourage the growth
of extremist groups standing on hateful or anti-democratic platforms. Of course, no one committed to liberal and democratic values wants to see these kinds of parties taking seats in the legislature.
But it would be wrong to rig our political system to exclude them
just because we disagree with their views. Proportional voting systems provide a democratic vent for populist anger and discontent,
creating clear incentives for mainstream parties to address underlying social problems and win back votes. We also have to remember
that small parties can play a valuable role in highlighting specific
issues that have been overlooked, as has often been the case with
"Green" parties. In any case, the European experience suggests that
there is no overall tendency for extremist parties to increase their
numbers over time under proportional systems.[36]

Countries with proportional representation tend to be multiparty
democracies, while the difficulties faced by smaller parties under
first past the post means that these countries are usually dominated
by two major parties. This points to the second reason why proportional representation is more "representative" than first past the
post. Two parties can never get close to representing the full range
of political views in society, and with just two viable options, lots of

people end up reluctantly voting for a party that isn't a good fit for their underlying values. Many stop voting altogether. In a multiparty democracy, by contrast, citizens are more likely to find a party that matches their political beliefs.[37]

Proportional voting systems also avoid the perverse situation, endemic to all countries with first past the post, where political influence is skewed towards so-called "marginal" or "competitive" constituencies—in other words, those with a realistic possibility of changing hands. If we measure "voter power" as the probability that someone's vote will change the outcome in their constituency, and hence influence the national balance of power, we find enormous differences between marginal and safe seats: in the UK, voters in the most marginal 10 per cent of constituencies wield roughly thirty times as much "power" as those in the safest seats.[38] As a result, politicians tend to focus their resources and attention on these areas: a study of the 2010 general election in the UK found that parties spent more than twice as much per vote in "ultra-marginal" con- stituencies (those won by less than 1 per cent of the vote) compared to safe seats; while in the 2014 election, marginal constituencies received almost three times as many donations as safe seats.[39] This problem is even worse in countries like the U.S.A. where politicians can shape constituency boundaries, and have used this power to create an ever-increasing number of safe seats, with the result that a growing number of citizens live in constituencies where incumbent politicians have very little incentive to respond to their constituents' concerns. Placing such control in the hands of politicians is a basic design flaw that any serious democracy should address.[40]

Proportional representation does, however, create some chal- lenges of its own. In countries with proportional representation, most governments are coalitions between different parties and policy is often the product of behind-the-scenes negotiations. This can make it harder for voters to hold parties to account for their decisions in government, since they can always blame their coalition partners; while the difficulties of forging stable coalitions can lead to instability, as has been the case in Israel, which in November 2022 held its fifth election in four years. By contrast, under first past the post, most governments are constituted from a single party, mak- ing it easier for voters to assess whether they have lived up to their manifesto commitments, and often leading to more stable government. Even so, it's important not to overstate the difference: a similar process of coalition-building is necessary under first past the post too—it's just that this mostly takes place *within* the major parties, which are themselves coalitions of various factions and interest groups, and as a result is largely hidden from public view.

Proportional systems can also make it harder to hold individual politicians to account. Under first past the post, voters in a constituency vote for a specific person and they can decide whether to continue supporting them at the next election. By contrast, under the traditional form of proportional representation where people vote for parties rather than individuals, there is no real mechanism for doing this. But we can incorporate mechanisms for individual accountability into a proportional voting system: instead of the so-called "closed list" model, where parties get to decide which candidates take up their seats, we can adopt the "open list" model, where citizens vote both for a party *and* for which candidates they want to take up that party's seats. We can also divide a country into smaller districts, each with its own list of candidates, with multiple seats that are allocated in proportion to the votes within each area—a kind of hybrid between first past the post and proportional representation.[41] Combining proportional representation with smaller multi-member constituencies also tends to reduce the total number of viable parties, which in turn can mitigate concerns that proportional systems will lead to fragmentation and instability.

Adopting proportional representation would be an important step towards political equality in countries like the UK and the U.S.A., but the success of any electoral system depends on citizens actually turning out to vote. A high level of turnout promotes meaningful political equality, since it helps to ensure a close connection between citizens and their representatives. Unfortunately, trends have been going in the wrong direction in most rich democracies: across the OECD, overall turnout fell from 75 per cent on average in the early 1990s to 65 per cent in the 2010s.[42] Even more worrying is the fact that turnout is so heavily skewed towards the rich: across the OECD, it is 12 percentage points higher among the richest 20 per cent than the poorest 20 per cent of the population, and this gap reaches 26 percentage points in America.[43]

As we have seen, the voting system itself is part of the problem here. The lack of choice under first past the post can leave many voters feeling alienated from politics, while voters in safe seats have little incentive to vote. Unsurprisingly, countries with proportional representation have significantly higher levels of turnout on average.[44] But whatever voting system we have in place, there are a range of other measures that all countries can and should take to maximize turnout and make it truly representative.

First, we should make voting as easy as possible by ensuring there are enough polling stations, extending voting hours and facilitating early and postal voting. As is already the case in most countries—though not the UK and U.S.A.—elections should be held on weekends or on special public holidays. We should also adopt automatic and universal voter registration, since easier registration increases turnout and makes it less biased towards the wealthy. Many democratic countries have already adopted some form of this, but the UK and the U.S.A. still require citizens actively to register prior to elections.[45] Voter identification laws—where citizens are required to show photo ID in order to vote—represent yet another unnecessary barrier to participation. In America, where such laws are common, their main effect has been to reduce turnout among Black, low-income and other marginalized voters, with little or no meaningful benefits in terms of reducing fraud. The introduction of voter ID requirements in the UK in 2023 is a clear step in the wrong direction.[46]

Alongside measures to make voting easier, turnout could be enhanced through compulsory voting backed up by modest fines. Compulsory voting already exists in twenty-eight countries, and the evidence suggests that it increases turnout by as much as 10 or 15 percentage points, while also reducing the gap in turnout between rich and poor.[47] Of course, compulsory voting is not a panacea, and it should not distract us from addressing the reasons why so many people are disengaged from politics in the first place. But it is a legitimate tool in the democratic toolkit. Critics rightly point out that this would in some sense limit freedom. But while the right to vote is a true basic liberty, the right *not* to vote is less important:

just as we require people to pay their taxes, or to take part in jury service, we should be able to require people to vote, if doing so is an effective way to advance an important public interest. And what could be more important than maintaining a strong and healthy democracy?[48]

FIXING DEMOCRACY'S "CRITICAL INFRASTRUCTURE"

The first step towards democratic renewal is to strengthen the electoral mechanisms that are the key to a healthy representative democracy. But, as we saw at the start of the chapter, democracy is about more than voting and elections—it also means ensuring that everyone has an equal opportunity to contribute to the much wider process of democratic deliberation and debate. In this context, equality depends on both enlightened understanding and effective participation. In other words, everyone must have the chance to come to an informed position about important political questions, to make their views heard, and to persuade others and indeed be persuaded by them.

In a modern representative democracy, these opportunities are inevitably mediated through certain institutions, the most important of which are political parties and the news media. These institutions, in turn, are underpinned by certain basic rights, like freedom of speech and association, without which they could not serve their democratic function. But guaranteeing these rights is not enough. Our failure to think carefully and creatively about how to regulate and fund parties and the news media has allowed the rich to dominate them, with disastrous consequences. Fixing this critical democratic infrastructure is a vital aspect of any serious agenda for political reform.

Political Parties

Let's start by looking at political parties. They are essential for organizing democratic deliberation, and for developing valuable technical and political expertise. They are also a forum where people with similar values and interests can come together and figure out societies' problems and how to solve them. Finally, they are one of the most important vehicles through which citizens can collectively advocate and campaign for their ideas. As a result, political equality depends on everyone having the same opportunities to influence parties. And yet the reality today is that such influence lies disproportionately in the hands of rich donors and powerful corporations.

The activities of political parties—running election campaigns, developing new ideas and policies—cost money, and in many countries a significant proportion of it comes from private donations, creating a direct channel through which the rich can gain extra political influence. Some countries cap donations at a relatively low level, thereby limiting the influence of any single individual. In Belgium, for example, individual donations to political parties are capped at €500 per year. But in many countries donations are capped at a level that is well beyond the reach of most citizens: in the U.S.A., for example, the limit is set at $30,000 per person; while in the UK and twelve other OECD countries there is no limit whatsoever. More than two thirds of OECD countries also allow corporate donations. Some countries, including the UK, try to limit the role of money in politics by imposing restrictions on total spending, but without caps on individual donations, parties have a strong incentive to raise money from a few large donors.[49]

Although international evidence on who actually gives money to parties is hard to come by, the available data shows that donations are heavily skewed towards rich individuals and large corporations. A study by the economist Julia Cagé found that in France and the UK just 10 per cent of all donors account for more than two thirds of all donations.[50] More than any other advanced democracy, though, it is America which stands out for the sheer amount of private money in politics, and the extent to which this gushes from a rich and unrepresentative "donor class." Elections in America are eye-wateringly expensive—spending in the 2020 presidential and congressional elections topped $14 billion, with the average cost of winning a seat hitting nearly $20 million for the Senate and more than $2 million for the House of Representatives (in both cases, an increase of more than 170 per cent in real terms since records began in 1986).[51] Almost all of this money comes from private donations, since although there are limits on individual contributions, these can be circumvented by giving to supposedly independent "Political

Action Committees," or PACs. (Since a Supreme Court ruling in 2010, PACs have been allowed to spend unlimited amounts in support of their preferred candidates.) Political donations in America are dominated by the ultra-rich: just one tenth of one tenth of 1 per cent of Americans provided almost half of the money spent in the 2012 federal elections, while 132 megadonors gave more than $10 million each to Political Action Committees, together surpassing the total raised from more than 3.7 million small donations to the rival Obama and Romney presidential campaigns.[52] As you might expect, the donor class is richer, whiter and more male than the population overall; and its members tend to hold more "conservative" opinions than the average American.[53]

The role of private money in funding political parties distorts democracy in all sorts of ways. Part of the problem is that rich donors are able to secure direct benefits in return for their donations—sometimes legally, sometimes not. In the UK, it is surely no coincidence that so many people who have gifted large sums to parties are given knighthoods or elevated to the House of Lords, while in America ambassadorships are routinely awarded to political donors.[54] For corporations, the prize for generous donations is typically more favourable regulation. But the impact of all private donations on politics is much more pervasive than this kind of direct quid pro quo. Anecdotal evidence from the U.S.A. suggests that members of Congress spend up to half of their time on fundraising activities.[55] Sometimes parties deliberately tailor their platform or choice of candidates to appease donors, but the influence of the donor class also reflects a more unconscious process of social and intellectual osmosis that occurs when politicians spend so much time around this deeply unrepresentative group. And, of course, donations don't just affect who stands for office and on what platform, they shape who wins and eventually holds power.[56]

So how can we break the hold of private money over politics? The first step is to introduce tight restrictions on donations. If we want everyone to have a reasonably equal opportunity to influence parties in this way, then individual contributions need to be capped at a level that is within everyone's reach, say in the low hundreds of pounds. Politicians would then have to appeal to the full range of potential voters rather than focusing their efforts on a small and unrepresentative elite. Corporate donations should be banned outright, though there is a case for permitting contributions from trade unions and other mass-membership advocacy groups. In any case, restrictions on donations should include non-monetary gifts and contributions in kind, which corporations sometimes use to win political influence.

Placing strict limits on political donations would be controversial. In America, the Supreme Court has repeatedly struck down legislation seeking to introduce them, on the basis that this would violate First Amendment rights to free speech. These rulings have made it almost impossible to curb the growing role of private money in American politics, and similar arguments are often deployed to defend the status quo in the UK and elsewhere. Whatever the merits of these judgements as an interpretation of the U.S. Constitution—and there is some debate about this—they are based on the flawed premise that one basic freedom (in this case, free speech) should have an absolute priority over another (political equality). As we touched on in Chapter 1, both freedom of speech and political equality are vital basic liberties, and we need to balance them in a way that best protects our overall interest in living in a free and democratic society. A cap on donations is undoubtedly a precondition for meaningful political equality, but does nothing to limit the content of speech, and would not directly favour any particular point of view.[57]

Since small voluntary contributions alone are unlikely to sustain the vital activities that parties perform, these limits should be combined with a system of public funding. This concept is widely accepted, and nearly every country in the OECD has some form of it.[58] But its generosity and adequacy is extremely variable, and the trend in recent years has been in the wrong direction, with countries including the U.S.A., Italy, and Canada slashing or even abolishing state subsidies.[59]

At a time when trust in politicians is so low, it's not easy to argue for spending *more* on politics. But doing so is essential for true political equality. The key challenge is to make sure that subsidies are allocated independently from the government of the day, otherwise incumbent politicians could abuse the system to favour their own party. To get around this, most countries allocate state funding based on previous election results, so that whichever party won the most seats gets the most money.[60] But this retrospective system tends to favour the incumbents, and creates something of a "catch-22" for new parties: they need funding to win elections, but they need to win elections to secure funding.[61]

The system that would get us closest to political equality is to put funding directly into the hands of citizens, in the form of a "democracy voucher"—an annual allowance of, say, £50, that each citizen could contribute to the party or candidate of their choice.[62] This could exist alongside a system of private donations capped at a low level, or it could replace them entirely. Democracy vouchers would transform our political system: they would give everyone an equal opportunity to influence political parties through donations; they would give parties an incentive to engage with the widest possible spectrum of voters; and they would encourage popular engagement in politics more widely, sparking conversations among friends and families about which party has the best ideas and who should get their voucher. This model also has the potential to make fundraising a community affair—a pub quiz or fundraising dinner for 100 people with £50 vouchers could raise as much as £5,000.[63] And they would make it much easier for new parties to emerge: since vouchers would be issued on an annual basis, party funding would respond quickly to changes in public opinion.

While democracy vouchers have been discussed in policy circles for some time, they are no longer simply a philosopher's pipe dream.[64] In 2017, Seattle introduced the first democracy-voucher scheme for local elections, following a citywide referendum. During each election cycle (every two years), every resident is awarded four $25 vouchers which they can donate to registered candidates of their choice. Candidates can decide whether to participate in the scheme and agree not to accept private donations in excess of $250. There have now been three elections under this system, and on each occasion almost all of the candidates used it. A study of the first two election cycles by economists at the University of Washington found that the number of individual donors rose by a massive 350 per cent, many of whom had never made political donations before. These elections were also more competitive, with the scheme leading to an 86 per cent increase in the number of candidates and more challengers beating incumbents.[65] The time has come to introduce this sort of scheme at a national level.

Even so, this wouldn't entirely eliminate the unfair influence of rich individuals and corporations, who would still be able to influence parties by funding lobbying, advocacy and interest groups. These types of organisation can also play a valuable democratic role, by helping citizens to come together and make their views heard, and by providing legislators with useful information and expertise, for example, about how new environmental regulations might affect a particular industry, or how new roads or housing will affect specific communities. But their activities are inevitably shaped by whoever is paying for them—which, as things stand, is mostly large businesses and rich individuals. The most reliable (and worrying) data on this topic comes from the U.S.A., where for every dollar spent on lobbying by labour unions and public interest groups in 2012, large corporations and their associations spent $34.[66] The consequences should concern us all: according to an OECD review of more than 300 studies, lobbying has "led to the misallocation of public resources, reduced productivity and perpetuated social inequalities," holding back action to address some of the most important public policy issues of our time, from regulating the tobacco industry and addressing obesity to financial regulation and, of course, addressing climate change.[67]

If we are serious about political equality then, at the very least, we need maximum transparency about the interactions between lobbying and advocacy groups, civil servants and politicians.[68] But transparency alone is not enough. As the political scientist Lee Drutman has pointed out, the influence these groups have comes not only, or even mainly, from giving money, but by shaping the way our representatives think—providing information and expertise that they lack the time and resources to develop for themselves. If we want to reduce lobbyists' influence then we need to provide more generous funding for in-house research and expertise, and invest more in truly independent organizations that can supply legislators with impartial information on a range of policies—like the House of Commons Library in the UK and the Congressional Research Service in the U.S.A.[69] We should also try to rebalance the weight of lobbying activity itself, so that it better reflects public opinion rather than who has the deepest pockets—by, for example, placing limits on how much corporations can spend on lobbying, and exploring innovative ways to subsidize advocacy on under-represented issues.[70]

The Media

Alongside political parties, the media—newspapers, broadcasters and, increasingly, social media platforms too—are an essential part of democracy's critical infrastructure. These are both a vital forum for public deliberation and advocacy, and a key source of facts and information, or "news." Of course, there are all sorts of news, some of which, like the latest celebrity gossip, has little relevance to democracy. From the perspective of political equality, what matters is the production and dissemination of what we might call "public interest news," including facts about the problems we face as a society and how we might address them; about the operation of government, and whether our political leaders are living up to their promises; and about what our fellow citizens think.

For the media to fulfil its democratic role, it obviously needs to be free from government interference or censorship: people need to be free to speak their minds and to criticize the government without fear; and, as we saw in the previous chapter, Rawls's basic liberties principle sets a very high bar for legal restrictions on political speech. But in a healthy democracy we also need a media system which is a *reliable* source of information, and which is *diverse*, in the sense that it reflects the variety of views that exist in society and, crucially, is not controlled by a small elite.[71]

The media market is unlikely to deliver these qualities on its own. The news, like facts and knowledge more generally, is what economists call a "public good"—a good whose availability is not diminished through use, and from which it is difficult to exclude people: my reading the news does not reduce your ability to do so, and it is hard (though not impossible) to prevent people from accessing the news once it has been produced. Markets tend to under-provide public goods, and the news is no exception. Producing news—as opposed to merely disseminating it—is a time-consuming and expensive activity: at the very least, it involves paying for experienced and knowledgeable reporters who have the time and expertise to analyse and interpret what is going on around us. Some of the most valuable public interest news comes from investigative reporting, such as uncovering secret meetings between politicians and business leaders. This can be hugely expensive, with individual stories often running into hundreds of thousands of pounds, and those who create original news often struggle to cover their costs, since other outlets can typically reproduce it for free.

From an economic perspective, then, there is always a danger that the market will fail to deliver enough public interest news. In practice, the production of news has historically depended on reader subscriptions and advertising revenues. This model has hardly been ideal, since it has given large companies the ability to shape the news by threatening to withhold advertising revenue. But the rise of the internet has blown this model apart, as readers and advertising have moved online. Some organizations have been able to adapt by introducing online subscriptions and paywalled websites; while others have been able to cut costs through new technologies and by collaborating on large investigations with different outlets. But the big picture is that the resources available for producing public interest news have plummeted. In the U.S.A., the number of "newsroom" employees across newspapers, broadcast radio and TV, and online dropped by 26 per cent between 2008 and 2020.[72] The problem is most severe for local news organizations: in the UK, 321 local papers have closed in the past ten years; while, in America, one in five local papers have closed since 2004, leaving 5 million Americans with no local newspaper and 60 million with just one.[73] The decline of local newspapers is associated with increased corruption, lower turnouts at elections, fewer people standing for office, and incumbents being more likely to win.[74]

Alongside the economic challenges of creating public interest news is the fact that it isn't always easy to distinguish between accurate and false or misleading information, or "fake news."[75] This is a growing problem, thanks in large part to the ease with which misinformation can spread on social media. The result is that it has become more difficult to establish the shared basis of facts that is so vital in any democracy, with increasingly serious consequences.[76]

The continued spread of false and misleading information about the 2020 U.S. presidential election, actively encouraged by President Trump and much of the Republican Party, means that nearly two years later most Republicans still refuse to accept that President Biden was legitimately elected.[77] In the context of the Covid pandemic, misinformation about vaccines has been deadly.[78]

Closely related to the issue of fake news is that of hyperpartisanship within the media. Media organizations don't simply present facts, they also select and interpret them, often according to a particular political agenda. There is nothing wrong with partisanship per se. The problem arises when the boundary between facts and opinions becomes blurred, making it difficult for citizens to tell the difference, as is increasingly the case with major American cable news networks like Fox and MSNBC.[79] The trend towards increased partisanship is no accident—it is a predictable consequence of how countries like America have chosen to regulate the media, leading to an overriding focus on profit, which in practice often means generating extreme and sensationalist content.

We cannot simply rely on the media market to provide us with reliable facts, nor can we rely on it to deliver pluralism and diversity. Indeed, there is a natural tendency for the media market to be dominated by a handful of large players. In part, this reflects significant "economies of scale," where the cost of producing news tends to be lower for larger organizations. It also reflects so-called "network" effects—people want to be reading the same newspaper, or to be on the same platform, as everyone else.[80] Although the internet has reduced the costs of accessing and distributing information, leading to a proliferation of smaller online outlets (many of which simply recycle news created elsewhere), TV bulletins and news websites continue to be the most popular sources, and are often dominated by a handful of major players.[81] In the UK, just five companies account for some 80 per cent of the combined print and online national newspaper market, while five conglomerates account for 80 per cent of all local news titles.[82]

Most worrying of all is that these companies are often controlled by a few rich individuals, with political agendas and interests of their own. In the UK, six billionaires either own outright or have a majority of voting shares in most of the national newspapers, including Rupert Murdoch, whose News UK owns the *Sun* and *Sun on Sunday*, *The Times* and the *Sunday Times*, and Lord Rothermere, who chairs the Daily Mail and General Trust which owns the *Daily Mail*, the *Mail on Sunday*, the *Metro* and the *i*.[83] The economic difficulties faced by media outlets over the last decade have, if anything, exacerbated this problem, with news organizations increasingly reliant on the largesse of the super-rich who are willing to take on struggling or even loss-making organizations in exchange for prestige and political influence, like Amazon founder Jeff Bezos who bought the *Washington Post* in 2013.[84] This troubling concentration of ownership also affects social media, the most recent example being Elon Musk's acquisition of Twitter in 2022, giving the world's richest person control over the world's most politically influential social media platform.

We urgently need to find an economic model which can promote the production of reliable public interest news and a healthy degree of pluralism and diversity. A return to primarily advertising-based revenue is neither likely nor obviously desirable, given the way this creates incentives to chase clicks, often at the expense of quality or accuracy; the subscription-based model is at best a partial solution; and the recent growth of philanthropic funding is a mixed blessing, putting more power in the hands of a wealthy few, however well intentioned. Any long-term solution will almost certainly have to include a significant role for public funding. And yet, although many democratic countries have some kind of public media subsidy, these systems are often far from ideal.[85]

The central challenge is to design a mechanism for providing public money without compromising the freedom and independence of the press. One option is to directly fund state-owned news media, along the lines of the UK's BBC. We can define the remit of a public media corporation in a way that will best support democracy: so, for example, we can use this approach to make sure that there are dedicated journalists to report on government, both centrally and locally, and to fund original analysis and investigative reporting. A public media corporation can also be required to abide by especially stringent standards in terms of factual accuracy and political impartiality, helping to provide a trusted source of information for all. Finally, this model can also satisfy the need for diversity by providing what is known as "internal pluralism," where a single institution curates a wide variety of views. For this approach to work, however, we also need to ensure that any publicly funded media corporation is truly independent. We don't have to look far to see how such organizations can become the tool of incumbent politicians—the state-owned Russia Today is a particularly egregious example. While far from perfect, the BBC has been largely successful in this respect, and continues to be the most widely trusted source of news information in the UK, providing a template on which we can build.[86]

Even if we could guarantee the political independence of a public media corporation, in a healthy democracy we need not just internal but also external pluralism. In other words, we need multiple outlets with different outlooks, approaches and even political agendas. The best way to achieve this would be to introduce a system of media vouchers.[87] As with democracy vouchers, citizens would each be given a certain amount of money that they could direct towards eligible news outlets. Since the purpose of the scheme would be to promote accurate and reliable public interest news, we would need to find a way to restrict eligibility to organizations that produce relevant content (there is no need to subsidize gardening or car magazines!). At the same time, we should make subsidies conditional on adhering to certain independently monitored standards of factual accuracy, integrity and respect for the law.[88] The scheme could also be designed with the explicit purpose of promoting media pluralism—say, by limiting the amount of voucher money going to any single firm.

Media vouchers should be tied to certain minimum standards of factual accuracy, but should they also be conditional on political impartiality? While we need some impartial sources of news—and a public media corporation can help fulfil this function—there is no need for every outlet to be impartial. What matters is that citizens know what they are getting.[89] At the very least, we should require news organizations to be transparent about their funding and any direct political allegiances. Beyond this, we could adopt a tiered regulatory framework, as proposed by the media expert Lara Fielden. She suggests three tiers: legally regulated broadcasters with a remit to promote impartiality; "ethical private media," which agree to voluntary self-regulation and a high degree of integrity and accountability; and "baseline private media," which would be held to the minimum legal standards, say in relation to dangerous speech, libel and privacy.[90] These tiers would be accompanied by a mandatory kite-marking scheme, so that consumers know what to expect from different providers. We could then incentivize providers to adopt the high standards associated with "ethical private media" by restricting vouchers to this tier, thereby promoting public interest news without violating freedom of speech or introducing any form of censorship.

Alongside a new model of public funding, we should also explore new models of media ownership which would disperse power more widely, breaking the hold of wealthy tycoons. The for-profit company is not necessarily a good fit for news organizations whose purpose, after all, is to provide an important public good. For example, we could encourage—or even require—news organizations to be run on a non-profit basis, where shareholders would be replaced with individual donors who would contribute to news organizations in return for tax deductions, as has been suggested by Julia Cagé. We could also change the corporate governance rules for media organizations in order to give small investors more influence, thereby tilting control away from larger shareholders; and we could set maximum limits on the stake that any single individual could hold.[91]

BEYOND ELECTIONS

Even if we implement everything talked about so far—embracing proportional representation and transforming the way we fund political parties and the media—elections would still be a rather crude way of communicating our views and holding politicians to account. Our representatives would continue to enjoy considerable discretion over which policies to support, which they could use to pursue their own interests, and they would inevitably still be influenced by the network of unelected administrators, civil servants, lobbyists and advisers who surround them.[92] To counterbalance the tendency for professional politicians to become detached from the people they are meant to represent, we should embrace new forms of direct participation so that "ordinary" citizens can make their views heard independently of the political class. The combination of electoral and direct democracy will bring us closer to true political equality than either system by itself.

Increasing direct participation in politics has other benefits too. Above all, it can lead to better-informed and more-effective decision making: while professional politicians may possess technical and political expertise, we also need to draw on the knowledge of ordinary citizens. The value of this is most obvious at the local level, where residents will often have a better grasp of how policies might play out in reality, whether they are changes to local infrastructure, such as new roads or housing, or the delivery of public services, such as buses and schools. The experience of participation itself can also have wider benefits for individuals and society at large—fostering a sense of agency and community, and bolstering the values on which democracy depends.

Fortunately, new methods of participation are already beginning to reinvigorate democratic thinking and practice around the world. Working out how to integrate them fully within large-scale democracies represents an exciting new frontier for democratic renewal.

One of the most promising of these ideas is "participatory budgeting," where local communities are given control of budgets and decide in open public meetings how to spend them. This was first pioneered in Porto Alegre, a city of about 1.5 million inhabitants in southeast Brazil, where, since 1988, a significant proportion of local government public spending has been allocated according to a public participatory process.[93] First, citizens meet in "plenary" assemblies, open to all residents, which are organized both by neighbourhood and around specific citywide issues such as public transport and culture. At these assemblies, citizens deliberate and then choose delegates who form councils tasked with formulating more specific spending priorities. These councils hold their own open meetings with residents and civil society associations throughout the city, to hear their ideas and consider specific projects, before presenting proposals back to the original plenary assemblies. Once these have been approved, each assembly elects delegates to a city-wide council which develops an integrated citywide budget that is, finally, submitted to the city's elected mayor for approval.

The Porto Alegre model has led to an explosion of interest in and practical experimentation with participatory budgeting—a 2019 study identified more than 11,000 real-world examples across seventy-one countries. While South America long led the world, Europe now has the most programmes.[94] In the U.S.A., the first trial was launched in Chicago in 2009; and since 2011 the number of participants and dollars involved around the country has roughly doubled each year.[95]

The success of direct participatory schemes such as these depends, as ever, on careful design. The most important priority is to try to ensure that participants are broadly representative of the wider population. We also need to find a way to incorporate the kinds of expertise that citizens typically lack—in drawing up budgets, and in the details of specific policy areas, from neighbour-hood planning to addressing poverty. Finally, if we are serious about engaging citizens in democratic politics, then we need to be willing to hand over real decision-making power, otherwise people simply won't bother taking part.

Porto Alegre's experience shows that these conditions can be met. Its scheme has achieved an impressive level of popular engagement, with around 8 per cent of adults attending at least one meeting in a typical budgetary cycle.[96] This might not sound like very much, but it is a vastly higher level of direct participation than is found in almost any electoral democracy. This has not been confined to educated elites: poorer citizens—as well as Indigenous and Afro-Brazilians, who tend to participate less in ordinary electoral politics—are well-represented, and the scheme has led to a significant shift in spending towards poorer parts of the city.[97] The inclusion of rep-resentative elements—namely, the election of delegates—means that this smaller group who are responsible for developing specific policies can acquire the necessary expertise, with support from civil servants. Most of these citizen-representatives are also actively involved in charities and community groups, and a rich network of civil society organizations has been vital to the overall success of the programme.[98] Crucially, what distinguishes Porto Alegre from many other participatory budgeting projects is that it gives citizens real power over important local decisions.

We should expand participatory decision-making more widely. This works best at a reasonably small scale, with Porto Alegre's population of about 1.5 million probably near the upper limit of what is feasible. As a result, it also depends on the existence of a political system in which considerable power is held at a local level. In some countries, this is already the case; but in others, like the UK, where power is highly centralized, it would have to form part of a wider process of decentralization. There is a separate debate to be had about which decisions should be made at what level: decisions about national security, macroeconomic policy and the generosity of the welfare system, for example, are best made at a national level; while those concerning local housing, infrastructure and public services may be better made at a regional, city or more local level. The extent of direct participation also depends on how keen people are to devote themselves to the democratic process. We should approach this question with an open mind, testing the popular appetite as we go.

Just as direct democracy can help to revitalize local politics, random selection can do so nationally. As we have seen, despite its intuitive appeal as a way of achieving political equality at scale, random selection is not a credible substitute for the electoral model in its entirety because it fails to give citizens as a whole a final say over democratic decisions. For this reason, it is best used in a more "advisory" capacity, with its proposals subject to approval by elected representatives or in a referendum. Looked at this way, the key advantage of this method is the insight it can give into what a reasonably representative sample of the population thinks about a particular issue, which in turn can help to improve the quality of democratic deliberation and debate. Of course, we can find this out more quickly and cheaply using ordinary opinion polling. But random selection offers insight into not just people's existing political opinions, but the conclusions they would reach after considered reflection.[99] The results of this kind of exercise can give each of us a better idea both of what our fellow citizens think and of what *we* might think if we had time and access to experts, and if we talked to people beyond our immediate social group.*

Although neglected for many years, this forgotten democratic method is making a comeback.[100] The Canadian province of British Columbia embarked on the first large-scale modern experiment with random selection in 2004, when it convened a "citizens' assembly" of around 100 people to develop a proposal for electoral reform. After meeting every other weekend for more than a year, their recommendation was put to a referendum. (Although it won the support of a majority of voters, it was never implemented because the vote failed to reach the required 60 per cent turnout threshold.) Since then, a number of other countries, including Iceland, the Netherlands and Ireland, have taken a similar approach to address a range of important constitutional questions. In Ireland, propositions put forward by citizens' assemblies played a crucial role in persuading a historically socially conservative population to vote in favour of legalizing same-sex marriage in 2015 and abortion in 2018.[101] A similar approach could offer a way through equally fraught issues in countries like America, where popular views about abortion, say, are considerably more nuanced than those expressed in mainstream political debate, suggesting a group of "ordinary" citizens might be able to find a solution that could secure wide support.[102]

The argument for random selection depends on the participants being representative of the wider population.[103] This can be achieved through a carefully designed invitation process, alongside practical measures to ensure that everyone who is invited is able to take part, such as paying people for their time, requiring employers to grant leave from work, and support for those with caring responsibilities.

---

* The case for random selection is especially strong when it comes to questions about the political process itself, which we have been discussing in this chapter. Generally speaking, an incumbent party will want to maintain the system that put it there, and may obstruct popular reforms that could threaten its hold on power. Random selection also has advantages in addressing long-term issues like climate change or an ageing population which may be neglected given the short-term incentives of the electoral cycle.

We also need to think carefully about how we can foster an informed and respectful debate in which everyone feels comfortable to speak. So, for example, the discussion should be guided by experts who can provide unbiased information about the subject at hand, and by trained facilitators who can create an environment where everyone has the chance to contribute, not just the loudest and most confident people. Contrary to the concerns raised by pessimists, the evidence is clear that ordinary citizens are perfectly capable of engaging in thoughtful debate about complex policy issues, and that many people change their minds after taking part in such a process.[104]

How can we incorporate random selection into the ordinary workings of democratic government? There are two basic approaches we can pursue. The first is to expand and formalize its use to address specific issues and as part of the standard voting process. At present, the decision about whether to initiate a citizens' assembly on a given issue, and whether any proposals are ultimately put to a vote, is in the hands of elected politicians. Instead, we could allow citizens to convene an assembly, much in the same way that many American states allow citizens to initiate a referendum by securing a certain number of supporters. We can also integrate this method into elections and referendums. In the American state of Oregon, for example, referendum proposals (or "Citizens' Initiatives") are first submitted to a "Citizens' Initiative Review," which brings together twenty to twenty-five representative voters to listen to advocates for and against the measure that is due to be put to a popular vote, as well as the views of experts. The group meets for four or five days, and sets out in a report what they consider to be the key arguments on either side, which is then sent to every citizen ahead of the vote.[105] We could adopt a similar process ahead of elections, by asking a panel of randomly selected citizens to produce a report on the major party manifestos.

The second, more ambitious approach would be to establish a randomly selected "citizens' chamber," to form part of the legislature. It could either have an advisory role, not unlike the House of Lords in the UK today, or a shared right of ratification, similar to the way in which the U.S. House of Representatives and the Senate are both required to approve legislation before it can become law. Of course, there would be many details to work out—how exactly to select representatives and how long they should serve for, how to facilitate high-quality deliberation, how to prevent participants from being co-opted by moneyed interests and so on.[106] But this kind of hybrid parliament would retain the advantages of the electoral model while embedding random selection in the heart of our modern democratic structures.

For all the flaws in our current political systems, support for the democratic ideal is alive and well, and there are a host of exciting new ways in which we can better achieve political equality. The proposals in this chapter—proportional representation, democracy vouchers, more direct participation—would break the hold of rich donors and increase popular engagement in collective decision-making. Reforming our democracy in this way is both essential in its own right, and a precondition for overcoming the inevitable resistance to any wider programme of social and economic renewal. And yet even the best-designed political system would struggle in the face of the extreme inequalities of income and wealth that exist in most rich countries today. Ultimately, as Rawls argued, if we are committed to political equality, then we also need to reduce these inequalities directly.[107] Having looked in detail at the implications of Rawls's first principle, in the chapters to come we will look at how his second principle can guide us in accomplishing precisely this— bringing about true equality of opportunity and ensuring that society really will work to "the greatest benefit of the least advantaged."

6

Equality of Opportunity

We have seen how Rawls's first principle can help defend our basic freedoms and reinvigorate democracy. And yet, vital though this is, it is not enough to address the justified discontent with our societies today. This discontent is rooted above all in a broken economic model which is pushing the natural world to the brink of disaster, which continues to allow class, race and gender to shape people's opportunities, and which increasingly channels the benefits of economic activity into the hands of a privileged few.

There is growing recognition that our economic system needs far-reaching reform, but there is little agreement about what this would look like, or what exactly we should be aiming for. As we saw in the Introduction, over the past few decades our political discourse has been dominated by a harsh and individualistic neoliberalism, combining a single-minded focus on economic efficiency and growth with an almost religious faith in the benefits of free markets. This way of thinking has crowded out alternative ideas of what a fair and sustainable economy would look like: as the philosopher Fredric Jameson famously said, it has often felt easier to imagine the end of the world than the end of capitalism.[1]

There are signs that this is starting to change. Questions about sustainability and inequality that had long been relegated to the sidelines of our public debate are firmly back on the agenda. Although our governments have singularly failed to address the climate and ecological emergency, there is at least a growing consensus that this is a defining challenge of our times, and plenty of ideas about what we need to do. There is also an increasingly urgent discussion about why inequality has increased so much in recent decades, and how we can reduce it.[2] But as we saw in the Introduction, we continue to lack an underlying ethical or philosophical framework which can bring all this together and offer a truly systematic alternative to neoliberalism.

This is why Rawls's ideas are so essential. Over the course of the final three chapters, we will see how they can guide us towards a new political economy that is at once unmistakably liberal and strongly egalitarian, and which puts sustainability at its core. It's important to remember here that the two aspects of his second principle—fair equality of opportunity, the difference principle—work together. For Rawls, economic justice is not only about ensuring that there is a fair competition for different positions, but about making sure that the "prizes" attached to those positions—income, wealth and social prestige—are fair. At the same time, everything we do to promote opportunity and increase the life chances of the least well off must respect our obligations towards future generations, including our fundamental duty to maintain the vital ecosystems on which society depends. As we shall see, it is when it comes to economic questions that the transformative potential of Rawls's ideas becomes fully apparent—both for how we understand liberalism, and for how we organize our society.

We'll begin, as Rawls does, by looking at how we can move beyond empty rhetoric and make good on the promise of equality of opportunity for all. As we saw in Chapter 1, *fair*—as opposed to merely formal—equality of opportunity depends on two things: first, jobs and positions should be allocated on the basis of talent, rather than nepotism or prejudice; and second, everyone should have an equal chance to develop their talents and abilities. In this chapter, we will look at how we can tackle the influence of class, race and gender on people's life chances. Of course, people also face discrimination and a lack of opportunity on account of their sexuality, religion, disability and more, but it is impossible to explore all the applications of this important principle in one chapter, and looking in detail at these three core categories should be enough to illustrate the approach. As we shall see, although equality of opportunity may be a familiar idea, putting it into practice will require profound changes to our society and economy.

MISSED OPPORTUNITIES

Just how far are we from fair equality of opportunity? To answer this question, we first need to understand how differences in parental or family resources—or what we might think of as "social class"—affect children's chances in life. There are lots of ways we could measure this: we could look at whether children with more educated parents receive more education themselves, or whether children born to parents with professional jobs are more likely to have similar jobs as adults. The most widely used and readily available measure is the relationship between parental income or earnings and what children go on to earn as adults. This is what is generally referred to as "social mobility" (or, to be precise, "intergenerational income mobility").

In a society with perfect equality of opportunity, we would expect to see a weak relationship between parental resources and children's earnings. Children from rich and poor backgrounds would benefit from the same kind of schooling, have access to the same universities, compete for the same kinds of jobs and hence end up with similar pay. As a result, we would expect high levels of social mobility: children born into poor families would have a similar chance of ending up rich as children born into rich families would have of ending up poor. Of course, even with perfect equality of opportunity, we might expect to find *some* relationship between parental resources and children's earnings: rich parents might pass on economically valuable genetic traits, or raise their children with values that lead them to prioritize work.[3] But, in general, a strong relationship between parental resources and children's earnings is a powerful indicator that society is failing to provide genuinely equal opportunities.[4]

This is exactly what we find across the world's rich democracies. Children born into rich households are much more likely to be rich as adults.* Looking across the OECD as a whole, fathers pass on about 40 per cent of any earnings advantage to their sons. In other words, if your father earns £10,000 more than your friend's father, on average you will yourself earn £4,000 more than your friend.[5] Although there are various estimates of the precise link between parental resources and children's earnings in rich democracies, this relationship is consistently strongest in the UK and U.S.A., where parents pass on about 50 per cent of their earnings advantage to their children; and weakest in Norway, Denmark and Finland, where this number falls to less than 20 per cent.[6] The fact that there is much greater social mobility in some countries is an important reminder that the transmission of inequality from one generation to the next is not an immutable fact of life, but something that can be shaped by public policy.

Looking beneath these headline figures, we find that mobility is especially low at the top and bottom of the income distribution.[7] In other words, we find "sticky" floors and ceilings: children born into rich families are much more likely to stay rich, while children born into poor families are much more likely to stay poor. By contrast, when we look at the middle of the income distribution, there appears to be rather a lot of mobility. Suppose we imagine society divided into five equal groups, or quintiles, from the richest to the poorest. In a society with perfect social mobility, children born in the poorest quintile would have the same chance—20 per cent—of ending up in any quintile, and the same would be true of children born into the richest quintile. In reality, in both the UK and U.S.A., more than 30 per cent of people who were born into the bottom quintile stay there, while fewer than 10 per cent reach the top quintile. Even more striking is the extent to which children born into the most privileged households tend to stay at the top: around 40 per cent of those born into the top quintile stay there, and fewer than 10 per cent fall into the bottom quintile.[8] This suggests we need a dual-track approach to

---

* In practice, most studies have looked at the relationship between the earnings of fathers and sons. This is partly for technical and data-related reasons, including the fact that women are now much more likely to work than their mothers were, but it also likely reflects the scarcity of female economists and the wider neglect of sex and gender within the discipline.

unlocking opportunity: first, to address the lack of opportunity for those growing up in the poorest households; and, second, to tackle so-called "opportunity hoarding" among the richest ones.

International comparisons also reveal that countries with the highest inequality, like the UK and U.S.A., tend to have the lowest mobility; while lower inequality is associated with higher mobility.[9] This is because parents with more income are generally able to provide their children with better opportunities, and in more unequal societies parents have stronger incentives to use their money to give their offspring a competitive edge. In the U.S.A. and UK, where incomes are so unequal, and where getting into a top university can lead to truly enormous differences in income and social status, it is no wonder that rich parents go to great lengths to secure the best opportunities for their children, often spending tens or even hundreds of thousands of pounds on private education in the process.[10] By contrast, in relatively equal countries, like Norway or Denmark, parents can be more confident that their children will have a decent standard of living no matter what, and hence this imperative isn't nearly so strong.

The fact that more unequal countries have lower mobility reminds us that although it may be helpful to distinguish between equality of opportunity and equality of outcome, in practice the two are always closely related: parents' outcomes are children's opportunities, and as long as some children grow up in poverty, equality of opportunity will remain an elusive goal. After all, it's impossible for children to make the most of being at school if they are living in overcrowded housing or don't have enough food to eat, and poverty makes it much more difficult for parents to offer their children the love and support they need. There is clear evidence, for example, that economic hardship leads to parental stress and conflict as well as harsh parenting, all of which can hold back children's development and lead to behavioural problems. One study found that when a parent loses their job, the chances that their child is held back a year in school increase by 15 per cent; another found that children whose mothers had unstable jobs had more behavioural problems.[11] Although in the following section we will focus on the role of the education system, if we are serious about equality of opportunity we also need to eliminate poverty and reduce inequality directly. How to do this will be the subject of the final two chapters, when we turn to the implications of Rawls's difference principle.[12]

EDUCATION AND OPPORTUNITY FOR ALL

Our failure to provide children with equal opportunities is reflected in the large gaps in educational achievement that exist between those born into rich and poor families. These appear before children even start school, typically widening as they grow older and culminating in vast differences in their skills and qualifications as adults. In the UK and France, children born into the richest 20 per cent of families are three times more likely to get a degree than those born into the poorest 20 per cent, while in America they are five times more likely.[13] These differences in educational attainment have enormous consequences, not just for people's incomes, but for their social status and access to cultural and indeed political life.

Closing these gaps must start with the so-called "early years"— roughly the first five years of life. There is now a very large body of evidence which attests to the critical importance of this period for children's development, their ability to benefit from formal schooling, and their economic opportunities as adults.[14] And yet the difference in "school-readiness" between the richest and poorest children by age five is a shocking nineteen months in the UK, and as high as twenty-two months in the U.S.A., meaning it would take nearly two extra years for the poorest American children to catch up with their wealthy peers.[15]

These inequalities among very young children are largely driven by their experiences at home. As we touched on above, this partly reflects differences in material living conditions, like access to decent food, housing and healthcare. These in turn shape and interact with differences in parenting ability and styles. In fact, more than anything else, children's development during their crucial early years depends on how far their parents or primary carers create a nurturing and stimulating environment.[16] We know, for example, that children with close relationships with their parents, and those with more regular bedtimes, are less likely to develop behavioural problems, and that simple activities like reading and talking to children can have a big impact on their cognitive development.[17] In addition to implementing measures to alleviate poverty and insecurity, which we will discuss in the next chapter, we must do more to help parents directly during this period, including expanding access to parenting classes, better mental-health care for parents with young children, and home visits from health professionals and social workers—all of which have been shown to be effective.[18] These kinds of services would ensure that all parents have access to the information they need, and would help identify those that might need more intensive support.

And yet there are clearly limits to how far the state can intervene in day-to-day family life. This brings us back to the crucial role of the education system in establishing a level playing field and compensating for some of the differences that children inevitably experience at home, starting with early years education, or "preschool." One of the earliest and best-designed studies to demonstrate the potential of early years education is the Perry Preschool Project, implemented in Michigan in the 1960s for a group of poor Black families whose children were at high risk of failing in school. Follow-up interviews forty years later found that its former participants were more likely to have completed high school and gone to college, less likely to have been arrested, and had more savings, higher earnings and better relationships with their families.[19] Other studies and experiments, including those looking at large-scale and even universal programmes, have confirmed the basic finding that high-quality preschool programmes—with well-trained staff, low student-to-staff ratios and a strong focus on learning and development—can lead to increased educational attainment, higher earnings, lower welfare dependency and less crime.[20] Moreover, children from the poorest families tend to benefit the most from such initiatives, thereby increasing social mobility. In Norway, a major expansion of subsidized childcare in the mid-1970s is estimated to have reduced the link between parental and child incomes—already among the lowest in the world—by a further 10 per cent.[21]

The past few decades have seen a significant expansion in early years education in many advanced democracies. And yet, despite its importance for children's development, public spending on it is much lower per child than on schools and universities.[22] Children from poor families are still much less likely to participate too, even though they stand to benefit the most. In some countries, the gap is really very large: in both France and Ireland, children under the age of three from high-income families are more than four times as likely to be enrolled in formal early years education.[23] One of the most important reasons for this situation is that, in contrast to compulsory schooling which is generally paid for by the state, families often have to shoulder some or all of the upfront costs of preschool, and many on low incomes simply cannot afford it.

If we really want to level the playing field for the youngest children then we must establish a universal legal entitlement to high-quality early years education, possibly starting as early as the point at which parental leave comes to an end, as is done in several European countries, including Denmark, Germany, Finland and Norway.[24] The most direct way to encourage widespread participation, especially of children from disadvantaged backgrounds, would be to make this free for everyone. But a more targeted approach can also work, as is found in Denmark where early years education is offered free to the poorest households, and then at heavily reduced rates to those with moderate incomes.[25] Denmark is one of only a handful of countries where children from low-income families are as likely to attend early years education as those from high-income ones. While targeted subsidies are typically the cheapest way to ensure equal access for disadvantaged households, we might still want to consider making early years education free for all because of the other benefits this can have. In particular, such an approach could help promote both gender equality (a topic we will come back to later in this chapter), and economic growth, since even small improvements in a child's early development can end up paying for themselves through their impact on attainment in school and university, and in turn on future earnings.[26] Either way, ensuring broad access to high-quality early years education will require significant public spending: in Denmark, this accounts for about 1.3 per cent of GDP, nearly double the OECD average of 0.7 per cent, and dwarfing the measly 0.3 per cent spent in the U.S.A.[27]

In most countries, investing more in early years education should be the top priority for promoting equality of opportunity, since this is where current policy is furthest from where it needs to be. But we also urgently need to rethink the school system where, despite the advent of publicly funded universal education, rich parents are often able to secure better opportunities for their children.

The most egregious problem in many countries is the role of private "fee-paying" schools.[28] These are typically unaffordable for most parents. In the UK, fees for private day schools were around £15,700 a year on average in 2020/21, rising to more than £44,000 for the most expensive and prestigious boarding schools like Eton—while median household annual disposable income stands at around £31,400.[29] As a result, most private-school students come from the richest 10 per cent of households.[30] These children benefit from a much higher overall level of investment in their education: private schools in the UK have about three times more resources per pupil than the typical state school, which they use to pay for more highly qualified teachers, smaller class sizes and a wider range of extracurricular activities. Children at these schools also benefit from the positive "peer effects" of being around other children who have often been selected on the basis of academic ability (which, as we have seen, is itself shaped by their family background and opportunities before school).[31] For those lucky enough to get a private education, the experience typically has lifelong advantages: in the UK, former private-school students earn 41 per cent more on average in their early thirties than their otherwise similar state-educated peers. They also dominate most elite professions, accounting for 63 per cent of lawyers, 59 per cent of bankers and financiers, and 52 per cent of journalists, despite making up just 7 per cent of the population.[32]

How should we address the impact of fee-paying schools on equality of opportunity? At the very least, we should remove the public subsidies that fee-paying schools benefit from in many countries, such as the tax advantages they get from being registered as charities in the UK. But if we are serious about equality of opportunity, it would be better to abolish fee-paying schools entirely. This isn't about judging parents for wanting the best for their children, but about designing the school system in a way that is consistent with our commitment to giving every child a fair start in life.[33]

To see how this might be done, we can look to Finland, which changed its constitution in the early 1970s to ban schools from charging tuition fees for "basic" or compulsory-level education. Prior to the reform, Finland had a large private-school sector, accounting for more than half of upper secondary-school students.[34] After the reform, most of these schools were gradually brought into the public sector (while a small number of Finnish schools are still run by private companies, they cannot charge fees). Today, the Finnish education system is widely regarded as one of the most successful in the world, outperforming many countries in international test scores for science, mathematics and reading, including ones with large privately funded systems. It is also one of the world's most equitable: an OECD study concluded that "No other country has so little variation in outcomes between schools—and the gap within schools between the top and bottom-achieving students is extraordinarily modest."[35] Of course, the absence of fee-paying schools is not the only reason why Finland's education system is so successful, but the Finnish experience shows that this need not come at the expense of quality overall—if anything, it is likely to have the opposite effect.[36]

While most of us readily accept that the state can ban or regulate obviously "bad" activities like pollution, the idea of stopping people from spending their money on something "good" like education can feel rather counter-intuitive. Critics of abolishing private schools point out that this would restrict parental freedoms. But is the freedom to spend money on a private education more important than achieving fair equality of opportunity? Although Rawls didn't comment on this specific issue, it is precisely the kind of question that his basic liberties principle is designed to address. This principle singles out some economic freedoms, like the right to own personal property and choose your occupation, as being so important that they take priority even over equality of opportunity. These freedoms are basic liberties because they are a truly essential precondition for living a free life and pursuing our dreams and ambitions. But the freedom to spend large amounts of money on a private education, or indeed to pass on unlimited amounts of wealth through gifts and inheritances, simply doesn't have the same importance.

A closely related worry is that banning fee-paying schools might be a slippery slope towards more intrusive and worrying kinds of interventions. If we are willing to prevent parents from spending money on education, then what should we do about activities such as reading young children bedtime stories, or introducing teenage ones to well-connected friends—activities that give some children advantages which others don't have, but which no right-minded person would want to ban? As we saw in Chapter 1, the basic liberties principle can help us determine the limits on how far the state can go in order to promote equality of opportunity. Parents should be free to read their children bedtime stories and introduce them to friends, because, unlike private schooling, having these kinds of freedoms is vital for healthy parent–child relationships.[37]

Banning fee-paying schools would address the most direct way in which the rich can use their wealth to secure educational advantages for their children. But even within the state-funded system, rich families are often able to gain access to better schools. The problem is particularly acute in countries such as the U.S.A., where about 45 per cent of funding for public schools comes from local sources (mainly from property taxes). As a result, schools in the poorest American neighbourhoods spend about 15 per cent less per pupil, equating to roughly $1,500 a year.[38] Even in countries such as the UK, where funding is more centralized, rich parents are effectively able to "buy" a place at the best schools by moving within the relevant school "catchment area," while poorer households are often priced out—houses near the highest-rated schools cost about 12 per cent more than similar houses near the worst ones.[39]

What would a fair system of school funding look like? At first sight, spending the same amount on every child might seem like an attractive goal, and in many countries this would be an improvement on the status quo. But equal funding is not enough to address the disadvantages that children from poorer and less-educated households and neighbourhoods face at home. If we are serious about fair equality of opportunity, then we need to spend more money on children from the least advantaged backgrounds. This was the purpose of the "pupil premium" introduced in England in 2011, which was a grant paid to schools with children from low-income families, as well as the new "national funding formula," introduced in England in 2018, which aims to allocate school funding in a consistent way across the country, taking into account various measures of need.[40] A "weighted funding formula" like this is surely the right way to go, offering a consistent way to target educational resources to where they are needed most.[41] Estimates using American data suggest that educating disadvantaged students to the same level as their more privileged peers could require anywhere between 25 per cent to 100 per cent extra per pupil.[42] In the UK, the most deprived schools currently receive about 25 per cent extra per pupil (down from 30–35 per cent in 2009/10), and gaps in educational attainment remain large, indicating the real cost could easily be towards the upper end of this range.[43]

Just as important as the level of funding is how it is spent. There is growing evidence about how best to design an education system to support children from disadvantaged backgrounds. So, for example, making children who have fallen behind repeat a year appears to be especially damaging. We also know that segregating students by ability at a young age—as advocated by proponents of grammar schools in the UK, and as is standard practice in both Austria and Germany, where academic selection starts at the age of ten—tends to have a negative impact on the lowest performing and often most disadvantaged children, without raising average performance. Instead, we should embrace the "comprehensive" model where children of different abilities attend the same schools, and avoid separating by ability until a later age. We should also encourage integration between different socioeconomic and racial groups, since children from disadvantaged backgrounds tend to do better in more socially mixed schools.[44] We could, for example, make it harder for rich parents to buy access to better schools by widening catchment areas and providing transport for children who live further away; and we could use lotteries for allocating places in oversubscribed schools.[45]

Targeted help for disadvantaged students is also essential. One-to-one tuition has been proven to make a significant difference in helping poorer students fulfil their potential. Numerous studies have also confirmed just how important it is to have good teachers, including one which estimated that replacing a bad teacher with an average one for a single year of schooling would increase each student's lifetime income by as much as $80,000.[46] Yet, in most countries, more experienced teachers are less likely to work in challenging schools. With the right policies, though, we can get the best teachers where they are needed most: in Korea, a combination of higher salaries, smaller class sizes, less teaching time and faster promotion means that disadvantaged students are more likely to be taught by high-quality maths teachers compared to their more fortunate peers.[47]

We also need to think about post-secondary or tertiary education. While this encompasses both vocational training and academic learning, it is the expansion of the latter that has dominated public policy in recent decades, and having a university degree has become one of the most important determinants of people's economic prospects. Graduates tend to earn significantly more than those who haven't gone to university—across the OECD, people with a degree who are working full time earn 50 per cent more, on average, than those without, rising to almost 90 per cent for those with a master's or a PhD.[48] At the same time, graduate-level jobs tend to offer more personal autonomy and greater job satisfaction.[49]

As things stand, tertiary education systems often amplify the unequal opportunities available to children at home and in school. It's not just that people from rich families are more likely to go to university, they are also much more likely to go to the most selective institutions, which are the gateway to the best-paid and most prestigious jobs. In the UK, someone from the richest 20 per cent of families is more than six times as likely to go to a highly selective university as someone from the poorest 20 per cent.[50] At America's most elite "Ivy League Plus" universities—private institutions whose annual fees can be as high as $65,000—there are more students from the top 1 per cent of the income distribution than from the entire bottom 50 per cent.[51] The dominance of academic higher education by those from privileged backgrounds is even more worrying given the widespread neglect of vocational education and training, and the fact that around half of young people in most rich countries don't go to university—a topic we will address in more detail in the next chapter.[52]

If we want to improve access to higher education for children from disadvantaged backgrounds, then we need to redouble our efforts to close the gaps in attainment that open up at school. But even if we could close these gaps entirely, this wouldn't be enough:

in France, about 30 per cent of the difference in university participation between those from rich and poor backgrounds remains even after we account for differences in attainment at school, while high-income students in America are 34 per cent more likely to attend selective colleges than low-income students with the same test scores.[53] In other words, we also need to reform the higher education system itself, so that young people with the same ability on leaving school have the same chance to get a degree.

Part of the problem here is that young people from poorer backgrounds who could go to university don't apply—whether because they think they won't get in or fit in, or because the application and funding systems are too complicated.[54] And even once admitted, these students are more likely to drop out. A combination of outreach programmes and extra support for disadvantaged students would help address these issues. But more than anything else, equality of opportunity in higher education means making sure that participation depends on ability, rather than on ability to pay. As the number of people attending university and indeed other forms of tertiary education has expanded in recent decades, this has become an increasingly important policy issue, with public opinion polarized between "free" university tuition where the costs are borne by taxpayers in general, and a loan-based system or graduate tax, both of which would shift some or all of the costs on to individual graduates.

Free tuition is the norm in continental Europe, where the state typically pays most of the direct costs of studying and sometimes provides grants to cover living costs and other expenses.[55] While this clearly enables equal access irrespective of family income, it is expensive—and, as we shall see, it may not be the fairest approach. Historically, the main alternative to free tuition has been for the state to provide loans that operate much like a mortgage, with fixed monthly repayments, as is the case in the U.S.A. and Canada. But this makes going to university very risky—graduates who end up with relatively low earnings can find themselves with debts they simply cannot afford to repay, especially if they suffer periods of ill-health or unemployment. In America, around 15 per cent of student loans are in default at a given time, affecting 9 million borrowers, who often struggle to buy a home or car, or get a credit card as a result.[56] This prospect is often enough to deter young people from poor backgrounds from going to university altogether.

Mortgage-style student loans are patently incompatible with fair equality of opportunity. But a growing number of countries have adopted income-contingent loans, whereby students pay back the cost of their education out of their future earnings, but only if these are above a certain threshold. This approach was pioneered by Australia in 1989, and has subsequently been implemented in around ten countries, including New Zealand, the UK (except Scotland) and the Netherlands.[57] In August 2022, President Biden announced plans to adopt a similar model in the U.S.A.[58] In the UK, for example, graduates start making repayments once their annual income exceeds £25,000, with 9 per cent of income above this threshold automatically going towards paying off student debt—in effect, a "temporary" graduate tax.* Outstanding loan balances are cancelled after forty years, and about 70 per cent of future graduates are currently expected to repay their loan in full.[59] Income-contingent loans take much of the risk out of going to university, since no one is in danger of losing their home or being declared bankrupt if they cannot afford their repayments.

Unlike traditional mortgage-style student loans, income-contingent loans are compatible with equality of opportunity. England is a useful case study here. Having previously offered free university education, it introduced fees in 1998, initially at a relatively low level—up to £1,000 per year, covering just a fraction of the overall cost of going to university. In 2012, the maximum fee was increased to £9,000 per year, creeping up to £9,250 since then, and typical tuition fees in England are now higher than almost any other country in the world, including America.[60] Perhaps surprisingly, however, enrolment rates have continued to increase, while the gap in participation between rich and poor students has remained

---

* The fundamental difference between income-contingent loans and a graduate tax is that the latter would see graduates pay a higher rate of tax in perpetuity. As a result, the highest-earning graduates could end up paying significantly more, well beyond the cost of their fees. While there are good reasons for higher taxes on the highest earners, these should apply across the board, not just to those who have been to university.

stable, and by some measures even slightly fallen. Of course, the gap remains much too large, but tuition fees—even at this relatively high level—don't seem to have made it worse, and it is far from clear whether abolishing them would necessarily make it much better.[61]

How can we decide between free tuition and income-contingent loans? Since both appear to be compatible with equality of opportunity, we can look to the difference principle for guidance. In other words, we should ask ourselves what system would be best for the least well off, which for the most part means non-graduates. On the one hand, since graduates typically earn more and have better jobs, it seems reasonable that they should contribute towards the cost of their education; and rather than spending public money to subsidize them, we could use it to benefit non-graduates directly. On the other hand, public subsidies that encourage people to go to university help to create a more dynamic and productive economy, which in turn tends to increase tax revenues, and may lead to higher wages or employment among non-graduates. The UK has probably gone too far in putting the burden on students: once we account for the fact that some people will never repay their loans, public funding accounts for less than 25 per cent of all spending on tertiary education in the UK, the lowest of any OECD country and well below the average of around 66 per cent.[62] It would also be better to adopt a more progressive repayment schedule: rather than asking everyone to pay 9 per cent of their income above £25,000, repayments could begin at, say, 1 per cent of income, and then increase gradually with earnings, as is the case in Australia.[63] But it seems likely that the fairest system would still involve splitting the cost between students and the state through a mix of free tuition and income-contingent loans.

Whatever this mix, financial support must be comprehensive. First, it should cover living expenses as well as the cost of fees, otherwise higher education will remain out of reach for those from low-income backgrounds. Second, it should encompass both public and private institutions, with limits on the fees that the latter can charge. Third, it should include vocational as well as academic study, addressing the existing tendency to neglect those who don't go to university. Fourth, financial support should be available for post-graduate degrees, which have become an increasingly important route to the best-paid jobs but have often been overlooked, leaving individual students to cover the costs. Finally, this should all be available irrespective of age, recognizing that some people may not want to study immediately after leaving school, and that in a fast-changing global economy many people will want or need to retrain during their lifetime.

RACE

These reforms to schooling and higher education would radically weaken the link between social class and children's opportunities. But differences in parental resources are not the only factors that unfairly shape people's life chances today: our societies continue to tolerate serious racial injustices, whose roots lie in long histories of outright exploitation and oppression. The failure of liberal societies to address this legacy fully, and the tendency for some liberals to insist on a strictly "colour-blind" approach to public policy—not to mention the fact that many canonical liberal thinkers from Hume and Kant to Mill endorsed explicitly racist ideas—have led some to question or even reject liberalism altogether.[64] This scepticism has sometimes extended to Rawls, with critics arguing that his theory is simply too abstract and ahistorical to help us grapple with the challenges of racial exploitation and discrimination.[65]

While it is true that Rawls said relatively little about race, his principles provide us with a powerful and recognizably liberal framework for thinking about what we mean by racial justice, and how we can bring it about. The basic liberties principle affirms that all citizens are entitled to individual freedom and political equality, irrespective of the colour of their skin.[66] While all democratic states now recognize this fundamental principle, ethnic minorities continue to face racial bias and discrimination from the state: police brutality in America, where Black men are two and a half times more likely than white men to be killed by police during their lifetime, is just the most visible example.[67] The most basic priority for achieving genuine racial justice is to ensure that our public institutions *actually* treat citizens from ethnic minorities with the same dignity and respect as everyone else.

While the basic liberties principle provides the foundation for racial justice, it is Rawls's principle of fair equality of opportunity

which has the most far-reaching implications. In a society organized according to this principle, everyone would have the same
chance to develop their talents and to compete for jobs and positions irrespective of their ethnicity, and there would be no systematic inequalities between different racial groups.[68] Of course, most
countries continue to fall well short of this ideal, albeit to differing
degrees, reflecting both different histories of racial exploitation and
discrimination, and the extent to which they have tried to address
that past. These inequalities are perhaps most stark—and most thoroughly documented—in America, where the median income for
Black households is about half that of white ones. The wealth gap is
even larger: the median Black household's wealth is just 12 per cent
of its white counterpart's—a total of around $16,000 compared to
$140,000 for a typical white household. Despite the progress in terms
of formal legal equality and protections from discrimination, these
racial differences in income and wealth have barely changed since
before the civil rights era in the 1960s.[69] Significant racial inequalities exist in other countries too: in the UK, the median income of
Black households is about 80 per cent of that for white ones, while
Pakistani households have the lowest income on average, at just
65 per cent of the median for white ones.[70]

In part, these inequalities reflect the impact of current racial discrimination. Overtly racist beliefs and attitudes grounded in con-
scious racial prejudice or in patently false beliefs about biological
inferiority have declined significantly, though they haven't disappeared entirely. But racial stereotypes and unconscious biases persist.[71] The result is that ethnic minorities often face unfair treatment
in education, housing, employment and elsewhere. So-called "CV
studies"—where researchers send out otherwise-identical CVs with
different names—consistently find that applicants with traditionally
Black or ethnic minority names are much less likely to be invited
for an interview. In a widely cited American case, job applicants
with "white names" (Greg Baker and Emily Walsh) had to send
out ten CVs on average to secure one callback, while those with
"African-American names" (Lakisha Washington and Jamal Jones)
needed to send around fifteen. The authors calculated that having
a white-sounding name was equivalent to an extra eight years of
experience.[72] Similar results have been reported across a range of

industries and countries.[73] And, of course, racial discrimination goes well beyond the world of work. A recent study of private rental housing in Boston found that white applicants secured a viewing 80 per cent of the time, compared to 48 per cent for Black applicants with the same financial credentials.[74]

Anti-discrimination laws are clearly necessary. But most countries have had them in place for decades, and racial discrimination continues to be widespread. Stronger enforcement may be part of the solution—we should do more to make sure that victims can access legal support, and we should impose tough penalties on guilty individuals or companies. But the inherent difficulty of proving that a particular decision is the result of racial discrimination means this punitive approach can take us only so far.[75] We should combine these laws with other policies, such as requiring companies to publish information about racial gaps in employment and pay, mandating name-blind application forms, and encouraging firms to put in place strategies and training to address unconscious racial biases.[76] Alongside top-down regulations, we need to do much more to empower workers to address issues that are specific to their workplace, through institutions like unions and works councils (topics we will explore in more detail in Chapter 8).

Alongside such targeted interventions, there is a broader role for the state in trying to change the underlying attitudes that sustain racial inequalities. As we saw in Chapter 4, the state cannot simply ban racist ideas; and, even if it could, this would not affect the subtler forms of bias and stereotyping that are important drivers of racial inequality. But it can use its "expressive" powers to criticize these ideas and foster a truly inclusive and multiracial sense of patriotic identity, through public awards, holidays, monuments and so on. As ever, schools are essential and should teach children about the diversity of the societies they live in, and the history of slavery, empire and segregation. Equally important (if not more so) is to create an environment in schools that enables different social groups to mix. As we have seen, social contact is one of the best ways to reduce prejudice, and we should design school admissions policies to stimulate racial integration.

One of the most controversial questions in debates about race is whether there is a role for "positive discrimination," or "affirmative action." By "positive discrimination," I mean situations in which race (or, indeed, class or gender) is explicitly taken into account when allocating a given position, even if it isn't directly relevant.* So, for example, universities might set a lower academic threshold for admitting Black or ethnic minority students; or they might go further and adopt a quota of places for a particular group.

At first sight, positive discrimination appears to go against the principle that positions should be allocated on the basis of relevant ability, and many liberals have opposed it on this basis.[77] In an ideally just society positions *would* be allocated simply on the basis of ability, and positive discrimination would be wrong. But we live in societies where long histories of oppression continue to shape opportunities in profound ways. In this context, positive discrimination can be justified if it helps to move us closer to fair equality of opportunity, by breaking down racial stereotypes about who goes to university, say, or who does particular types of jobs, or by providing role models to young people from under-represented groups.[78] Even so, we should use these kinds of policies sparingly. Positive discrimination is often a crude way to level the playing field: Black children growing up in more affluent households, for example, may have had more opportunities than their poor white counterparts. The sense of unfairness this can arouse can be exploited to drive a wedge between different racial groups, as it arguably has been in America, where the use of affirmative action in college admissions is deeply controversial.[79] But when other policies have failed, or are likely to take an intolerably long time to make a difference, positive discrimination can be justified.

Still, even if we could eliminate discrimination entirely, large racial inequalities would continue to exist. The cumulative impact of long and violent histories of racial injustice means that Black and other minority ethnic children in many countries are much more likely to be born into poor families. In America, more than one in four Black and one in five Hispanic or Native American children grow up in poverty, compared to fewer than one in ten white ones.[80]

---

* Race might be directly relevant to some roles: a community centre dedicated to supporting Black children might have good reason to want to recruit a Black teacher.

In the UK, child poverty rates are almost twice as high for Black children compared to white ones, and even higher for Pakistani and Bangladeshi families.[81] As we have seen, children from poor families have worse opportunities to develop their skills and abilities, and hence are more likely to be poor as adults. In this context, bringing an end to racial discrimination would simply mean that poor Black children would have the same meagre opportunities as poor white ones. Although racial gaps in income and wealth would eventually disappear, this could take a very long time.

If we want racial justice, then we need to combine efforts to tackle discrimination with policies that can break the link between poverty and life chances, such as universal access to early years education, targeted school funding for disadvantaged children and comprehensive financial support for tertiary education. These will help to reduce racial inequalities even when they are not explicitly designed with that purpose in mind. But we can and should complement "race-neutral" policies with "race-conscious" ones that are explicitly designed to address the specific challenges faced by children from disadvantaged ethnic groups. What this might look like would, of course, depend on the circumstances in particular countries and communities. In America, where there is a high degree of residential segregation between poor Black communities and the wider population, any attempt to tackle persistent racial inequalities would have to include major public investment in these neighbourhoods—not just in schools, but in housing and local amenities (such as parks), public safety, and employment.

As we have seen, Rawls's principles justify measures not only to address discrimination at an individual level but also to reform our social and economic institutions in order to guarantee fair opportunities for all. But does this go far enough? For many progressives, especially in America, the notion of "reparations" is increasingly at the heart of debates about racial justice. Some employ the term to denote largely symbolic actions that would recognize and apologize for past wrongs; but for most it expresses the belief that the state should make cash payments to compensate the descendants of slaves and other victims of state-sanctioned racial violence, segregation and discrimination for the injustices perpetrated against their predecessors.

Rawls's principles don't appear to have much to say about reparations, and he has been criticized for his silence on this issue. But as the philosopher Tommie Shelby has argued, this reticence reflects the fundamentally "forward looking" nature of his project, rather than indifference or opposition to the idea. Rawls's aim was to define an ideally just society so that we could see more clearly what was wrong with our existing institutions, and how to fix them—including how to end racial injustice. By contrast, the question of reparations is ultimately "backward looking"—it is about how we as a society can make amends for past injustices.[82] This is not to say that reparations are unimportant: we surely have a moral obligation to acknowledge and provide redress for past injustices, especially where these have been directly perpetrated by the state.[83] In other words, some form of "corrective" or "compensatory" justice is surely called for. But working out what this would look like raises difficult moral questions about the extent to which people living today can be held accountable for the wrongs of their forebears, and about what it would take to compensate for them. These are questions that Rawls's framework is simply not designed to answer.[84]

Rawls's critics—most notably the philosopher Charles Mills—have sometimes suggested that since his principles do not directly address the question of reparations, they cannot help us to overcome the historical legacy of racial injustice in countries such as America, and so are in some sense complicit in perpetuating racial injustice. But this is simply not the case. Fair equality of opportunity calls on us as a society to do everything we can to address the way slavery, segregation and past discrimination continue to blight the life chances of young Black people today. Substantial payments to Black citizens could certainly help achieve this goal, and may, for example, be the only way to eliminate the vast racial wealth gap that exists in America.[85] But whereas calls for reparations tend to focus on cash payments alone, fair equality of opportunity demands a much wider set of policies to dismantle the structures that perpetuate racial inequality today, from housing to education and employment. Although fair equality of opportunity is not the same as compensating for the racial injustices of the past, it would remove the socio-economic burdens that racial minorities continue to shoulder because of that history.[86]

GENDER

Beyond the disparities of class and race, there remain large inequalities between men and women.[87] Across the OECD as a whole, women earn around 25 per cent less than men on average. In part, this reflects the fact that fewer women are in paid work, but those who are also tend to have lower hourly wages than men: women are nearly three times as likely to be working in part-time jobs, which are typically less well paid; and even women employed full time earn around 15 per cent less than men on average.[88] Women are also much less likely to reach senior management or board-level positions—just 5 per cent of CEOs are women, and they hold around 20 per cent of board seats.[89] Although the gap between men and women in terms of total employment has continued to decline over the past decade, progress in terms of hourly wages has largely stalled. As ever, some countries do better than others: the smallest gaps are found in Denmark, Iceland and Norway, while the U.S.A. and UK are somewhere in the middle of the range—reminding us that these inequalities are far from immutable.[90]

For most of the twentieth century, gender inequalities in employment and pay could mostly be put down to the vastly unequal educational opportunities available to men and women and outright discrimination in the labour market. On both fronts, the second half of the century saw enormous progress. Rules and conventions which used to bar women from certain universities or occupations have been abolished or prohibited, and most countries have laws that mandate "equal pay for equal work." Across the world's rich democracies, girls now outperform boys in terms of literacy as teenagers, and are more likely to go to university—in 2014, 57 per cent of bachelor's and master's degrees were attained by women.[91]

This is cause for celebration, but the fact that women on average are better educated than men makes the persistent gaps in terms of employment and pay even more troubling. After all, on the basis of education alone, we would expect women to be paid *more* than men, not less. Part of the explanation is that, despite the headline improvement in educational attainment, women's opportunities continue to be constricted by gendered stereotypes. By the age of fifteen, twice as many boys as girls expect to work as engineers, scientists or architects; and girls are much less likely to study for lucrative STEM subjects (Science, Technology, Engineering and Mathematics), despite having similar ability in science. In some of these fields, the gaps are very large indeed: across the OECD, fewer than 20 per cent of new entrants into university-level engineering programmes are women.[92] The influence of gender stereotypes in education in turn helps to explain why certain types of jobs—especially caring occupations like nursing and preschool teaching—continue to be performed overwhelmingly by women, often for very low pay.

There is undoubtedly more we can do as a society to make sure that the educational opportunities open to boys and girls reflect their individual interests and abilities, rather than gendered norms. We should begin by making this an explicit goal of the education system, as they have in Sweden, where the preschool curriculum was revised in 2010 to affirm that children "should have the same opportunities to develop and explore their abilities and interests without having limitations imposed by stereotyped gender roles." Other measures could include financial incentives to attract female teachers into male-dominated subjects, a concerted effort to remove gendered assumptions from teaching materials, and more direct teaching about the history of gender discrimination and inequality.[93]

Women also continue to face discrimination at work. In one famous study, several U.S. orchestras introduced gender-blind auditions by asking musicians to play from behind a screen, leading to a significant increase in the number of women being hired.[94] Other "CV studies"—similar to the ones we discussed in the context of race—looking at a wide range of jobs have confirmed that women face discrimination in male-dominated occupations, especially if they have children.[95] This helps explain why women often do different, lower-paid jobs. But women also face unequal treatment even when they are doing the same kinds of jobs as men. As the #MeToo movement has shown sexual harassment continues to be an all-too-familiar part of working life, and academic studies in the U.S. have shown that more than half of women have experienced sexual harassment at work.[96] As with racial discrimination, we must use the full range of legal and "expressive" powers available to the state to enforce anti-discrimination laws and to change the attitudes and beliefs that drive discrimination—from mandatory reporting of gender pay gaps to quotas and other forms of positive discrimination where necessary.[97]

As the education gap between men and women has narrowed and even reversed, and as overt discrimination has declined, the spotlight has shifted to the gendered division of labour within the home. Looking across the OECD as a whole, women spend two full hours more per day than men caring for children and parents and doing housework. This in turn helps to explain the differences in employment and pay which we have been discussing, which in most countries only really emerge once women start having children.[98] In the UK, for example, the difference in men's and women's hourly wages increases from about 10 per cent on the arrival of a first child to almost 33 per cent after twelve years.[99] This partly reflects the impact of taking time out of work to raise children: by the time a woman's first child reaches twenty, she will, on average, have spent four more years out of paid employment altogether than an equivalent man; and, of the time spent working, much more will have been in part-time roles.[100] Since women accumulate less experience, they end up missing out on opportunities for training and promotion. The impact of raising children on the amount that women earn also reflects the fact that mothers are much more likely to take on flexible roles with less responsibility and pay, and to work in "family friendly" sectors like retail and care where wages are relatively low.

In order to reduce gender inequality in employment and pay, either men need to take on a more equal share of raising children and other unpaid activities, or we have to find ways to mitigate the impact of an unequal division of labour on women's earnings—or some combination of the two. This raises some complicated philosophical questions about what a fair division of labour within the home would look like, and what the state can and should do to bring this about. Families should obviously be free to make these kinds of choices for themselves—no one seriously thinks the state should force men and women to devote an equal amount of time to raising their children, and to do so would violate their basic liberties. But some people think that as long as these choices are made freely, in the sense of being made without coercion, we don't need to worry about the fact that women do so much more unpaid care work, or about the economic inequality to which this leads.

We must reject this idea. As Rawls argued, even if choices about who looks after children are "free" in this sense, this doesn't necessarily make them fair.[101] In order to be fair, these decisions must also be made in a context where men and women have genuinely equal opportunities: there is nothing fair about a situation in which women "choose" to take on the bulk of unpaid care work because they face discrimination at work or in education, as has so often been the case. At the same time, even in a perfectly just society, women might still choose to spend more time raising children than men. Although the role of biology has often been exaggerated, the experience of being pregnant and giving birth may lead women to want to devote more time to child-rearing, and breast-feeding makes it more likely that women will take on the primary care role for very young children. Some people also hold religious or moral commitments to traditional gender roles, and even in a society where men and women have equal opportunities in education and work, these beliefs would shape their choices.

In principle, then, the gendered division of labour can be fair without being perfectly equal. But the vast differences in unpaid care work between men and women today are far from fair. As we have seen, people's decisions about who will look after the children continue to be shaped by discrimination and gendered norms in education and at work, such that women often earn less than their male partners. On top of this, parental leave policies actively reinforce traditional gender roles. In many countries, while mothers are entitled to around fifteen to twenty weeks of paid leave, fathers typically get just a couple of paid weeks off.[102]

If we are committed to fair equality of opportunity, then rights to parental leave should be gender-neutral. Rather than effectively requiring women to take the bulk of the time off work needed to raise young children, we should leave these decisions to families. So, for example, we could give families an overall allocation of parental leave and allow them to divide this as they see fit. The same principle should apply to all statutory entitlements to part-time and flexible work, which should be offered on an equal basis to men and women.

Beyond these statutory entitlements, employers should be required by law to offer additional benefits to parents on a gender-neutral basis.[103]

Even in countries with this kind of shared parental leave, however, women continue to take the vast majority of it.[104] We shouldn't be surprised by this: the gendered division of labour is the product not only of unequal rights and opportunities, but of prevailing social norms which influence both what men and women want to do, and what they feel they can do without attracting social opprobrium. We can see the impact of these norms in the economic data: even in households where a woman is earning more than her male partner, she is still more likely to reduce her hours of paid work after having children.[105] As we move towards a world in which women have the same rights and opportunities as men, we would expect these norms to evolve in a more gender-neutral direction. But these kinds of cultural changes often happen slowly, and a growing number of countries have taken a more proactive role in trying to encourage men and women to share childcare on more equal terms. Eight European Union countries now offer incentives for fathers to take more time off work to care for young children, either through "use it or lose it" policies where a fixed amount of leave is reserved for fathers, or through bonus leave for parents who use it in a more equal way.[106]

These kinds of policies have been more effective in increasing the amount of leave taken by fathers, and have an obvious appeal for those of us who are concerned about gender equality.[107] But is it really fair to penalize households where women decide to do the bulk of the child-rearing? On the one hand, it seems right that the state should leave families to make these choices for themselves, in light of their particular circumstances, preferences and beliefs. And yet there is a case for policies like these which try to loosen rigid gender norms about raising children while leaving parents with the final say. For a start, it's worth remembering that these norms were formed in societies where women were denied fair opportunities to participate in education and paid work, and even the right to vote. We also have to remember that, in a society where women do almost all the childcare, those who don't want children—or who want to have children and continue to work full time—may face discrimination because employers wrongly assume that they will take time out to raise children; while men who want to take parental leave may find it hard to exercise their rights in practice.

Alongside measures to address the unfair burden of unpaid care work which currently falls on women, we should do more to support parents and carers irrespective of gender.[108] More generous subsidies for early years education, along the lines we discussed earlier in this chapter, would not only reduce gender inequality by enabling mothers to work, but also help all parents juggle raising children with having a career. We must also ensure that unpaid carers can participate fully in social, economic and political life. After all, as Rawls put it, "reproductive labor is socially necessary labor," and the same is true of looking after the disabled, sick and elderly.[109] Unfortunately, Rawls's principles are designed to help us think about conventional paid work, and a full account of how we should organize and reward caring would take us too far afield.[110] But at the very least, we need to make sure that unpaid carers can maintain a sense of independence. All too often carers, mostly women, have found themselves financially dependent on male partners and vulnerable to domination, violence and abuse. Alongside subsidized childcare, generous rights to flexible working can make it easier to combine unpaid caring with paid work; while divorce laws can help protect the rights of partners who have devoted their lives to raising children and making a home. We should also try to change the way we organize work, so that people can go part-time without effectively giving up on decent wages and opportunities for career progression, as is typically the case today.[111] Doing so would help all of us to strike a better balance between working, caring and the many other things we want to do with our lives.

There is much work to be done if we are to make good on the promise of equality of opportunity. And yet, for Rawls, this is only the first step in creating a fair and sustainable economy. In the final two chapters, we will see how the difference principle, combined with the just savings principle, can lead us towards an even more fundamental rethinking of our economic institutions.

7

Shared Prosperity

•———————————————•

Inequality is a reality we are all familiar with—we see it in the vast differences between rich and poor neighbourhoods; in the gaps between well-paid lawyers and low-paid cleaners; and in the way society is reflected back to us through popular culture. And yet the numbers still have the capacity to shock. In Europe, 30 per cent of all national income goes to the top 10 per cent, while just 24 per cent goes to the *entire* bottom half—and this is after we account for the equalizing effect of taxes and transfers. Inequality is even more extreme in America, where the top 10 per cent receive 39 per cent of national income, compared to just 19 per cent for the bottom half. These differences translate into massive disparities in living standards. In America, the income of someone in the top 10 per cent is ten times as much on average as that of someone in the bottom half, while the average income for someone in the top 1 per cent is just over $1 million, more than eighty-five times the average of someone in the bottom 20 per cent.[1] Inequality has increased in most advanced economies since the 1980s, and in the UK, U.S.A. and Canada has reached highs not seen since before the Second World War.[2]

There is a lot of talk today about the need to address inequality, and the importance of building a more "inclusive capitalism" which can deliver "shared prosperity." But these terms are often used in a rather loose way, and it's not entirely clear what they mean, or how much poverty or inequality we should tolerate as a society. Rawls's principles can help us to move beyond such platitudes by offering a more precise definition of what a fair distribution of resources would be. Our first priority must be to ensure that every citizen has access to the minimum level of material resources they need to meet their basic needs. This is the most elemental feature of any decent society. But economic justice is about more than alleviating poverty. For Rawls, a just society is one in which the distribution of resources as a whole is fair, in the sense that it can be justified to everyone, right down to the least well off. And this brings us back to the difference principle.

According to the difference principle, inequalities are justified only if everyone ultimately benefits from them—say, because they provide incentives which in turn encourage innovation and economic growth. More specifically, we should organize our economy so that the living standards of the least well off are higher than they would be under any alternative system. As we shall see, this provides a powerful justification for a broadly market-based economy, since markets—at least when they are properly regulated—have proven themselves to be the most effective system for generating economic prosperity. But as the experience of the past few decades has made abundantly clear, there is nothing inherent to how markets work that means economic resources will be widely shared, let alone that they will maximize those available to the least well off.[3] Indeed, there is little doubt that in most (if not all) rich countries inequality far exceeds the level that can be justified according to the difference principle. After all, since no country has sought to design its economic system with such an egalitarian goal in mind, we can be pretty sure that none has achieved it.

As we saw in Chapter 1, the difference principle not only provides a powerful argument for a more equal society, it also offers the basis for a broader and more humane perspective on what we mean by inequality in the first place. There is a tendency in both political and philosophical debate to focus on the distribution of income and (to a lesser extent) wealth, and the difference principle has sometimes been interpreted in this way too. Of course, having a decent income is a precondition for living a free and independent life, and in a market economy how much money we have determines how far we share in the prosperity of society overall. But thinking about inequality solely in terms of financial resources misses so much of what is wrong with our economic system and to apply the difference principle in this limited way is to miss its transformative potential.

Properly understood, the difference principle is concerned not just with the distribution of income and wealth, but with the concentration of economic power and control, and with the extent to which people have opportunities for self-respect, including through work.[4] This has far-reaching practical implications—indeed, it is no exaggeration to say that it justifies a fundamental transformation of our economic institutions. In particular, by putting power, control, dignity and self-respect at the heart of our economic thinking, this principle exposes the limitations of the welfare state paradigm that has long dominated liberal and progressive economic thinking. This paradigm rests on the idea that the problem with capitalism is the unequal distribution of material resources, and that we can address this through redistribution—whether in the form of cash benefits, or the direct provision of goods and services, such as education, housing and healthcare. But redistribution alone cannot address the extreme concentration of power in the hands of owners that is characteristic of capitalism as we know it; nor can it address the importance of paid work as a source of agency, social recognition and individual meaning. Indeed, Rawls argued that "welfare state capitalism" could never fully realize his principles of justice.[5] This doesn't mean we need to dismantle the welfare state—but that we need to build on it, by doing more to equip citizens with the skills and resources they need to play a productive role in economic life, and by bringing about a fundamental shift in the balance of power at work.

Our debate about how to organize our economy is often framed as a choice between capitalism and socialism. But this binary approach often obscures more than it reveals. For a start, the terms "capitalism" and "socialism" are used in such vague and contradictory ways that people frequently end up talking past one another. More importantly, it falsely narrows the range of options that are available to us.[6] Economic systems differ along multiple dimensions, including the extent to which we rely on markets and how they are regulated, the balance of private and public ownership, the level of taxation and the role of the state in providing public services. Rather than thinking about the form of our economy as a choice between rigid alternative "systems," like capitalism or socialism, we should be more creative and recognize the potential to combine these different elements in entirely new ways.

The difference principle can help us to transcend this false dichotomy and to open up a richer and more nuanced conversation about our economic structures. As we explore what this would look like in practice, we will have to go well beyond what Rawls himself explicitly said about these questions—even more so than in previous chapters.[7] But with the difference principle as our guide, we can start to assemble a new and inspiring political economy that is an alternative both to the statist socialism of the past and the market fundamentalism of the present. Whether the result is best described as a kind of "liberal socialism" or a form of "inclusive capitalism"—or with some entirely different label, such as Rawls's "property owning democracy"—is, in a sense, beside the point.

SUSTAINABILITY AND THE ECOLOGICAL EMERGENCY

Before we look at how we can create shared prosperity, we need to consider how we can make the transition to a truly sustainable economy. As we saw in Chapter 1, justice is not only about our obligations to our fellow citizens here and now, but about how our actions today affect future generations, and Rawls developed the just savings principle to address this issue. The most fundamental duty that we have towards future generations is to preserve the stable climate, diverse ecosystems and vital natural resources that are the basis for life as we know it. This commitment to ecological sustainability defines the natural limits within which our society and economy must operate.

Unfortunately, as things stand, we are spectacularly failing to live within these limits. The elimination of wild spaces and our relentless extraction of natural resources are pushing fragile ecosystems to the point of collapse: extinction rates are 100–1,000 times higher than the historical baseline, and many scientists believe we are in the early stages of the sixth mass extinction event in the history of planet Earth.[8] Our addiction to fossil fuels and relentless emission of greenhouse gases have already led to an increase of more than 1°C in average global temperatures compared to pre-industrial levels. On our current trajectory, this is set to soar to nearly 3°C—a level at which we face the prospect of irreversible and truly catastrophic climate and ecological breakdown.[9]

It is difficult to overstate the severity and urgency of these inter-locking crises: they pose a threat not just to our material standard of living but to peace, stability and the survival of humanity itself. We are already experiencing the effects of climate change in the form of increasingly frequent and severe floods, storms, droughts and heat-waves. And this is only a taste of what is to come. At 3°C of warm-ing, we would expect to see a massive rise in sea levels which, in combination with higher temperatures and more extreme weather, would lead to global shortages of food and fresh water. Large parts of the planet would in effect be rendered uninhabitable, prompting a wave of conflict and mass migration that could destabilize the entire world.[10] We may still be able to avoid the worst effects of cli-mate change if we can limit temperature increases to no more than 1.5°C. But decades of inaction mean this will require massive and immediate reductions in emissions: according to the Intergovern-mental Panel on Climate Change (IPCC), we need greenhouse gas emissions to peak by 2025, then fall by more than 40 per cent by 2030 and reach "net zero" by 2050 if we are to have a fighting chance of meeting this target.[11] There is currently no credible plan in place to reduce emissions at this pace or scale.[12]

Transforming our economy and society so that we can live within the limits of our finite planet is the most urgent challenge that we face. The choices we make over the next few years will shape the future of life on Earth, and each of us bears a profound moral responsibility, not just to change our individual behaviour, but to take political action so that our governments recognize the gravity of this crisis and do everything in their power to avert it. This will require a collective mobilization of resources and changes in culture and behaviour on a scale that has rarely been seen outside wartime—matching, if not exceeding, those seen during the Covid pandemic. While there is much to be gained from establishing a new and more harmonious relationship with the natural world, it is quite possible that as we do so, total economic output as we commonly measure it will have to grow more slowly, or even decline—especially in rich countries that have both the responsibility (because of their historic emissions) and the capacity to shoulder the greatest burden.[13] If this is what it takes to secure a sustainable future for our children and grandchildren, then this is what we must do.[14]

The scale of the ecological crisis is so profound that it is sometimes suggested that we need an entirely new economic model. On one level this is right: the transition to a sustainable economy will require a transformation not just of how we generate energy but of almost every aspect of our societies, from where we live and how we travel to what we eat. But some environmental advocates have argued that we need to abandon our commitment to markets altogether and move beyond an economy in which the profit motive is so central. There is no doubt that, in the absence of careful regulation, markets tend to deplete natural resources in an unsustainable way, because market prices fail to capture the full impact of economic activity on the natural world—something we will come back to shortly. But with the right regulations in place, we can not only ensure that markets operate within safe ecological limits, but also harness their dynamism and efficiency to help bring about this transition.

How can we create a truly sustainable economy? A complete answer to this hugely complex question deserves a book of its own, and rests on detailed technological considerations about which we should keep an open mind. We will focus instead on the core institutions needed to support this transition. Our first priority must be to put in place an overarching legal framework which defines the natural boundaries within which our society must operate, and compels the government to develop a strategy to live within them.[15] The UK's pioneering Climate Change Act of 2008 provides one model of what this might look like. This law requires the government to restrict the total amount of carbon emissions from the UK economy in line with its long-term goal of "net zero" emissions by 2050, and to produce five-year "carbon budgets," which cap emissions in the short-to-medium term, backed up by credible plans for achieving these goals. The process is overseen and informed by an independent Climate

Change Committee consisting of experts, who provide regular progress reports to Parliament. Crucially, the act provides a legal mechanism for citizens to hold the government to account: in a landmark ruling in 2022, the UK's High Court ruled that the government had breached its obligations and would have to revise its climate strategy in order to demonstrate how it would fulfil them.

The Climate Change Act may not be perfect—the UK still needs to do much more to meet its climate goals, and a new government could in theory simply repeal it. But the UK is closer to meeting its international climate obligations than many other European countries; and the act is surely a major reason why it has been so much more successful in reducing greenhouse gas emissions than in tackling other environmental issues, such as water pollution or soil degradation, where there is nothing equivalent in place.[16] We should build on this model by introducing something like a "Sustainable Economy Act" which is more difficult for the government to repeal or ignore, and which extends beyond the climate to encompass other crucial aspects of the natural environment. This would instigate a much-needed debate about what we as a society regard as safe limits for biodiversity, pollution, the exploitation of finite raw materials and so on, and the mechanisms that would bring them into effect.[17]

What kinds of measures might this involve? Environmental taxes are almost certainly part of the solution. A "carbon tax," for example, would increase the price of activities that generate carbon dioxide and other greenhouse gases. In doing so, it would ensure the competitive advantage of renewable energy; it would give firms across the entire economy an incentive to reduce their energy consumption and develop energy-saving innovations; and it would encourage all of us as consumers to change our spending habits in a more sustainable direction. This idea has almost universal support among economists; and in 2022 there were already thirty-seven different carbon taxes around the world, alongside a similar number of cap-and-trade schemes (a close cousin of the carbon tax), including the EU-wide Emissions Trading Scheme.[18] We know both approaches can reduce emissions, but existing schemes are nowhere near ambitious enough. According to the International Monetary Fund, we need a global carbon price of around $75 for every ton by 2030 to have a decent chance of limiting warming to 1.5–2°C, but four fifths of global emissions still remain unpriced and the average emissions price is just $3 per ton.[19]

Carbon taxes and other "price-based" mechanisms can help us harness the benefits of markets in service of a more sustainable economy. But markets alone cannot deliver the changes we need in the time that we need them, so we must combine carbon taxes with a much more direct role for government. In some cases, this means using regulation to phase out certain products and activities (such as petrol-fuelled cars, and gas boilers), to limit our use of finite raw materials, or to protect wild spaces from further development. We also need to mobilize the resources of the state to invest in new technologies from hydrogen fuels and electric batteries to more efficient farming methods. Above all we need the state to embark on a once-in-a-generation programme to transform the basic infrastructure of our economy and society, including investing in renewable energy capacity and the electrification of almost everything, expanding public transport, insulating housing and a complete overhaul of how we produce and distribute food. This will require an unprecedented and genuinely collective effort which cannot be left to markets.

Without careful thought, however, the transition to a more sustainable economy could easily worsen existing social inequalities. Take the example of a carbon tax. Although carbon emissions tend to rise with income, meaning the rich would pay more in absolute terms, poorer households spend a bigger proportion of their income on carbon-intensive essentials, such as energy and transport.[20] As a result, a carbon tax would also represent a larger share of their income, making inequality worse. And with or without a carbon tax, moving to "net zero" is going to require the almost total elimination of fossil-fuel extraction as well as major changes in sectors such as transport and farming. While there are real opportunities here to create better and more enjoyable jobs, we have to recognize the very real human costs for the livestock farmers and oil-extraction workers whose jobs will disappear or change in fundamental ways, and the impact this will have on their communities. Making this transition in a fair and inclusive way is not only a moral imperative but a precondition for building a viable political movement for change.

In the case of a carbon tax, for example, we could redistribute the revenues in the form of an annual "carbon dividend" to all citizens. In the U.S.A., a carbon tax of around \$50 per ton of CO_2 could fund an annual dividend of around \$500. Thanks to the dividend, although the price of food, energy and transport would go up, all but the highest 30 per cent of earners would see an increase in their overall standard of living.[21] Alternatively, we could use some or all of the money raised by a carbon tax to support individual retraining programmes and to help communities that are currently dependent on fossil-fuel extraction to develop new, sustainable industries. Addressing these challenges bring us back to the need for a much wider agenda to address inequality and bring about genuinely shared prosperity.

THE CASE FOR MARKETS

The inequality that is tearing apart our societies today reflects, to a large extent, the embrace of free-market ideology since the 1980s. Many on the left are sceptical of or outright hostile to markets and the way in which they prioritize profits rather than the needs of people or the planet. Some would do away with markets altogether. But this would be a serious mistake.

For a start, critics on the left sometimes overlook the vital importance of markets for individual freedom. A "market," after all, is simply a space in which people are free to buy and sell things, and this freedom of exchange is valuable in its own right. As the economist and philosopher Amartya Sen has put it, "to be *generically against* markets would be almost as odd as being generically against conversations between people."[22] Crucially, markets allow us to exercise some important basic liberties. The existence of a "labour market," where people are free to sell their labour and buy that of others (within certain limits), is more or less a precondition for exercising our freedom of occupational choice, and the basic liberties principle immediately rules out a society where the state simply tells people what jobs to do.[23] More broadly, our basic right to own personal property suggests that we should be free to decide how to spend our income—to choose what food to eat, what clothes to wear, and how to prioritize between all of the things that we may want or need. We should rely on markets to distribute most consumer goods and services because the alternative would be some form of state-controlled rationing.[24]

The case for markets also rests on their efficiency as a way of coordinating work and production—in other words, their ability to harness the skills and resources available to society to produce things that people actually want and need, and hence to promote economic growth and prosperity. Since around 1800, average incomes in Western Europe and America have increased somewhere in the region of 2,000–3,000 per cent, transforming people's access to everything from food and housing to education and healthcare, culture and art. While only part of the story, there is no question that the embrace of markets played a critical role in this truly astonishing improvement in living standards.[25] From the perspective of the difference principle, if markets can increase the total wealth of society, then, with the right institutions in place, they can also help to raise the living standards of the least well off.

Why do markets promote economic efficiency and prosperity? In a market economy, activity is guided in a decentralized way by prices and the profit motive. Market prices give firms a signal of what consumers want—if people wish to eat out more or to buy more plant-based foods, then the relevant prices will tend to increase, which in turn will encourage more people, say, to open restaurants or for farmers to shift from rearing animals for slaughter to growing plants. Similarly, market prices encourage firms to produce things efficiently, by economizing on relatively scarce resources—raw materials that are in short supply tend to be expensive, and firms will try to find alternatives or to develop leaner production methods. Although most businesses are primarily motivated by the desire to make profits, competition helps to keep this in check—companies that charge excessive prices will be undercut by their competitors, pushing prices for consumers down towards the costs of production. Competition also means that inefficient firms tend not to survive very long, while the opportunity to make more money by developing new technologies and products is a constant spur to innovation, which in turn is the ultimate driver of long-term economic growth.

Of course, markets only produce things people want if they can also pay for them. This can have the perverse effect of directing production towards luxuries for the rich—expensive gadgets, yachts and so on—while essential needs, like decent housing and nutritious food, go unmet. But the real problem here lies with the unequal distribution of income, rather than an inherent flaw with markets. If income was distributed more equally—as it would be in a society organized according to the difference principle—then we would see a shift in production away from luxuries and towards things like food and housing which are the priority for most people.

The alternative to a market economy is a planned one, where the state directly coordinates production using a central plan based on some assessment of what people want and what firms are able to produce. For much of the twentieth century, there was a lively debate about the advantages of markets versus planning. This played out in real life in the Soviet Union, China and, to a lesser extent, India, all of which adopted largely planned economies for much of the second half of the century.[26] Although no one really supports the notion of a full-blown planned economy today, the idea helps us to see the advantages of markets more sharply.

One problem with a planned economy is that it puts an enormous amount of power in the hands of the state. As we saw in the Soviet Union, there is a real danger that politicians or bureaucrats will organize the economy to create what they think people want or need, rather than what people actually want and need. But even if we could guarantee that the state would try to promote people's real interests, it's far from certain that it could ever collect the information it would need to do so in an efficient manner, let alone process it and come up with an "optimal" plan.[27] In general, individuals are better placed to know what they want and need, and businesses typically have a better idea about how to respond to consumer demand, and how to make things in the most cost-effective way. Planned economies also face particular difficulties when it comes to innovation, since the constant incentives to improve and innovate provided by competition in a market economy are largely lacking. By contrast, markets—at least, when they are working well—coordinate activity in a way that takes advantage of the decentralized knowledge of millions of individual consumers and companies.[28] The theoretical argument for markets over planning is largely supported by the actual experience of the Soviet Union and other planned economies in the twentieth century, which suffered from chronic shortages, poor-quality products and low overall rates of innovation and growth.[29]

While a market-based economy has some pretty decisive advantages over a planned one, this leaves open the question of who should own the means of production. As we have seen, Rawls's basic liberties principle guarantees a fundamental right to own personal property, but there is no such right to own or work in a private firm; and although markets have conventionally been associated with private ownership, this need not be the case. In theory, state-owned firms could compete for customers in a market much like private ones, while profits would ultimately flow to the government, which could use them to pay for public services or distribute them directly to citizens—this is the essence of market socialism, which we touched on in Chapter 3.[30] For Rawls, the question of whether businesses should be owned by shareholders, by the state or even by workers ultimately depends on which model is best able to balance prosperity with equality and hence improve the prospects of the least well off.

Although the case for markets rests on their superior efficiency, this does not mean we should embrace a laissez-faire approach to economic policy—far from it. Left to their own devices, markets are far from perfect even from the narrow perspective of economic efficiency.[31] The textbook idea of perfectly competitive markets is nothing more than a helpful fiction, and much of modern economics is concerned with identifying the various ways in which actual markets fail by this standard and exploring how we can address these failings.

For a start, the beneficial properties of markets depend on healthy competition. But the rise of large tech monopolies in recent years is a timely reminder that this is not something we can take for granted, but something which has to be maintained through carefully designed and vigorously enforced regulation.[32] And in some sectors, such as energy and the railways, where there are enormous economies of scale, meaningful competition may not be possible at all, and it often makes more sense to rely on direct public provision instead.

But simply maintaining competition is not enough. Markets are only efficient when prices are a good measure of the social value of different activities. But many economic activities involve what economists call "externalities," where there is a gap between market price and social value. Perhaps the most serious example is the fact that there is typically no market price associated with emitting carbon dioxide or other greenhouse gases into the atmosphere, despite the enormous social costs associated with climate change. Since businesses don't have to shoulder these costs, they tend to emit more than we would want. In other cases, such as investing in education, or developing new medicines or technologies, market prices fail to reflect all of the positive social value that these activities generate, meaning we end up with less education, fewer medicines and slower innovation than would be "efficient" from an economic point of view. When it comes to so-called "public goods" such as national defence, roads or clean air, we often cannot rely on markets at all.[33] Similarly, while certain relatively straightforward public services such as waste collection and street cleaning can and have been successfully delivered by the private sector, the benefits of public sector outsourcing have frequently been overstated. In more complex cases, such as healthcare, prisons and welfare support, it is likely to do more harm than good.[34] Finally, market economies suffer from cyclical booms and busts which create unemployment and economic hardship.

Preventing and compensating for these "market failures" are among the most important tasks for any government, and doing so is a vital precondition for making the most of what markets have to offer. In fact, since these failures are such a pervasive feature of economic reality, the question is not *whether* markets should be left to their own devices, but rather *how* they should be regulated in different contexts. There is, of course, much more to say about such matters—about how best to promote competition in an increasingly digital world; how to encourage the innovation that is the source of long-run economic growth; how to address externalities and provide public goods, from public transport to healthcare and national security; and how to manage fluctuations in employment. Important though these issues are, for the remainder of this book we will put them to one side. Although the difference principle justifies an active role for the state in regulating markets—and hence provides an alternative to the laissez-faire dogmas of neoliberalism—how exactly we should do this is the bread and butter of modern economic debate. We should adopt a pragmatic and evidence-based approach, resisting both the naive faith in the efficiency of markets that is common on parts of the right and the instinctive hostility towards them found on parts of the left. Our focus here is not the familiar question of how we can make our economy efficient. Rather, it is how we can make it fair.*

MEETING BASIC NEEDS:
THE CASE FOR A UNIVERSAL BASIC INCOME

The most fundamental requirement of a fair economy is that everyone can meet their basic needs, and we cannot rely on markets for this task. We can see this by looking at people's "pretax" or "market" incomes—that is, their incomes before taxes and transfers, which for most people are mainly earnings from work. In most countries, if people had to rely on their market income alone, somewhere between 20 per cent and 30 per cent of households would be living in "relative income poverty," defined as having less than 60 per cent of average income.[35]

One way to address this is to help people to increase their earnings, say by investing in education or establishing mandatory minimum wages, and we will look in detail at how we might do this in the next section. But there is a limit to how far we can raise minimum wages without creating unemployment, and in any society some citizens will be unable to support themselves through work because they have caring responsibilities, or because of sickness or

---

* Of course, measures designed to promote efficiency can also enhance fairness (and vice versa). Tackling the monopoly power of large companies like Apple and Amazon, for example, would not only foster competition and innovation, but also prevent shareholders from benefiting financially from their monopoly power, and hence reduce the unfair inequalities that exist between them and everyone else. But even if we could create a perfectly efficient economy, this would not make it fair—at least, not if we think about fairness in terms of the difference principle.

disability. As a result, we will always need some system for topping up people's market incomes. What should this system look like? Most rich countries have adopted some combination of "social insurance" and "means-tested" benefits. The basic idea of social insurance is that individual citizens pay taxes (or make insurance "contributions") in return for receiving an income during periods when they are unable to work because of sickness, involuntary unemployment, or old age.[36] Means-tested benefits, by contrast, are paid on the basis of need rather than prior contributions, usually to people whose incomes fall below a certain threshold. They are also typically conditional on the recipient proving that either they are actively taking steps to find employment or are unable to work. The balance between these two systems varies from one country to the next—social insurance plays the primary role in most continental European countries; while in the UK, U.S.A. and other anglophone countries, means-tested benefits tend to be more important.[37]

The most pressing problem with existing welfare systems is that benefits are typically well below what people need to meet their basic needs. In the UK, the standard unemployment benefit for a single adult is around £75 per week, barely above what is considered to be a "destitution" income of £70, and far below the £230 per week that most people consider to be the minimum for a socially acceptable standard of living.[38] Across the OECD as a whole, minimum-income benefits for a single person, including benefits related to housing, amount to about 35 per cent of median household income.[39] As a result, even after we account for taxes and transfers, about 17 per cent of people live in relative income poverty in both the UK and the EU, rising to about a quarter of the population in America.[40] Poverty rates tend to be even higher among households with children—in the UK, around 23 per cent of children are currently living in poverty, increasing to more than 30 per cent once we take housing costs into account.[41] As we discussed in the previous chapter, child poverty not only undermines children's health and well-being, but prevents them from fully developing their talents and abilities, making equality of opportunity all but impossible to achieve.

At the very least, then, we need to increase the generosity of existing benefits to meet widely accepted poverty standards. This would be a significant improvement on the status quo. But it would be better to pursue a more fundamental transformation of how we go about meeting basic needs, by introducing a universal and unconditional basic income, or UBI. As we shall see, doing so would realize Rawls's powerful vision of economic justice to an even greater degree.[42]

A UBI is defined as a regular cash payment to every citizen, with two key features: it is "universal" in the sense that it would be paid to everyone, no matter how rich or poor; and it is "unconditional" in the sense that it would be paid without any requirement to be in, or looking for, work. Part of the appeal of a UBI is that it could replace most existing transfers and benefits, but it doesn't necessarily have to be sufficient to meet people's basic needs on its own, and the appropriate level at which it should be paid will depend both on how we define basic needs, and on what other systems are in place to help citizens meet those needs.[43] At the very least, we would still want to have additional support for the severely disabled, and the state would continue to fund core services such as education and healthcare, given their vital role in ensuring equality of opportunity.

At first sight, a UBI might appear to be an expensive and wasteful way to meet basic needs. If our aim is simply to make sure that everyone has access to a minimum level of income, then we can always do this more cheaply by targeting support towards the poor, and by requiring those who can work to do so. In fact, the difference principle would appear to suggest precisely this kind of approach— after all, if we can meet people's basic needs at a lower overall cost, then we can have lower taxes, and this in turn will tend to promote economic dynamism and growth that can benefit everyone.

The justification for a UBI rests on the importance not just of income but of dignity and self-respect. While means-tested and conditional benefits may be an efficient way to boost the incomes of the least well off, they can profoundly undermine people's sense of self-respect. Means-testing inevitably creates a distinction between those who do and don't receive benefits, and people who are dependent on welfare are frequently demonized in politics and popular culture.[44] At the same time, having to meet the various conditions that come with these benefits can itself be intrusive and humiliating, depriving citizens with the lowest incomes of agency and independence, and putting some of the most vulnerable people in society in a position of almost total reliance on an often impersonal bureaucracy. For people who are able to work, this means proving that you have tried and failed to secure a decent job, which in our work-obsessed culture can itself feel humiliating.[45] For those who cannot work, it often means enduring intrusive and personal questions, such as, "Can you cope with going alone to places you know?" or "How bad is your incontinence?"[46]

A growing body of research attests to the damaging impact that this whole process can have on people's mental health: the threat of having one's benefits withdrawn leads to anxiety, fear and insecurity; and when benefits actually are withdrawn, this rarely leads people to find a job, and frequently worsens existing physical and mental illnesses.[47] As one British benefits adviser put it, in a moving plea for a more humane approach, this system "tramples on privacy and self-respect in a way inconceivable to anyone outside the benefit system. It creates a noxious fog of suspicion which clouds neighbours' understandings of each other and poisons their relationships. It leaves people—fellow-citizens, human beings—living in perpetual fear . . . For often-isolated people, what fears could be more insidious than inability to pay for food, warmth and housing, or the suspicious eyes of neighbours?"[48]

Means-tested benefits can also make it more difficult for those on the lowest incomes to take paid work. On the one hand, they create well-known "poverty traps," where benefits are rapidly withdrawn as people earn more, so that those on low incomes can find themselves losing 80p or 90p in reduced benefits for every extra £1 of earnings. Once we take into account costs such as travel and childcare, they may actually end up with less than if they had stayed at home. Alongside this is the so-called "precarity trap."[49] For many on low incomes, job opportunities are frequently short-term, even more so in recent years with the development of the "gig economy." The complexity of most welfare systems, combined with delays before payments are made, can lead some people to refuse jobs they would otherwise like to do, since even a short period without an income can be catastrophic.

A UBI would eliminate these problems at a stroke—meeting basic needs in a way that supports rather than undermines the independence and self-respect of the least well off. Since it would be paid to everyone, a UBI would end the stigma associated with receiving benefits and banish the need for intrusive and demeaning assessments. It would also make it easier and more financially rewarding for those on the lowest incomes to work, with all the wider advantages this can have. In the words of the philosophers and basic income advocates Philippe Van Parijs and Yannick Vanderborght, whereas a means-tested welfare system provides "a safety net that fails to catch a great many people it should catch, and in which many others get trapped," a UBI "provides a floor on which they can all safely stand."[50]

A UBI would also transform power relations in society more widely, especially those between workers and employers. In our current welfare system, the unemployed typically have to accept the first job they are offered on pain of losing their benefits. And while those in work can theoretically threaten to quit, this is rarely credible, since in many countries people who voluntarily leave work are denied access to benefits, and often have to accept another job with the same poor conditions. All this would change with a UBI in place: no one would be forced to take a job simply to survive, and even the lowest-paid would be able to say "no" to degrading work or an abusive employer.[51]

Critics sometimes argue that a UBI is at odds with recognizing the importance of work as a source of self-respect and social recognition, as if its introduction would lead us to abandon any effort to improve the availability or quality of work and simply pay people to sit at home instead. But, if anything, the opposite is true: it is in large part because of its potential to transform work for the better that a UBI is so desirable. With a UBI in place, employers would have to pay higher wages for the least attractive jobs (no one would clean toilets unless they were paid a decent wage to do so) or find other ways to make these jobs more pleasant. The prospect of paying higher wages would, in turn, encourage businesses to find ways to make those jobs more productive, say by investing in on-the-job training or new technologies. A UBI would also make it easier for people to study outside work, with potentially far-reaching benefits in terms of productivity; and it would support those who want to start a new business, encouraging innovation. Finally, a UBI would allow people to say "yes" to work that is intrinsically satisfying or socially useful but might not pay very well, such as creative or care work. In this way, it could make meaningful work more widely available, especially for those on the lowest incomes, while leaving it up to individuals to decide exactly what that means or how much it matters to them.

The need for a UBI is only strengthened by recent labour market trends. It would allow people to make the most of the flexibility that comes with the gig economy, while guaranteeing a baseline of financial security for all. Looking further ahead, although the future path of new technologies like artificial intelligence is difficult to predict, there is a real possibility that automation will lead to a long-term decline in wages or employment as machines come to replace humans in a wider range of tasks.[52] In a world where large numbers of people are unable to meet their basic needs through work, something like a UBI would be essential.

A UBI would also transform power relations well beyond the world of paid work. It would be a source of financial independence for those who cannot undertake paid employment, whether because they have caring responsibilities, or because of illness or disability. And it would enable people to escape bad relationships of all sorts, providing an exit route for young gay or trans people whose families or communities cannot accept their sexuality, or for women suffering from domestic violence or being pushed into forced marriages.

Is It Fair?

There is a lot, then, to be said in favour of a UBI. But as critics have pointed out, it has an obvious, and rather serious, moral drawback—namely, that some people might stop working altogether and simply freeride on the hard work of others. This strikes most people as unfair, and it goes against the spirit of reciprocity at the heart of Rawls's approach to economic justice. Indeed, Rawls himself was critical of a UBI for this reason, arguing that in a fair society everyone should be expected to "do [their] part in society's cooperative work" and that "we are not to gain from the cooperative efforts of others without doing our fair share."[53]

While this is a valid concern, it doesn't mean we should abandon the idea.[54] We have to look at the case for a UBI in the round: no economic policy or institution is perfect, and as Rawls himself said, "the best available arrangement may contain a balance of imperfections, an adjustment of compensating injustices."[55] It is true that, in the absence of any work-related conditions, a UBI would allow some people to stop working altogether. But, as we shall see, this number is likely to be small, and we have to remember that it is precisely because a UBI is unconditional that it has such enormous potential for bolstering the self-respect of the least well off in society—by eliminating the need for intrusive and humiliating assessments, and fundamentally altering the balance of power at work. We cannot have it both ways: the transformative benefits of a UBI depend in large part on the fact that everyone, and not just the rich, would be able to say "no" to demeaning or degrading work. The risk that a small number of people might choose to stop working altogether is a price worth paying.

How can we be confident that most people would make a fair contribution to society through paid work, even with a UBI in place?[56] Despite critics' fears, there is no reason to think that people would leave work en masse. Some of the best evidence comes from a series of real-life experiments with so-called "negative income taxes" in America and Canada between 1968 and 1980.*[57] A negative income tax is a close cousin of a UBI which involves topping up people's income to a guaranteed minimum level, irrespective of whether they are working or looking for work. Studies of these trials should help to assuage concerns about freeriding: participants only slightly reduced the amount of time spent in work, by about two to four weeks of full-time employment per year on average. Moreover, where people did work less, this was often because they took slightly longer to find a new job, or because they were studying or looking after children. There is no evidence of people permanently withdrawing from paid employment.[58]

---

* President Richard Nixon nearly succeeded in introducing a version of a negative income tax in the early 1970s. The so-called "Family Assistance Plan" was overwhelmingly approved by the House of Representatives but ultimately failed to secure the backing of the Senate, and was eventually shelved.

These findings are consistent with a large body of research looking at "unconditional cash transfer" programmes around the world. A recent review of this literature concluded that these kinds of schemes either have no impact on how much people work or lead to only a small decrease, while they are associated with significant improvements across a whole range of measures, including mental and physical health, educational outcomes, parenting, and crime.[59] None of this should come as a surprise: most people want to have more than a basic income; and as we have already discussed, paid work is more than just a source of income—it is a source of meaning, identity and self-respect. Many of the richest people in society, who could easily choose a life of leisure, work for just these reasons.

Although fears about freeriding appear to be overblown, we could consider hybrid forms of UBI that maintain an element of conditionality but without anything like the harsh and punitive regimes that exist in many countries today. The economist Tony Atkinson proposed a basic "participation income" in return for making a minimum social contribution, defined broadly to include not just paid work but other caring or charitable activities too.[60] The choice between this and a full-blown UBI is not an easy one: a participation income would mitigate concerns about freeriding, but it would add a costly layer of administrative complexity and draw the state into vexed questions about what activities would merit payments.

Can We Afford It?

The main practical challenge with introducing a UBI is the cost. There is no escaping the fact that it would be very expensive. Most discussions focus on simple back-of-the-envelope calculations of the gross cost—the amount paid to each person multiplied by the number of people in the country. The total will obviously depend on the level at which the UBI is paid, which in turn will depend on how it sits alongside other benefits and public services. For simplicity, let's consider the most generous kind of UBI, namely, one that is sufficient to eliminate poverty on its own. As a rough rule of thumb, the gross cost could be as high as 20–25 per cent of GDP.[61] But of course a UBI would also replace many existing benefits and tax allowances, and these savings could reduce the cost by between a third and a half, bringing the net additional cost to around 10–15 per cent of GDP.[62]

A poverty-level UBI, then, would require a significant increase in taxes. But it's important to remember that although everyone would pay more tax, they would also receive a basic income in return. In fact, most of the headline cost of a UBI involves giving and taking money from the same people. Once we account for the combined effect of the extra income and the higher taxes needed to pay for it, most people would be "net beneficiaries"—they would receive more from the UBI than they would pay in additional taxes; while only a minority would be "net contributors," paying back more than they receive.[63]

From an economic perspective, the true "cost" of a UBI is measured by whether it would reduce total output, or GDP, and hence make society poorer overall. This calculation depends on how people respond both to receiving an unconditional income and to the increase in taxes needed to pay for it. As we have already seen, most people would keep working even if they received a UBI; and as we shall see later in this chapter, increasing taxes tends to have a much smaller impact on how much people work than we commonly think. But the truth is that the full economic consequences of a UBI are difficult to predict, and for this reason it would make sense to proceed by introducing it gradually while phasing out existing benefits.[64]

We should also be open to possibilities that could achieve some of the aims of a UBI more cheaply. For a start, a UBI need not be all-or-nothing. Even a partial UBI, which would not in itself be enough to live on, could provide a vital source of stability and bargaining power for the poorest people in society. Another option would be a time-limited UBI, which people could draw on for, say, five years over their lifetime, providing a cushion in times of real need. We could also maintain an element of means-testing, by making payments only to people whose income falls below a certain level. As we have seen, if we pay for a UBI by increasing taxes on income, then we end up with a back-and-forth where most people end up paying some of it back in higher taxes. But we could skip all this, and simply make a single payment to net beneficiaries, while levying a tax on net contributors. This is the idea behind the negative income tax that we touched on before.[65] We could design this so that the overall impact on people's incomes and work incentives would be the same as with a UBI, but since we would only need to make payments to net beneficiaries, this would require a much smaller increase in headline tax rates.[66] From a political point of view, this is a big advantage—although since payments would be targeted at the poor, it might fail to encourage the same spirit of universality and solidarity as a truly universal basic income.

A UBI is clearly not the only way we can ensure that every citizen is able to meet their basic needs. But it is, on balance, the most attractive way because of how it would strengthen the independence and self-respect of those who have the least, and because of its potential to transform the balance of power between workers and employers. And even if we don't adopt a full-blown UBI, we should move towards a more universal and less conditional welfare system.

SHARED PROSPERITY AND PREDISTRIBUTION

While meeting basic needs is the most fundamental requirement of economic justice, the difference principle is concerned with designing an economic system in which the benefits of prosperity are widely shared, and where the living standards of the least well off are higher than they would be under any other system. Crucially, we cannot rely on redistribution alone to achieve this goal. As we have already seen, Rawls explicitly rejected "welfare state capitalism" which would focus on "the redistribution of income to those with less at the end of each period," in favour of a "property owning democracy" where the state would ensure "the widespread ownership of productive assets and human capital (that is, education and trained skills) at the beginning of each period."[67]

In effect, Rawls argued for what has come to be known today as "predistribution"—the idea that we should try to prevent market inequalities from emerging in the first place, rather than relying on taxes and transfers to ameliorate them. This way of thinking has attracted growing interest from academics and politicians, and for good reason.[68] The increase in overall income inequality since the 1980s has been driven above all by a sharp rise in pretax or market inequality rather than by a decline in redistribution.[69] Differences in pretax inequality are also key to understanding why some countries are so much more unequal than others, often more so than differences in the progressivity of taxes or the generosity of the welfare state.[70]

These differences in market income inequality can be very large indeed. In America, the pretax income of the poorest 50 per cent is just $21,000 on average, compared to $29,000 in Denmark—despite both countries having similar overall income per capita. Similarly, the top 10 per cent of Americans earn a whopping $353,000 on average, compared to $237,000 among their Danish counterparts.[71] As a result, America would have to do much more redistribution than Denmark if it wanted to achieve the same level of final or "disposable" income inequality—in other words, money in people's hands, which is what ultimately matters.[72] However, the fact that pretax income inequality is so much lower in Denmark suggests that unequal countries like America or the UK could do much more to tackle this problem at source. After all, there is no deep economic reason why the poorest 50 per cent should earn so much more in Denmark than in America—both countries are at similar levels of development and have access to much the same technologies. This doesn't mean it would be easy for America to increase the earnings of the bottom half to the level found in Denmark—these differences are rooted in different education systems, different approaches to economic regulation, differences in the bargaining power of workers, and no doubt much more. But there is no question that market incomes can be shaped by public policy, and this is what "predistribution" is all about.

Before we look at *how* we can increase the pretax incomes of the least well off, I want to say a little more about *why* we should do this. Some of the interest in predistribution in recent years reflects the idea that it offers a way of reducing inequality on the cheap, without having to increase taxes to pay for more redistribution. This is obviously politically attractive, and all else being equal, lower taxes are better for economic efficiency and growth.[73] But we cannot just wave a magic wand and bring about a more equal distribution of market incomes. While there are some ways to do this without increasing taxes (such as higher minimum wages and stronger trade unions), most of the things we can do to increase the pretax income of the least well off—from investing in skills and education to bringing about a more equal distribution of wealth—will also require higher taxes.

From the perspective of Rawls's principles, the importance of predistribution stems from the importance of reciprocity and self-respect in the context of work. By focusing on increasing market incomes, especially from employment, predistribution helps to maintain the healthy connection between contribution and reward that might be lost if we relied too heavily on redistribution. At the same time, it takes seriously the importance of work for people's sense of self-respect: whereas redistribution simply aims to top up people's income, predistribution is focused on equipping everyone with the skills and resources to play an active role in economic life.[74] The importance of predistribution for reciprocity and self-respect helps to explain not only its intuitive moral appeal, but also its political potential: while many people are sceptical about increasing taxes to pay for redistribution, there is often greater support for minimum wages, vocational training and other policies which would increase people's income through work.[75]

Raising Wages

There are two key sources of pretax or market income: income from labour, or earnings; and income from capital—profits, rents, interest and so on. For most people, and especially for those with the lowest incomes, earnings are the most important, and so we should look first at how we can increase them.

In a market economy, how much someone can earn depends above all on their skills, or "human capital," and any strategy to raise the wages of the least well off has to start here. This brings us back to the education system, which we have already discussed in relation to fair equality of opportunity.[76] Making sure that everyone has the same chances to develop their abilities would itself bring about a much more equal distribution of skills, and hence wages: if everyone with the potential ability to go to university were able to do so, this would increase the supply of graduates and reduce the wage premium they typically receive. But we also need to think about the education system from the perspective of the difference principle. In other words, how can it promote the life prospects of the least well off?[77]

This is particularly relevant when it comes to thinking about vocational education and training, a topic we only touched on in Chapter 6. Although there has been a massive expansion in academic higher education since the 1970s, educational opportunities for the half or more of the population who don't go to university have been largely overlooked. This isn't universally true—some countries, like Germany, have a long tradition of excellent vocational education. But in countries such as the UK and U.S.A., vocational education is fragmented and of variable quality, and often seriously underfunded. A 2012 study found that average public funding per full-time student in the UK was around £2,150 per year for vocational courses, compared to almost £8,400 for university undergraduates.[78]

This focus on academic as opposed to vocational education is sometimes justified on the basis it will yield a bigger return in terms of economic growth. There is, however, some debate about whether this is actually the case.[79] And even if public subsidies for academic degrees have a bigger impact on growth, this wouldn't excuse the current neglect of vocational education. This is, in effect, the educational equivalent of trickle-down economics—it justifies policies that mostly benefit those with higher earnings, while simply assuming that some of the rewards will find their way to lower-earning non-graduates too. While investing in academic higher education *can* have indirect benefits for non-graduates, in the form of higher employment or more generous redistribution, if we really want to increase the earnings of this group we should do so by investing *directly* in their skills and, therefore, their earning potential.

At the very least, those who want to pursue vocational routes should have access to funding on the same basis as those who want to follow an academic path. We could, for example, give everyone a lifetime education budget which they could spend on academic learning or vocational training over the course of their career.[80] The UK appears to be moving in this direction with plans to give everyone access to a "Lifelong Loan Entitlement" from 2025 which they could use to fund both academic or vocational training.[81] From the perspective of the difference principle, we might even want to offer more generous subsidies for vocational routes than for academic ones, given that the former are more likely to benefit lower earners.

Beyond funding, we need institutional reform to raise the status and quality of vocational education, following the example of countries such as Germany. The most successful models combine a number of key features: a well-defined set of pathways for vocational learners, leading to widely recognized qualifications; a strong focus on apprenticeships and other forms of work-based learning; a highly qualified workforce, with both teaching skills and industry experience; and close engagement from employers to ensure that people are learning genuinely useful skills.[82] We should provide generous public subsidies for on-the-job training, and consider tilting this towards lower-skilled workers: while organizations currently spend more on training highly skilled employees, larger subsidies for less-skilled workers could help reverse this pattern.[83]

Investing in education would help increase wages for lower earners. But wages don't depend on skills alone, they also depend on the relative bargaining power of workers vis-à-vis employers.[84] Recognizing this leads us towards a broader agenda to reform our labour market institutions, the most important of which are minimum wages and trade unions.

Legally binding national minimum wages have proved to be a powerful tool for raising the earnings of the least well off, and in many countries there is room to increase them further. An independent review, commissioned by the UK government and written by the leading economist and minimum-wage expert Arindrajit Dube in 2019, concluded that even relatively high minimum wages—up to two thirds of median pay—would probably "significantly increase the earnings of low paid workers" while having a "modest" impact on overall employment, if any.[85] A handful of countries, including France, New Zealand and Portugal, already have minimum wages set at more than 60 per cent of median earnings, and in 2020 the UK government made a commitment to increase the minimum wage to two thirds of median earnings. But in countries like America, where the federal minimum wage currently stands at around 30 per cent of median earnings, this would represent a radical shift in public policy with large benefits for the lowest earners.[86]

Still, there is a limit to how far national minimum wages can go before they start to have a negative impact on employment. In part, this is because they have to be set at a level that works for the least productive sectors. If we want to push wages above this lowest common denominator, we urgently need to strengthen the role of trade unions and other wage-bargaining institutions which can push for higher wages in a way that is sensitive to the circumstances of specific firms and industries. This is especially important in countries like the UK and U.S.A. where, since the 1980s, trade unions have come under concerted attack, losing much of their power and membership—a shift which is widely recognized as a key factor behind the increase in inequality over this period.[87]

Increasing the power of unions does not mean entering a world of constant industrial conflict: in many countries, unions play a fundamentally constructive role, and the evidence suggests that collective bargaining—if designed well—can reduce inequality without harming productivity.[88] Perhaps the most important design feature that the most successful systems have in common is that negotiations are conducted at the sector or industry level, rather than taking place within individual firms, as is currently the case in about two thirds of OECD countries, including the UK and U.S.A.[89] Sector-based wage bargaining is common in continental Europe and has recently been reintroduced in New Zealand.[90] In this system, unions typically meet with employer organizations and negotiate wage agreements that apply to a range of different jobs within a given industry, such as retail or banking, while leaving room for businesses to tailor these agreements to their particular circumstances.[91] According to the OECD, it is in this kind of model that "the best outcomes in terms of employment, productivity and wages seem to be reached."[92] Its key advantage is that it creates a level playing field for all the businesses in a given sector: since wages are relatively fixed across similar firms, companies have to focus on increasing productivity, rather than cutting wages, in order to gain a competitive edge.[93] Another advantage is that wage deals can automatically be extended to all workers in the relevant industry, which is especially important given the recent increase in gig work and other forms of non-standard employment which make unions difficult to organize.

Better training, higher minimum wages and stronger trade unions would all significantly increase wages for the lowest-paid workers. But we also need to make sure that people can find a job in the first place. We know that involuntary unemployment takes a very heavy toll on people's well-being, far beyond what we can account for by the loss of income alone.[94] As Rawls put it, "Lacking a sense of long-term security and the opportunity for meaningful work and occupation is not only destructive of citizens' self-respect but of their sense that they are members of society and not simply caught in it." The special importance of paid work as a source of independence, identity and social recognition means the state should consider itself the "employer of last resort."[95]

There are different ways we can put this into practice. At the very least, we should use the familiar tools of fiscal and monetary policy—public spending and interest rates—to maintain a high level of overall demand for labour and to mitigate the impact of recessions on employment.[96] Alongside an employment-oriented approach to fiscal and monetary policy, we need more targeted help for people who are struggling to find work. The most direct approach would be a "jobs guarantee," where the state would offer employment to anyone who cannot secure work in the normal way, if needs be by creating jobs that wouldn't otherwise exist. Although there are significant practical challenges with this, a review of such programmes found that, when they are designed carefully, they seem to be able to "increase employment . . . and produce genuinely valuable output."[97]

Our primary focus, however, should be on supporting unemployed workers to find jobs where there is existing demand. Some countries do this better than others. Many European nations already invest heavily in job-transition or "active labour market" programmes, including help with retraining. Denmark has probably the most well-developed system, devoting as much as 2 per cent of GDP to it, and the rate at which displaced workers find new jobs in Denmark is significantly faster than in other OECD countries. By contrast, spending on active labour market programmes is 1 per cent of GDP in France, and as little as 0.11 per cent in the U.S.A.[98] Even if there was a UBI to give low-paid workers the financial breathing space to retrain and find an appropriate job, there would still be a place for job-to-job support, especially for those who need to undertake significant retraining. In light of the rapid pace of technological change today, and the urgent need to shift from polluting to sustainable industries, these kinds of policies are more important than ever.

Shared Wealth

It's clear that there is much more we could do to increase the earnings of the lowest-paid workers. But if we want to reduce the vast inequalities in our societies, we also need to look at the distribution of wealth, which is and always has been even more unequal than income. The wealthiest 10 per cent of the population hold 61 per cent of all personal wealth in Europe, and 71 per cent in America. By contrast, the poorest 50 per cent have almost nothing: just 3 per cent of the total in Europe, and 1.5 per cent in America.[99] These massive inequalities are mirrored in the distribution of "capital income"— from profits, interest payments, rents, dividends and so on—which in most countries accounts for about 30–40 per cent of total pretax income.[100] If we are serious about predistribution then we also need to increase the wealth of the bottom 50 per cent, and bring about a more equal distribution of wealth overall.* This isn't only about raising people's purchasing power—having wealth can also be a vital source of security and stability, providing a cushion in hard times, and a springboard for trying new things like going to college or starting a business.

There is some scope to increase wealth among the poorest 50 per

---

* Another way to reduce inequality would be to increase the overall proportion of income that is paid out in wages (the labour income share) and reduce that which is paid out to owners (the capital income share). A combination of policies that increased workers' bargaining power alongside more robust enforcement of anti-monopoly laws would probably achieve this. But, in the end, the distribution of income between labour and capital—or workers and owners—depends mostly on technological forces that are largely beyond our control, such as the growing importance of machines due to automation. If we want to build a more equal society, then our primary focus should be changing the underlying distribution of capital itself, so that everyone shares in the profits that currently go to a small class of owners.

cent of people by encouraging private savings: we could limit the fees charged by financial intermediaries, offer guaranteed minimum interest rates to small savers, or introduce a reduced rate of tax on savings for those with lower levels of capital income.[101] But if we seriously want to change the overall distribution of wealth, we need something more radical.

One option would be a "universal minimum inheritance"—a one-off transfer of wealth to every citizen when they reach adulthood, funded by taxes on large inheritances and the very wealthy. This idea was first proposed in a pamphlet published in 1796 by Thomas Paine, a prominent figure in the American and French revolutionary movements, who argued that every citizen should be paid a fixed sum on reaching the age of twenty-one.[102] Although his proposal was never implemented and largely forgotten, recent years have seen a revival of interest. In the UK, the New Labour government introduced a form of minimum inheritance in the early 2000s known as the "Child Trust Fund." Under this scheme, the government paid £250 into a tax-free savings account for every child at birth, with an extra £250 for poorer families, and the fund was topped up with an extra £250 on a child's seventh birthday. Although a helpful proof of concept, the Child Trust Fund was phased out in 2011, and in any case the sums involved were much too small to make any meaningful difference.

The first proposal for a substantial minimum inheritance scheme was developed by the legal scholars Bruce Ackerman and Anne Alstott in the 1990s, who argued that every American citizen should receive an $80,000 lump sum on reaching the age of eighteen, funded by a 2 per cent annual tax on personal wealth.[103] More recently, the economist Thomas Piketty has proposed a minimum inheritance equal to 60 per cent of average adult wealth—equivalent to around €120,000 in Western Europe—funded by a combination of inheritance taxes and an annual wealth tax which between them would raise around 5 per cent of national income per year.[104]

A universal minimum inheritance on this scale would fundamentally alter the distribution of wealth in society. In addition to making capital income more equal, it would be a powerful tool for bolstering the agency and independence of the least well off, much like a universal basic income. A minimum inheritance would be universal, and hence, like a UBI, free of the stigma associated with means-tested benefits; and, in principle, it would enable everyone to support themselves, at least for a period of time—creating a buffer for people who want to quit their job or take their time finding a new one. It would also open up the possibility of making large one-off investments, like starting a company or buying a house, in a way that wouldn't be possible with a UBI. But even with a generous minimum inheritance, we would still require some kind of system for meeting basic needs, both to support people who cannot work as a result of disability or caring responsibilities, and to step in if people who have spent their minimum inheritance fall on hard times.[105]

An alternative that fits better with the proposal for a universal basic income would be to establish a "citizens' wealth fund" that would be owned by, and managed on behalf of, the population as a whole. As with the minimum inheritance, the resources for building up this fund would come from progressive taxes on wealth. But rather than transferring the proceeds directly to citizens, the state would buy shares in private companies and other valuable assets, which in turn would generate an income. This could be a source of revenue for general spending, but since the underlying motivation is to create a more equal distribution of wealth—and the security and independence that come from possessing wealth—it would make more sense for it to be paid directly to citizens on an equal basis, in the form of an annual "citizens' dividend." If used in this way, the fund would effectively help to pay for a UBI.

A citizens' wealth fund would provide an automatic mechanism through which all citizens would share in the income that would otherwise go to a small minority of rich investors; and with a large fund, we could afford to be much more relaxed about the inevitable shifts in the balance of income between capital and labour that occur as technology changes over time. In addition to contributing towards the cost of a UBI, a wealth fund has some important economic advantages compared to a minimum inheritance. With a minimum inheritance, there is a risk that if most people decide to spend rather than save their money, there will be less money available for investment, which in turn could reduce productivity and wage growth in the long term. By contrast, a citizens' wealth fund offers a way to have a more equal distribution of wealth while maintaining a high overall level of savings.

How big a fund should the state try to accumulate? The answer ultimately depends on the consequences of building up a large, state-owned share in the economy and of raising the taxes to pay for the fund in the first place. But we should be open to the state accumulating a very large fund. The Nobel Prize–winning economist James Meade, whose work was an important influence on Rawls, suggested that in the long run we should aim to establish a fund equivalent to around 50 per cent of national wealth.[106] While it would probably take many decades to build a fund of this size, it could eventually cover a significant portion of the cost of a UBI, reducing the burden on income taxes.

While a citizens' wealth fund would no doubt face fierce political resistance from the rich, there are no serious practical difficulties to establishing one. Indeed, we already have a working template in the form of the "sovereign wealth funds" that operate in more than eighty countries.[107] Some of these are very large indeed: Norway's sovereign wealth fund—first established in 1990 and now the biggest in the world—was valued at nearly $1.4 trillion in 2021, almost three times Norway's annual GDP.[108] The scheme whose design comes closest to a citizens' wealth fund is the Alaska Permanent Fund, which was created in 1976 through an amendment to the state constitution requiring that 25 per cent of the rent and royalties from the state's mineral, oil and gas resources be deposited into a fund. Each year, a portion of the fund's income is distributed directly to Alaskan residents on an equal basis, with payments averaging around $1,500 in recent years, and the rest is reinvested so that the fund keeps growing.[109] The fund is hugely popular, and has helped Alaska to buck the trend of rising inequality: it is the only state in America where incomes became more rather than less equal during the 1990s and 2000s.[110]

Although a citizens' wealth fund would represent a significant expansion of a certain sort of public ownership, it would not be a return to the top-down nationalization of the post-war period. Businesses would continue to be privately run and managed, making their own decisions about which products to create, what technology to use, whom to hire and fire and so on. In this way, the wealth fund would be compatible with the decentralized decision-making that is the essence of a healthy and dynamic market economy. While the state might face political pressure to use its influence as a shareholder, we can put safeguards in place to prevent excessive interference—for example, the Norwegian sovereign wealth fund is prohibited from holding more than 10 per cent of voting shares in any individual company.[111]

While it is important to guard against too much interference in individual companies, the fund need not be an entirely passive investor. In fact, a citizens' wealth fund could be a powerful tool for directing investment towards important public priorities that might otherwise be neglected by the market: it could invest in renewable technologies, deprived geographical areas, or life-saving medicines. Unlike most sovereign wealth funds today whose investment strategy is opaque and only loosely subject to democratic oversight (if at all), a citizens' wealth fund should itself be fully transparent and subject to democratic control.[112]

TAXES

Like many of the proposals outlined over the course of this book, a citizens' wealth fund would be expensive. If we want to establish a proper system of public funding for the democratic process, to invest more in education and training and to create a universal basic income, we would almost certainly need to increase taxes. How far depends on the precise combination of policies that we decide to pursue, but this would probably require taxes in the region of 45–50 per cent of national income.[113]

This is high by both historical and international standards. Across the OECD as a whole, taxes represent about 34 per cent of national income. In the UK, taxes are just below the OECD average at 33 per cent, while the U.S.A. stands out among rich nations for its low level of overall taxation, at just 25 per cent of GDP.[114] But it is not without precedent. There are already seven European countries where the government collects more than 40 per cent of GDP in taxes; in both France and Denmark, tax revenues exceed 45 per cent of GDP.[115] While an overall tax rate of 45–50 per cent of GDP would imply a significant increase in most rich countries, changes of this scale have happened before. At the start of the twentieth century, taxes typically accounted for less than 10 per cent of national income, and the level of taxes that we take for granted today would surely have seemed almost unimaginable. And yet by 1980 this share had more than tripled to roughly its current level.[116]

Building support for higher taxes is a long-term political project. It will succeed only if we are able to articulate a positive vision of the kind of society that this would create, whether that be fixing our broken political system or achieving equality of opportunity. We also need to address the spectre of authoritarian socialism which inevitably emerges in debates about higher taxes: in other words, to make clear that the aim is not to give the state more control over how we live, but to ensure that each of us has a fair share of the resources we need to shape our own lives.

Wouldn't increasing taxes to 45–50 per cent of national income undermine economic dynamism and prosperity? The idea that taxes are bad for growth was the driving force behind the tax cuts introduced by Ronald Reagan, Margaret Thatcher and others in the 1980s, and more recently by Donald Trump and Liz Truss; and it continues to be one of the most intuitive and powerful arguments against any proposal to increase taxes today. We should take this concern seriously: we can all benefit from a growing economy, and financial incentives have an important role to play in driving innovation and prosperity. But we need to keep this in perspective: even if higher taxes reduce growth—and as we shall see below, it's far from clear that this is the case—this would not be a conclusive argument against them. We always have to balance the potential costs of higher taxes in terms of economic efficiency with their benefits in terms of equality and justice. From the perspective of the difference principle, what ultimately matters is not the size of the economic pie overall but the absolute size of the slice that goes to the least well off.

So what is the relationship between taxes and economic prosperity? The massive increase in tax rates over the course of the twentieth century, and the fact that different countries raised taxes at different times and to different degrees, provides a rich source of evidence— and the reality is more complex, and less concerning, than we are typically led to believe. If taxes were bad for growth, then we would expect countries which increased taxes more than others to have experienced lower long-run growth rates. But economic growth has been much the same in America as in countries like Belgium, Denmark and Finland, which had similar levels of income per capita and taxes as the U.S.A. in the 1960s, but which subsequently increased their tax take by 10–15 per cent of GDP more than America did.[117] This isn't simply the result of cherry-picking a few favourable examples: in a hugely influential study of twenty countries over more than 140 years, the economic historian Peter Lindert concluded there was no evidence that higher social spending, and therefore taxes, were systematically associated with less economic output or slower growth—a result which has been widely corroborated.[118] Although there surely comes a point at which higher taxes would have such a damaging impact on work incentives and innovation that they would reduce growth, there is no evidence that even high-tax countries like Denmark and France have reached this point.

The fact that higher taxes seem not to come at a cost in terms of economic growth will come as a surprise to many. Indeed, it surprised Lindert, who referred to it as the "free lunch puzzle," since it appears as if we can have all the benefits of higher social spending— better health, education, infrastructure and so on—without paying any cost in terms of the prosperity of society overall.[119] Part of the answer is that countries with high levels of tax have deliberately sought to construct their tax and benefit systems in ways that minimize the negative impact on financial incentives to work (something we will come back to). But it is also increasingly clear these incentives don't matter nearly as much as we often assume, or as advocates of lower taxes and trickle-down economics would have us believe. People's motivations to work are about much more than making money—an insight backed up by a large body of economic literature looking at the ways taxes affect people's decisions about how hard to work, how much to save, or whether to start a new business. While there is some evidence that people work less in response to higher taxes, what stands out is just how small this effect is. This is especially true for people with high levels of education and income, whose decisions about whether and how much to work appear to be almost completely unresponsive to changes in the tax rate.[120] This is not to say we can just increase taxes without worrying about the consequences: people who are on the margins of the labour market, such as the lowest-paid, as well as single parents and "second earners" (the lower-earning person in a couple, most of whom are women), are more sensitive to changes in their take-home pay; and we need to take this into account when designing the tax (and benefit) system.[121] But increases in tax rates along the lines we are discussing are unlikely to have a dramatic effect on whether or how hard most people work.

In part, then, the explanation for the "free lunch puzzle" is that economists have systematically overstated the importance of financial incentives for economic activity. But just as important is that the conventional focus on incentives only looks at one side of the story. In particular, it ignores the fact that tax revenues are often spent in ways that actually *increase* productivity and growth. Most obviously, they can be used to pay for productivity-enhancing infrastructure such as roads and energy, or for research and development that would otherwise be underfunded by the market.[122] But policies whose primary aim is to promote fairness and equality—such as spending more on schools in disadvantaged areas, and increasing the resources available to low-income families—also tend to be good for growth, since they help people to acquire the skills and good health they need to play a full and productive role in economic life.[123] This is crucial to understanding why high-tax countries haven't fallen behind: whatever the negative effects of higher taxes on work incentives in countries like France and Denmark, these have been balanced out by the benefits of spending more on things like health and education.[124]

Taxes on Income

Increasing taxes to 45–50 per cent of GDP would allow us to transform our society and increase the living standards of the least well off without seriously undermining economic growth—indeed, with the right policies in place, it might even increase it. But how can we raise taxes to this level?

The obvious place to start is by increasing taxes on those with the highest incomes—the top 10 per cent, and especially the top 1 per cent. Yet the trend since the 1980s has been in the opposite direction:

across the OECD as a whole, the average top income-tax rate fell from 62 per cent in 1981 to 35 per cent in 2015.[125] These cuts were justified by the claim that top earners are the engines of innovation, hence lower taxes for them would unleash a new era of economic growth that everyone would benefit from. While this is plausible in theory, in reality tax cuts for very high earners have coincided with a slowdown in growth: in the U.S.A., which saw some of the largest tax cuts for the rich, the average rate of economic growth fell from 1.7 per cent per year in the 1960s and 1970s to 1.4 per cent per year since the 1980s.[126] It's possible that growth would have been *even* lower without these tax cuts, but there is little evidence to support this: countries which pursued larger tax cuts for the rich over this period did not experience faster economic growth.[127] Indeed, the claim that cutting top rates of tax will boost growth is a prime example of what the Nobel Prize–winning economist Paul Krugman has referred to as "zombie economics"—"ideas that have failed repeatedly in practice, and should be dead, but somehow are still shambling around, eating policymakers' brains."[128]

In reality, most estimates suggest that high top rates of tax can raise significant revenue without harming growth. Just how far we can go is the subject of debate: credible estimates for the revenue-maximizing top tax rate range from around 55 per cent to 80 per cent, reflecting uncertainty about how much high earners would reduce their taxable income in response.[129] On closer inspection, however, there is not as much uncertainty as it seems. In fact, there is a general consensus that taxes have relatively little effect on *real* economic activity among high earners—how much they work and save, or the likelihood they will start a business. In an authoritative and widely cited survey, Emmanuel Saez, Joel Slemrod and Seth Giertz—three of the world's leading tax economists—concluded "there is no compelling evidence to date of *real* economic responses to tax rates at the top of the income distribution."[130] The problem is that when taxes go up, high earners start doing everything they can to avoid paying them, from relabelling income as dividends, which benefit from lower tax rates, to hiding money altogether. The good news, though, is that the extent of tax avoidance is not an immutable fact of economic nature, but something which depends on how we design the tax system itself. Emmanuel Saez and his fellow economist Gabriel Zucman argue that if we do everything we can to close off opportunities for tax avoidance, the revenue-maximizing marginal tax rate on the top 1 per cent of incomes in America is in the vicinity of 75 per cent, and would be levied on income above a threshold of around $500,000 per year. With this tax in place, the top 1 per cent would pay roughly 60 per cent of their total income in taxes, around double the current average tax rate. Saez and Zucman estimate that this would raise about four percentage points of national income, or more than $900 billion in 2021.[131]

Critically, the success of this proposal depends on clamping down on (legal) tax avoidance and (illegal) tax evasion. This is partly about enforcement. Public regulators are often seriously underfunded: in the U.S.A., the Internal Revenue Service employed fewer than 10,000 auditors in 2017—less than at any time since the mid-1950s, when the country's population was half what it is today—and those in the top 1 per cent have seen their chances of being audited decline by more than 70 per cent since 2010 alone. In the words of Saez and Zucman, "when it comes to regulating the tax dodging industry, the IRS brings a knife to a gunfight."[132] Even with extra resources, regulators face a constant struggle to keep on top of all the new schemes dreamt up by clever and well-paid tax advisers. For this reason, we need to tilt the law in favour of tax enforcement agencies: there should be a presumption that any transaction with the sole purpose of dodging taxes is illegal, while businesses should be required by law to report new tax-planning products, on pain of large fines.[133] Finally, we need to clamp down on the tax havens, which the very rich often use to hide their wealth and evade taxes, including by empowering regulators to levy sanctions or punitive taxes on secretive countries or financial institutions.[134]

The more fundamental challenge, however, is to simplify the tax system itself and eliminate loopholes. And this brings us to the second key part of creating a fairer and more progressive tax system, namely the need to increase taxes on capital income. The past few decades have seen many rich countries reduce tax rates on corporate profits and individual income from capital, so that these are often less than for income from work.[135] In the UK, for example, the higher rate of income tax on earnings is 40 per cent, compared to 32.5 per cent for income paid in the form of dividends, and

20 per cent for income from capital gains.[136] These differences in how income from labour and capital are taxed have encouraged architects, lawyers, doctors and other highly paid professionals to cut their tax bills by registering as businesses and paying themselves dividends rather than a salary. They also tend to increase inequality, since rich people are much more likely to have significant capital income, and they are the reason we find ourselves in the ludicrous situation where Warren Buffett pays a lower overall tax rate than his secretary, despite being one of the richest men in the world.[137] Lower tax rates on capital income have often been justified on the grounds that they will promote investment and growth, but the evidence is weak.[138] In light of this, there is growing support among economists for taxing labour income and capital income at a similar, if not the same, rate.*[139]

Increasing taxes on high earners and corporations would go a long way towards funding the predistributive and redistributive pro-grammes that we discussed earlier in the chapter. But if we want to increase the overall level of taxation to 45–50 per cent of national income, then we need to think about taxes beyond the richest 1 per cent or 10 per cent. After all, even in America, where the top 1 per cent have such a large share of pretax income, taxes on them can probably raise about 10 per cent of national income at most; and as

---

* Any serious strategy for increasing taxes on capital income must also include a plan for taxing corporate profits. This would ideally involve international cooperation, and the past few years have seen some prog-ress on this front, with 136 countries representing more than 90 per cent of global GDP agreeing to impose a minimum corporate tax of 15 per cent on the largest companies—though the U.S. now looks unlikely to follow through. But there is plenty that countries can do unilaterally. The UK could, for example, impose a minimum corporate tax of, say, 25 per cent on "domestic" companies. If a British company like BP were to book $1 billion of its profits in a tax haven like Barbados, where the corporation tax rate is just 5 per cent, the UK could levy a 20 per cent tax on those profits to make up the difference. The UK could also tax companies that relocate to tax havens. Suppose, for example, that BP moved its headquar-ters to Barbados, but continued to make 10 per cent of its global sales in the UK. The UK could then decide to levy its own corporate tax rate on 10 per cent of BP's global profits.

a general principle, broad-based taxes levied at a lower rate tend to be better for economic growth.

Some economists, including Saez and Zucman, argue that income taxes should bear most, if not all, of the burden of raising tax revenues, because they can be made "progressive" by design (in the technical sense that the tax rate increases with income). On this view, if we want to increase tax revenues beyond the very rich, then we should simply levy higher income taxes on low- and middle-income earners too. But we should also explore the potential for raising revenue through taxes on consumption. General consumption taxes such as Value Added Tax (VAT) already play an important role in most rich countries—across the OECD as a whole, they account for around 30 per cent of overall tax revenues.[140] Many economists argue that they represent a more "efficient" or growth-friendly way to raise large amounts of revenue.[141] There is also a strong case for consumption taxes that aim to discourage socially harmful activities, such as a carbon tax, which we discussed earlier in the chapter. We don't need to get into the details of whether consumption taxes are more efficient than income taxes here, but with taxes as high as 45–50 per cent, questions about economic efficiency are clearly of first-order importance. While taxes like VAT are less progressive than income taxes, and may even be regressive, in the sense that poor people end up paying a higher proportion of their income, we should always think about the tax system in the round. In the end, what matters isn't whether an individual tax is progressive or regressive, but the combined impact of taxes and spending overall. Thinking about the tax system in the round brings us to a crucial, and often overlooked, source of tax revenues: wealth.

Taxes on Wealth

If we want to realize the ambitious policies we've explored in this chapter, we will need higher taxes on the stock of wealth itself, in addition to those levied on the flow of income that is generated by holding wealth, such as dividends and profits. Whereas taxes on capital income are simply part of a fair and progressive system of income taxation, taxes on wealth would help us to prevent the accumulation of very large fortunes that threaten to undermine the democratic process, and make sure that everyone has a fair share in the benefits that come from holding wealth, through a universal minimum inheritance or a citizens' wealth fund.

There are two main types of taxes on wealth, inheritance taxes and annual wealth taxes, and there is a case for both. Inheritance taxes are levied on transfers of wealth when someone dies. These mostly affect the very rich, and hence would help to reduce inequality: across the OECD, the inheritances and gifts reported by the wealthiest 20 per cent of households are nearly fifty times higher than those reported by the poorest 20 per cent.[142] They also represent a relatively efficient way to raise revenue, in the sense that they appear to have a minimal effect on people's decisions about how much to save or work.[143] Although most advanced economies have some kind of inheritance tax, as with other taxes that mostly affect the rich, these have declined over time, falling from 1.1 per cent of tax revenues among OECD countries in 1970 to 0.4 per cent today.[144]

Our first priority should be to reverse this trend. While inheritance taxes should be levied at a low rate for most people, they should rise sharply for the largest fortunes. Thomas Piketty has proposed a tax which starts at 5 per cent on fortunes worth more than half of average wealth (currently around £150,000 in the UK), rises to 50 per cent for bequests worth five times the average (around £1.5 million) and goes as high as 80 or 90 per cent for billionaires.[145] As well as increasing inheritance-tax rates, we should reform the tax base. In most countries, these taxes are levied on transfers made only after someone dies, while transfers made during someone's lifetime are exempt. This creates obvious opportunities for tax avoidance, especially among the rich, who can afford to "gift" houses and savings to their children while they are still alive. It would be much fairer to levy a tax on lifetime gift receipts, as has been the case in Ireland since 1976: everyone would be entitled to a tax-free allowance of, say, £150,000 per person, but gifts past this level would be taxed, and the tax rate would increase with the total amount received.[146]

Alongside a more progressive inheritance tax, we should introduce an annual wealth tax on the largest fortunes. This would provide a faster way to tackle the extreme concentration of wealth, and to make serious progress towards paying for a minimum inheritance or citizens' wealth fund. At the same time, it would effectively allow us to limit how much wealth any single individual can accumulate during their lifetime. Beyond a certain point, very large concentrations of wealth not only are difficult to justify from the perspective of the difference principle, but pose a direct threat to democratic political equality. Although it's not entirely obvious where we should draw the line, it's hard to see how we could possibly justify the existence of billionaires, let alone the $203 billion accumulated by Elon Musk, co-founder and CEO of Tesla and the world's richest man at the time of writing, or Amazon founder Jeff Bezos's $126 billion.[147] An annual wealth tax should be levied at a rate that effectively makes it impossible for anyone to accumulate so much.

In working out the appropriate tax rate we have to remember that wealth taxes would ideally sit alongside taxes on capital income. Once we take into account their combined effects, even a seemingly low annual wealth tax of 1–2 per cent could see some people paying most if not all of their capital income in taxes.[148] This isn't necessarily a problem—after all, one aim of wealth taxes is to reduce the size of the largest fortunes. But it does mean these taxes should be reserved for the very rich. The scheme proposed by Senator Elizabeth Warren, a prominent candidate for the 2020 Democratic presidential nomination, would be a good start: a 2 per cent annual tax on fortunes worth more than $50 million, increasing to 6 per cent for assets above $1 billion.[149] And there are grounds for going further: we could extend this to include the wealthiest 1 per cent (in America, those with around $4 million or more), and we could impose even higher rates at the very top.[150]

Would these taxes blunt the spirit of innovation and entrepreneurialism that is so important to long-term economic growth? Would they, for example, have deterred Mark Zuckerberg from inventing Facebook? We don't know for sure, but it seems unlikely. Most entrepreneurs are motivated by much more than money, and from the perspective of someone starting a new business, the chances of becoming a multimillionaire are already so small that the prospect of having to pay higher taxes in that scenario is unlikely to be a major consideration. Although hard evidence is limited, the handful of studies which exist do not find evidence of a substantial negative effect.[151] Wealth taxes could even have a positive effect on innovation, by encouraging the super-rich to invest in high-return start-ups rather than spending their money on luxury goods.[152] Critics also worry that wealth taxes could discourage savings, which might reduce business investment. But most studies have found only a small effect, and we can compensate for any decline by using the tax revenue to encourage other forms of saving, such as a citizens' wealth fund.[153]

The success of a wealth tax does, however, depend on minimizing avoidance.[154] Historically, wealth taxes have often been riddled with exemptions, while enforcement has been lax, typically relying on self-reported wealth.[155] As a result, they have raised relatively little revenue, and since the 1990s the number of countries with wealth taxes has fallen from twelve to just three (Switzerland, Norway and Spain). But rather than abandon the idea, we should learn from these experiences. It's clear, for example, that wealth taxes should be applied to all forms of wealth, with few, if any, exemptions; and that enforcement should rely on third-party reporting—in other words, banks and financial institutions should be required to report wealth to the tax authorities. Finally, significant taxes on wealth would make it all the more important to empower tax regulators and crack down on secretive tax havens.

What about the possibility that the rich themselves will move to another country altogether? Despite some high-profile instances, such as Facebook co-founder Eduardo Saverin who gave up his U.S. citizenship in favour of Singapore not long before Facebook's shares went public in 2012, there is little evidence of wealthy people moving country to avoid such taxes.[156] Of course, this could become more common if we significantly increase them, but we can mitigate this by imposing "exit taxes" on very wealthy people. This is already the case in the U.S.A., where any individual worth more than $2 million who renounces their citizenship is assumed to have done so for tax-avoidance reasons and is subject to additional taxes.[157] Others have proposed going further, such as restricting the right to return for tax exiles except in cases of compassionate leave.

Although none of these policies are without their challenges, there is no fundamental economic or practical obstacle to raising the overall level of taxation to 45–50 per cent of national income, nor to significant increases in the top rates of tax on income and wealth—and most people would be materially better off as a result. And yet the ideas we have discussed up to now represent only one half of the economic transformation that we so urgently need. They would do nothing to address the enormously unfair concentration of economic power and control in the hands of shareholders which is such a defining feature of capitalism as we know it. Taking this seriously would lead us to an even more profound change in the structure of our economic system—one that would transform the world of work to the benefit of us all.

8

Workplace Democracy

———•———•———

The idea that companies should be controlled by their owners rather than their employees is so familiar that few of us ever stop to question it. In most countries, the precedence of owners or shareholders over workers—the "shareholder primacy model"—is set down in law.* Under this system, shareholders have the exclusive legal right not only to any profits that the firm might make but to appoint the board of directors, which in turn is ultimately responsible for all the key decisions about how it is run. In larger companies, shareholders typically delegate most of their decision-making powers to a chief executive officer (CEO) and other senior managers. But since managers ultimately report to the board of directors, and directors are appointed by the shareholders, it is shareholders who have the final say.[1] And since business ownership is so heavily concentrated in the hands of the rich, this means that a relatively small class of wealthy individuals (and the financiers who manage their wealth)

---

* I will use the terms "owner" and "shareholder" interchangeably. In publicly traded companies, shares can be bought and sold on a stock exchange. Most companies, however, are "privately held." These can be owned by a founder, who could be the sole shareholder (and may also be a director and manager), or by private investors who have bought shares in the company.

has an enormous amount of control over the organization of economic activity and the nature of work—and hence over how most of us spend a very large part of our lives.

The decisions made by owners often have very real consequences for their employees. It is owners rather than workers who decide whether workplaces are organized in a spirit of collaboration or cut-throat rivalry; whether employees are treated with dignity as human beings, or as a mere "input" whose cost is to be minimized; and whether individual jobs provide opportunities for creativity, variety and autonomy, or are mind-deadeningly dull. On a more practical level, owners determine not just wages but the length of the working day, whether there are opportunities for training and development, and much more. Crucially, they have the power to fire workers, with all the consequences this can have for people's income, sense of purpose and identity. Of course, owners' decisions are constrained by the realities of market competition—workers obviously have to agree to wages and working conditions too—but inasmuch as there is any discretion about these matters, this lies with owners.

The almost total concentration of formal power in the hands of shareholders means that firms are, in the words of the philosopher Elizabeth Anderson, effectively a kind of mini-dictatorship: "The vast majority [of workers] are subject to private, authoritarian government, not through their own choice, but through laws that have handed nearly all authority to their employers."[2] Of course, the analogy isn't perfect. For a start, employment law sets some basic limits on the control that owners have over workers. And even if the formal power structure of the modern firm resembles a dictatorship, this doesn't mean that work is terrible for everyone, or that workers are totally powerless. Many companies are run as more or less benevolent dictatorships and take pride in treating their employees well, whether because they actually care about them or because it's just good business or, often, somewhere between the two. This is especially true of companies that employ highly skilled workers: Google is famous for offering its employees significant autonomy—encouraging them to spend 20 per cent of their time working on "what they think will most benefit Google"—alongside a dizzying array of perks, from free food and "nap pods" to generous health insurance and parental leave.[3] And many businesses choose to involve their employees in decision-making through dedicated forums and committees. It is also easier to quit your job than it is to leave your country permanently; and if owners treat their employees badly, they will struggle not only to motivate their workforce but to find anyone who is willing to work for them at all.

While the analogy between firms and dictatorships may not be perfect, it reminds us that in most countries we have chosen to give a small group of owners an extraordinary amount of power over our working lives—power that they are free to exercise in pursuit of their own interests, and without any meaningful input or accountability from the people most affected by their decisions. Even with trade unions, which historically have provided a vital source of countervailing worker power, owners still hold all the formal levers of control; and in many countries, decades of anti-union legislation have left them in a seriously weakened state. The result is that the workplace, for many people, is a sphere of subservience and powerlessness quite unlike any other domain of life in a modern democratic society. In both Europe and America, fewer than half of employees say they are consulted most or all of the time about important decisions that will affect their work, or even about their own work objectives.[4] Many workers want more influence: in the UK, fewer than half feel satisfied with the amount of involvement they have in decision-making in their company; while a recent survey in America found that, across a whole range of issues from benefits and pay to the impact of new technology, a majority want more influence than they currently have.[5] Unsurprisingly, those with the lowest pay and least skills tend to have the least voice: across Europe, just a third of low-skilled workers say they are involved in decisions that affect their work, compared to four-fifths of managers.[6]

This lack of influence is a problem in its own right, but it is also detrimental to people's wider health and well-being. It's not just that low-paid workers frequently lack fulfilment at work: many live in a state of perpetual insecurity leading to chronic anxiety and stress—even more so with the fracturing of traditional employment relationships and the rise of the gig economy.[7] Others are forced to accept degrading working conditions, like Amazon warehouse staff who are reportedly subject to such gruelling performance requirements that some have ended up peeing in a bottle rather than take a toilet break, or truckers who are routinely subject to twenty-four-hour tracking and surveillance.[8] In some cases, the result is outright abuse: one third of UK employees report being afraid at work; while one in five American workers report recent instances of verbal abuse, humiliation, bullying, unwanted sexual attention, or harassment.[9]

Although the concentration of power within the workplace affects us all, it has been largely absent from mainstream political debate, while serious discussion of more democratic alternatives has been confined mostly to the socialist left.[10] And yet, while they have kept such ideas alive, the association with socialism means proposals for greater democracy at work have often been dismissed as fundamentally illiberal or unworkable. But there is nothing unworkable about workplace democracy, and liberals would do well to heed the concerns of socialists on these issues.

In any case, the matter is becoming harder to ignore. The malaise sweeping across today's liberal democracies is about more than money—it reflects a more profound crisis of dignity and meaning which is closely tied to changes in the nature of work over recent decades, from the decline in industrial jobs and communities to the rise of automation and the gig economy.[11] And further disruption appears to be on the horizon, including the development of increasingly intrusive forms of workplace surveillance and the potential for artificial intelligence to lead to massive automation. While low-paid workers may be the first in line, these changes will affect us all.

In Rawls's difference principle, we have the basis for a nuanced and unmistakably liberal solution to this predicament.[12] As we saw in Chapter 1, instead of calling on us to abolish workplace hierarchies altogether (as some socialists have done), it recognizes that a degree of hierarchy between owners and workers, and between managers and ordinary employees, can be justified—but only if there are compensating benefits for the least well off, say in terms of greater productivity and hence higher incomes. And as we shall see, it demands a much greater role for democracy at work. By "democracy at work" I don't just mean reviving trade unions, valuable though this would be. Nor is this about taking firms into public ownership, which on its own would simply transfer power from private shareholders to the state, and do little to empower most employees. Instead, we must reinvent the internal structure of companies themselves, so that workers have the legal right to participate in decision-making on much more equal terms.

Greater democracy within the workplace would also expand opportunities for meaningful work, which, as Rawls argued, is such a vital source of self-respect. Of course, many people are perfectly happy to work just for money and to find their meaning and satisfaction elsewhere. But, as we have seen, paid work has a special importance, both because we spend so much of our lives doing it, and because it is the most important way most of us make a productive contribution to society. This isn't just armchair philosophy: when people from seventeen advanced economies were asked what gave them a sense of meaning in their lives, "occupation and career" was ranked second, after "family and children," but ahead of a long list of other things, including "physical and mental health," "friends and community" and "spirituality, faith and religion."[13] Other studies show that people's experiences at work really do matter for their overall sense of well-being: according to the distinguished economist and "happiness" expert Richard Layard, "quality of work" is the second most important factor explaining differences in how happy people in the UK feel, after mental illness and ahead of both income and physical health.[14] While many people already find meaning from their work, these opportunities tend to be concentrated among the well-educated and highly paid.[15] A recent European survey found that the least skilled jobs had the "lowest levels of creativity . . . and task variety," and that almost half of workers were stuck in monotonous or repetitive jobs.[16]

Many people instinctively agree that the availability of meaningful work is something we should care about as a society, but it's not immediately clear what, if anything, we—or, more specifically, our governments—can do about it. While politicians and commentators say they want to increase the availability of "good jobs," serious practical measures are few and far between: all too often, their solutions amount to little more than appealing to the good conscience and enlightened self-interest of employers. But we cannot simply impose meaningful work from the top down either. After all, what makes work meaningful will differ from one person to the next—some look for variety, while others want to develop deep expertise—and people also differ in terms of the priority they attach to meaningfulness compared to, say, a higher salary. In any case, the practical details of reconfiguring jobs to make them more fulfilling will inevitably be specific to individual companies, and it is neither desirable nor feasible for the state to micromanage in this way—no one seriously wants a Department for Meaningful Work telling employers how to make jobs more varied or creative.[17]

Although we cannot create meaningful work by government diktat, we can achieve this by empowering employees to shape their workplaces so that they better reflect their priorities. To do so, we need to combine the power of "exit" with the power of "voice."[18] We can think of the proposal for a universal basic income in the previous chapter as giving workers a meaningful "exit" option—when even the lowest-paid can make a credible threat to quit, employers are more likely to take their concerns seriously. But it would be a mistake to rely on "exit" alone, and in this chapter we will look at how we can strengthen workers' "voice," enabling them to change companies from within. In fact, "voice" may be too weak a term—it suggests that workers will have to rely on persuasion, when we must go further and give them formal rights to influence the decisions that affect them at work.

For Rawls, changing the nature of work was crucial for bringing about a more just society. In a society organized on the basis of his principles, he argued, "no one need be servilely dependent on others and made to choose between monotonous and routine occupations which are deadening to human thought and sensibility. Each can be offered a variety of tasks so that the different elements of his nature find a suitable expression."[19] And yet he said almost nothing about what this would look like in practice, making just a few passing comments about the possibilities of worker cooperatives, meaning this aspect of his theory has often been overlooked.[20] Over the course of this final chapter, we will see how living up to this ideal would revolutionize the world of work.

EMPLOYMENT RIGHTS

If we really want to change work for the better, then new forms of workplace democracy must be underpinned by laws that guarantee a minimum level of safety, decency and dignity for all. In the same way that the constitution establishes certain basic rights like freedom of speech which place limits on the democratic process, employment law should define certain rights that all workplaces—even democratic ones—have to respect. There is no need for workers to negotiate these minimum standards in every company, and a baseline that all firms have to respect can help to prevent a race to the bottom.[21]

At the very least, we should put in place health and safety regulations that protect workers from avoidable risks at work, as well as rights to paid breaks during working hours. All employees should also benefit from the protections against harassment and discrimination that we discussed in Chapter 6. More broadly, employment law should limit the power that employers and managers have over individual employees to situations where this serves a legitimate business purpose. In America, employers often have wide leeway to fire workers for things they say or do outside work—including political activities, their choice of sexual partner, smoking, the use of alcohol, and taking recreational drugs—and in many countries there is an ongoing debate about whether employers should be able to sack workers for things they post on social media.[22] As a general rule, these kinds of powers should be limited to those rare situations where workers' actions outside work seriously affect their company's reputation—something that will generally only apply to the most senior figures; or where they blatantly reject the basic civic equality of their colleagues and fellow citizens, say by posting neo-Nazi materials. There should also be a general presumption against noncompete clauses which prevent workers from moving to, or starting, a competing business within a certain period after leaving a job. And we urgently need a legal framework to regulate the rapid growth of workplace surveillance: at the very least, employers should be required by law to notify and consult workers before introducing new forms of surveillance, which should, of course, be limited to working hours.[23]

Employment law has a vital role to play in protecting people's rights to leisure and a decent life outside work. These should include minimum entitlements to paid holiday and sick pay; reasonable regulations of the length of the working day, overtime and anti-social hours; and rights to flexible working and parental leave (which, as we saw in Chapter 6, have a vital role to play in advancing equality of opportunity by making sure that *all* parents, and not just the rich, can spend time with their children). These kinds of protections are commonplace in most advanced democracies, with the exception of America, where most workers have no legal entitlement to paid holidays, parental leave or flexible working.[24]

One of the most important and difficult questions for employment law to answer is how easy it should be to dismiss workers. Different countries have adopted very different approaches, ranging from the American "at-will" model, where employers can terminate an employee for almost any reason and without warning, to the French model, where they have to justify dismissals according to specific criteria and are often required to make significant severance payments. We should take very seriously the importance that most people, and especially those on low incomes, place on job security. Workers across the OECD are three times more likely to say that job security is "very important" compared to high wages or promotion opportunities.[25] Moreover, we know that insecurity at work can contribute to anxiety and depression, with knock-on effects for productivity.[26] And, of course, job security is about more than having a stable income—the sense of community and identity that many people find at work is typically tied to a particular workplace and the skills and relationships they develop within it. As a result, even with generous unemployment benefits or a universal basic income, we would still want to maintain a degree of job security. But we also have to recognize the importance of flexibility for economic dynamism and productivity: we can all gain from living in a society where employers are able to change their workforce to suit their needs, and where successful companies can grow and failing ones can shrink. The best solution is probably a version of the "flexicurity" model, most closely associated with Denmark. In other words, it should be reasonably easy to dismiss workers (though stopping well short of the American model) but those who lose their jobs would be entitled to generous income support and opportunities for retraining.

CO-MANAGEMENT

With basic employment rights in place, we can start to think about how to bring greater democracy to the workplace. The concentration of power in the hands of owners is often accepted without question, as if it simply follows from the definition of ownership. After all, in everyday usage, to say that someone "owns" something implies that they have a more or less exclusive right to decide what to do with it. So, for example, to say that "I own my car" means that I am free to decide what to do with my car without consulting anyone else—I can drive it to Scotland, paint it pink, rent it out, or indeed sell it to someone else who would then become the owner of the car with all of the rights that I currently have. Of course, the law always sets some limits on what we can do with our property—I cannot drive my car on the wrong side of the road, or into another person. But within these limits, the ordinary idea of ownership implies that owners can do more or less what they like with their property, while other people have no such rights—my neighbour cannot decide to paint my car a different colour, no matter how much they might dislike pink.

Proponents of the shareholder primacy model sometimes appeal to these common-sense ideas of ownership to support their position. They argue that just as car owners are entitled to decide what to do with their cars, shareholders, as "owners" of a company, should have the exclusive right to decide how it is run. On this view, it would be wrong to give workers a say, as this would violate the rights of shareholders as owners. But a moment's thought reveals that ownership is a more complex concept. For a start, the common-sense view implies that ownership is a more or less binary phenomenon—you either own something, or you don't. But it makes more sense to think of ownership as something that comes in degrees and entails a bundle of different legal rights, which differ depending on the nature of the item in question. In the case of most "personal property," including cars, but also clothing, food, housing and so on, this bundle is typically very extensive—we really do have almost exclusive rights of control, and there are good reasons for this.[27] But owning shares in a firm is quite different. Even in countries that follow the shareholder primacy model, the rights that shareholders have are much more limited than the ones we generally have over our personal property: shareholders of Ford cannot simply turn up and demand entry to a Ford factory whenever they like, nor can they help themselves to a car and drive it to Scotland.

In thinking about the rights of workers versus owners, it's helpful to distinguish two distinct aspects of ownership. The first are income rights, or "beneficial ownership." The beneficial owners of a business have a right to any residual income or profits once it has met its commitments to workers, suppliers and so on. The second are control rights, or the right to decide how a company is run. The distinctive feature of the shareholder primacy model is that it combines both income and control rights in the hands of investors. There are some good reasons why we might want to do this: since shareholders are entitled to the firm's profits (and liable for its losses) they have strong incentives to use their control rights in a way that will maximize profitability; and, as we saw in the previous chapter, the pursuit of profit is a key aspect of what makes markets work well.[28] Moreover, if shareholders were deprived of all control, they probably wouldn't be willing to invest in the first place. But, at least in principle, these different aspects of ownership—income and control rights—can be separated. In fact, we have already encountered an example of this in the discussion of the citizens' wealth fund, where the state would become a beneficial owner by buying shares in many firms, but without having, or at least without exercising, control rights over them.

The purpose of this discussion is not to make the obvious point that owning a car is different to owning shares in a company, but to highlight that what it means to own something is not as simple as it might seem, and that the rights we have as owners—whether of a car or a firm—are social choices. It makes little sense to defend the shareholder model by simply asserting that shareholders "own" firms, since this simply begs the question of what rights the owners of a firm should have in the first place. In the end, it is up to us as a society to decide how to distribute income and control rights between workers and shareholders, and the difference principle is there to guide us in these matters. From this perspective, the appropriate balance ultimately depends on what would best promote the long-term interests of the least well off, not just in terms of income and wealth, but in terms of access to positions of authority and opportunities for meaningful work.

Once we think about things in this way, there is a strong case for bringing about a much more equal distribution of power between workers and owners. The most promising model for achieving this is known as "co-management," which, as the name suggests, involves owners and workers sharing certain control rights within a given company.* Adopting this model in its fullest form would transform the balance of power within the workplace and give all citizens a meaningful say over their working lives.

Co-management first originated in the aftermath of the First World War in Germany, which continues to have the most established and extensive system of power sharing between owners and workers.[29] Indeed, the term "co-management" comes from the German word *Mitbestimmung*, often translated as "codetermination." In the second half of the twentieth century, a number of other countries—most notably Austria and the Nordic states of Sweden, Denmark, Norway and Finland—followed suit, and today most European countries have some form of co-management, albeit typically less extensive than in Germany.[30]

There are two key aspects of the European model of co-management. First, it gives workers the right to elect a certain share of seats on the board of directors, which as we have seen is responsible for setting a company's overarching vision and strategy—what to produce and where, how much to invest in new machinery, whether to pursue mergers and acquisitions, and so on—and which appoints the CEO and other executives who are responsible for implementing this strategy.[31] In doing so, co-management breaks the exclusive grip that shareholders have over firms, and creates a mechanism through which employees can shape decisions at a strategic level.

In Germany, employees have the right to elect one third of the board in all businesses with more than 500 employees, and half the board in those with more than 2,000.[32] In total, fifteen European countries—more than half of the twenty-seven EU states, plus

---

* We will focus on how this would work within the private sector, but a similar model should also be extended to public-sector organizations, where workers would share control rights with their employer, namely the state.

Norway—grant workers widespread rights to elect board-level representatives in both the private and public sector, while a further four grant employees more limited rights, mainly in state-owned companies. The extent of workers' representation varies: the most common arrangement is for staff to have one third of the seats on the board, though in France just one or two seats are reserved for them, while Germany is the only country where some firms are required to give employees equal representation alongside shareholders.[33] In most countries, rights to board-level representation are restricted to companies over a certain size, with the threshold varying from as few as twenty-five employees in Sweden to 1,000 in France.[34]

Alongside putting workers on boards—which are focused on strategic questions and can feel rather remote—we need to ensure that employees can shape their workplaces on a more day-to-day level. This brings us to the second feature of the European co-management model and what are typically referred to as "works councils." Under the shareholder primacy model, companies often establish employee forums and committees, but this is usually at the discretion of employers, who can choose to ignore them. And while workers can try to increase their influence by joining trade unions, in most countries coverage is patchy, and unions have limited rights. By contrast, with works councils we could immediately establish a body in every workplace with a legal mandate to represent employees' interests in discussions and negotiations with their management. What's more, while unions are accountable only to their members, works councils could be democratically accountable to the entire workforce, giving every worker an equal right to elect their representatives and hence to shape company policy.*

Unlike voluntary employee forums, works councils would have explicit rights and powers set down in law. In Germany, where works

---

* Even with works councils in place, trade unions would still have an important role to play, both in supporting councils within individual firms, and in negotiating wage agreements. Indeed, as we shall see below, co-management appears to work best when unions take the lead in negotiating industry-wide wage agreements, while works councils focus on other aspects of working conditions, as is the case in Germany.

councils have the most far-reaching powers, employers have to share a whole range of information about the economic and financial situation of the company, from profitability and plans for investment to proposed mergers.[35] When it comes to the composition of the workforce and the design of individual jobs, employers have to consult works councils, but can ultimately reject their suggestions. The most extensive rights are reserved for decisions relating to working conditions, including issues ranging from pay structures and the use of bonuses, working hours, holiday arrangements, and workplace facilities like canteens. In these cases, works councils often have full co-management rights, meaning owners cannot act without their approval. In situations that involve major changes to the workforce, like a plant closure, works councils have the right to draw up a "social plan" to compensate employees, including through redundancy payments. If a works council and employer cannot reach agreement on an issue where they share co-management rights, the matter is decided by a conciliation committee with a neutral chair and the power to enforce a binding decision on both sides.

A lot has now been written on how co-management works in practice, and, as you would expect, co-managed companies generally have better working conditions.[36] Perhaps the most consistent finding is that they tend to offer greater job security: during the 2008–9 recession, for example, co-managed businesses were less likely to fire workers, and more likely to find other ways to get through, such as reducing wages or working hours. Co-management is also associated with more family-friendly policies, such as flexible working, parental leave and childcare provision. Recent studies have found that workers in co-managed firms in Finland have better overall job quality, taking into account factors such as job interest, stress levels and whether individuals felt supported by managers, while in Germany businesses with workers on their board were less likely to outsource labour and more likely to increase skill levels over time than those without.[37] While co-management appears to have either no effect or a small positive impact on average wages, it tends to reduce inequality within companies, mostly by increasing the wages of the lowest-paid.[38]

From the perspective of the difference principle, the main concern with co-management—at least in theory—is that it might reduce productivity and growth, and hence lead to lower living standards over time. There are undoubtedly some direct costs associated with co-management, such as paying worker representatives for their time; and there is a risk that having to seek workers' approval will make it harder for companies to reach quick decisions about, say, whether to expand into a new market or how to respond in a crisis. More importantly, detractors worry that if workers push for higher wages, expensive benefits or laid-back working conditions, then profits will decline and investment will fall, leading to a long-term reduction in productivity which ultimately makes everyone worse off.[39]

In practice, however, these fears have failed to materialize. What stands out from the academic literature on co-management is that the overall impact on company performance—whether that be investment, productivity, profits or longevity—appears to be small, and is as likely to be positive as negative.[40] The most rigorous studies tend to be more upbeat: a recent examination of workers on boards in Germany found that this led to *more* investment and higher productivity, without harming revenue or profitability.[41] This encouraging picture is reinforced by surveys which show that most company directors and managers in co-managed firms are positive about their experiences.[42] To understand these findings, we need to appreciate the potential benefits of co-management for companies. Sharing information and power can foster greater trust and collaboration between employers and workers, and in doing so can improve productivity to the advantage of both.[43] If an employer controls what information to share, then their workers might not believe them when, for example, they claim that cuts are necessary in order for the company to survive—even if this is true. By contrast, if an employer has a legal duty to share information with workers, then it's more likely that both sides will work together to find a way through a genuine crisis. Similarly, workers are more likely to share ideas about how to make their workplace more productive, or to engage in company-specific training, such as mastering a new piece of machinery or custom software, if they are confident that they will benefit from any increase in profits. The evidence suggests these productivity benefits are very real, and more than compensate for any costs.

While the advantages of co-management have often been

under-appreciated, the advantages of the shareholder model have been seriously exaggerated. The primary justification for the latter is that shareholders will maximize the long-term profitability of their companies, which in turn will promote productivity and economic growth. But there is an emerging consensus among economists and business leaders that shareholder primacy, at least in its current form, may actually be having the opposite effect.[44] In reality, shareholders often know very little about the businesses they own shares in, and have a worrying tendency to prioritize short-term profits over long-term success—preferring, for example, to pay themselves large dividends rather than invest in new products and technologies. In a context where the average holding period of shares on the New York Stock Exchange is just five and a half months, workers may have more of a stake in the lasting success of a given company than its owners.[45]

In light of this evidence, the argument for replacing the shareholder model with some form of co-management is pretty decisive, at least from the perspective of the difference principle—after all, co-management, at least in its current form, increases worker power without any significant cost in terms of productivity and growth. In fact, we should look to go further and adopt a maximal model of co-management, with a general presumption that owners will share power with workers on equal, or nearly equal, terms.[46] In practice, this would mean giving workers half the seats on the board in most if not all companies.* After all, if workers have a minority of seats on the board—as is currently the situation everywhere except the largest German companies—then shareholders can always outvote them.[47] It would also mean empowering works councils with meaningful decision-making powers, at least when it comes to working conditions, rather than merely having the right to be informed or consulted, as is so often the case.[48]

We could also explore variations of this model. So, for example,

---

* We might want to exempt the smallest or newest businesses from the full requirements of equal co-management, so as not to deter entrepreneurship, and to ensure that fledgling companies can act quickly and nimbly—a topic we will come back to in the discussion of worker cooperatives below.

rather than asking workers and shareholders to elect separate representatives, they could jointly elect a single set of board members in a "mixed assembly" where workers and shareholders each have 50 per cent of the votes.[49] Since workers and shareholders would choose from the same list of candidates, potential directors would have an incentive to appeal to both sides, helping to foster a more collaborative approach. Another model, put forward by the political scientist and sociologist Isabelle Ferreras, proposes a dual or "bicameral" board structure, with one board comprising worker representatives and one comprising shareholder representatives, and major corporate decisions would have to be agreed to by both.[50]

Whatever the details, for co-management to work well, a few safeguards would need to be in place. Since the primary aim is to democratize the workplace, worker representatives on boards and in works councils should be elected on a "one worker, one vote" basis. They should also be paid for their time, and have legal protections from dismissal so that they can do their job without fear of retaliation. We also have to think about the wider context. For example, the success of co-management in Europe appears to rest, at least in part, on the fact that wage bargaining mostly takes place at the sector or industry level, rather than within individual firms.[51] Taking the question of wages off the table in this way appears to encourage boards and works councils to focus on areas of mutual advantage. This not only reinforces the case for sector-based wage bargaining, which we explored in the previous chapter, but is a helpful reminder that we always need to think about how policies and institutions interact with one another.

Embracing such a thoroughgoing form of co-management would, to some extent, be a step into the unknown. Even in Germany, this would see rights that are currently reserved for the largest firms extended to most of the workforce. For countries like the UK and U.S.A., it would be nothing short of an economic revolution.[52] As with any change of this scale, the full consequences—both positive and negative—are hard to predict.[53] Given this uncertainty, it would make sense to introduce these policies gradually, perhaps extending the fullest powers to workers in the largest companies first, or to those in certain industries.

Employee Share Ownership and Profit Sharing

Even though there is little evidence that co-management undermines productivity or economic growth, if we are looking to implement a maximal version then we need to take the possibility seriously. One way to ameliorate the chances of this happening would be to ensure that employees directly benefit from their company's profits. This would give workers a financial incentive to apply themselves and share new ideas with management; and by bringing about a closer alignment between the interests of workers and owners, it could help to foster the collaborative relationships that are so vital to the success of co-management.

There are two models we can build on here. The first is to encourage employees to own shares in their company, so that they benefit from its success through dividends and rising share values. In America, for example, a growing number of companies have adopted an Employee Share Ownership Plan, or ESOP, where employees are granted shares in the company—which are held in a trust managed on behalf of employees as a whole—usually in return for tax breaks.[54] Partly as a result, America now has one of the highest rates of employee share ownership of any country in the world, with about 20 per cent of private-sector employees owning some form of company stock, compared to fewer than 5 per cent in Europe.[55]

The second model is to encourage formal "profit sharing" agreements, where owners agree to pay a fraction of their profits to their employees, usually according to a pre-specified formula. This plays a particularly prominent role in France where, since 1967, companies with more than fifty employees have been required by law to implement such a scheme. Profit-related bonuses kick in only when annual profits exceed 5 per cent of a company's equity, and companies have some discretion about whether these are paid equally to all employees, or in proportion to salary. In 2018, 9 million French employees—representing 50.9 per cent of private-sector workers—had access to some kind of profit sharing scheme, and companies paid out a total of €19.4 billion, equivalent to 3.4 per cent of total private-sector wages.[56]

There is now a large body of evidence showing that these collective forms of "financial participation" or "shared capitalism" tend to benefit both workers and owners. From the perspective of workers, these schemes are associated with increased job security, higher job satisfaction and well-being, more investment in training and generally more positive attitudes towards their companies. They also seem to increase workers' total income, with extra payments being made on top of (rather than instead of) ordinary wages.[57] These schemes also appear to improve—or at least not reduce—productivity. A review of more than 100 studies, covering fourteen countries and almost 60,000 different firms, found that employee ownership was associated with a small but statistically significant positive impact on company performance; while a similar synthesis of studies found that companies with a profit sharing scheme in place had higher productivity on average.[58] Part of the explanation for this is that workplaces which adopt these schemes appear to develop a culture that encourages higher levels of effort and commitment, and where slacking off is generally frowned upon.[59]

Employee share ownership and profit sharing work best in companies that involve their workers in decisions, and which prioritize things like training and job security.[60] As such, we should think about co-management and financial participation as part of a mutually reinforcing whole. In most countries, the latter are voluntary and encouraged via public subsidies and tax breaks, some of which can be very substantial—in America, tax subsidies can cover 30–40 per cent of the total cost of transferring shares into an Employee Share Ownership Plan.[61] But if we move towards a system of extensive co-management, we should consider a mandatory model, like the one in France, where firms would be required to put in place some kind of profit sharing or share ownership scheme, with the details subject to mutual agreement between workers and owners.

WORKER COOPERATIVES

There is plenty of scope to empower workers even within conventional "capitalist" or shareholder-owned firms. But why not replace shareholders with workers altogether?[62] This is the idea behind the worker cooperative. From the perspective of the difference principle, worker cooperatives have an obvious appeal since formal power and control are shared equally on a "one worker, one vote" basis.[63] In small cooperatives, members might come together to make decisions in person—a kind of direct workplace democracy; in larger cooperatives, it is usually necessary to elect representatives to a board that exercises control on behalf of employees (much as shareholders elect directors in a conventional company). In both cases, it is up to the workers as a whole to agree on the overarching strategy of their company as well as how to put this into practice.

Whereas shareholders tend to focus narrowly on profits, only taking issues of job quality into account as far as they help support the bottom line, worker cooperatives usually adopt a broader perspective. When asked to define success, respondents to a survey of cooperatives in Canada mentioned not just decent wages and profitability but also meaningful work, personal development and creating products that served some kind of social purpose.[64] Some cooperatives organize work in radically different ways compared to conventional firms, like the British whole-foods cooperative Suma, whose 200 employees are each paid the same wage and do a range of different jobs every week, from truck driving or cooking to accounts.[65] Other cooperatives, and especially larger ones, look more familiar, with hierarchical pay and management structures and significant specialization at the individual job level. What matters is that workers decide how things are done. Either way, worker cooperatives consistently offer greater job security, and wages tend to be more equal, while employee ownership more broadly is associated with more autonomy, better training, a stronger sense of loyalty and pride, increased job satisfaction and lower staff turnover.[66]

From a purely economic perspective, worker cooperatives have some important advantages compared to co-management. The most important is that they combine both income and control rights in the hands of workers, much as conventional firms combine them in the hands of shareholders. As a result, the risk with co-managed firms that workers will prioritize higher wages and benefits without considering the long-term implications for the business largely disappears. Although workers in a cooperative can decide to improve their conditions, they also have to shoulder the costs of doing so. At the same time, cooperatives can realize the advantages that come from co-management and profit sharing to an even greater degree, since their workers have even stronger incentives to work hard, share information and invest in company-specific skills.

Of course, cooperatives aren't perfect, and sceptics often highlight a number of potential issues. As with co-management, they worry that cooperatives will be weighed down by endless meetings and cumbersome decision-making. Other concerns are more specific to the cooperative model. A central worry is that cooperatives will be less willing to make long-term investments, such as opening a new plant, since workers often don't expect to be around long enough to reap any benefits (though, as we have seen, shareholders are often guilty of short-termism too). Similarly, big investments are often risky—new products might not catch on; new machinery might not be as good as expected—and workers are likely to be more wary of these kinds of risks than wealthy investors, who can spread their money over a range of investments. Finally, there is a danger that the current members of successful cooperatives will be tempted to start hiring new workers on standard employment contracts, rather than as full members with rights to a share of profits, in order to keep the extra income for themselves—to the extent that these companies stop being cooperatives in any meaningful sense (this is known as "degeneration").

Fortunately, few of these fears are borne out in reality. Most studies find that cooperatives perform well compared to conventional firms.[67] There is no evidence that they are systematically less productive—in fact, in industries where both types of company exist, cooperatives tend to be more productive and survive longer than their conventional capitalist counterparts. Neither do cooperatives appear to take a short-term perspective on investment decisions. And while some cooperatives have "degenerated" by hiring non-members, or have even sold out to private investors, this is rare, and in most cases cooperatives are governed by rules that prevent this from happening.

The potential of the cooperative sector is perhaps best illustrated by the enormous success of the Mondragon group of cooperatives in the Basque region of Spain and the Lega cooperative federation in the Emilia-Romagna region of Italy. The Mondragon group, founded in 1854, is probably the most famous cooperative collective in the world. It currently consists of ninety-five separate cooperatives employing around 80,000 people, including a highly successful cooperative bank, a large network of food and retail stores, a university, and companies making all manner of consumer and industrial products, from outdoor clothing to electrical conductors.[68] The Lega federation was founded in 1886 and operates as a loose umbrella organization for a number of cooperative associations. Much like Mondragon, the Lega has firms operating across an impressively wide range of sectors, from agriculture and wine-making to housing and social services, and today around 6 per cent of the workforce in Emilia-Romagna are members of worker cooperatives.[69] Although far from typical, these two organizations are proof that cooperatives can flourish on a large scale and in a variety of industries.

But if cooperatives are so good, why are they so rare?[70] Although data is hard to come by, they account for a tiny fraction of employment in most countries. In the UK, there were an estimated 500 worker cooperatives in 2012, employing around 80,000 people, or 0.3 per cent of total employment (much of which is accounted for by the John Lewis Partnership, which, strictly speaking, is not a cooperative because workers do not exercise full control over management).[71] In the U.S.A., there are just 300–400 fully democratic workplaces employing around 7,000 people.[72] A number of European countries, however, have larger cooperative sectors: there are roughly 2,600 worker cooperatives in France, 17,000 in Spain and 25,000 in Italy. But even in Italy they probably represent less than 1 per cent of all companies.[73]

Critics argue that the small number of cooperatives is evidence either that workers don't want to work in them or that their apparent productivity advantages are peculiar to small firms or specific industries. But a careful inspection of the evidence points to a different explanation. According to the economist Gregory Dow—perhaps the world's foremost authority on the economics of cooperatives— the rarity of cooperatives is rooted in the challenges they face in getting started in the first place. A study looking at the creation of new companies in France found that, between 1979 and 2002, on average just 167 new cooperatives were created annually, compared to more than 250,000 conventional firms.[74]

The first and most obvious obstacle is raising money for investment.[75] Starting a new company is expensive: even such a relatively small-scale and low-capital enterprise such as a shop requires considerable money up front—to rent a space, to buy computers and build up a stock of products, and of course to hire other people, all while establishing a reputation and a customer base. The investment required would obviously be even higher for workers who wanted to start a company in a capital-intensive sector such as manufacturing wind turbines. Workers rarely have enough money to finance a new business themselves, but cooperatives often find it especially difficult to secure external funding. An entrepreneur who wants to start a conventional capitalist firm can raise money by issuing shares to investors, but this option isn't open to cooperatives, since investors are typically willing to buy shares only if they come with voting rights; and cooperatives, by definition, only give voting rights to employees. This leaves the option of borrowing from, say, a bank. But cooperatives often struggle to borrow money too. In part, this reflects a lack of familiarity among banks and other lenders about how cooperatives work. But there is also a deeper problem: lenders usually want some kind of deposit or collateral as security in case of default, especially with risky investments like a new company; while workers who want to start a cooperative rarely have this kind of collateral available. Workers who want to organize a buyout of their employer and convert it into a cooperative face similar difficulties in securing the necessary funds.

A second challenge is that most entrepreneurs want to create conventional firms rather than cooperatives. The prospect of being in control of one's own business is one of the reasons why many people want to start a company in the first place. And for new companies in particular, concentrating control in the hands of a single owner makes it easier to define a clear vision and to be nimble and decisive in the crucial start-up phase of creating a new business. Entrepreneurs also have strong financial incentives to opt for a conventional structure where they own all or most of the shares, since they can cash these shares in if the firm does well. By contrast, in a cooperative, entrepreneurs would have to hire new workers as partners with a share of both income and control rights from the start.

Finally, entrepreneurs who do want to start a cooperative, or workers who want to convert an existing firm into a cooperative, have to overcome coordination problems not faced by conventional companies. If you want to set up a conventional business, you have to find the right investors and employees—in themselves not easy tasks. But if you want to establish a new cooperative, you need to find a group of like-minded people who not only have the right skills but also share a particular vision for the company, are able to work together, and have enough money to get the venture off the ground—a much more complicated endeavour. A related set of difficulties faces those wanting to organize a worker buyout. This usually relies on a small number of committed individuals who are willing to take the lead. But even where every employee would benefit from converting a conventional company into a cooperative, and even if financing is available, it might not happen because no one is willing to take on the rather thankless task (at least financially) of organizing a worker buyout.

Expanding the Cooperative Sector

The challenges that cooperatives face in getting started are not simply the result of inertia or a lack of familiarity with the cooperative model—they reflect some inherent challenges faced by worker-owned businesses.[76] As a result, they do not represent a viable wholesale alternative to the conventional shareholder-owned firm, despite their many advantages. But this doesn't mean we should settle for the marginal role that cooperatives currently play. Encouraging the cooperative sector is an important part of giving workers a real choice over the kind of company they work for, and we should aim for an economy in which everyone has a reasonable opportunity to work in a truly democratic workplace.

Fortunately, with the right set of policies in place, we can expect cooperatives to flourish.[77] The first step is to create a supportive legal framework, learning from countries such as Italy and Spain. Cooperatives should be required by law to reinvest a minimum share of their profits: in Italy, where this is the case, there is no evidence of underinvestment—indeed, cooperatives often reinvest significantly more than the required minimum.[78] The law should also set an upper limit on the proportion of non-members in the workforce in order to prevent the most profitable cooperatives from "degenerating" into conventional firms, as well as stopping them from selling out to private investors.

These reforms would help already existing cooperatives to survive, but the real key to expanding the cooperative sector is to encourage the creation of new cooperatives. The most important thing we can do here is make it easier to raise external investment. The Mondragon group and the Lega federation can show us the way here. At the heart of their success has been the development of financial institutions dedicated to lending to cooperatives: the Mondragon corporation established its own cooperative bank, which is now the third-largest credit union in Spain; while the Lega federation developed a specialized financial consortium for funding cooperative investments. In both cases, one of the most important sources of capital has been requiring member cooperatives to deposit a share of their profits and reserves in a fund used to lend to other cooperatives. There is much to be said for this model, but on its own it would severely limit the overall availability of finance, and hence the rate at which the cooperative sector could grow. We should go further and establish a cooperative investment bank, funded through a mix of private and public capital (a citizens' wealth fund would be an ideal source of the latter). This bank should also take a more proactive approach than a traditional one, like the Mondragon group's bank, which tightly monitors the performance of individual cooperatives, and even has the power to replace their management or impose a recovery plan when difficulties emerge.[79]

Alongside a cooperative bank, we should create a network of cooperative federations with a remit to provide a range of other services, including legal support, accounting, human relations and management consulting. This has been integral to the success of the Mondragon and Lega federations, so much so that one study concluded that "if one factor can be singled out as responsible for the success of the Mondragon cooperatives, it is that even the smallest of them is both assisted and disciplined by a battery of management services on a scale appropriate to a company as big as the whole group."[80] Federations could adopt different models—some could operate under strong central control, as is the case with Mondragon, whereas others could follow the Lega's looser, more decentralized set-up—and each could be endowed with enough seed funding to make a meaningful impact on the overall size of the sector.[81]

Even with these reforms in place, it seems likely that most new firms would continue to be run and owned by an entrepreneur backed by shareholders and other external investors. This isn't necessarily a problem: we all benefit from entrepreneurial innovation and dynamism, and we should be careful not to put too many obstacles in the way of people wanting to start new companies. But although the conventional corporate model has particular advantages in the early stages of a firm's life, these are less obvious for established businesses where, as we have seen, cooperatives tend to perform as well as their traditional counterparts. If we want to significantly expand the cooperative sector, we should also make it much easier for workers to convert shareholder-owned firms into worker-owned ones.

The key to making this happen is to give workers the legal right to initiate employee buyouts. A limited version of this already exists in Italy under the Marcora Law, introduced in 1985, which gives workers the option to buy their firm if it is threatened with closure and allows them to claim a lump sum worth up to three years of future unemployment benefit to help finance the acquisition. But there is no need to restrict this to failing businesses. Instead, we should give employees the right to initiate a takeover at any time, such that if enough of them (say 10 per cent) are in favour, this would trigger a binding referendum on the issue.[82] Given the advantages of the conventional model for new businesses, it would make sense to limit this right to companies over a certain size in terms of employment or revenue.

This right will make a meaningful difference, though, only if we combine it with a practical mechanism for financing buyouts.[83] As a general rule, existing owners should be paid the market value of their shares, or close to it—this is crucial for maintaining the financial incentive for entrepreneurs to set up new businesses.[84] Moreover, since most of the benefits of working in a cooperative are enjoyed by its employees, they should cover most of the overall cost. This would also help to ensure that firms are converted into cooperatives only if the current employees genuinely believe there will be some overall advantage to them. Owners would be able to make counter-offers, such as raising wages, improving conditions or instituting other forms of workplace democracy, and so the threat of being converted into a cooperative would itself raise workers' bargaining power. In general, workers won't have enough money to buy the firm outright, and would need to purchase it gradually through a combination of loans and wage deductions at a rate agreed with the workforce. There is also a strong argument for a degree of public subsidy, say in the form of cheap loans, to reflect the wider benefits to workers from having a meaningful option to work in a democratic workplace. As we have seen, the tax subsidies for owners who transfer their shares to an Employee Share Ownership Plan in America can amount to 30–40 per cent of the cost. A similar level of subsidy might easily be justified for worker-led transitions to cooperatives.

The combined impact of these measures could, over time, substantially increase the size of the cooperative sector. Together with the proposals for co-management, they would revolutionize the world of work, with far-reaching benefits for us all. In doing so, they would address our persistent failure as a society to take responsibility for the structures that govern our working lives—a failure that has contributed to the profound crisis facing rich liberal democracies today. We *can* change these structures, and we have a vital interest in doing so. With these reforms in place, we can ensure that everyone is treated with the dignity and respect they deserve, and that each of us has the chance to find a sense of meaning, community and personal accomplishment through our work. By recognizing the essential importance of work, these ideas not only fill a gap in liberal economic thinking, they open up an exciting new frontier on the journey towards a truly fair society.

Conclusion

·————————·

> A map of the world that does not include Utopia is not
> worth even glancing at, for it leaves out the one country at
> which Humanity is always landing. And when Humanity
> lands there, it looks out, and, seeing a better country, sets
> sail. Progress is the realisation of Utopias.
>
> Oscar Wilde, "The Soul of Man under Socialism"[1]

Throughout history, utopian dreams of a better society have been
a vital force for progress. Many of the things we take for granted
today—freedom from slavery, universal suffrage, the existence of
the welfare state—were once nothing more than figments of the
imagination of idealistic social reformers. While we cannot change
the world with dreams alone, moral ideas about justice, freedom and
equality, backed up by practical ideas about how we can change our
institutions, can and have been a source of inspiration, guidance and
courage, helping to bring people together to change their societies
for the better.

As the democratic world stands at a crossroads, we need such
ideas today more than ever. And yet, in a moment that calls for creativity and boldness, all too often we find timidity or, worse, scepticism and cynicism—a sense that democratic politics is hopelessly
corrupt and that capitalism is beyond reform. The result has been a
surge of support for illiberal and authoritarian populists, creating a
palpable sense of uncertainty about the future of liberal democracy
itself.

There is, then, an urgent need for a compelling vision that can
renew faith in liberal and democratic ideals and galvanize people
to build a better society. Rawls's ideas represent an unparalleled
resource for taking up this challenge—an astonishingly coherent

and constructive body of work which has already transformed philosophy, and which can reinvent progressive politics for the twenty-first century.

Over the course of this book, we have seen how these ideas can deliver both a searching critique of our existing institutions and—most importantly—an inspiring account of how we can do better. We have seen how Rawls's basic liberties principle, and his commitment to a distinctively "political" liberalism, can help us to protect our basic freedoms while navigating the so-called "culture wars"—including by enshrining those freedoms in a written constitution, strengthening the independence of the judiciary and nurturing a truly inclusive sense of patriotic identity. This same principle, with its affirmation of our essential right to meaningful political equality, can also guide us to reinvigorate democracy: adopting proportional representation, getting money out of politics and embracing new forms of direct participation.

While the basic liberties principle shows us how we can reimagine liberal democracy, the combination of fair equality of opportunity, the difference principle and the just savings principle, set us on the path to transforming, or even transcending, capitalism as we know it. This must begin by taking immediate action to address the climate and ecological emergency and recast our economy so that it can operate within safe ecological limits. Creating a legal framework to enforce these limits is a critical first step, and developing a more detailed plan for how we can curb emissions and protect fragile ecosystems is the most urgent policy imperative of our time.

But sustainability must go hand in hand with the wider task of addressing inequality and achieving economic justice. If we want meaningful equality of opportunity, we need to embrace far-reaching changes to our education system—from expanding early years education to abolishing private schools—and to redouble our efforts to tackle entrenched racial and gender inequalities. Beyond this, our goal should be to build a society that is not only more equal but more humane; one in which even the lowest-paid workers are treated with dignity and respect, and where each of us has a real opportunity to find work that can be a source of creativity, community and personal fulfilment. A universal basic income would provide a vital foundation of security and independence for all. But we cannot simply compensate for market inequalities through taxes and transfers. Rather, we must change the underlying structure of our economy itself: empowering workers to increase their earnings, giving everyone a fair share of society's wealth through a citizens' wealth fund, and embracing new forms of democracy at work.

In exploring these proposals we have taken seriously Rawls's commitment to building a "realistic utopia," taking people as they are, and institutions as they might be.[2] None of these ideas depend on speculative changes in technology or a transformation in "human nature." And although I have argued for specific policies and reforms, these should not be interpreted as a rigid blueprint, but as a contribution to a more open and imaginative public conversation about how we should organize our society. We should try to maintain an open mind, avoiding the dogmatism that so often stymies fruitful debate about these questions, and adopting an experimental attitude to the task of institutional reform—testing new ideas, and adjusting our approach in light of new evidence.

While the agenda developed in this book is realistic in the sense that the policy proposals are feasible, it is utopian in the sense that we have imagined the best that our societies could be and put to one side the question of how we could bring this about. We needed to do this in order to develop a clear idea of where we want to get to. But in the end, for any of this to become a reality we need to build a broad-based political movement capable of winning elections and using the power of the state to fundamentally change our political and economic institutions.

What are the prospects for creating such a movement? Across the world's advanced democracies, basic liberal and democratic values are under threat and there is a sense that our societies are more divided than ever. But there is reason to hope. After a period of decline, mainstream progressive parties—the most likely vehicle for a programme of this kind—have come to power in countries from America and Germany to Australia, Brazil and Spain; and in the UK, at the time of writing, the Labour Party seems likely to win the next election. The result is a moment rich with possibility. We are living in one of those rare periods in which established norms and allegiances have been thrown into question, and when, as the philosopher Antonio Gramsci famously put it, "the old is dying and the new cannot yet be born."[3] Just as the 1980s saw the triumph of neoliberalism over the post-war social democratic settlement, we are living through another era of transition—a period of intense ideological struggle, the outcome of which will define the shape of political discourse and public policy for a generation. For all its challenges, this moment represents an opportunity to break with neoliberalism once and for all and to set society firmly on the course of justice, fairness, freedom and equality.[4]

And yet, seizing this opportunity will require a kind of moral and political leadership that has been missing in recent years. In the face of serious electoral setbacks, mainstream progressive parties have all too often fallen back on triangulation, guided by opinion polling and calculations of short-term gain rather than any deeper sense of direction or values. This approach has fostered a transactional politics, where individual policies often feel like a bribe—or, as politicians would say, an "offer"—aimed at a particular group rather than part of a coherent agenda. As a result, many voters are unclear about what exactly it is that progressive parties really stand for, and those parties have struggled to forge strong bonds with individual voters or social groups, leaving them vulnerable in an increasingly volatile political climate.

There is no question that parties need to respond to voters' current concerns and think about their own immediate electoral prospects—after all, they can only change society if they can win elections. But taken too far, this approach reduces parties to merely tactical organizations pursuing electoral advantage, rather than truly political organizations trying to advance a particular set of values or a vision of society.[5] It also seriously underestimates the extent to which they can shape rather than merely respond to the political conditions around them. The divisions that run through our politics today, epitomized by the so-called "culture wars," are not the inevitable result of inexorable social and economic forces. They are, to a large extent, the product of our politics itself, and the ways in which politicians choose (or feel compelled) to frame the various issues we face as a society.[6]

Progressive parties need to lead rather than to follow—to regain a sense of political agency and make a fundamentally moral argument about why and how we can change society for the better. No doubt some people will dismiss appeals to moral values as hopelessly idealistic. But values have always mattered in politics, and they may matter now more than ever. While broadly progressive parties were once able to rely on the fairly consistent support of "working-class" voters, and more recently on the votes of marginalized groups including ethnic minorities and the LGBTQ+ community, the link between how people vote and their objective economic circumstances—and indeed their other social identities, such as race, gender or sexuality—has become much weaker over time.[7] Across the world's rich democracies, progressive parties have come to be dominated by educated professionals and alienated from lower-income and non-college-educated voters, making it increasingly difficult to win elections. In this context, putting values centre stage is not empty idealism, but an essential part of any serious political strategy, since they provide the glue that can bind disparate groups together. Rawls's ideas offer a truly universal moral vision with the potential both to cut across social and cultural divisions and to address once and for all the economic concerns of long-neglected lower-income voters.

Putting values at the heart of politics doesn't mean floating away into lofty abstraction. Politicians are unlikely to get elected by giving speeches explaining the original position thought experiment. The art of politics is to connect abstract values with the tangible realities of people's daily lives—with people's desire to practise their religion freely and to choose whom to love, with the imperative every parent feels to secure a decent education for their children, and with the yearning we all have to be treated with dignity and respect at work, and so on. And while we need a clear idea of where we ultimately want to get to, we must not let the best be the enemy of the good. Rawls's ideas provide us not only with a destination, but with a direction of travel; and even though our present moment seems ripe for an ambitious and transformative politics, incremental change is usually better than no change at all.

Finally, while political parties have a vital role to play, we cannot simply sit back and leave it to them. Politicians are unlikely to adopt such a far-reaching agenda of their own accord; and even if they did, they would face fierce opposition from those who benefit from the status quo—whether that be rich political donors, powerful corporations or monopolistic media moguls. We should call out such self-serving behaviour for what it is. But our societies will only change when we, the people, demand it. Each of us has a responsibility for making this happen—not just by voting, but by joining political parties and standing for office, by taking to the streets, and by coming together to build a wider social movement.

In the end, there is no guarantee that the ideas set out in this book will become a reality. Indeed, there is no guarantee that liberal democracy itself will survive. This isn't cause for pessimism or despair, but a reminder that it is within our power to change our world, for better and for worse. My aim has been to help us recover a sense of possibility about the future. But it is up to us, both individually and collectively, to build a society in which we are, at last, truly free and equal.

AFTERWORD: FROM WHAT TO HOW

In the year since this book was first published, its reception has brought home to me just how eager people are for a galvanizing vision of a better society. And yet, in the many conversations I've had, the discussion often turns from *what* such a society would look like to *how* we can bring it about.

By "how," I'm not talking about which policies we need, but about politics—about how to build a movement that can win elections and put this programme into practice. This is really a topic for another book—after all, Rawls provides us with a theory of justice, not a theory of change. And there are good reasons for addressing "what" and "how" separately: all too often, our capacity to imagine what a truly fair society would look like is stymied by the inevitable self-censorship that comes from thinking about short-term electoral realities. The result is a politics that lacks the ambition needed to inspire people and bring about meaningful reform.

Still, if we are serious about changing society, then we need to engage with these realities. As we saw in the Conclusion, mainstream progressive or centre-left parties—which are the most likely to take forward the ideas in this book—have won important victories in recent years. But this revival still looks rather uncertain, and is based more on dissatisfaction with the alternatives than a wave of popular enthusiasm. And it comes after a decade in which centre-left parties around the world saw their vote share decline, often to historic lows. This collapse in support was most striking in Europe, starting with PASOK in Greece, which lost three quarters of its vote share in the May 2012 election, followed five years later by the Dutch Labour Party and French Socialist Party, both of which saw their support drop into single digits, and Germany's Social Democrats, which achieved their worst result of the post-war era. Even in the UK, where the first-past-the-post electoral system means voters have few alternatives, the Labour Party saw a steady decline in support for most of the 2000s, and won fewer seats in the 2019 election than at any time since 1935.[1]

Alongside this fall in vote share has been a destabilizing shift in who votes for centre-left parties, not just in Europe but across the world's advanced democracies: a decline in support from lower-income, less-educated and working-class voters, and an increase in the importance of more-educated and affluent middle-class voters, especially those with university degrees.[2] There is also a growing sense that progressive parties have come to be dominated by younger and more urban people with socially liberal values, and disconnected from older citizens living in towns and rural areas with a more traditional outlook. Party affiliations and loyalties have become weaker too: the share of people in Western Europe who say they feel close or very close to a political party has declined from around 70 per cent in 1960 to around 30 per cent; and in the UK, nearly half of all voters did not vote for the same party in the three general elections held between 2010 and 2017.[3]

How, in this shifting and uncertain context, can centre-left parties build a truly broad-based electoral coalition? The answer will inevitably depend on the specific challenges and opportunities in each country. But the more I've talked about the book, the clearer it has become to me that even though Rawls's ideas may not provide a road map for winning elections, they can help us answer some of the big strategic questions facing mainstream progressive parties, laying the foundations for a popular political movement that could change our societies for the better.

They do this, in part, by pointing us towards a politics with certain distinctive characteristics. First, as we touched on in the Conclusion, progressive parties should be guided by strong values, and a transformative long-term vision. In other words, they should be *principled*. This might sound detached from the realities of electoral politics, but the opposite is true. People typically decide who to vote for not by assessing the details of individual policies, but on the basis of a more nebulous sense of what each party or candidate stands for and how this aligns with their own values, interests and identities.[4] As old party loyalties decline and as new generations come of age, putting values at the heart of politics is essential for building the affective bonds with voters that are so crucial for electoral success.

In practical terms, this means political parties cannot simply present themselves as more competent managers than their opponents, with better solutions to specific problems. While competence matters, this technocratic approach leaves many voters cold, and leads to a politics focused simply on responding to the latest crisis, rather than on advancing towards a vision of a better society. Nor can politicians rely on triangulating to match the views of "centrist" voters. This strategy can yield short-term benefits, and was at least partly responsible for the success of "third way" parties in the 1990s and 2000s, such as New Labour under Tony Blair in the UK, the Democrats under Bill Clinton in the U.S.A. and Gerhard Schröder's Social Democrats in Germany. But by watering down their distinctive ethos and ideology, those parties alienated many once-loyal voters without forming lasting connections to new ones, often leading to a long-term decline in support.[5]

While progressive political parties should be guided by clear values and a long-term vision, they should also be *pragmatic* about the pace at which this can be achieved, and the compromises that are often necessary to win elections. This doesn't mean abandoning principles, but being serious about putting them into practice in the democracies we actually live in, however slowly or imperfectly. Of course, winning elections isn't everything—radical parties and factions with little chance of forming a government can help push mainstream ones to go further and faster. But in a democracy, electoral success is a precondition for changing our basic institutions, and this means prioritising policies that will have a reasonably quick impact on people's lives, and accepting that change will typically come through pursuing reforms that fall short of our ultimate goals.

We should approach questions about electoral strategy based on the evidence. This means avoiding two pitfalls. On the one hand, we should reject the idea, common among political radicals, that having a more far-reaching policy programme is necessarily a sign of a deeper commitment to progressive values, or that politicians who advocate a more incremental agenda have betrayed the cause. There is little point in standing on a transformative platform if this consigns a party to electoral oblivion. On the other hand, as we have seen, we must not simply assume that adopting a more "moderate" platform is the most likely route to power. Progressive parties should harness and amplify support for larger changes where this exists, as it clearly does today: a recent survey of citizens in seventeen advanced democracies found that, on average, more than half said their political and economic systems needed major reforms or to be completely overhauled.[6]

The case for reform over revolution is not only about electoral politics—it is also about policy. Populist politicians like to suggest that there are obvious solutions to our problems. But many of the challenges we face—from raising the achievement of disadvantaged children to addressing the climate emergency—are genuinely complicated. This doesn't mean we should keep things as they are, and in some cases, like the climate emergency, we have no option but to pursue radical change, even if we cannot fully grasp the consequences. But a more piecemeal and experimental approach will often serve us best, testing new policies and institutions and adjusting in light of the evidence—something we can encourage by devolving real power to sub-national and local governments.[7]

Embracing reformism doesn't mean abandoning the goal of social transformation: over time, incremental changes can amount to something truly revolutionary. For this to happen, we should pursue what the philosopher André Gorz referred to as "non-reformist reforms"—those which pave the way for a fundamental shift in our political and economic structures.[8] So, for example, while the immediate impact of putting one or two workers on the boards of major companies, or creating a small citizens' wealth fund, might be modest, if expanded in the ways described in this book, these would genuinely transform how our economy works.

In a democratic society there will always be reasonable disagreement when it comes to politics—both about our basic values, and the policies most likely to achieve them. This brings us to the third feature of an effective Rawlsian politics: it should be *pluralist*.

Perhaps the best way to understand the idea of pluralism is to compare it with its opposite: populism. The essence of populism is the claim that populist parties, and especially their often charismatic leaders, represent the true voice of "the people" against corrupt elites and outsiders. As we have seen, in most democratic societies the rich really do exert enormous political influence. But by insisting that "the people" have just one point of view—the one expressed by populist politicians—populists undermine the belief in legitimate political disagreement that is the essence of any healthy democracy.

This attitude is most evident today among right-wing demagogues like Donald Trump in the U.S.A., Marine Le Pen in France and Jair Bolsonaro in Brazil, who routinely dismiss criticism as "fake news," and rely on a narrow conception of "the people"—typically based on race or religion—to delegitimize other perspectives. In the UK, populist champions of Brexit like Boris Johnson and Nigel Farage often claimed to represent the authentic voice of the British people, dismissing "remainers" as an out-of-touch metropolitan elite, even though they comprised 48 per cent of voters in the referendum. But liberals and progressives are not immune from this way of thinking: the idea that people who voted for Brexit were either stupid or bigoted is a case in point. More broadly, there is a troubling tendency on parts of the left to assume that even those who vote for centre-right parties are misguided, selfish or evil—rather than simply people with different but reasonable moral and political beliefs.

Worryingly, these intolerant attitudes appear to be on the rise. A recent global survey found that young people in advanced democracies were much more likely to think that "you can tell if a person is good or bad if you know their politics," or that "the people I disagree with are just misinformed."[9] And there is some evidence that they may be more prevalent among those on the left: in the UK, Labour supporters are more likely than Conservatives to say the other side are selfish, hypocritical and close-minded, and that they would find it hard to make friends with them.[10]

This moral self-righteousness is deeply unattractive: as Rawls put it, "Those who suppose their judgements are always consistent are unreflective or dogmatic; not uncommonly they are ideologues and zealots."[11] Rather than dismiss or condemn those we disagree with, we must recognize that moral and political questions are genuinely difficult, and that good people will reach different conclusions about them. It is also a serious obstacle to electoral success: if we are to have any chance of improving our societies, we must be willing to engage in the difficult work of listening and persuading that is essential for changing minds and winning votes.

While people will always disagree about politics, we should nonetheless seek to articulate a *unifying* vision for society grounded in genuinely universalist values, such as fairness, freedom and equality. As we have seen, a commitment to universalism is at the heart of Rawls's philosophy; it also provides an alternative to divisive forms of "identity politics" on both left and right.

I want to be clear that in critiquing identity politics I am not questioning the fundamental importance of struggles for equality and justice for groups that have been denied them on the basis of their physical characteristics or beliefs. Overcoming these injustices is integral to Rawls's philosophy, and must be central to any progressive agenda. My aim is not to question these goals, but a particular approach to achieving them.

The most extreme form of identity politics, and the one we should be worried about, is the idea that democracy is simply a battle to advance the interests of specific groups—Black people, white people, women, Christians—rather than the pursuit of equal justice for all. While the accusation of pursuing identity politics is typically levelled at the left, this sort of "tribalism" is and always has been primarily an ideology of the radical right.[12] Its roots lie in the racist philosophies that emerged in eighteenth- and nineteenth-century Europe and America to justify empire and slavery in the face of universalist Enlightenment ideals.[13] Today, ethnic and religious nationalists like Donald Trump in America and Narendra Modi in India are united in the idea that identity is the true basis of political authority and community.

And yet there are worrying parallels in some progressive circles, where it has become fashionable to reject the universalism of the Enlightenment as "white" or "Eurocentric," and little more than a tool for masking power and legitimizing injustice.[14] While it's important to call out how these ideals have been abused right from their conception, we must not confuse our failure to live up to them with their emancipatory power or ethical validity. And we must remember that, historically, highlighting the gap between professed ideals and actual reality has been a powerful force for progress—from the Haitian Revolution of 1791–1804, whose leaders first pushed the logic of the French Declaration of the Rights of Man to its radical conclusion in rejecting empire and slavery, to Martin Luther King's framing of the U.S. Constitution in 1963 as a "promissory note" on which America had "defaulted."[15]

Most people who support movements like #MeToo and Black Lives Matter surely see themselves as seeking to fulfil the promise of universal justice to those who have long been denied it. In contrast to far-right nationalists, they typically support what we might call "strategic" identity politics: the idea that, just as we might think people on lower incomes should take a lead in combating poverty and exploitation, discriminated-against groups should lead their own struggles. In fact, when the Combahee River Collective—a group of Black feminist socialists—first popularized the term "identity politics" in 1977, this is what they had in mind, arguing that "the only people who care enough about us to work consistently for our liberation are us."[16]

Organizing around our separate identities has been essential to minorities achieving justice, often in the face of the indifference or even outright hostility of mainstream political parties and trade unions, and it continues to have an important role today. But we must be careful not to let this kind of organizing become an end in itself, or an obstacle to building coalitions that cut across these groups. While Black people, women, LGBTQ+ people and so on clearly have unique insights into their experiences of discrimination and the structures that enable it, we should resist the increasingly popular idea that personal identity is the most important—or only—basis of political authority, and the tendency to relegate those who don't share a particular identity to the status of mere "allies," rather than equal participants in a common struggle.

The basis for a genuinely unifying politics—and what distinguishes it from identity politics—is a commitment to shared values, rather than to class, race, gender or any other identity. The task of progressive parties—and where Rawls can show us the way—is to connect the struggles of minorities to genuinely universal values, and to foster a mode of organizing that can build solidarity between groups with different priorities.

One of the things I love most about Rawls's ideas is that they are fundamentally *hopeful*. This is the fifth and final characteristic that should shape our approach to politics if we want to bring about real change. Of course, we must have a clear analysis of the problems with our existing institutions, and Rawls's principles can help us develop such a critique. But we also need a positive vision, underpinned by a firm belief in the possibility of progress.

This would provide a clear alternative to the apocalyptic narratives of societal decline so often favoured by right-wing populists. But it would also counter the deep pessimism that has come to dominate certain parts of the left, especially among more radical critics of the status quo. This often manifests in a tendency to underplay historic achievements, or to suggest that we can never overcome deep injustices, as with the claim that racism is "part of America's DNA."[17] Of course, most activists believe that change *is* possible (otherwise they wouldn't be activists), and such claims are typically motivated by a desire to show how reassuring stories of progress have been used to mask the continued existence of serious injustices. But pervasive pessimism about the possibility of progress is liable to become a self-fulfilling prophecy.

By encouraging us to focus on a vision of a truly just society, Rawls's philosophy provides a vital antidote to this way of thinking. This doesn't mean embracing the naive belief that progress towards liberal and democratic ideals is inevitable, or that change will be easy. Hope is not the same as optimism: whereas optimists believe that good things are more likely to happen, to hope is to believe that good things *can* happen, even if they might be unlikely, and that it's possible to make them more likely by taking the right kinds of actions.

Whereas optimism can ring hollow, hope is a clarion call that motivates people to get involved in politics. It was a message of hope that inspired millions to campaign for Barack Obama to become U.S. president in 2008. And it was the same belief in the possibility of a better future that energized so many in the late 2010s to get behind democratic socialists like Jeremy Corbyn in the UK and

Bernie Sanders in the U.S. And yet Obama's inspiring rhetoric was not always matched with practical ambition, while Corbyn and Sanders failed to convince a sceptical electorate that their ambitious policies were credible. The challenge we face is to combine a bold and hopeful vision with a realistic agenda for change. In many ways, that is the purpose of this book.

A Rawlsian politics, then, would be principled, pragmatic, pluralist, unifying and hopeful. But having these qualities alone won't be enough for centre-left and progressive parties to bridge cultural divides and win back disaffected lower-income voters. To achieve this, they must also adopt a policy programme that would both tackle inequality and create a truly inclusive society.

It's easy to interpret the electoral decline of centre-left parties since the 1980s as evidence of waning support for a more equal society. But this gets things the wrong way around. It's not that people stopped caring about inequality or supporting the welfare state—in fact, in most rich nations public concern about inequality has increased significantly since the 1980s, and today around 80 per cent of people in OECD countries think the gap between rich and poor is too large.[18] What's changed is that mainstream progressive parties (and much of the media) largely stopped talking about these issues. There is now a substantial body of evidence that this rightward shift has alienated those parties' traditional supporters, many of whom have simply stopped voting.[19] And it has been the rejection by right-wing populists of free-market economics in favour of more interventionist policies which has been responsible for the surge in their support since the 2010s, especially among poorer and less-educated voters.[20]

This doesn't mean going back to the statist ambitions of post-war socialism, with its emphasis on public ownership and central planning. Nor does it mean reviving the "third way" formula of market-driven growth and redistributive taxation. Instead, Rawls points us towards a modern progressive economics: one that is comfortable celebrating aspiration, entrepreneurship and the benefits of a broadly market-based economy, but that is committed to harnessing the benefits of markets for all, not primarily through redistribution but by investing in skills, establishing new institutions like citizens' wealth funds and creating a "partnership economy" where workers and owners share power on much more equal terms. This is an economic agenda that would address the justified concerns of long-neglected lower-income voters, not simply for higher incomes (important though that is) but for dignity, respect and an opportunity to contribute to society.[21]

What about the so-called "socio-cultural issues"—gender, race, immigration, sexuality, climate—that have increasingly come to dominate political debate? Progressive parties have championed these matters in recent decades, achieving major legislative victories from anti-discrimination laws to equal pay and gay marriage. And yet it's frequently claimed that in doing so they have driven a wedge between middle- and working-class voters, pushing the latter into the arms of the populist right.[22] Some appear to want to downgrade or even ignore these topics, as if we could turn back the clock to a simpler era when politics was dominated by a single left–right economic dimension; while others have argued that progressive parties should adopt a more socially conservative approach.

I believe either approach would be a huge mistake. Questions about sexual and reproductive freedom, racial and gender equality and sustainability are not the frivolous concerns of a metropolitan elite, but fundamental issues of social justice. The prominence of these issues in our political debate is not a passing fad, but a consequence of the democratic empowerment of disadvantaged groups, and vacating this space will only allow illiberal voices to dominate. The problem is not that centre-left parties have supported justice for minorities, but that they have failed to combine this with an egalitarian economic agenda that could unite these groups. One of the great strengths of Rawls's philosophy is that it provides a unified framework for addressing both socio-cultural and economic questions, and hence for navigating the multiple dimensions of modern politics.

Fortunately, the idea that championing these issues represents a fundamental obstacle to electoral success is simply not supported by the evidence. It's not just that, as we saw in Chapter 4, large and growing majorities in most advanced democracies support liberal positions on sexuality, gender, race and national identity. The popular narrative that progressive parties' positions on these matters have driven working-class voters to embrace right-wing extremists is flatly contradicted by the evidence: only a small minority of former centre-left voters have moved to the far right—most have gone to the Greens and to other left parties, or to the mainstream right; and far right parties still win only a small share of the working-class vote.[23] Moreover, the widespread tendency to depict lower-income and less-educated voters as a monolithic, typically white and male, authoritarian block is increasingly detached from reality. The modern working class includes many women and ethnic minorities, and while its members are often sceptical about the benefits of immigration, many hold liberal attitudes on moral and cultural questions.[24] In fact, a growing body of research has found that a "left-authoritarian" strategy combining economically left-wing policies with illiberal positions on socio-cultural questions risks driving away potential progressive voters, while "left-liberal" programmes attract the most support.[25]

This is not to deny that the growing prominence of socio-cultural issues creates challenges for centre-left parties. Potential progressive voters are often more divided about these questions than economic ones; and right-wing parties have successfully built new coalitions of socially conservative voters who might otherwise disagree about economics. But we should reject the idea that we face a binary choice between liberal and authoritarian positions. While healing our fractured societies will require considerable political skill, most people's attitudes are more nuanced than our polarized political debate would suggest, and as we have seen on issues ranging from gay rights and religious freedom to immigration and liberal patriotism, Rawls's ideas offer a principled way to bridge apparent divides.[26]

There is, of course, much more to say about how we can build a broad-based political movement for change—about how to approach politics in an age of social media and misinformation, about the role of social movements and organizations such as trade unions, and about how to counter the power of corporate interests and financial markets to obstruct economic reforms. But we must start by developing a clear moral vision and a transformative practical programme. This, in turn, will help us to overcome the divisions—ideological, tactical and personal—that have so often held back progressive politics, and persuade our fellow citizens that a better society is not only desirable, but achievable.

ACKNOWLEDGEMENTS

I want to start by thanking my brilliant agent Georgina Capel, as well as Irene Baldoni, Rachel Conway and the rest of the team, for taking a chance on me and getting my proposal into the hands of my dream publishers at Allen Lane. It means a great deal to know I can always pick up the phone and find encouragement, enthusiasm and a sense of humour at the other end. I feel extraordinarily lucky to have Chloe Currens as my editor and I cannot thank her enough for her faith in me as well as the project, her patience and insight during many long discussions about the ideas, her careful editing and beautifully written suggestions, and for always supporting me to write the book I wanted to write. Kit Shepherd's meticulous copy editing helped sharpen my arguments and streamline my prose, improving every single paragraph, and I am thrilled to be working with Isabel Blake and Julie Woon on taking the book out into the world. I am also grateful to Jim Stoddart for the beautiful cover design, and to everyone else at Penguin Press who has helped along the way, including Thea Tuck, Thi Dinh, Anna Wilson and David Bond.

In the U.S., I want to thank Erroll McDonald at Knopf for believing in and fighting for this book, and being so ambitious about the impact it could have. Brian Etling also deserves a special mention for holding everything together so brilliantly, and I feel very lucky to now be working with Jess Purcell, Elka Roderick and Abigail Endler to bring the book to as many people as possible.

In the very early stages of this project, I benefited hugely from the advice of Alice Whitwham, Will Hammond, David Evans, Susannah Otter and Jack Ramm about how to get started. Throughout the process various friends and colleagues gave their time to discuss the book, including Will Attenborough, Ed Blain, Alex Bryson, Pawel Bukowski, Emma Hogan, Nicola Lacey, Michael Jacobs, Soumaya Keynes, Ed Miliband, Martin O'Neill, Oscar Rickett, Jonathan Rutherford and Martha Spurrier. Johann Hari in particular offered invaluable writerly wisdom at moments of crisis. Special thanks to Toby Regbo, Ricky Power Sayeed, Cain Shelley, Daniel Susskind, Florence Sutcliffe-Braithwaite, Mike Webb and Tommy Wide, all of whom provided detailed comments on the manuscript and/or discussed the ideas at length. I am grateful to Nikhil Krishnan who generously organised a workshop on the book, and to all those who came along, including Harry Kingdon, John Maier, Geraldine Ng, Veronica Salazar-Restrepo and especially Callum MacRae and Jack Hume, who gave written feedback. I am particularly grateful to Samuel Freeman for agreeing to formally review the manuscript, and to Angus Deaton and Stuart White, both of whom went above and beyond, offering helpful comments on the entire draft text.

I started this book midway through my PhD in Economics at the London School of Economics, and I want to thank Tim Besley, my supervisor, for encouraging me to pause my PhD to pursue the idea, and for providing me with an inspiring model of what an economist can be. Over the years I have benefitted from many great teachers, including Lynne Gavin, Richard Blanch, Jillian Leddra and Catherine Manson, each of whom had a profound impact on my time at school and as a teenager. I first encountered Rawls as a History undergraduate at Cambridge in a course led by the brilliant Melissa Lane, and I was lucky to have other fantastic supervisors including Richard Drayton, Jon Parry and Simon Szreter, who helped build my confidence and shaped my thinking in important ways. I was able to pursue my interests in political philosophy and economics during a year at Harvard where I had the incredible privilege of studying under one of my greatest intellectual heroes, Amartya Sen; and then at the LSE, first through an MSc, under the guidance of Richard Bradley, and then during my PhD, where Kai Spiekerman and Chandran Kakuthas welcomed me into the political theory group.

Writing this book sometimes seemed impossible, and I feel very lucky to have wonderful friends who patiently listened to my worries and offered their support, especially Grace Chatto, Max Colson, Matt Knott, Jesse Nicolls, Jack Patterson and Bea Philips. I want to offer my deep thanks to Liam Smith and Luba Shkabara who helped in vital practical ways, and to all those who have given me psychological and spiritual guidance over the years, including Rohan Barua, Anna Bhushan, Meredith Churchill, Wainwright Churchill, Dr. ALV Kumar, Sarah Litton, Publio Valle, Priyanka Wali and Maestros Damian Pacaya, Rojelia Gonzalez, Anita Tananta, Tony Lopez and Ida Pacaya at the Temple of the Way of Light; as well as my great uncle David Bateman, who was such an important influence in my life; and Moses, who I love very much.

None of this would have been possible without my amazing family: my brilliant and open-hearted brother Leo and his wonderful partner Frankie Reid, my inspiring and generous sister Jess, my ever-thoughtful brother-in-law Geirmund, my gorgeous niece and nephew Martha and Charlie, and my amazing parents Nicki and Simon, who have given me so many opportunities and whose unconditional love and support is the foundation for everything else in my life. My biggest thanks go to my partner Simon, for his unbelievable patience in listening to me go round in circles talking about every single aspect of this book, for his insight about how to make it better, for making it possible to take my time and, beyond the book, for helping me to grow and flourish in so many ways. I feel so lucky to have found you, and love you more than I can possibly express here. Thank you.

NOTES

PREFACE

1 John Rawls, *Justice as Fairness: A Restatement,* ed. Erin Kelly (Cambridge, MA: Harvard University Press, 2001), 2.

INTRODUCTION

1 Roberto Mangabeira Unger, *What Should the Left Propose?* (London: Verso, 2005), 1.

2 Cas Mudde, "The Real Threat to Liberal Democracy Isn't the Right. It's the Ideological Vacuum at Its Own Heart," *Prospect,* 6 December 2019.

3 With the possible exception of the economist Thomas Piketty, whose work has helped to galvanize a new conversation about how we can address the enormous inequalities that disfigure our societies: see *Capital in the Twenty-First Century,* trans. Arthur Goldhammer (Cambridge, MA: Harvard University Press, 2014), and *Capital and Ideology,* trans. Arthur Goldhammer (Cambridge, MA: Harvard University Press, 2020).

4 Although Rawls didn't use this exact phrase, he described his theory as "realistically utopian" on numerous occasions. See, for example, John Rawls, *Justice as Fairness: A Restatement,* ed. Erin Kelly (Cambridge, MA: Harvard University Press, 2001), 4–5.

5 Joshua Cohen, "The Importance of Philosophy: Reflections on John Rawls," *South African Journal of Philosophy* 23:2 (2004), 114–15.

6 The following discussion of Rawls's biography draws on Samuel Freeman, *Rawls* (Abingdon: Routledge, 2007), 1–12, and Thomas Pogge, *John Rawls: His Life and Theory of Justice*, trans. Michelle Kosch (Oxford: Oxford University Press, 2007), 3–27.

7 Pogge writes that Tommy also died after contracting pneumonia from the young Rawls: see Pogge, *Rawls*, 5–6. But according to Rawls's wife, Margaret (in personal correspondence with Professor Samuel Freeman in December 2021 which was relayed to the author), while Rawls may have thought he was responsible for Tommy's death, and perhaps said so to Pogge, she did not think this was the case.

8 Pogge, *Rawls*, 7.

9 For a detailed look at the development of Rawls's thinking, see Andrius Gališanka, *John Rawls: The Path to a Theory of Justice* (Cambridge, MA: Harvard University Press, 2019), and Katrina Forrester, *In the Shadow of Justice: Postwar Liberalism and the Remaking of Political Philosophy* (Princeton: Princeton University Press, 2019), 1–39.

10 Forrester, *In the Shadow of Justice*, 104.

11 Marshall Cohen, "The Social Contract Explained and Defended," *New York Times*, 16 July 1972; "Five Significant Books of 1972," *New York Times*, 3 December 1972.

12 See, for example, Cohen, "The Social Contract Explained and Defended": and Robert Nozick, *Anarchy, State, and Utopia* (New York: Basic Books, 1974), 183. For a wider discussion of how Rawls's ideas were received, and the impact they have had on contemporary political thought, see Forrester, *In the Shadow of Justice*, 104, as well as Sophie Smith, "Historicizing Rawls," *Modern Intellectual History* 18:4 (2021), 906–39.

13 G. A. Cohen, *Rescuing Justice and Equality* (Cambridge, MA: Harvard University Press, 2009), 11.

14 "Remembering Rawls," in Michael J. Sandel, *Public Philosophy: Essays on Morality in Politics* (Cambridge MA: Harvard University Press, 2006), 251. For similar sentiments and anecdotes, see Samuel Freeman, "John Rawls: Friend and Teacher," *Chronicle of Higher Education*, 13 December 2002; and Joshua Cohen, "The Importance of Philosophy," 113.

15 Peter Laslett, "Introduction," in Peter Laslett (ed.), *Philosophy, Politics and Society: First Series* (Oxford: Basil Blackwell, 1956), vii. While there is no question that Rawls fundamentally reshaped political philosophy, to say that it was "dead" may be an overstatement, and his ideas obviously did not emerge in a vacuum—see Smith, "Historicizing Rawls."

16 Samuel Freeman, "A New Theory of Justice," *New York Review of Books*, 14 October 2010. See also Kymlicka, who wrote at the start of his widely respected introduction to political philosophy that "It is generally accepted that the recent rebirth of normative political philosophy began with the publication of John Rawls's A Theory of Justice in 1971": Will Kymlicka, *Contemporary Political Philosophy: An Introduction*, second edition (Oxford: Oxford University Press, 2002), 10.

17 Nozick, *Anarchy, State, and Utopia*, 183. In an essay to mark the fiftieth anniversary of the publication of *A Theory of Justice*, the commentator Dylan Matthews wrote: "A philosopher once described European philosophy as essentially 'a series of footnotes to Plato'; it would be no exaggeration to describe the history of political philosophy over the past half-century as a series of footnotes and responses to John Rawls." Dylan Matthews, "The Most Influential Work of Political Philosophy in the Last 50 Years, Briefly Explained," *Vox*, 9 December 2021.

18 Freeman, *Rawls*, 457.

19 For examples of "third way" thinkers in the UK who engaged with Rawls's ideas, see the then Labour MP and shadow cabinet member Bryan Gould's *Socialism and Freedom* (London: Macmillan, 1985), and the then deputy leader of the Labour Party Roy Hattersley's *Choose Freedom: The Future for Democratic Socialism* (London: Penguin, 1987).

20 This isn't to say Rawls has had no influence over politics. Many politicians will have encountered his ideas as students, and Barack Obama, for example, appears to have been influenced by them (see, for example, "Obama's Rawlsian Vision," *The Economist*, 19 February 2013). But it is very rare indeed to hear politicians directly reference Rawls as a source of inspiration.

21 Rawls's aversion to public awards was so obvious that his wife, Margaret, apparently declined the Kyoto Prize, which comes with a $500,000 award, without even consulting him. See Freeman, "John Rawls: Friend and Teacher." According to philosopher Martha Nussbaum, to whom Rawls was a mentor, his aversion to playing the role of public intellectual was grounded in his belief that he lacked the necessary abilities as a speaker and writer, rather than due to a lack of interest in politics, and he told her that those who possessed these talents had a duty to use them for the public good. See Martha Nussbaum, *Philosophical Interventions: Reviews, 1986–2011* (Oxford: Oxford University Press, 2012), 1.

22 While Rawls is often criticized today for being too abstract, he was closely engaged with work in economics and moral psychology, and was careful to demonstrate that his ideas were compatible with the prevailing theories in these disciplines, something that set him apart from many of his peers. See, for example, Marshall Cohen, "The Social Contract," which praised Rawls for "reviv[ing] the English tradition of Hume and Adam Smith, of Bentham and of John Stuart Mill, which insists on relating its political speculations to fundamental research in moral psychology and political economy."

23 Rawls's ideas have often been misunderstood, especially by those on the left, as at best a justification for an expanded welfare state and at worst an apology for trickle-down economics and neoliberalism. But as Rawls said in the 1990s, "I would find it very difficult to see how anyone who has lived in [America] for the past decade or so could think that it is a just or nearly just society as I define justice." And most rich countries have only moved further from Rawls's ideal since then. See Rawls quoted in Martin O'Neill, "Social Justice and Economic Systems: On Rawls, Democratic Socialism, and Alternatives to Capitalism," *Philosophical Topics* 48:2 (2020), 161. Rawls has also been criticized for saying relatively little about race, gender, disability, and climate justice; but, as we shall see, with the possible exception of disability, his theory provides a powerful framework for addressing these questions too.

24 Freeman, *Rawls*, 458.

25 To a lesser extent, these criticisms also apply to a longer "classical liberal" tradition going back to thinkers like John Locke and Adam Smith. Neoliberals have frequently positioned themselves as the heirs of this tradition, but in doing so, they have often seriously distorted it. Smith, for example, was far from being the anti-state ideologue that he is sometimes portrayed as today, and his thinking was grounded in a nuanced and sophisticated understanding of human nature. Jesse Norman, *Adam Smith: What He Thought, and Why It Matters* (London: Penguin, 2018).

26 Just as Friedman and Hayek can point to a long and respected lineage of classical liberal thinkers going back to Locke and Smith, today's "liberal egalitarians" (as they are typically referred to in academic circles) can point to an intellectual lineage that originates with John Stuart Mill—the great progressive liberal of the nineteenth century—and encompasses the British "new liberals" (also known as "social liberals") of the late nineteenth and early twentieth centuries, such as Thomas Green, Leonard Hobhouse and John Hobson, and the

great early twentieth century American philosopher John Dewey (to mention just those in the Anglophone tradition). See Samuel Freeman, "Capitalism in the Classical and High Liberal Traditions," *Social Philosophy and Policy* 28:2 (2011), 19–55.

27 As we shall see, Rawls's principles often point towards policies similar to those advocated by democratic socialists today like higher taxes on the rich and more democracy at work. And yet, while Rawls sometimes reached similar conclusions, he did so by drawing on the distinctively liberal, rather than on socialist values and concepts. See Pablo Gilabert and Martin O'Neill, "Socialism," in Edward N. Zalta (ed.), *The Stanford Encyclopedia of Philosophy* (fall 2019 edition), sect. 3.2.5, https://plato.stanford.edu/cgi-bin/encyclopedia/archinfo.cgi?entry=socialism. Rawls regularly gave lectures on Marx, and was at pains to show how his own theory could respond to Marx's critique of capitalism. See "Lectures on Marx," in John Rawls, *Lectures on the History of Political Philosophy*, ed. Samuel Freeman (Cambridge, MA: Harvard University Press, 2008), and "Addressing Marx's Critique of Liberalism," in Rawls, *Justice as Fairness*, 176–9.

28 Certainly there is nothing in the recent socialist tradition that can rival Rawls's theory in terms of scope and ambition. For much of the twentieth century, socialists had a reasonably clear vision of what a socialist society would look like: drawing on Marx, most favoured replacing markets with central planning, and private with public ownership. But few of them advocate such a programme today. The focus tends to be on reforms that would reduce inequality while leaving the basic structure of a capitalist market economy intact, such as more progressive taxes or public ownership of key utilities. While it's common to describe these policies as the first steps towards a more fundamental transformation, the ultimate objective is far from certain. For interesting discussions of socialist ideas and politics, as well as thoughts on how to reformulate socialism for the twenty-first century, see Axel Honneth, *The Idea of Socialism: Towards a Policy of Renewal*, trans. Joseph Ganahl (Cambridge: Polity Press, 2017), and John E. Roemer, "What Is Socialism Today? Conceptions of a Cooperative Economy," *International Economic Review* 62:2 (2021), 571–98.

29 David Goodhart, *The Road to Somewhere: The New Tribes Shaping British Politics* (London: Penguin, 2017). For an analysis of how progressive parties have increasingly come to be dominated by more educated voters, see Amory Gethin et al., "Brahmin Left Versus Merchant Right: Changing Political Cleavages in 21 Western Democracies, 1948–2020," *Quarterly Journal of Economics* 137:1 (2021), 1–48.

30 Thomas Nagel, "Rawls on Justice," *Philosophical Review* 82:2 (1973), 234. Nagel went on to say: "Yet the hope has a basis, for Rawls possesses a deep sense of the multiple connections between social institutions and individual psychology. Without illusion he describes a pluralistic social order that will call forth the support of free men and evoke what is best in them. To have made such a vision precise, alive, and convincing is a memorable achievement."

1. WHAT'S FAIR?

1 John Rawls, *A Theory of Justice*, revised edition (Cambridge, MA: Harvard University Press, 1999), 3.

2 Ibid., 88.

3 Rawls formulated his two principles in slightly different ways in different publications. The quoted text is taken from John Rawls, *Political Liberalism*, expanded edition (New York: Columbia University Press, 2005), 5–6, except for the final clause, "consistent with the just savings principle." This comes from Rawls's statement of the two principles in *A Theory of Justice* (266) which says that social and economic advantages should be "to the greatest benefit of the least advantaged, consistent with the just savings principle." I have added this because, although Rawls did not always explicitly include the just savings principle when stating his two principles together, it is always assumed to apply. For an overview of the key aspects and major formulations of the two principles, see Pablo Gilabert, "The Two Principles of Justice (in Justice as Fairness)," in Jon Mandle and David Reidy (eds.), *The Cambridge Rawls Lexicon* (Cambridge: Cambridge University Press, 2015), 845–50.

4 "If Rawls had achieved nothing else, he would be important for having taken seriously the idea that the subject of justice is what he calls 'the basic structure of society' . . . Rawls's incorporation of this notion of a social structure into his theory represents the coming of age of liberal political philosophy." Brian Barry, quoted in Robert E. Goodin et al. (eds.), *A Companion to Contemporary Political Philosophy*, second edition (Oxford: Blackwell, 2007), 100.

5 John Rawls, *Justice as Fairness: A Restatement*, ed. Erin Kelly (Cambridge, MA: Harvard University Press, 2001), 11.

6 The status of the family, and whether or not it is properly considered to be part of the basic structure, is the subject of some debate. Rawls himself argued that the family is part of the basic structure because of its role in the "orderly production and reproduction of society and its

culture from one generation to the next": Rawls, *Political Liberalism*, 467. This means that the state has a legitimate role in recognizing and supporting the family in some form, and this applies to any family unit that can raise children, whether heterosexual, homosexual, single parent and so on. But Rawls's principles are clearly not meant to determine the internal dynamics of family life, and parents don't have to distribute resources within the family according to the difference principle. See S. A. Lloyd, "The Family," in Mandle and Reidy (eds.), *The Cambridge Rawls Lexicon*, 279–83.

7 Rawls developed a separate theory and set of principles to address these questions, which he called "the Law of Peoples": see John Rawls, *The Law of Peoples* (Cambridge, MA: Harvard University Press, 1999). But his ideas on this topic are less widely accepted, even among those of a broadly Rawlsian persuasion. In fact, a number of philosophers have argued, *contra* Rawls, that his principles, including the difference principle, should be directly applied on a global level, meaning we have an obligation to maximize the prospects of the least well off, not within our own country but in the world at large. For a more general discussion of debates about global justice, including Rawls's ideas and influence, see Gillian Brock, "Global Justice," in Edward N. Zalta (ed.), *The Stanford Encyclopedia of Philosophy* (summer 2022 edition), https://plato.stanford.edu/entries/justice-global/.

8 One might wonder whether we can really separate global and domestic justice in this way. For the most part, I think we can. Even if global justice calls for a wholesale transformation of international economic structures, and even if this comes at a significant economic cost to rich countries, the case for basic rights, democracy and fair economic structures *within* those countries would remain broadly the same.

9 Rawls himself tended to divide the basic liberties into five categories: liberty of conscience and freedom of thought; freedom of association; the rights and liberties that protect the integrity and freedom of the person; the equal political liberties; and the rights and liberties associated with the rule of law. See Rawls, *Political Liberalism*, 291. I have grouped the first three as "personal" liberties, and refer to the final two as "political" and "procedural" liberties respectively.

10 Rawls defined "fair value" as follows: "Citizens similarly gifted and motivated have roughly an equal chance of influencing the government's policy and of attaining positions of authority irrespective of their economic and social class": Rawls, *Justice as Fairness*, 46. For an explanation of why Rawls guaranteed the fair value of only the political liberties, and not of all the basic liberties, see ibid., 150–53.

11 As Rawls commented: "Historically one of the main defects of constitutional government has been the failure to insure the fair value of
political liberty. The necessary corrective steps have not been taken,
indeed, they never seem to have been seriously entertained. Disparities in the distribution of property and wealth that far exceed what
is compatible with political equality have generally been tolerated by
the legal system." Rawls, *A Theory of Justice*, 198–9.

12 In the same way that the first (basic liberties) principle takes priority
over the second, fair equality of opportunity also takes priority over
the difference principle. This ranking of principles is a distinctive feature of Rawls's theory and a major contribution in its own right. See,
for example, Bernard Williams's 1972 review of *A Theory of Justice*,
reprinted in his *Essays and Reviews, 1959–2002* (Princeton: Princeton
University Press, 2015), 82–6. As Williams explained, before Rawls,
philosophy was divided into two camps: pluralistic theories that recognized multiple moral values like freedom, opportunity and equality, but left us to balance them in an ad hoc way (what Rawls called
"intuitionism"); and then utilitarianism, which reduced everything
to a single value, namely utility. For Williams, the merit of Rawls's
approach was that, by making space for multiple values *and* giving
us a straightforward way to rank them, it was "at once complete and
humane enough to satisfy moral demands, and rigorously unified
enough to meet the rational requirements of one who wants more
than disconnected insights" (ibid., 83).

13 Freeman, *Rawls*, 51.

14 Rawls, *Justice as Fairness*, 2. For a recent history of some of these
debates, see Annelien de Dijn, *Freedom: An Unruly History* (Cambridge, MA: Harvard University Press, 2020).

15 For a discussion of liberal resistance to universal suffrage, see Edmund
Fawcett, *Liberalism: The Life of an Idea* (Princeton: Princeton University Press, 2014), 146–59. De Dijn argues that liberal opposition to
democracy was often grounded in the desire to protect private property and prevent economic redistribution, rather than a concern for
personal freedoms of religion and conscience. See De Dijn, *Freedom*,
3–5.

16 Neoliberal thinkers have often been sceptical or outright opposed
to parliamentary democracy. As Thomas Piketty points out, Hayek
rejected universal suffrage in favour of a "legislative assembly" comprising people aged over forty-five with proven ability who would
be elected through professional associations "such as Rotary Clubs."
See Thomas Piketty, *Capital and Ideology*, trans. Arthur Goldhammer

(Cambridge, MA: Harvard University Press, 2020), 706–9. Recent years have seen a growing number of thinkers openly call for limits on democracy in order to curb the influence of supposedly ignorant and irrational voters, such as the libertarian philosopher Jason Brennan who has made the case for replacing democracy with "epistocracy," or "rule of the knowledgeable," by giving more educated people extra votes. See Jason Brennan, *Against Democracy* (Princeton: Princeton University Press, 2016). For a discussion and critique of Brennan and the wider context for these ideas, see Nathan Robinson, "Democracy: Probably a Good Thing," *Current Affairs*, 27 June 2017.

17 The political scientist Yascha Mounk refers to this as "rights without democracy," noting that independent agencies rather than elected legislatures are now responsible for the vast majority of new laws, rules and regulations in America. See Yascha Mounk, *The People vs. Democracy: Why Our Freedom Is in Danger and How to Save It* (Cambridge, MA: Harvard University Press, 2018), 65.

18 Amy Gutmann, "Rawls on the Relationship between Liberalism and Democracy," in Samuel Freeman (ed.), *The Cambridge Companion to Rawls* (Cambridge: Cambridge University Press, 2003), 168–99.

19 Freeman, *Rawls*, 46.

20 For a detailed discussion, see Rawls, *Political Liberalism*, 289–371.

21 Rawls also refers to these as the capacities to be "rational" and "reasonable": to be rational is to have a sense of what you want in life and how to pursue it; while to be reasonable is to be willing and able to cooperate with other people on fair terms. A democratic society depends on citizens having both capacities, since "Merely reasonable agents would have no ends of their own they wanted to advance by fair cooperation," while "merely rational agents lack a sense of justice and fail to recognize the independent validity of the claims of others." Rawls, *Political Liberalism*, 52.

22 As we have already discussed, we need the "procedural" freedoms— the rights and liberties associated with the rule of law—in order to exercise our personal and political liberties.

23 We will come back to public reasons in Chapter 2, but, in short, they are justifications grounded in widely held political values rather than in personal religious or moral beliefs. While non-basic freedoms such as commercial advertising—or (arguably) things like pornography, public nudity, or recreational drug use—can be limited on grounds of, say, public health they cannot be restricted simply because they might offend some (or even most) people's aesthetic, moral or religious sensibilities.

24 Frank Michelman, "Rawls on Constitutionalism and Constitutional Law," in Freeman (ed.), *The Cambridge Companion to Rawls*, 394–425.

25 There is room for debate about how extensive our rights over personal possessions need to be in order to secure our basic interests in living freely and developing our moral capacities, as well as about what count as "personal possessions" for these purposes. See, for example, Katy Wells, who argues that we could achieve the same underlying goals through a more limited set of rights, comparable to those we have over things that we rent. See Katy Wells, "The Right to Personal Property," *Politics, Philosophy & Economics* 15:4 (2016), 358–78.

26 In explaining the relationship between his first and second principles, Rawls distinguished between liberty and the "worth" of liberty. The first principle is meant to provide each of us with a guarantee of certain equal basic liberties, understood as formal legal freedoms to do or be certain things without interference from the state or other citizens. But the worth of these formal freedoms to us as citizens depends, crucially, on our access to resources like income and wealth. The aim of the second principle is to make sure that we each have access to a fair share of the resources we need to exercise our basic freedoms and to pursue our dreams and goals in life. Or as Rawls put it: "Taking the two principles together, the basic structure is to be arranged to maximize the worth to the least advantaged of the complete scheme of equal liberty shared by all. This defines the end of social justice." Rawls, *A Theory of Justice*, 179.

27 In other words, these countries have an "intergenerational earnings elasticity" of about 0.5: see Miles Corak, "Income Inequality, Equality of Opportunity, and Intergenerational Mobility," *Journal of Economic Perspectives* 27:3 (2013), 79–102.

28 Raj Chetty et al., "Race and Economic Opportunity in the United States: An Intergenerational Perspective," *Quarterly Journal of Economics* 135:2 (2020), 730.

29 Rawls summarized this idea as follows: "those who are at the same level of talent and ability, and have the same willingness to use them, should have the same prospects of success regardless of their initial place in the social system." Rawls, *A Theory of Justice*, 63.

30 R. H. Tawney, *Equality*, fourth edition (London: George Allen & Unwin, 1952), 109.

31 Universal healthcare is important not only for equality of opportunity but for making sure that everyone can exercise their basic liberties too, and for improving the prospects of the least well off. See Rawls, *Justice as Fairness*, 173–5, and Norman Daniels, "Health and Health

Care," in Mandle and Reidy (eds.), *The Cambridge Rawls Lexicon*, 332–5. For a more detailed discussion of a broadly Rawlsian approach to healthcare, which Rawls commented on approvingly, see Norman Daniels, "Health-Care Needs and Distributive Justice," *Philosophy & Public Affairs* 10:2 (1981), 146–79, and Norman Daniels, *Just Health Care* (Cambridge: Cambridge University Press, 1985).

32 As Rawls put it, "In all sectors of society there should be roughly equal prospects of culture and achievement for everyone similarly motivated and endowed." Rawls, *A Theory of Justice*, 63.

33 Nava Ashraf et al., "Mind the Gap: What Gender Differences in Pay Tell Us about Untapped Talent," Hub for Equal Representation in the Economy working paper (May 2021). See also Robert Lynch, "The Economic Benefits of Equal Opportunity in the United States by Ending Racial, Ethnic, and Gender Disparities," Washington Center for Equitable Growth (June 2021).

34 Rawls himself said relatively little about the rights of parents. The ideas here draw on important work by the philosophers Harry Brighouse and Adam Swift, whose approach fits well within a broadly Rawlsian framework. See Harry Brighouse and Adam Swift, *Family Values: The Ethics of Parent-Child Relationships* (Princeton: Princeton University Press, 2014).

35 Michael J. Sandel, *The Tyranny of Merit: What's Become of the Common Good?* (London: Penguin, 2020), 119.

36 According to the *Oxford English Dictionary* (online edition), the term "meritocracy" was first used in 1956 by Alan Fox in the journal *Socialist Commentary*, but Young's book brought the term into mainstream discourse. Young later expressed dismay about how the term had been so widely misused. See Michael Young, "Down with Meritocracy," *Guardian*, 29 June 2001.

37 Young's book is written in the voice of a fictional author in 2033 exploring the history of the meritocratic society in which he lives. Towards the end of the book, the narrator notes some social unrest among the "less intelligent" classes. The account later breaks off, and a footnote informs us that the author was killed in violent upheavals in May 2034. See Michael Young, *The Rise of the Meritocracy* (London: Thames & Hudson, 1958).

38 In a meritocratic society, Rawls argued, "There exists a marked disparity between the upper and lower classes in both means of life and the rights and privileges of organizational authority. The culture of the poorer strata is impoverished while that of the governing and technocratic elite is securely based on the service of the national ends

of power and wealth. Equality of opportunity [in this context] means an equal chance to leave the less fortunate behind in the personal quest for influence and social position." Rawls, *A Theory of Justice*, 91.

39 Sandel, *The Tyranny of Merit*, 24–31.

40 Rawls, *A Theory of Justice*, 64. The idea that we do not "deserve" our natural abilities in any deep moral sense was, for Rawls, "a moral truism. Who would deny it?" He continued, "Do people really think that they (morally) deserved to be born more gifted than others? Do they think that they (morally) deserved to be born a man rather than a woman, or vice versa? Do they think that they deserved to be born into a wealthier rather than into a poorer family? No." Rawls, *Justice as Fairness*, 74–5.

41 Rawls, *A Theory of Justice*, 65.

42 Ibid., 64–5. How far people can and should be held responsible for the amount of effort they put into an endeavour is hotly contested even within the broadly egalitarian liberal tradition. Indeed, this question is at the heart of debates around so-called "luck egalitarianism," the idea that inequalities are justified only if they are the product of choices which people can be held responsible for, rather than the result of unchosen circumstances. For a discussion of these ideas and their relationship to Rawls, see Samuel Scheffler, "What Is Egalitarianism?," *Philosophy & Public Affairs* 31:1 (2003), 5–39.

43 At first sight, this line of reasoning seems to culminate in the rather extreme conclusion that we cannot be held responsible for any of our actions. But this is not the point Rawls was trying to make. His aim was simply to show that if we want to organize a society around the meritocratic ideal, then we need to reach some agreement about what "merit" means, or what people morally deserve. And since people can only deserve things which they are responsible for in some way, this quickly leads us into the quicksands of one of the most intractable philosophical quandaries of all time—the debate about the nature of individual responsibility and free will. Rawls did not attempt to resolve this. Rather, he argued that since there is no prospect of reaching agreement, we should look for an alternative principle of economic justice.

44 Rawls, *Justice as Fairness*, 75–7.

45 Rawls's other principles also have implications for how much inequality we should tolerate as a society. The basic liberties principle justifies limiting inequality to whatever level is consistent with all citizens having a roughly equal influence over collective decision-making: while we can regulate donations to political parties, there is clearly a

limit to how far we can insulate the democratic process from wider inequalities. Similarly, if we are serious about fair equality of opportunity, we also need to reduce poverty and inequality directly, since there is a limit to how far the education system can make up for the different experiences that children have at home. Taken on their own, these principles already justify policies that would tackle the largest and most egregious inequalities in our societies, and they set an upper limit on how much inequality can be justified on the basis of the difference principle.

46 The idea that we have a collective moral duty to use the power of the state to help the poor is recognized across a whole range of political and philosophical views, including by almost every major thinker in the liberal tradition, even right-wing ones like Friedrich Hayek. However, while this duty has sometimes been conceived of as a matter of public charity, Rawls was clear that it is a question of basic justice. See Freeman, *Rawls*, 86.

47 As Rawls put it, "below a certain level of material and social well-being, and of training and education, people simply cannot take part in society as citizens, much less as equal citizens." Rawls, *Political Liberalism*, 166.

48 The basic liberties principle "may be preceded by a lexically prior principle requiring that basic needs be met, least insofar as their being met is a necessary condition for citizens to understand and to be able fruitfully to exercise the basic rights and liberties." Rawls, *Justice as Fairness*, 44. For a detailed discussion, see Rodney G. Peffer, "Basic Needs," in Mandle and Reidy (eds.), *The Cambridge Rawls Lexicon*, 50–54.

49 The difference principle is concerned with maximizing the living standards of the least well off *within the present generation*. It does not mean, as has been suggested by right-leaning Rawlsians like John Tomasi and Jason Brennan, that we need to maximize the prospects of the least well off in *future* generations. This would imply that we have an obligation to maximize the (sustainable) level of economic growth into the future. For a discussion of these issues, and a critique of Tomasi and Brennan, see Andrew Lister, "The Difference Principle, Capitalism, and Property-Owning Democracy," *Moral Philosophy and Politics* 5:1 (2018), 151–72. While the difference principle applies *within* generations, the just savings principle—which we will discuss at the end of this chapter—is concerned with justice *between* generations, and can help us think about the extent to which we should aim to increase the overall wealth of society over time.

50 As Rawls commented, we can think of the difference principle as providing "an interpretation of the principle of fraternity," which, compared to liberty and equality, had been largely overlooked within democratic theory. He argued that, in this way, his principles gave expression to all three concepts associated with the French Revolution and the wider democratic tradition: "liberty corresponds to the first principle, equality to the idea of equality in the first principle together with equality of fair opportunity, and fraternity to the difference principle." Of course, "fraternity" may also refer to a wider notion of social solidarity and civic friendship, with implications for how we treat our fellow citizens on a more personal level. For Rawls, the difference principle was a way of applying this concept to the question of how we organize our basic institutions. See Rawls, *A Theory of Justice*, 90–91.

51 As we shall see in Chapter 3, it's hard to find any socialists who actually endorse this idea in its strongest form.

52 Rawls, *Justice as Fairness*, 139.

53 Philippe Van Parijs, "Difference Principles," in Freeman (ed.), *The Cambridge Companion to Rawls*, 213–14.

54 Rawls has often been criticized for his failure to address these issues. For an explanation and defence of Rawls's approach, see Freeman, *Rawls*, 106–8. For an overview of how recent philosophers have taken up this question, including attempts to modify Rawls's approach, see Daniel Putnam et al., "Disability and Justice," in Edward N. Zalta (ed.), *The Stanford Encyclopedia of Philosophy* (fall 2019 edition), https://plato.stanford.edu/archives/fall2019/entries/disability-justice/.

55 Van Parijs, "Difference Principles," 211–16.

56 Rawls, *A Theory of Justice*, 74.

57 This is the essence of one of Robert Nozick's best-known criticisms of Rawls, the so-called "Wilt Chamberlain" argument. See Robert Nozick, *Anarchy, State, and Utopia* (New York: Basic Books, 1974), 160–64. For Rawls's response to this criticism, see *Political Liberalism*, 283.

58 Thomas Nagel, "Rawls and Liberalism," in Freeman (ed.), *The Cambridge Companion to Rawls*, 71.

59 This gap is even more shocking if we look at North America (U.S. and Canada) alone, where the top 1 per cent captured 35 per cent of growth, compared to 2 per cent for the bottom half. Across the world as a whole, the richest 1 per cent captured 27 per cent of the total increase in income, compared to just 12 per cent for the bottom half. "Pretax income" is defined as income before taxes and transfers, but

after the operation of the pension system. Facundo Alvaredo et al., *World Inequality Report, 2018* (Paris: World Inequality Lab, 2018), 48.

60 Rawls, *A Theory of Justice*, 87.

61 This feature of the difference principle has often been overlooked in popular discussions of Rawls's work, and even in some academic ones. As Samuel Arnold points out, Rawls is partly responsible for this, since he tended to illustrate his discussions of the difference principle by talking about wage levels: see Samuel Arnold, "The Difference Principle at Work," *Journal of Political Philosophy* 20:1 (2012), 94–118. But a careful reading of Rawls's work makes it clear that this is simply a heuristic device—a simplification to help us think through the principle's implications—and that, properly understood, the difference principle applies not just to the distribution of income and wealth but to the distribution of positions of power and responsibility, and the social bases of self-respect. See, for example, Rawls's comment that this principle "applies, in the first approximation, to the distribution of income and wealth and to the design of organizations that make use of differences in authority and responsibility" (*A Theory of Justice*, 53), and that "Eventually in applying the difference principle we wish to include in the prospects of the least advantaged the primary good of self-respect" (ibid., 312). There is now a broad consensus among Rawls scholars on this point: see, for example, Freeman, *Rawls*, 105–6, 113; Van Parijs, "Difference Principles," 211–12; and Martin O'Neill, "Free (and Fair) Markets without Capitalism: Political Values, Principles of Justice, and Property-Owning Democracy," in Martin O'Neill and Thad Williamson (eds.), *Property-Owning Democracy: Rawls and Beyond* (Chichester: Blackwell, 2012), 89–90.

62 Unfortunately, Rawls said very little about this vital primary good. For a thoughtful discussion of how we might interpret this idea, building on Rawls's brief comments, see Arnold, "The Difference Principle at Work."

63 For a detailed discussion of Rawls's ideas about self-respect, see Jeffrey Moriarty, "Rawls, Self-Respect, and the Opportunity for Meaningful Work," *Social Theory and Practice* 35:3 (2009), 441–59.

64 Rawls, *A Theory of Justice*, 386.

65 Rawls's most detailed discussion of self-respect can be found in *A Theory of Justice*, 386–92. I have broken this concept down into three distinct parts: meaningful work, social recognition, and agency. Rawls himself did not make these precise distinctions, but they are implicit in his discussion. He defined self-respect as having "two aspects."

First, it "includes a person's sense of his own value, his secure conviction that his conception of his good, his plan of life, is worth carrying out." This sense of self-worth in turn depends on "(1) having a rational plan of life, and in particular one that satisfies the Aristotelian Principle [as defined in the main text]; and (2) finding our person and deeds appreciated and confirmed by others who are likewise esteemed and their association enjoyed"—in other words, on having opportunities to exercise one's skills and capacities, or what I refer to as "meaningful work," and on "social recognition." Second, Rawls argued that, alongside a sense of self-worth, self-respect depends on having a sense of self-efficacy—"confidence in one's ability . . . to fulfill one's intentions"—or what I have referred to as a sense of "agency" or "independence."

66 Ibid., 377, 386.

67 Moriarty, "Rawls, Self-Respect, and the Opportunity for Meaningful Work," 449–53.

68 Rawls, *A Theory of Justice*, 386.

69 Ibid., 387–8.

70 Rawls referred to this as the "index problem," since it raises the question of how we should weight the different elements in an index of social and economic primary goods (*A Theory of Justice*, 113). See also Arnold, "The Difference Principle at Work," 113–14. As Arnold suggests, it seems entirely plausible that most low-paid employees would be willing to exchange a little income for more power and control, with all the benefits this might have in terms of job quality. This is even more likely to be true if the least well off had much higher incomes than they currently do, which they would if we put in place the policies required to realize the difference principle.

71 Rawls, *Justice as Fairness*, 137–8. For detailed discussions of Rawls's critique of "welfare state capitalism," see Freeman, *Rawls*, 219–35, and O'Neill, "Free (and Fair) Markets without Capitalism."

72 Lukas Meyer, "Intergenerational Justice," sect. 4.4, in Edward N. Zalta (ed.), *The Stanford Encyclopedia of Philosophy* (summer 2020 edition), https://plato.stanford.edu/archives/sum2020/entries/justice intergenerational/.

73 As Freeman summarizes, the just savings principle "requires current generations to set aside and save for the future as much as they would rationally want their predecessors to have saved for them *knowing* that they [the current generation] are obligated to provide the same amount for those who come after them": see Freeman, *Rawls*, 139.

74 Rawls, *Justice as Fairness*, 159.

75 Of course, we have to balance the welfare of the current generation against the aim of securing justice in the future, and so the savings rate—the proportion of income or wealth to be set aside for saving—should not be too high, especially at low levels of development. But if there was no obligation to save whatsoever, then poor societies would never attain the minimum level of prosperity needed to sustain just and democratic institutions. Rawls himself argued that "it is impossible to be very specific about the schedule of [savings] rates" that would be justified according to this principle, and sought only to set some broad limits on the range of savings that are required as a matter of justice. See Lister, "The Difference Principle, Capitalism, and Property-Owning Democracy." See Rawls, *A Theory of Justice*, 255.

76 As Rawls said, "It is a mistake to believe that a just and good society must wait upon a high material standard of life": Rawls, *A Theory of Justice*, 257.

77 "The difference principle . . . does not require continual economic growth over generations to maximize upward indefinitely the expectations of the least advantaged (assessed in terms of income and wealth). That would not be a reasonable conception of justice. We should not rule out Mill's idea of a society in a just stationary state where (real) capital accumulation may cease." See Rawls, *Justice as Fairness*, 63–4.

78 Meyer, "Intergenerational Justice," sect. 4.4. Whereas the just savings principle clearly requires us to maintain the minimum conditions that are needed for the existence of a just society over time, there is some debate about its implications beyond that.

79 Although he said very little about the environment, Rawls recognized that this was an essential part of the question of intergenerational justice, commenting that this topic included both "the question of the appropriate rate of capital saving and of the conservation of natural resources and the environment of nature." Rawls, *A Theory of Justice*, 118–19. A number of other thinkers have used, and in some cases extended, Rawls's ideas to develop a more thorough account of environmental justice and sustainability. See, for example, Russ Manning, "Environmental Ethics and Rawls' Theory of Justice," *Environmental Ethics* 3:2 (1981), 155–65; Catriona McKinnon, *Climate Change and Future Justice: Precaution, Compensation and Triage* (Abingdon: Routledge, 2012); John Töns, *John Rawls and Environmental Justice: Implementing a Sustainable and Socially Just Future* (Abingdon: Routledge, 2022).

80 This is the classic definition of sustainable development first put

forward in the Brundtland Report. See World Commission on Environment and Development, *Our Common Future* (Oxford: Oxford University Press, 1987).

81 The just savings principle implies a commitment to "strong" rather than "weak" sustainability. "Weak" sustainability seeks to maintain the overall wealth of society from one generation to the next, but allowing for an increase in material wealth (like the stock of industrial machinery or housing) to compensate for a decline in natural wealth (like stocks of essential minerals or fossil fuels). "Strong" sustainability, by contrast, recognizes that there are critical aspects of the natural world that cannot be substituted for by an increase in material wealth. Strong sustainability implies that our societies must operate within certain hard ecological limits, and in Chapter 7 we will look at how we can put this idea into practice. For a discussion of these concepts, see Eric Neumayer, *Weak Versus Strong Sustainability: Exploring the Limits of Two Opposing Paradigms*, fourth edition (Cheltenham: Edward Elgar Publishing, 2013).

2. A NEW SOCIAL CONTRACT

1 John Rawls, *Justice as Fairness: A Restatement*, ed. Erin Kelly (Cambridge, MA: Harvard University Press, 2001), 14–15.

2 Rawls argued that even among intelligent and well-informed people who honestly want to pursue the truth, disagreement about these kinds of questions is all but inevitable. This is a consequence of what he called the "burdens of judgement," including the complexity of evidence, vagueness of concepts, the way our experiences shape our understanding and the pluralism of basic values. The only way to eliminate such disagreement, he argued, would be through the oppressive use of state power, as in medieval Europe where religious conformity was enforced by the Catholic Church, and in authoritarian religious regimes today such as Saudi Arabia. See Rawls, *Justice as Fairness*, 32–8.

3 John Rawls, *Lectures on the History of Political Philosophy*, ed. Samuel Freeman (Cambridge, MA: Harvard University Press, 2008), 13; Fred D'Agostino et al., "Contemporary Approaches to the Social Contract," in Edward N. Zalta (ed.), *The Stanford Encyclopedia of Philosophy* (fall 2019 edition), https://plato.stanford.edu/archives/fall2019/entries contractarianism-contemporary/.

4 In the preface to *A Theory of Justice*, Rawls said his aim was to "generalize and carry to a higher order of abstraction the traditional theory

of the social contract as represented by Locke, Rousseau, and Kant" so that it was "no longer open to the more obvious objections often thought fatal to it"; and, in doing so, to provide "an alternative systematic account of justice that is superior [to] utilitarianism." See John Rawls, *A Theory of Justice*, revised edition (Cambridge, MA: Harvard University Press, 1999), xvii–xviii.

5 Ibid., 30–35. Rawls was able to transcend this divide by developing a clear ranking of different principles or values. See the discussion in Chapter 1, n. 12, above.

6 Michael J. Sandel, *Justice: What's the Right Thing to Do?* (New York: Farrar, Straus and Giroux, 2009), 141.

7 The parties in the original position are ignorant not only of facts about themselves but of most facts about the society they live in, such as if there is a dominant religious or ethnic group. For a detailed description of the original position, see Rawls, *Justice as Fairness*, 80–89, and Samuel Freeman, *Rawls* (Abingdon: Routledge, 2007), 141–98.

8 This example draws on Adam Swift, *Political Philosophy: A Beginners' Guide for Students and Politicians*, third edition (Cambridge: Polity, 2014), 24–5.

9 From the perspective of the original position, the parties know that unless they and their fellow citizens have the capacities for a conception of the good and for a sense of justice, society will be little more than a struggle for power and control, and that whatever their goals in life, they are more likely to be able to pursue them in a stable and cooperative society. For a more detailed discussion of the motivation of the parties in the original position, see John Rawls, *Political Liberalism*, expanded edition (New York: Columbia University Press, 2005), 304–24.

10 For a discussion of why primary goods are the appropriate "metric" for thinking about justice, see *A Theory of Justice*, 78–81, and *Justice as Fairness*, 57–61, 88. Rawls's most detailed account of these questions is contained in "Social Unity and Primary Goods" (1982), in John Rawls, *Collected Papers* (Cambridge, MA: Harvard University Press, 2001), 359–87.

11 Rawls, *Justice as Fairness*, 84–5.

12 Rawls, *A Theory of Justice*, 514.

13 Rawls referred to this as the "strains of commitment." See *Justice as Fairness*, 102–4, and Freeman, *Rawls*, 182–5.

14 As Rawls put it, the original position "models what we regard—here and now—as fair conditions under which the representatives of free

and equal citizens are to specify the terms of social cooperation in the case of the basic structure of society," and, as a result, the principles the parties would adopt "[identify] the conception of justice that we regard—here and now—as fair and supported by the best reasons." John Rawls, *Political Liberalism*, expanded edition (New York: Columbia University Press, 2005), 25–6.

15 Rawls, *Justice as Fairness*, 29–32. For a more detailed discussion of "reflective equilibrium" and Rawls's wider approach to justifying his principles, see Freeman, *Rawls*, 142–7, and T. M. Scanlon, "Rawls on Justification," in Samuel Freeman (ed.), *The Cambridge Companion to Rawls* (Cambridge: Cambridge University Press, 2003), 153–5. Thanks to Samuel Freeman for his helpful suggestions on this passage.

16 Rawls, *Justice as Fairness*, 94–5.

17 The following discussion reflects the "mature" version of Rawls's argument for why the parties in the original position would choose his principles, as set out in his later work *Justice as Fairness* (80–134). For an overview of how Rawls's presentation of this argument evolved over time, see Freeman, *Rawls*, 167–97. See also the comment in n. 23 below, which highlights one of the more significant changes.

18 For a detailed account of these criticisms and of Rawls's response to them, see Freeman, *Rawls*, 167–80. For Rawls's response itself, see *Justice as Fairness*, 106–10.

19 Rawls argued that the maximin rule is a rational way for people to make decisions when three conditions hold: first, they have no idea what the probability of different outcomes is, meaning they can't take an educated guess about the best way forward; second, there is an option where the worst-case scenario is a decent one; and third, some options could lead to outcomes that are completely intolerable. He argued that all three conditions apply to the choice faced by the parties in the original position: first, since they don't know who they will be in society, or even the relative size of its different groups, they cannot assign probabilities to how things will turn out for them under different principles; second, the worst-case outcome under "justice as fairness"—that is, being the worst off in a society regulated by Rawls's principles of justice—is a decent one; and third, as we have discussed in the main text, the worst-case outcome under utilitarianism would be truly intolerable. See *Justice as Fairness*, 97–101.

20 Rawls, *Justice as Fairness*, 105. Rawls only refers to religious freedom, but the same argument clearly applies to other basic liberties.

21 The argument for fair equality of opportunity from within the original position has been rather neglected, both by Rawls and by subsequent

commentators. See Anthony Simon Laden, "The Original Position," in Jon Mandle and David Reidy (eds.), *The Cambridge Rawls Lexicon* (Cambridge: Cambridge University Press, 2015), 583.

22 As we touched on in Chapter 1, although the just savings principle clearly applies to questions about the natural environment, Rawls himself focused primarily on the accumulation of material resources. See Rawls, *A Theory of Justice*, 251–8.

23 Rawls recognized that *A Theory of Justice* was not entirely clear on this point, later describing this as a "serious fault" (*Justice as Fairness*, 95 n. 17). In *Justice as Fairness*, he reformulated the argument within the original position into "two fundamental comparisons": one that focuses on the basic liberties principle, which relies on the maximin argument; and a second that focuses on the difference principle, which does not. The discussion in the main text here follows Rawls's revised approach.

24 For the argument against restricted utilitarianism, see Rawls, *Justice as Fairness*, 119–30, and Freeman, *Rawls*, 188–98.

25 See Anthony Simon Laden, "Difference Principle," in Mandle and Reidy (eds.), *The Cambridge Rawls Lexicon*, 211–16.

26 Rawls thought it was vital that any theory of justice be compatible with a reasonable account of the facts of human moral psychology, and the subject is at the heart of the (often overlooked) third part of *A Theory of Justice*. Here, Rawls set out an account of how citizens might come to develop a sense of justice, which draws in part on the work of the developmental psychologist Lawrence Kohlberg, starting with the way in which children develop a sense of reciprocity through their interactions with their family and then with a wider community. See Walter J. Riker, "Kohlberg, Lawrence," in Mandle and Reidy (eds.), *The Cambridge Rawls Lexicon*, 405–6, and David A. Reidy, "Moral Psychology," in ibid., 520–27.

27 Rawls, *Justice as Fairness*, 1, 192–5. Of course, this kind of compromise could just as easily lead to a contraction in our basic freedoms.

28 For the definition of an "overlapping consensus," see ibid., 32–8; and, for a discussion of how this might actually come about, and why it isn't simply "utopian," ibid., 192–4.

29 Rawls, *Political Liberalism*, 459.

30 Ibid., 11–15. These three features are common to any set of "political" principles, or to any "political conception of justice"—of which Rawls's is just one example (see the discussion about the family of reasonable political principles in note 32 on page 312).

31 For "comprehensive" utilitarians, the principle of maximizing total

happiness or "utility" is not only a principle for justifying political institutions, but a rule that we should follow in everything we do—in choosing our career, in deciding how much money to give to charity, and even in how we treat our family and friends.

32 Rawls argued that citizens would support reasonable political principles for two reasons. First, because, as we shall see, these principles are grounded in ideas drawn from the "public political culture," which they recognize as the only reasonable starting place for developing a shared idea of justice. Second, he also argued that citizens could support these principles for reasons that are rooted within their own comprehensive doctrine. So, for example, Christians might support liberal political principles because they follow from their commitment to the equal dignity of all human beings in the eyes of God; while secular liberals might support them because they promote the ideal of autonomy. In this way, citizens with different moral and religious outlooks can support the same political principles, but for different reasons. We can think of an overlapping consensus as being like a Venn diagram, where citizens' different comprehensive views are the circles, and the shared political principles are where they overlap. See Rawls, *Justice as Fairness*, 184–95.

33 Ibid., 5–7.

34 Ibid., 5.

35 "The public political culture is not unambiguous: it contains a variety of possible organizing ideas that might be used instead, various ideas of liberty and equality, and other ideas of society. All we need claim is that the idea of society as a fair system of cooperation is deeply embedded in that culture, and so it is not unreasonable to examine its merits as a central organizing idea." Rawls, *Justice as Fairness*, 25–6.

36 First, the parties in the original position are tasked with choosing principles for organizing society's basic structure—not with agreeing wider principles about how to live. Second, they are ignorant of their religious or moral beliefs, which means that whatever principles they choose will be justified independently of those beliefs. Finally, the whole construction of this thought experiment embodies familiar and intuitive ideas from the public political culture of democratic societies: the description of the parties reflects the idea of citizens as free and equal; while the fact that they are looking for principles that everyone could agree to reflects the idea of society as a fair system of cooperation.

37 Aristotle, *The Politics*, book VII, 1323a, translated by Ernest Barker

(New York: Oxford University Press, 1946), quoted in Sandel, *Justice*, 215.

38 Rawls recognized that we cannot develop any substantive theory of justice without *some* idea of what people's interests are, and hence *some* idea of "the good life" (often simply abbreviated to "the good"). But he argued that we could rely on a "thin" and distinctively political idea of the good (as defined by the notion of "primary goods") which is compatible with the many "thicker" ideas of the good held by real-life people. See Rawls, *Justice as Fairness*, 140–45.

39 This discussion draws on Thomas Nagel's review of Michael Sandel's book *Public Philosophy: Essays on Morality in Politics* (Cambridge, MA: Harvard University Press, 2006), "Progressive but Not Liberal," *New York Review of Books*, 25 May 2006. See also Sandel's response, in Michael J. Sandel, "The Case for Liberalism: An Exchange," *New York Review of Books*, 5 October 2006.

40 Note that this is a critique of grounding political principles in comprehensive liberalism, rather than of comprehensive liberalism per se. It is perfectly possible to be a comprehensive liberal, in the sense that you value autonomy as the highest good in life; *and* to be a political liberal, in the sense that you think that liberal institutions need to be justified on the basis of political ideas that most citizens can share, rather than with an ideal of autonomy that many people don't.

41 Richard Dawkins, *The God Delusion* (London: Bantam Press, 2006).

42 Rawls, *Political Liberalism*, 190–200.

43 Rawls and other liberals are sometimes criticized for being excessively "universalist," in the sense that they appeal to abstract values rather than to the values of any particular community. While these criticisms may apply to some extent to *A Theory of Justice*, in *Political Liberalism* Rawls was clear that we should think of his ideas as applicable to modern constitutional democracies and expressing values found in their public culture. For a discussion of this critique, see Stephen Mulhall and Adam Swift, "Rawls and Communitarianism," in Freeman (ed.), *The Cambridge Companion to Rawls*, 460–70.

44 Amartya Sen, *Human Rights and Asian Values*, Sixteenth Annual Morgenthau Memorial Lecture on Ethics and Foreign Policy (New York: Carnegie Council on Ethics and International Affairs, 1997).

45 For Rawls's most extensive and developed treatment of the ideas of civility and public reason, see *Political Liberalism*, 435–90. For

detailed discussions, see Freeman, *Rawls*, 381–401, and Jonathan Quong, "On the Idea of Public Reason," in Jon Mandle and David Reidy (eds.), *A Companion to Rawls* (Chichester: Wiley Blackwell, 2014), 265–80.

46 Quong, "On the Idea of Public Reason," 267.

47 Rawls, *Political Liberalism*, 243 n. 32 and 479.

48 The idea of the "reasonable" plays a central role in Rawls's philosophy. According to Rawls, reasonable people want to live with others on terms that everyone can accept as fair, and reasonable political principles are those which all reasonable people could accept. For a more detailed discussion, see Freeman, *Rawls*, 345–51.

49 Rawls, *Political Liberalism*, xlvi–xlvii, 6.

50 The idea that there is a family of reasonable political principles—or "political conceptions of justice"—plays an important role in putting into practice a distinction that Rawls draws between legitimacy and justice. According to Rawls, laws and institutions are "legitimate" when they are justified according to any member of the family of reasonable political principles; and we have a presumptive moral duty to obey legitimate laws. This is a weaker standard than justice, in the sense that laws can be legitimate without being fully just. For Rawls, laws are fully just only if they are grounded in the "most reasonable" conception of justice, namely his own principles of "justice as fairness." So, for example, a society that respects basic freedoms but does nothing to support the least well off beyond ensuring a basic minimum may be legitimate while still falling short of being fully just. From a practical point of view, this distinction explains why we should obey some laws even when we think they are unjust, since as long as laws meet the minimum standard of legitimacy, we have a presumptive duty to obey them. This is essential because if anyone could disobey any law they didn't think was just, a stable democracy would be impossible. See Freeman, *Rawls*, 371–81.

51 Rawls highlighted judges as an example of public reason in practice. In ruling on cases, judges have to appeal to commonly accepted legal principles and precedents, rather than their own personal moral or religious beliefs. In this way, the law provides judges with a source of public (rather than private) reasons. See Rawls, *Political Liberalism*, 231–40.

52 Rawls argued that when citizens reveal the religious or non-public reasons why they support certain political positions in this way, it can help reassure others that they are committed to a shared set of political values. Rawls, *Political Liberalism*, 462–6.

3. RAWLS AND HIS CRITICS

1 Samuel Freeman, "Capitalism in the Classical and High Liberal Traditions," *Social Philosophy and Policy* 28:2 (2011), 19–55.

2 Robert Nozick, *Anarchy, State, and Utopia* (New York: Basic Books, 1974), 230.

3 According to Nozick's obituary in the *Guardian*, his book, which had been translated into eleven languages by his death, "philosophically underpinned the free market, anti-welfarism of the . . . Reagan-Thatcher era." See Jane O'Grady, "Robert Nozick," *Guardian*, 26 January 2002.

4 Nozick, *Anarchy, State, and Utopia*, ix.

5 Ibid., 169.

6 Rawls argued that Nozick's libertarianism wasn't really a form of liberalism at all. For Rawls, any liberal view had to have the features that we discussed in Chapter 2: a precedence for certain basic liberties and a guarantee that everyone would be able to meet their basic needs. Since Nozick failed to guarantee the latter, this makes his ideas libertarian rather than liberal. As Rawls noted, this isn't an argument against Nozick's theory, it's just a helpful way of categorizing it, and of highlighting what makes it different from other more recognizably liberal theories. See John Rawls, *Lectures on the History of Political Philosophy*, ed. Samuel Freeman (Cambridge, MA: Harvard University Press, 2008), 13. For a more detailed discussion of what distinguishes liberalism from libertarianism see Samuel Freeman, "Illiberal Libertarians: Why Libertarianism Is Not a Liberal View," *Philosophy & Public Affairs* 30:2 (2001), 105–51.

7 Milton Friedman, for example, was willing to support some government policies that would make markets more efficient, and even some measures to address extreme poverty; but he opposed civil rights legislation banning race-based discrimination, on the grounds that employers should be free to hire whomever they like on more or less whatever terms they like. See Freeman, "Capitalism in the Classical and High Liberal Traditions," 44–5. Hayek similarly worried that any attempt by the state to bring about a particular distribution of resources would undermine freedom. See Michael J. Sandel, *Justice: What's the Right Thing to Do?* (New York: Farrar, Straus and Giroux, 2009), 61.

8 According to Jason Brennan, most libertarians today reject Nozick's natural rights approach and instead agree with Rawls, and with a long philosophical tradition which stretches back to David Hume,

that rights are fundamentally conventional or social rather than natural—in other words, they are the product of human choices and so must be justified rather than simply asserted. See Jason Brennan, "Libertarianism after Nozick," *Philosophy Compass* 13:2 (2018). As Milton Friedman put it, "The notion of property ... has become so much a part of us that we tend to take it for granted, and fail to recognize the extent to which just what constitutes property and what rights the ownership of property confers are complex social creations rather than self-evident propositions": quoted in Freeman, "Capitalism in the Classical and High Liberal Traditions," 34. A different approach, advocated by John Tomasi, is to argue that Rawls's own theory justifies a more extensive set of economic freedoms being counted as "basic liberties" than Rawls himself proposed: see John Tomasi, *Free Market Fairness* (Princeton: Princeton University Press, 2012). For a powerful critique of Tomasi and defence of the more conventional Rawlsian position, see Thad Williamson and Martin O'Neill, "Free Market Fairness," *Boston Review*, 5 November 2012.

9 For a contemporary defence of this kind of position, see N. Gregory Mankiw, "Spreading the Wealth Around: Reflections Inspired by Joe the Plumber," National Bureau of Economic Research Working Paper 15846 (March 2010).

10 Hayek, cited in Michael J. Sandel, *The Tyranny of Merit: What's Become of the Common Good?* (London: Penguin, 2020), 126–8. See also Andrew Lister, "Mankiw on Just Deserts," blog post, 12 May 2014, https://andrewlister.blog/2014/05/12/mankiw-on-just-deserts/.

11 Although neither Hayek nor Friedman described themselves as utilitarians, on closer inspection both appear to have believed that the ultimate justification for a strong commitment to property rights rests on the idea that these would promote economic efficiency, which in turn would promote social welfare. See Freeman, "Capitalism in the Classical and High Liberal Traditions," 23 n. 5, 35, 52.

12 Laura Spinney, "Will Coronavirus Lead to Fairer Societies? Thomas Piketty Explores the Prospect," *Guardian*, 12 May 2020. Piketty also refers to this as the "Pandora's Box" argument: "namely, that any challenge to private property will inevitably unleash uncontrollable chaos so that it is better never to open the box." See Thomas Piketty, *Capital and Ideology*, trans. Arthur Goldhammer (Cambridge, MA: Harvard University Press, 2020), 990.

13 Andrew Lister, "The 'Mirage' of Social Justice: Hayek Against (and For) Rawls," *Critical Review* 25:3–4 (2013), 431. As Lister notes, while Hayek's views are hard to piece together, at the level of abstract

principles his position appears to be remarkably similar to Rawls's. Hayek frequently argued that the case for free markets and private property was that, compared to the feasible alternatives, they would benefit everyone. Elsewhere he claimed that extensive property rights were justified because they would maximize the opportunities of any randomly selected member of society. According to Lister, most of the differences between Rawls and Hayek stem from the latter's extreme optimism about the operation of markets, and from under-argued "slippery slope" claims along the lines discussed here.

14 See André Azevedo Alves and John Meadowcroft, "Hayek's Slippery Slope, the Stability of the Mixed Economy and the Dynamics of Rent Seeking," *Political Studies* 62:4 (2014), 843–61. The authors conclude that, far from supporting Hayek's hypothesis, the evidence "shows conclusively that it is the mixed economy that has proved remarkably stable, whereas laissez-faire and totalitarian regimes have proved inherently unstable."

15 Raymond Geuss, quoted in Brian Leiter, "Geuss on Political Philosophy, Rawls, and the Circumstances of Philosophy," *Leiter Reports: A Philosophy Blog*, 14 August 2014, https://leiterreports.typepad.com /blog/2014/08/geussonpoliticalthoughtrawlsandthecircumstances -of-philosophy.html.

16 Paul Mason, "The Left, the Party and the Class: An Essay on the Future of the Labour Left," *Medium*, 25 July 2020. For a discussion (and rebuttal) of more academic criticisms of Rawls from the left, see Arthur DiQuattro, "Rawls and Left Criticism," *Political Theory* 11:1 (1983), 53–78.

17 For an overview of feminist criticisms directed at Rawls, and potential Rawlsian responses, see Martha C. Nussbaum, "Rawls and Feminism," in Samuel Freeman (ed.), *The Cambridge Companion to Rawls* (Cambridge: Cambridge University Press, 2003), 488–520. For a critical perspective on Rawls and race, see Charles W. Mills, "A Critique of Tommie Shelby," *Critical Philosophy of Race* 1:1 (2013), 1–27. And, for a defence of Rawls, see Tommie Shelby, "Race and Social Justice: Rawlsian Considerations," *Fordham Law Review* 72:5 (2004), 1697–1714, and Shelby's response to Mills, "A Reply to Charles Mills," *Critical Philosophy of Race* 1:2 (2013), 145–62.

18 John Rawls, *Justice as Fairness: A Restatement*, ed. Erin Kelly (Cambridge, MA: Harvard University Press, 2001), 170–71. For an overview of some of the ways in which different thinkers have tried to address these concerns, see Daniel Putnam et al., "Disability and Justice," in Edward N. Zalta (ed.), *The Stanford Encyclopedia of Philosophy*

(fall 2019 edition), https://plato.stanford.edu/archives/fall2019
/entries/disability-justice/, and Linda Barclay, *Disability with Dignity: Justice, Human Rights and Equal Status* (Abingdon: Routledge, 2018).

19 The term "socialism," like "liberalism"—and indeed any other "-ism"—means different things to different people. Many individuals who describe themselves as "socialists" use the term simply to indicate a commitment to equality, and a moral opposition to capitalism as we know it; and, at a philosophical level, it's often hard to distinguish this kind of socialism from Rawls's egalitarian liberalism. In the remainder of this section, I have focused on socialist arguments that follow Marx in focusing on the injustice of private ownership of the means of production. The discussion draws on the chapter on "Marxism" in Will Kymlicka, *Contemporary Political Philosophy: An Introduction*, second edition (Oxford: Oxford University Press, 2002), 166–207.

20 This paraphrases Kymlicka, *Contemporary Political Philosophy*, 176. Thomas Nagel makes a similar point in "Rawls and Liberalism," in Freeman (ed.), *The Cambridge Companion to Rawls*, 70.

21 "*Simple* equality, meaning everyone being furnished with the same material level of goods and services . . . is generally rejected as untenable . . . neither communism nor socialism . . . calls for absolute economic equality": Stefan Gosepath, "Equality," in Edward N. Zalta (ed.), *The Stanford Encyclopedia of Philosophy* (summer 2021 edition), sect. 3.1, https://plato.stanford.edu/archives/sum2021/entries/equality/.

22 Brian Leiter, "Why Marxism Still Does Not Need Normative Theory," *Analyse & Kritik* 37:1–2 (2015), 29. For Leiter, the failure to challenge capitalist relations of production is the defining feature of what he dismisses as "bourgeois practical philosophy."

23 For an example of this argument, see William A. Edmundson, *John Rawls: Reticent Socialist* (Cambridge: Cambridge University Press, 2017). Edmundson argues that, while Rawls leaves the choice between capitalism or socialism open in principle, in practice the basic liberties principle commits him to socialism since, according to Edmundson, it is impossible to secure political equality in a society with private ownership of the means of production.

24 The discussion here follows the interpretation set out in Kymlicka, *Contemporary Political Philosophy: An Introduction*, 177–87. For an overview of the debate about how to interpret this key Marxist concept, see Matt Zwolinski and Alan Wertheimer, "Exploitation," in Edward N. Zalta (ed.), *The Stanford Encyclopedia of Philosophy*

(summer 2017 edition), https://plato.stanford.edu/archives/sum2017
/entries/exploitation/.

25 Of course, some "capitalists" or owners also perform labour: for
example, in owner-managed firms where owners do "management"
work. Strictly speaking, from the perspective of the Marxist theory of
exploitation, there is nothing wrong with owners being paid for this
kind of work. The problem is that owners also receive income in the
form of profits, simply because they are owners.

26 Even if we accept the conventional Marxist account of exploitation,
we might still endorse something like Rawls's idea of a "property
owning democracy," where property is privately owned but ownership is very widely shared rather than full-blown socialism. In a such
a society, most citizens would have a substantial, or even roughly
equal, share in society's wealth, and consequently there would no
longer be a class of capitalists who live off the "surplus labour" of
everyone else. This would largely—if not entirely—address Marxist
concerns about exploitation, depending on precisely how we define
that term. Thanks to Stuart White for emphasizing this point.

27 Kymlicka, *Contemporary Political Philosophy*, 179.

28 Branko Milanovic makes this point in his "Ricardo, Marx, and Interper-
sonal Inequality," *Global Inequality and More 3.0* (Substack), 18 October 2021, https://branko2f7.substack.com/p/ricardo-marx-and
interpersonal-inequality?mc_cid=ae01f8df66&mc_eid=78087e0c17.
For an overview of the relative importance of income versus wealth
inequality, see Thomas Piketty, *Capital in the Twenty-First Century*, trans. Arthur Goldhammer (Cambridge, MA: Harvard University Press, 2014), 263. See also Maura Francese and Carlos
Mulas-Granados, "Functional Income Distribution and Its Role in
Explaining Inequality," IMF Working Papers 2015, no. 244, which
notes that most of the increase in inequality in recent decades is the
result of growing disparities between workers rather than a shift of
overall income from labour to capital.

29 Rawls has also been criticized—not unfairly—for having relatively
little to say about these questions.

30 Will Kymlicka, *Contemporary Political Philosophy*, 180, and G. A.
Cohen, "Marxism and Contemporary Political Philosophy, or, Why
Nozick Exercises Some Marxists More Than He Does Any Egalitarian
Liberals," *Canadian Journal of Philosophy Supplementary* 16 (1990),
363–87. Cohen's interpretation of Marx is disputed. For an alternative
account, see Stuart White, "Needs, Labour, and Marx's Conception
of Justice," *Political Studies* 44:1 (1996), 88–101.

31 Exploitation isn't the only concept which socialists have for thinking about justice. Another prominent one is Marx's maxim "From each according to his ability, to each according to his needs." For a discussion of the difficulties with this notion, and how it potentially conflicts with the Marxist account of exploitation, see Kymlicka, *Contemporary Political Philosophy*, 187–90.

32 A number of socialist thinkers, including Cohen and Roemer, have proposed a radical or "socialist" principle of equality of opportunity, according to which inequalities are fair if (and only if) they reflect choices that we can reasonably be held responsible for, rather than luck. As we saw in Chapter 1, n. 12, above, the same idea is often referred to as "luck egalitarianism," and has been supported by other philosophers, many of whom reject the "socialist" label. For an overview of these developments within socialist philosophy, see John Roemer, "Socialism Revised," *Philosophy & Public Affairs* 45:3 (2017), 297–303.

33 As with the idea of exploitation, there is some debate both about what Marx meant by alienation and about whether there are other, better ways to think about it. For a discussion of Marx's views, see Kymlicka, *Contemporary Political Philosophy*, 190, and Jonathan Wolff, "Karl Marx," in Edward N. Zalta (ed.), *The Stanford Encyclopedia of Philosophy* (winter 2017 edition), sect. 2.3, https://plato.stanford.edu/archives/win2017/entries/marx/.

34 These ideas haven't been ignored entirely. Adam Smith also wrote about the damaging effects that excessive specialization (the "division of labour") could have on workers, and John Stuart Mill advocated for worker cooperatives. More recently, there has been a resurgence of interest in these matters from a range of liberal perspectives. For an overview, see Nien-Hê Hsieh, "Survey Article: Justice in Production," *Journal of Political Philosophy* 16:1 (2008), 72–100.

35 See Jeffrey Moriarty, "Rawls, Self-Respect, and the Opportunity for Meaningful Work," *Social Theory and Practice* 35:3 (2009), 441–59.

36 Rawls, *Justice as Fairness*, 177, in direct response to Marx's critique of liberalism.

37 Communitarianism and its critique of liberalism are most closely associated with philosophers including Michael Sandel (whose ideas are discussed in more detail in the main text), and also Alasdair MacIntyre, Charles Taylor and Michael Walzer, all of whom wrote prominent books on this topic in the 1980s. For an excellent overview of these ideas and of the varied responses to them, see Daniel Bell, "Communitarianism," in Edward N. Zalta (ed.), *The*

Stanford Encyclopedia of Philosophy (summer 2016 edition), https://plato.stanford.edu/archives/sum2016/entries/communitarianism/. Recent examples of this broad line of argument include Francis Fukuyama, *Liberalism and Its Discontents* (London: Profile, 2022), and Patrick J. Deneen, *Why Liberalism Failed* (New Haven: Yale University Press, 2018). Although Fukuyama's book is ultimately a defence of liberalism, he argues that "belief in the sovereignty of the individual deepens liberalism's tendency to weaken other forms of communal engagement, and in particular turns people away from virtues like public-spiritedness that are needed to sustain a liberal policy overall" (63). Deneen's book is an outright critique, which states that liberalism's goal is "the liberation of the individual from particular places, relationships, memberships, and even identities—unless they have been chosen," and that it has "homogenized the world in its image" with devastating consequences (16–17). Whereas, for Fukuyama, the modern tendency towards excessive individualism is in some sense a perversion of important liberal values, for Deneen these flaws are inherent to liberalism and the reason we have to abandon it altogether.

38 For a detailed discussion of, and response to, the communitarian critique of Rawls, see Stephen Mulhall and Adam Swift, "Rawls and Communitarianism," in Freeman (ed.), *The Cambridge Companion to Rawls*, 460–87.

39 Michael J. Sandel, "The Procedural Republic and the Unencumbered Self," *Political Theory* 12:1 (1984), 81–96; Fukuyama, *Liberalism and Its Discontents*, 54.

40 Mulhall and Swift, "Rawls and Communitarianism," 461.

41 John Rawls, *A Theory of Justice*, revised edition (Cambridge, MA: Harvard University Press, 1999), 104. Inasmuch as the original position does reflect an underlying account of human psychology, it is one derived from a *political* conception of citizens and the capacities they need in order to participate in society.

42 John Rawls, *Political Liberalism*, expanded edition (New York: Columbia University Press, 2005), 27.

43 The description of the parties in the original position, and the reasons they have for choosing Rawls's principles, both also reflect the importance of community, albeit rather abstractly. As we saw in Chapter 1, the sense of belonging to a community which shares our outlook in life is, for Rawls, a crucial source of self-respect, and hence an important "primary good." Moreover, the parties choose to give precedence to certain basic liberties, including freedom of association, because

they know that for most people community of some form is among the most important things in life.

44 Rawls, *A Theory of Justice*, 229. The fact that our social context shapes our values and our sense of ourselves is one of the reasons why Rawls is so concerned with the basic structure of society in the first place, since we cannot escape its effects on who we are and what we want in life. See Rawls, *Justice as Fairness*, 22.

45 Rawls added that "[citizens] may regard it as simply unthinkable to view themselves apart from certain religious, philosophical, and moral convictions, or from certain enduring attachments and loyalties": Rawls, *Political Liberalism*, 31.

46 For a discussion of this distinction, see Bell, "Communitarianism," sect. 2, "The Debate Over the Self."

47 Rawls also developed his own account of the meaning of community, or "social union," as he often referred to it, which he defined as cooperating with others in order to achieve *shared* goals: see Rawls, *A Theory of Justice*, 456–64. He distinguished this from mutually beneficial cooperation, which is when we cooperate with other people simply because doing so helps us to advance our individual goals. Rawls gave the example of an orchestra: although individual musicians may take pleasure in playing their individual parts, an orchestra is a community because all its members wants to create a beautiful piece of music together. This idea of community as the pursuit of shared ends is intentionally broad: it encompasses the value not just of orchestras, but of religion, culture, friendships and family life. A family is a community not because it enables its members to pursue their individual goals, say by sharing the costs of housing and food, but because it enables them to pursue shared goals, such as raising children. Participation in such communities is, for Rawls, an essential part of human existence, "since it is only in active cooperation with others that one's powers reach fruition. Only in a social union is the individual complete" (*A Theory of Justice*, 460). For a discussion of Rawls's ideas on community, see Sibyl A. Schwarzenbach, "Social Union," in Jon Mandle and David Reidy (eds.), *The Cambridge Rawls Lexicon* (Cambridge: Cambridge University Press, 2015), 788–90.

48 Rawls also argued that even though a liberal society cannot be a community in the sense of pursuing a particular shared idea of how to live, its citizens still share the common aim of creating a just society, and this in turn is the basis for a sense of "political community."

49 This draws on Bell, "Communitarianism," sect. 3, "The Politics of Community."

50 The case for a proactive approach to supporting varied types of community, including via public subsidies, is grounded in the pervasive difficulties that citizens face in getting these forms of voluntary association off the ground. In particular, it reflects the tendency for some people to hold back from contributing towards the costs of setting up, say, a local or religious group if they can freeride on other people's hard work instead.

51 Raymond Geuss, *Philosophy and Real Politics* (Princeton: Princeton University Press, 2008), 23–30. For a detailed discussion of Geuss's criticisms, and a thorough response to them, see Samuel Freeman, "Review: Philosophy and Real Politics," *Ethics* 120:1 (2009), 175–84.

52 For example, Geuss rejects the original position for seeming to presuppose the "very naïve" idea "that one can in some way get a better grasp or understanding of the power relations in society and how they work by covering them up, ignoring them, or simply wishing them away": Geuss, *Philosophy and Real Politics*, 90. But, as Freeman points out, Rawls's aim is not to gain an "understanding [of] the political world," but to articulate an ideal of justice: see Freeman, "Review: Philosophy and Real Politics," 180–81.

53 Of course, it's possible that when politicians appeal to moral principles, this is really a mask for advancing their own interests. But as Rawls argued, "People are not so stupid as not to discern when . . . norms are being appealed to by certain groups and their leaders in a purely manipulative and group-interested fashion." See Rawls, *Lectures on the History of Political Philosophy*, 7.

54 See, for example, Jonathan Haidt, *The Righteous Mind: Why Good People Are Divided by Politics and Religion* (London: Penguin, 2012).

55 Self-interest and altruism obviously exist alongside reciprocity, and the balance between these motivations depends a lot on the context. This points towards the importance of designing our political and economic institutions in a way that is sensitive to, and indeed encourages, our basic capacity for reciprocity—for example, by ensuring that everyone has fair opportunities to contribute to economic life, and that what people earn depends to some extent on how hard they work. For an overview of the evidence about reciprocity from both psychology and anthropology, see Samuel Bowles and Herbert Gintis, "Reciprocity, Self-Interest, and the Welfare State," *Nordic Journal of Political Economy* 26:1 (2000), 33–53, as well as Samuel Bowles and Herbert Gintis, *A Cooperative Species: Human Reciprocity and Its Evolution* (Princeton: Princeton University Press, 2013).

56 See Amartya Sen, *The Idea of Justice* (Cambridge, MA: Harvard

University Press, 2009), and Amartya Sen, "What Do We Want from a Theory of Justice?," *Journal of Philosophy* 103:5 (2006), 215–38. For a detailed discussion of Sen's ideas, and a defence of Rawls, see Laura Valentini, "A Paradigm Shift in Theorizing about Justice? A Critique of Sen," *Economics and Philosophy* 27:3 (2011), 297–315.

57 Sen, *The Idea of Justice*, 52–3.

58 Ibid., 9.

59 Rawls, *A Theory of Justice*, 8. The distinguishing feature of ideal theory for Rawls is that it assumes "perfect compliance"—in other words, everyone in society abides by the rules and plays their part. The task of ideal theory is both to identify principles for such a society and to think through the broad outlines of the political and economic institutions that would best realize them. Non-ideal theory, by contrast, is concerned with problems that result from our failure to create just institutions such as the poverty that exists because of the inadequacies of existing welfare states, or with injustices that arise when people refuse to comply with just institutions, which is the focus of theories of criminal justice. For a detailed discussion of Rawls's account of ideal and non-ideal theory, see John A. Simmons, "Ideal and Non-ideal Theory," *Philosophy & Public Affairs* 38:1 (2010), 5–36.

60 John Rawls, *The Law of Peoples* (Cambridge, MA: Harvard University Press, 1999), 89.

61 For a discussion of the "target" (and "urgency") roles of ideal theory, see Zofia Stemplowska and Adam Swift, "Ideal and Nonideal Theory," in David Estlund (ed.), *The Oxford Handbook of Political Philosophy* (Oxford: Oxford University Press, 2012), 373–90. For an overview of the different elements of non-ideal theory, and a brilliant example of this kind of work, see Tommie Shelby, *Dark Ghettos: Injustice, Dissent, and Reform* (Cambridge, MA: Harvard University Press, 2016), 10–14.

62 In other words, although Sen is right that simply having a picture of a perfectly just society is neither necessary nor sufficient for making the comparative judgements we are normally faced with, Rawls's theory provides us with much more than this. See Valentini, "A Paradigm Shift in Theorizing about Justice?," 304–9, for a similar argument. To return to the Everest analogy, we don't need to know how high Everest is to work out which of two smaller peaks is taller than the other. But, to stretch the analogy, Rawls's ideal theory is not simply telling us which mountain is the highest, it tells us what kind of mountain we should be looking for in the first place. After all, mountains have many characteristics other than their height—some are more

beautiful, others have better weather or more varied wildlife. The purpose of ideal theory is not only to describe the perfect mountain, but to help us to work out which characteristics of the mountain—or of society—we should care about in the first place.

4. FREEDOM

1 Economist Intelligence Unit, *Democracy Index 2021: The China Challenge* (London: Economist Intelligence Unit, 2022), 25–6. Data collected by Freedom House paints a similar picture, with almost all regions witnessing a decline in "freedom of expression and belief" and "personal autonomy and individual rights" over the past fifteen years. See Sarah Repucci and Amy Slipowitz, *Freedom in the World 2021: Democracy under Siege* (Washington, DC: Freedom House, 2021), 16.

2 Graeme Reid, "Hungary's Path Puts Everyone's Rights in Danger," Human Rights Watch, 6 October 2021, https://www.hrw.org/news/2021/10/06/hungarys-path-puts-everyones-rights-danger.

3 Yascha Mounk, *The People vs. Democracy: Why Our Freedom Is in Danger and How to Save It* (Cambridge, MA: Harvard University Press, 2018), 47.

4 Ian Millhiser, "Where Will Abortion Still Be Legal Now That Roe v. Wade Has Been Overruled?," *Vox*, 11 April 2022; Joan E. Greve, "Contraception, Gay Marriage: Clarence Thomas Signals New Targets for Supreme Court," *Guardian*, 24 June 2022.

5 For global trends on attitudes towards homosexuality, see Jacob Poushter and Nicholas O. Kent, *The Global Divide on Homosexuality Persists* (Washington, DC: Pew Research Center, 2020). For a snapshot of opinion about religious expression, see Richard Wike and Katie Simmons, *Global Support for Principle of Free Expression, but Opposition to Some Forms of Speech* (Washington, DC: Pew Research Center, 2015).

6 Laura Silver et al., *Diversity and Division in Advanced Economies* (Washington, DC: Pew Research Center, 2021).

7 The following discussion draws on Thomas Nagel, "Progressive but Not Liberal," *New York Review of Books*, 25 May 2006, and Thomas Nagel, "Rawls and Liberalism," in Samuel Freeman (ed.), *The Cambridge Companion to Rawls* (Cambridge: Cambridge University Press, 2003), 74–5.

8 This closely paraphrases Nagel, "Rawls and Liberalism," 74.

9 There is, of course, much more to say about this complex issue, and

Rawls's own comments are mostly contained in a brief footnote in his book *Political Liberalism*, expanded edition (New York: Columbia University Press, 2005), 243 n. 32. In this note—which must be one of the most widely discussed footnotes in the history of political philosophy—he argues that every woman should have "a duly qualified right to decide whether or not to end her pregnancy in the first trimester" (i.e. during the first twelve weeks of pregnancy). For a discussion, reformulation and defence of Rawls's position, see Robbie Arrell, "Public Reason and Abortion: Was Rawls Right After All?," *Journal of Ethics* 23:1 (2019), 37–53. Rawls's position corresponds with the law in most European countries, where abortions are typically limited to twelve weeks, except in specific circumstances such as when the mother's health or life is at risk. In England, Scotland and Wales, the limit is twenty-four weeks, roughly the point of foetal viability (i.e. when a foetus can survive outside the womb), which until recently was also the basis for abortion rights in the U.S.A. See "Legal Time Frames Surrounding Access to Abortion in Selected European Countries in 2020," *Statista*, accessed 9 August 2022, https://www.statista.com/statistics/1268439/legalabortiontimeframesineurope/.

10 This refers to the *Dignitatis humanae* (Of the Dignity of the Human Person) declaration issued by the Second Vatican Council in 1965. See Rawls, *Political Liberalism*, 477 n. 75. For historical examples of respect for religious freedom under both Buddhist and Islamic rulers in the Indian subcontinent, see Amartya Sen, *Human Rights and Asian Values*, Sixteenth Annual Morgenthau Memorial Lecture on Ethics and Foreign Policy (New York: Carnegie Council on Ethics and International Affairs, 1997). For a recent discussion of religious freedom within the Islamic tradition, and a comparison with the Catholic experience, see Daniel Philpott, *Religious Freedom in Islam: The Fate of a Universal Human Right in the Muslim World Today* (Oxford: Oxford University Press, 2019).

11 The legal scholar and philosopher Andrew Koppelman has also criticized the tendency towards absolutism in debates about gay rights versus religious freedom, and has argued for an approach that recognizes the legitimate interests at stake on both sides. See Andrew Koppelman, *Gay Rights vs. Religious Liberty? The Unnecessary Conflict* (Oxford: Oxford University Press, 2020).

12 "LGBT Rights," Gallup poll, 3–18 May 2021, https://news.gallup.com/poll/1651/gay-lesbian-rights.aspx.

13 Note that these statistics come from different surveys and hence are not directly comparable. For a discussion of these surveys in the

context of longer term trends in public opinion, see Ben Clements and Clive D. Field, "The Polls—Trends: Public Opinion Toward Homosexuality and Gay Rights in Great Britain," *Public Opinion Quarterly* 78:2 (2014), 523–47 (the surveys cited in the text can be found on pp. 526, 537 and 529 respectively).

14 The distinction between vertical and horizontal applications of Rawls's basic liberties principle comes from Frank Michelman, rather than from Rawls. See Frank Michelman, "Rawls on Constitutionalism and Constitutional Law," in Freeman (ed.), *The Cambridge Companion to Rawls*, 415–20.

15 In America, the relevant case is *Masterpiece Cakeshop v. Colorado Civil Rights Commission*, which according to the legal scholar Erwin Chemerinsky "received more attention or raised more important issues" than any other case in front of the Supreme Court in the 2017–18 session. The Colorado Civil Rights Commission had found that the Masterpiece Cakeshop had violated anti-discrimination laws by refusing to design and bake a cake for a gay wedding. The Supreme Court eventually overturned that ruling, but on narrow procedural grounds: the justices claimed that the commission had expressed impermissible hostility towards religion in reaching its decisions. The ruling has left open the underlying question of whether religious belief is a legitimate basis for refusing to serve certain types of customers, and it is almost certain to return to the court in the near future, with potentially far-reaching consequences. For a brief overview, see Erwin Chemerinsky, "Not a Masterpiece: The Supreme Court's Decision in *Masterpiece Cakeshop v. Colorado Civil Rights Commission*," *Human Rights* 43:4 (2017), 11–15 For a thoughtful discussion of the underlying moral issues, see T. M. Scanlon, "A Framework for Thinking about Freedom of Speech, and Some of Its Implications," 2018, https://www .law.berkeley.edu/wp-content/uploads/2018/10/Freedom-of-Speech -Berkeley.pdf. A similar case in the UK (*Lee v. Ashers Baking Company Ltd*) involved a cake shop in Northern Ireland which refused to bake a cake with a message in support of gay marriage. In the end, the UK Supreme Court sided with the cake shop's right not to have to promote a political view it disagreed with, arguing that the shop had not violated antidiscrimination laws since it would have refused to bake such a cake even if the customers were not gay. See "'Gay Cake' Row: What Is the Dispute About?," *BBC News*, 6 January 2022.

16 These brief quotations borrow from Nelson Tebbe, *Religious Freedom in an Egalitarian Age* (Cambridge, MA: Harvard University Press, 2017), 2. Tebbe's book provides perhaps the most thorough and

detailed attempt to address the tension between religious freedom and equality protections in a broadly Rawlsian spirit.

17 Tebbe highlights widespread scepticism among legal scholars, especially on the right, who claim that "a rational approach to religious freedoms is *necessarily* impossible"; and he argues that this in turn is closely related to the growing sense of political conflict and polarization around these issues. See Nelson Tebbe, "McElroy Lecture: How to Think about Religious Freedom in an Egalitarian Age," *University of Detroit Mercy Law Review* 93:3 (2016), 353–68, and the discussion in the preface to Tebbe, *Religious Freedom in an Egalitarian Age*.

18 See, for example, Tebbe, *Religious Freedom in an Egalitarian Age*.

19 These restrictions should be both effective in protecting other basic freedoms and necessary, in the sense that we have exhausted other possibilities which don't require limiting our basic freedoms. For a detailed discussion of these issues, see Joshua Cohen, "Freedom of Expression," *Philosophy & Public Affairs* 22:3 (1993), 207–63.

20 Rawls's most extensive discussion of free speech, specifically in relation to freedom of political speech, can be found in *Political Liberalism*, 340–55. He argued that we should limit political speech only where it poses a real and imminent threat to the survival of liberal democracy itself, and there is no other reasonable way to protect democratic institutions—a threshold that he argued had never been crossed in the history of the U.S.A., not even during the Civil War. Rawls never commented directly on so-called "hate speech" laws, and although it seems likely that he would have adopted a similar position, there is some disagreement. For example, Freeman argues that hate speech might not warrant the same level of protection since, unlike political speech, it's harder to argue that it is really necessary for developing our moral capacities: Samuel Freeman, *Rawls* (Abingdon: Routledge, 2007), 72. This argument would seem to apply most strongly to direct harassment and so-called "fighting words" (face-to-face insults that might lead to violence), but it's not clear whether it could justify the almost total ban on certain points of speech which is common under hate speech laws.

21 Garton Ash suggests that we should be guided by "a modernised version of the Brandenburg test." See *Free Speech: Ten Principles for a Connected World* (New Haven: Yale University Press, 2017), 132–8.

22 The term "dangerous speech" comes from the scholar and free-speech advocate Susan Benesch, who defines it as "any form of expression (e.g. speech, text, or images) that can increase the risk that its audience will condone or participate in violence against members of

another group." She argues that this is a more helpful and precise term than "hate speech," and has developed a sophisticated framework for identifying "dangerous speech," taking into account the message, speaker, audience, context and medium. See Susan Benesch, *Dangerous Speech: A Practical Guide* (The Dangerous Speech Project, 2021). From the perspective of Rawls's theory, the state clearly has a legitimate interest in combating "dangerous speech," but, as we shall see, banning it should typically be the last resort.

23 The classical debate about free speech is concerned with whether and when the state can directly restrict certain forms of speech. But contemporary debates are increasingly concerned with situations in which the behaviour of private individuals or organizations could pose a threat to freedom of speech. The question here is not whether the state can intervene to *ban* speech, but whether it should intervene to *protect* it in certain situations. So, for example, should firms be able to fire their employees for expressing their religious or political views at work, or indeed outside it? Should universities be able to restrict speech on campus? Should social media companies be able to ban viewpoints that they consider to be offensive or anti-democratic or dangerous? Each of these questions raises specific issues; but, at least in principle, there is a legitimate role for state intervention to protect free speech in them all. Social media companies and other firms are not beyond the law simply because they are "private" organizations, and we can regulate their activities if this is essential for protecting our fundamental interest in living in a society where we can freely exercise our moral capacities.

24 In Denmark, hate speech laws ban speech "by which a group of people is threatened, insulted or degraded," while in Spain the law bans speech that is a "provocation" to discrimination, hate or violence against groups. In England, Scotland and Wales, the law proscribes speech that is intended or likely to "stir up" racial hatred, and in the Netherlands the law applies to any statement which someone "knows or should reasonably suspect to be offensive to a group of persons on the grounds of their race, religion, personal beliefs, or their hetero or homosexual orientation." See Garton Ash, *Free Speech*, 215.

25 "Sex-Based Hostility Should Be Hate Speech, Recommends Report," *BBC News*, 7 December 2021.

26 See Corey Brettschneider, *When the State Speaks, What Should It Say? How Democracies Can Protect Expression and Promote Equality* (Princeton: Princeton University Press, 2012), and, for a summary, his "When the State Speaks, What Should It Say? The Dilemmas of

Freedom of Expression and Democratic Persuasion," *Perspectives on Politics* 8:4 (2010), 1005–19. Although Brettschneider doesn't explicitly develop his ideas as an application or extension of Rawls's theory, they are broadly consistent with it.

27 The state should restrict itself to promoting the most fundamental liberal and democratic values rather than promoting a detailed conception of justice (the state should obviously not be trying to indoctrinate children into blindly endorsing Rawls's theory of justice!). For the most part, it should reserve its criticism for those who seek to change the law in ways that would deny the basic equality of all citizens. So, for example, it should strongly criticize religious groups who call for laws banning homosexuality, but it should hold back from censuring organizations which respect the equal civil and political rights of gays and lesbians but which nonetheless hold that being gay is a sin in the eyes of God. For a more detailed discussion of these and related issues, see Brettschneider, *When the State Speaks, What Should It Say?*, 71–108.

28 As Brettschneider notes, some liberals argue that the liberal commitment to free speech is grounded in a deep commitment to neutrality. On this "neutralist" view, the reason that the state should not ban hateful and anti-democratic speech is because it should be neutral not just on moral and religious questions but on political ones too. It would therefore also be wrong for the state to criticize any such hateful and anti-democratic views, or to promote political values of freedom and equality through the education system. But Rawls does not share the neutralist position; and Brettschneider develops a powerful argument for why we should reject it. See Brettschneider, *When the State Speaks, What Should It Say?*, 71–82.

29 See Garton Ash, *Free Speech*, 220.

30 Susan Benesch, "Should Dangerous Speech Be Censored or Banned?," Dangerous Speech Project, accessed 9 August 2022, https://dangerousspeech.org/faq/.

31 For some examples, see Garton Ash, *Free Speech*, 225–9.

32 At a conceptual level, the limits of public reason are defined in terms of the ideas that we can reasonably expect other reasonable citizens to accept. The practical implications aren't entirely straightforward. For Rawls, as we saw in Chapter 2, these limits are defined by the family of reasonable political conceptions of justice, all of which would give special precedence to a set of basic liberties, and a guarantee that everyone would be able to meet their basic needs. They would also satisfy the three criteria that make any set of principles "political,"

namely: they would be narrow in scope, concerned only with how we organize the basic structure of society; independent of any single comprehensive moral doctrine; and derived from ideas in our public political culture.

33 For an overview of these problems, and an urgent argument for shifting the focus towards the substantive challenges faced by transgender people, see Shon Faye, *The Transgender Issue: An Argument for Justice* (London: Allen Lane, 2021).

34 In the UK, for example, the government announced a blanket ban in 2022 on transgender women with male genitalia being housed in women-only prisons (unless signed off by a Minister), citing concerns about the risk of sexual assaults. This is despite a 2021 High Court ruling that "There is no reliable statistical case that transgender women prisoners pose a disproportionate risk of harm to non-transgender women prisoners," and that existing laws already allow for case by case risk assessments (meaning a transgender women who is considered a risk because, say, they have a prior rape conviction, could be denied access to a women-only prison). See Amber Pierce, "Transgender Prisoners May Be Excluded from Women's Prisons," *The Justice Gap*, 16 September 2022.

35 John Rawls, *Justice as Fairness: A Restatement*, ed. Erin Kelly (Cambridge, MA: Harvard University Press, 2001), 145–8.

36 "Hungary: Freedom in the World 2019 Country Report," Freedom House, 2019, https://freedomhouse.org/country/hungary/freedom world/2019.

37 David Cole, "Keeping Up Appearances," *New York Review of Books*, 15 August 2019.

38 These criticisms were part of the motivation for the UK leaving the European Union, even though the European Convention on Human Rights is governed by the Council of Europe and the European Court of Human Rights in Strasbourg (which the UK continues to be a member of) and not the EU.

39 This headline related to a 2016 Supreme Court ruling that the government could not withdraw from the EU without Parliament's explicit permission to do so. In a further case, the Supreme Court ruled in 2019 that Prime Minister Boris Johnson had unlawfully suspended (or "prorogued") Parliament in an attempt to push through his preferred Brexit deal.

40 For a discussion of proposed plans to replace the Human Rights Act with a "British Bill of Rights," see "Explainer: Liberty's Guide to the Government's Plan to 'Overhaul' the Human Rights Act,"

Liberty, 7 March 2022, https://www.libertyhumanrights.org.uk /issue/explainer-libertysguide-to-the-governments-plan-to-overhaul -the-human-rights-act-2/. For a brief overview of changes to (ordinary) judicial review introduced in April 2022 via the Judicial Review and Courts Act, see "Judicial Review Reform," The Law Society, 28 April 2022, https://www.lawsociety.org.uk/topics/human-rights /judicial-review-reform.

41 According to the think tank Freedom House, Orbán has used his large parliamentary majority not only to undermine the courts but to "impose restrictions on or assert control over the opposition, the media, religious groups, academia, NGOs" in what amounts to a "sustained [attack] on the country's democratic institutions." See "Hungary: Freedom in the World 2019 Country Report."

42 Rawls distinguishes between constitutional restrictions on majority rule, which limit the *extent* of political freedoms by placing certain topics out of bounds, and measures that would undermine the *equality* of our political freedoms (such as giving some people more votes than others), which go against the spirit of the basic liberties principle in a more fundamental way. See Rawls, *A Theory of Justice*, revised edition (Cambridge, MA: Harvard University Press, 1999), 200–201. For a discussion of the place of majority rule within Rawls's theory, see Amy Gutmann, "Rawls on the Relationship between Liberalism and Democracy," in Freeman (ed.), *The Cambridge Companion to Rawls*, 187–92.

43 I want to thank Stuart White for emphasizing this important point.

44 There is also the question of whether the courts or the legislature should have the power to resolve "horizontal" clashes between different basic freedoms, such as how to balance the demands of religious freedom and gay rights. Rawls's view appears to be that we should leave fairly wide (though not unlimited) discretion to ordinary legislative bodies in these situations, rather than relying too heavily on the courts. See Michelman, "Rawls on Constitutionalism and Constitutional Law," 415–20.

45 Rawls, *A Theory of Justice*, 174.

46 For a critical perspective on the role of constitutions, see Ian Shapiro, *Politics against Domination* (Cambridge, MA: Harvard University Press, 2016), 40–45, 173–8. For a defence of the constitutional model, see Tom Ginsburg and Aziz Z. Huq, *How to Save a Constitutional Democracy* (Chicago: University of Chicago Press, 2018).

47 In these other countries, the "constitution" consists of a smaller number of relevant texts. James Melton et al., *To Codify or Not to Codify?*

Lessons from Consolidating the United Kingdom's Constitutional Statutes (London: University College London Constitution Unit, 2015), 4.

48 This was not an isolated incident. As Maddy Thimont Jack et al., *A Framework for Reviewing the UK Constitution* (London: Institute for Government, 2022), argues, politicians in the UK have increasingly been willing to challenge constitutional norms and conventions. The case for codification has only been strengthened by a series of major constitutional changes in recent years and decades, including the creation of devolved governments in Scotland, Wales and Northern Ireland in the late 1990s, the introduction of the Human Rights Act in 1998, and Brexit in 2020.

49 Even with a codified constitution there will always be room for interpretation, and the success of any constitutional democracy will depend on politicians, judges and bureaucrats respecting unwritten norms and conventions. In this sense, written rules and unwritten norms are complements rather than substitutes. For a discussion of the importance to democracies of unwritten norms and how they are increasingly under threat in America, see Steven Levitsky and Daniel Ziblatt, *How Democracies Die: What History Reveals about Our Future* (London: Viking, 2018).

50 Rawls appears to have supported the idea that some parts of a constitution should be beyond revision, arguing that the U.S. Supreme Court would be right to reject a constitutional amendment designed to undermine the basic protections for free speech enshrined in the First Amendment. See Rawls, *Political Liberalism*, 234–7. For a discussion of entrenchment clauses, see Ginsburg and Huq, *How to Save a Constitutional Democracy*, 173–5. Germany's so-called "eternity clause" insulates Article 1 (which relates to human dignity and basic rights) and Article 20 (which establishes the democratic and federal nature of the German state, and respect for the rule of law) of the German "Basic Law." See Ulrich Preuss, "The Implications of 'Eternity Clauses': The German Experience," *Israel Law Review* 44:3 (2011), 429–48.

51 See "The Constitution," The White House, accessed 28 October 2022, https://www.whitehouse.gov/about-the-white-house/our -government/the-constitution/.

52 Ginsburg and Huq, *How to Save a Constitutional Democracy*, 173–5; Independent Commission on Referendums, *Report of the Independent Commission on Referendums* (London: University College London Constitution Unit, 2018), 29.

53 Ginsburg and Huq, *How to Save a Constitutional Democracy*, 218.

State-level judicial appointments are also highly politicized, typically relying on some combination of popular elections and/or appointment by state governors. For an overview of judicial selection procedures at the state level, see "Judicial Selection: Significant Figures," Brennan Center for Justice, 4 October 2021, https://www.brennancenter .org/ourwork/researchreports/judicialselectionsignificantfigures.

54 For many years, the American system actually worked quite well. It was quite common for Supreme Court judges to be approved unanimously by the Senate and votes were rarely split simply along party lines: between 1790 and 2010, of 397 "important" decisions by the court which had at least two dissenting justices, in only two was the division partisan. But as American politics has become more polarized, and as the legislative system has become gridlocked, both the appointment and voting patterns of judges in the Supreme Court have become intensely political. See Cole, "Keeping Up Appearances."

55 Ginsburg and Huq, *How to Save a Constitutional Democracy*, 190.

56 One proposal, developed by law professors Roger Cramton and Paul Carrington, would allow each new Congress to appoint one judge to the Supreme Court, with only the nine most recent justices actively deciding cases. For a discussion, see Larry Kramer, "Statement of Larry Kramer to the Presidential Commission on the Supreme Court of the United States," 14 July 2021, https://www.whitehouse.gov /wpcontent/uploads/2021/07/Kramer-Testimony.pdf. Recent years have also seen growing support among Democrats for increasing the total number of justices in order to address the conservative imbalance created by the Republican Party's refusal to confirm Merrick Garland, President Obama's nomination in 2016. Whatever the merits of "court-packing" as a response to Republican abuses of power, this is clearly not a solution to the politicization of the Supreme Court—indeed, quite the opposite.

57 See Daniel Epps and Ganesh Sitaraman, "How to Save the Supreme Court," *Vox*, 6 September 2018, and Matt Ford, "A Better Way to Fix the Supreme Court," *New Republic*, 4 June 2019.

58 Richard Wike et al., *Globally, Broad Support for Representative and Direct Democracy* (Washington, DC: Pew Research Center, 2017), 28.

59 Richard Wike and Shannon Schumacher, *Democratic Rights Popular Globally but Commitment to Them Not Always Strong* (Washington, DC: Pew Research Center, 2020), 13, 15.

60 Mounk, *The People vs. Democracy*, 5. Young people are more likely to support technocratic government too: see Wike, *Globally, Broad Support for Representative and Direct Democracy*, 25. They are also

more likely to think that those they disagree with politically are "bad people," and less willing to believe that decent, well-informed individuals could reach differing political points of view: see R. S. Foa et al., *Youth and Satisfaction with Democracy* (Cambridge: Centre for the Future of Democracy, 2020), 23–4.

61 John Rawls, *Justice as Fairness: A Restatement*, ed. Erin Kelly (Cambridge, MA: Harvard University Press, 2001), 195–8.

62 Derek Heater, "The History of Citizenship Education in England," *Curriculum Journal* 12:1 (2001), 103–23. James Madison, one of the founding fathers, argued that "a people who mean to be their own Governors must arm themselves with the power which knowledge gives," while George Washington declared that "the education of our youth in the science of government" should be a "primary object" of America's education system. See Mounk, *The People vs. Democracy*, 245.

63 Rawls, *Justice as Fairness*, 157. For a detailed examination of Rawls's approach to civic education, see M. Victoria Costa, *Rawls, Citizenship, and Education* (Abingdon: Routledge, 2010).

64 This excessive focus on the vocational aspects of education has also led many countries to neglect its wider social and cultural role in encouraging healthy relationships, nurturing creativity and enabling people to participate in and benefit from art, music and culture.

65 Danielle Allen, *Education and Equality* (Chicago: University of Chicago Press, 2016), 7–8.

66 See Scott Warren, "At Long Last, Civics Education Is Making a Comeback. But What Exactly Is It, and How Do We Do It Right?," *The 74*, 6 March 2020. There is some evidence that this has got worse over time: while high-school students in the mid-twentieth-century U.S.A. were given three courses in civics, this has fallen to one single-semester course for approximately 85 per cent of students. See Danielle Allen, "Here's One More Question Parents Should Think about during Back-to-School Season," *Washington Post*, 5 September 2019.

67 House of Lords Select Committee on Citizenship and Civic Engagement, "The Ties That Bind: Citizenship and Civic Engagement in the 21st Century," HL Paper 118 (April 2018), 30. See also James Weinberg and Matthew Flinders, "Improving Citizenship Education," in Henry Tam (ed.), *Whose Government Is It? The Renewal of State-Citizen Cooperation* (Bristol: Bristol University Press, 2019), 177–94.

68 European Commission, European Education and Culture Executive Agency, *Citizenship Education at School in Europe, 2017* (Luxembourg: Publications Office of the European Union, 2018), 10.

69 This discussion of the aims of civic education draws on Danielle Allen, *Education and Equality*, 38–43.

70 Allen, *Education and Equality*, 43–9.

71 This is the essence of the "intergroup contact hypothesis" first put forward by Gordon Allport in the 1950s. According to Allport, there are four broad conditions that need to be met for exposure to other groups to have the desired effects. Members of each group must (1) have relatively equal status in the context where contact takes place; (2) work together in pursuit of common goals; (3) have incentives to cooperate. Finally (4) authority figures must encourage better intergroup understanding. See Yascha Mounk, *The Great Experiment: How to Make Diverse Democracies Work* (London: Bloomsbury, 2022), 87–92. These conditions are especially likely to hold in a well-designed school setting.

72 Simon Burgess and Lucinda Platt, "Integrating the Next Generation: How School Composition Affects Inter-Ethnic Attitudes," *LSE British Politics and Policy Blog*, 22 May 2018, https://blogs.lse.ac.uk/politics andpolicy/integrating-the-next-generation-school-composition/.

73 Mounk, *The Great Experiment*, 31–50.

74 Keith Banting and Will Kymlicka, "Introduction: The Political Sources of Solidarity in Diverse Societies," in Keith Banting and Will Kymlicka (eds.), *The Strains of Commitment: The Political Sources of Solidarity in Diverse Societies* (Oxford: Oxford University Press, 2017), 1–10.

75 There is no settled agreement on the distinction between patriotism and nationalism. I will use the term "patriotism" here to suggest a specifically *political* kind of identity, associated with living in a particular country under a single unified state; in contrast to "nationalism," which we can think of as grounded in cultural, ethnic or religious identities.

76 The liberal patriotism set out here draws on, and closely resembles, the "constitutional patriotism" developed by thinkers including Jan-Werner Müller and Jürgen Habermas. For a detailed discussion and defence of this idea, see Jan-Werner Müller, *Constitutional Patriotism* (Princeton: Princeton University Press, 2007).

77 Laura Silver et al., *Views about National Identity Becoming More Inclusive in U.S., Western Europe* (Washington, DC: Pew Research Center, 2021), 6.

78 Rawls, *Justice as Fairness*, 199 n. 20.

79 Post-war Germany is another classic example, and the idea of "constitutional patriotism" was mostly developed in this context. See Müller, *Constitutional Patriotism*, 15–45.

80 Danielle Allen, "The Flawed Genius of the Constitution," *The Atlantic,* 10 September 2020.

81 Carlos Vargas-Silva and Cinzia Rienzo, "Migrants in the UK: An Overview," The Migration Observatory, 2 August 2022, https://migrationobservatory.ox.ac.uk/resources/briefings/migrantsinthe ukanoverview/; "Refugee Crisis in Europe," UNHCR, https://www .unrefugees.org/emergencies/refugee-crisis-in-europe/.

82 A full account of what we owe people from other countries is a vital task for political philosophy, but one which, as we discussed in Chapter 1, lies beyond the scope of Rawls's principles, and therefore this book. While Rawls addressed questions about global justice in *The Law of Peoples* (Cambridge, MA: Harvard University Press, 1999), he said very little about the implications for immigration policy, except to note that each country (or "people") "has at least a qualified right to limit immigration" (39). Rawls's position is rejected even by some who are broadly sympathetic to his ideas about "domestic justice," such as Thomas Pogge and Charles Beitz; and Joseph Carens has used Rawlsian arguments to argue for "open borders." See Joseph H. Carens, "Aliens and Citizens: The Case for Open Borders," *Review of Politics* 49:2 (1987), 251–73. For an overview of recent debates about immigration within a broadly liberal philosophical perspective, see Shelley Wilcox, "The Open Borders Debate on Immigration," *Philosophy Compass* 4:5 (2009), 813–21.

83 Rawls, *The Law of Peoples,* 38–9.

84 Martin Ruhs and Carlos Vargas-Silva, "The Labour Market Effects of Immigration," University of Oxford Migration Observatory Briefing (December 2020). Lowest earners refers to those in the tenth percentile of earnings, while highest earners refers to those in the ninetieth percentile. For a discussion of the evidence across a range of countries, see Giovanni Peri, "Do Immigrant Workers Depress the Wages of Native Workers?," IZA World of Labor, May 2014, http://dx.doi.org/10.15185/izawol.42.

85 For an overview of the impact of migration on the public finances, see OECD, *International Migration Outlook, 2021* (Paris: OECD Publishing, 2021), 111–39.

5. DEMOCRACY

1 "Number of Democracies and Non-Democracies, World," *Our World in Data,* accessed 29 October 2022, https://ourworld indata.org/explorers/democracy?facet=none&country=~OWID

_WRL&Dataset=BoixMillerRosato&Metric=Democracy&Submetric
=Number+of+democracies, based on data from Carles Boix et al.,
"A Complete Data Set of Political Regimes, 1800–2007," *Comparative Political Studies* 46:12 (2013), 1523–54. For an overview of the unprecedented growth in democracy, and recent concerns about a reversal, see Martin Loughlin, "The Contemporary Crisis of Constitutional Democracy," *Oxford Journal of Legal Studies* 39:2 (2019), 436, and Larry Diamond, "Facing up to the Democratic Recession," *Journal of Democracy* 26:1 (2015), 141–55.

2 Jan-Werner Müller, *Democracy Rules* (London: Penguin, 2021), 179.
3 In this study, "developed democracies" are defined as those in Europe, North America, Northeast Asia and Australasia. R. S. Foa et al., *Global Satisfaction with Democracy 2020* (Cambridge: Centre for the Future of Democracy, 2020).
4 Richard Wike and Shannon Schumacher, "Democratic Rights Popular Globally but Commitment to Them Not Always Strong" (Washington, DC: Pew Research Center, 2020), 18–19.
5 OECD, *How's Life? 2020: Measuring Well-Being* (Paris: OECD Publishing, 2020), 186. The Organisation for Economic Co-operation and Development (OECD) is an intergovernmental organisation whose membership is comprised of 38 mostly rich countries that are committed to democratic government and a market economy, including most European countries, the United States, Canada, Japan, Korea, Australia and New Zealand. It is a fantastic source of reliable and internationally comparable data, which I will use frequently in the rest of this book.
6 Richard Wike and Janell Fetterolf, "Global Public Opinion in an Era of Democratic Anxiety," Pew Research Center, 7 December 2021, https://www.pewresearch.org/global/2021/12/07/global publicopinion-in-an-era-of-democratic-anxiety/.
7 International Institute for Democracy and Electoral Assistance, *The Global State of Democracy, 2021: Building Resilience in a Pandemic Era* (Stockholm: International IDEA, 2021), 15–16.
8 Freedom House, *Freedom in the World, 2021: Democracy under Siege* (Washington, DC: Freedom House, 2021), 2. According to the International Institute for Democracy and Electoral Assistance, "Democratically elected governments, including established democracies, are increasingly adopting authoritarian tactics": see International IDEA, *The Global State of Democracy, 2021*, 1. The same broad picture is evident across all international studies, including the Economist Intelligence Unit's *Democracy Index 2021: The China Challenge*

(London: Economist Intelligence Unit, 2022), and the V-Dem Institute's *Democracy Report, 2022: Autocratization Changing Nature?* (Gothenburg: V-Dem Institute, 2021). For a broader discussion, see Diamond, "Facing up to the Democratic Recession."

9 Many other political philosophers and democratic theorists have defined democracy in terms of political equality, including Robert Dahl, who is possibly the most widely respected theorist of democracy of the twentieth century: see Robert A. Dahl, *On Democracy* (originally published 1998), second edition (New Haven: Yale University Press, 2015), 35–43. For a more recent perspective along similar lines, see Müller, *Democracy Rules*, 42–7. Of course there are other ways to define and indeed to justify democracy. For a discussion, see Tom Christiano and Sameer Bajaj, "Democracy," in Edward N. Zalta (ed.), *The Stanford Encyclopedia of Philosophy* (fall 2021 edition), https://plato.stanford.edu/archives/fall2021/entries/democracy/.

10 For brilliant unpacking of the Rawlsian idea of political equality, see Joshua Cohen, "Money, Politics, Political Equality," in Alex Byrne et al. (eds.), *Fact and Value: Essays on Ethics and Metaphysics for Judith Jarvis Thomson* (Cambridge, MA: MIT Press, 2001), 47–80, and T. M. Scanlon, *Why Does Inequality Matter?* (Oxford: Oxford University Press, 2018), 74–94. Cohen highlights three distinct aspects of Rawlsian political equality: that it is about the *opportunity* for influence rather than actual influence; that it is about *equal* opportunities for influence rather than, say, guaranteeing a minimum opportunity for influence; and that it is about opportunities for *political* influence, defined as influencing legislative decision-making, which is broader than merely electoral influence, but narrower than "public influence," which is concerned with influencing people's views in the informal public sphere.

11 "The fair value of the political liberties ensures that citizens similarly gifted and motivated have roughly an equal chance of influencing the government's policy and attaining positions of authority irrespective of their economic and social class": John Rawls, *Justice as Fairness: A Restatement*, ed. Erin Kelly (Cambridge, MA: Harvard University Press, 2001), 46. He went on to note that "the worth of the political liberties to all citizens, whatever their economic or social position, must be sufficiently equal in the sense that all have a fair opportunity to hold public office and to affect the outcome of elections, and the like": ibid., 149.

12 It's worth highlighting some of the distinctive features of this way of thinking about democracy. First, the case for democracy rests on the

intrinsic value of political equality, and on the way the democratic process reflects the fundamental equality of citizens: everyone should have an equal chance to shape the laws that govern their lives, and no one is so superior that they should simply be given the power to tell other people how to live. Of course, we might also value democracy for instrumental reasons, on the basis that it tends to produce positive results such as protecting basic freedoms or promoting peace and prosperity. But the Rawlsian way of thinking, which highlights the intrinsic value of the democratic process, helps to immunize democracy against those who argue that we should adopt a different form of government—such as an idealized version of China's technocratic authoritarianism—simply because this would be better for prosperity: See Müller, *Democracy Rules*, 43. We can also distinguish Rawls's approach from the idea that democracy is justified because it gives equal consideration to everyone's views or interests. This cannot be all that democracy is about: after all, an unelected technocracy could, in principle, give equal consideration to everyone's views or interests by using opinion polling, or by developing policy based on a particular theory about what people's *real* interests are. But no one would think this was a democratic way to govern, and we should reject these alternatives because they fail to provide equal opportunities to participate, which, as we have seen, are valuable in their own right.

13 This discussion is influenced by Dahl's five-part schema in *On Democracy*, 37. Dahl set out five basic criteria which any democratic association, of any size, would have to meet: voting equality, effective participation, enlightened understanding, control of the agenda and inclusion of adults. For simplicity I have taken inclusion of adults as given throughout; and we can think of "control of the agenda" as part of "effective participation."

14 Müller makes a similar point about the "dual nature" of democracy involving both periodic voting and a much wider process of deliberation: see Müller, *Democracy Rules*, 94.

15 Of course, the distinction between understanding and participation is somewhat artificial: the process of working out what we think is closely related to that of expressing and advocating for our positions. But it is useful for thinking about the wider institutions of democracy beyond the ballot box.

16 Müller, *Democracy Rules*, 90–91. Parties and the media clearly aren't the only institutions that matter in a democracy. There are, for example, many ways to participate in politics beyond parties, including business associations, trade unions and other advocacy groups. But

as Müller argues, while all these matter, we can at least imagine a democracy without them, which is not the case with parties and the media: see ibid., 205 n. 1.

17 For a discussion of the difficulties of measuring political equality, see Larry M. Bartels, "Political Inequality in Affluent Democracies: The Social Welfare Deficit," Center for the Study of Democratic Institutions Working Paper 5–2017 (March 2017).

18 At first sight, it might seem as if differences in voting behaviour simply reflect a failure among members of these groups to take advantage of opportunities that are available to everyone. But even if everyone has an equal right to vote, this doesn't mean they have the same opportunity to exercise it: there are, for example, often fewer polling stations in poorer areas, and it is usually harder for the low paid to take time off work to vote. More importantly, the fact that poorer people are less likely to vote is itself the result of unequal opportunities for influence: as we shall see, the influence of rich donors leads politicians to neglect the interests and concerns of disadvantaged voters.

19 Martin Gilens and Benjamin I. Page, "Testing Theories of American Politics: Elites, Interest Groups, and Average Citizens," *Perspectives on Politics* 12:3 (2014), 564–81. See also Benjamin I. Page and Martin Gilens, *Democracy in America?: What Has Gone Wrong and What We Can Do about It* (Chicago: University of Chicago Press, 2017). This database was first put together by Gilens in a study which compared the influence of rich, average and poor citizens, defined as those at the ninetieth, fiftieth and tenth percentiles of the income distribution, respectively. As in their joint study, Gilens found that the preferences of rich Americans have a much stronger influence over policy outcomes than those of poorer citizens. See Martin Gilens, *Affluence and Influence: Economic Inequality and Political Power in America* (Princeton: Princeton University Press, 2012).

20 These results do not mean that average citizens never get the policies they want. Rich and average voters often want the same things, and hence there is a fairly strong relationship between the preferences of average citizens and public policy in general. What Gilens and Page show is that, when rich and average voters want *different* things, it is usually the rich who have their way. In other words, rich voters have more *influence* on the direction of public policy. As Gilens and Page argue, if ordinary citizens' wishes are met just because they happen to overlap in significant ways with those of the rich, this is simply "democracy by coincidence." See Gilens and Page, "Testing Theories of American Politics," 573.

21 For a review of this literature, see Robert S. Erikson, "Income Inequality and Policy Responsiveness," *Annual Review of Political Science* 18 (2015), 11–29. Erikson estimates that "the richest Americans enjoy at least 2.5 times the political influence of the poorest Americans. Considering all the resources of voters in different economic strata, the ratio could actually be far greater": ibid., 23.

22 Page and Gilens, *Democracy in America?*, 53–89.

23 Bartels takes a slightly different approach to Page and Gilens, looking at data on the relationship between public opinion and aggregate spending on pensions, health, education, and unemployment benefits in thirty affluent democracies over the past three decades. See Larry Bartels, "Political Inequality in Affluent Democracies: The Social Welfare Deficit." Other studies, which more closely replicate Gilens and Page's methodology, produce similar findings: see Wouter Schakel, "Unequal Policy Responsiveness in the Netherlands," *Socio-Economic Review* 19:1 (2021), 37–57, and Lea Elsässer et al., "Government of the People, by the Elite, for the Rich: Unequal Responsiveness in an Unlikely Case," Max Planck Institute for the Study of Societies MPIfG Discussion Paper 18/5 (2018). The fact that we find similar problems to the U.S.A. in European countries with much tighter limits on political donations suggests that achieving meaningful political equality will involve not just campaign finance reform, but looking again at the nature of the voting system, the role of the education system, the funding and regulation of advocacy and lobbying groups and the media, and no doubt much more.

24 Some of this suspicion reflects the history of elections, which were first introduced as a way of maintaining elite control, since the right to vote was typically restricted to rich, male property owners. But while elections may have first been introduced as a way of avoiding true democracy, they were subsequently adopted by committed democrats as a revolutionary tool for achieving democracy at scale. For a brief discussion, see Dahl, *On Democracy*, 103–5.

25 Even in an ideal system, elections would still be a relatively blunt tool for conveying the views of the population and for holding representatives to account. This is why, as we shall see, the best political system probably combines elections with forms of direct participation.

26 Although the Greeks coined the term "democracy," women, foreigners and slaves were excluded, and most people nowadays would consider universal suffrage to be an essential feature of any democratic political system.

27 For some of its proponents, the case for direct democracy rests on

the idea that active participation in politics is good in itself, and we should design our political institutions in order to encourage more of it. This way of thinking, which Rawls referred to as "civic humanism," has roots often traced back to Aristotle, who famously argued that "man is by nature a political animal," and that we can only realize our true nature through active engagement in politics. For Rawls, by contrast, political participation is ultimately a means to an end: engaged citizens help bolster the legitimacy and stability of a democratic society, and can prevent power from falling into the hands of a detached and self-serving elite. While some individuals will derive a sense of meaning and fulfilment from politics, for most people their other commitments—family, religion, work and so on—are probably more important. From this perspective, how much popular participation we should aim for ultimately depends on the extent to which this promotes political equality and good government.

28 Mogens Herman Hansen, "Democracy, Athenian," in Simon Hornblower and Antony Spawforth (eds.), *The Oxford Classical Dictionary*, fourth edition (Oxford: Oxford University Press, 2012). Thanks to Kit Shepherd for directing me to this source.

29 Random selection came to play a particularly important role in Athenian democracy in the fourth century B.C., partly in response to the disastrous Peloponnesian War (431–404 B.C.) and the desire for a kind of safety break on the decisions taken by the assembly. During this period, random lots were used to select members to three key bodies: the "Council of 500," which set the agenda for the assembly and decided which proposals could be debated; the *nomothetai*, who had to approve any laws made in the assembly; and a special court (the *graphe paranomon*) responsible for monitoring assembly debates, which could prosecute those responsible for illegal or unwise proposals. See James Fishkin, *Democracy When the People Are Thinking: Revitalizing Our Politics through Public Deliberation* (Oxford: Oxford University Press, 2018), 51–4.

30 See, for example, David van Reybrouck, *Against Elections: The Case for Democracy* (London: Bodley Head, 2016), and Brett Hennig, *The End of Politicians: Time for a Real Democracy* (London: Unbound, 2017). For a more philosophical discussion, see Alexander A. Guerrero, "Against Elections: The Lottocratic Alternative," *Philosophy & Public Affairs* 42:2 (2014), 135–78.

31 The discussion of random selection draws on Müller, *Democracy Rules*, 47–89. While part of the appeal of random selection is that it can overcome some of the difficulties with holding elected representatives

to account, it also suffers from its own accountability problems. If we replaced elected representatives with randomly selected ones, they would still wield an enormous amount of power, but there would be no mechanism for holding them to account through elections.

32 This discussion draws closely on Müller, *Democracy Rules*, 78–89.

33 International Institute for Democracy and Electoral Assistance, "Electoral System for National Legislature," *International IDEA Electoral System Design Database*, accessed 4 November 2022, https://www.idea.int/data-tools/question-view/130355. The claim about established democracies uses data from 1997/8 and comes from "The Global Distribution of Electoral Systems," *ACE Encyclopaedia* Version 1.0, accessed 10 August 2022, https://aceproject.org/main/english/es/esh.htm. "Established democracies" are defined as states with a population of more than 250,000 which have held continuing free elections for over twenty years. Of the thirty-six established democracies, twenty-one (59 per cent) have proportional representation. However, first past the post accounts for 71 per cent of the population, since this group include both the U.S.A. and India.

34 Although I believe the balance of arguments strongly favours proportional representation, there is a case to be made for first past the post as compatible with political equality. See, for example, Charles R. Beitz, *Political Equality: An Essay in Democratic Theory* (Princeton: Princeton University Press, 1990), 123–40, and James Lindley Wilson, *Democratic Equality* (Princeton: Princeton University Press, 2019), 193–215.

35 While first past the post often creates obvious difficulties for smaller parties, it can lead to large gaps between the share of votes and seats for larger parties too: in the 2019 UK general election, the most recent at the time of writing, the Conservative Party won 45 per cent of the vote, but secured 58 per cent of seats. See Patrick Dunleavy, "First-Past-the-Post: Normal (Disproportionate) Service Has Resumed," *LSE British Politics and Policy Blog*, 19 December 2019, https://blogs.lse.ac.uk/politicsandpolicy/first-past-the-post-ge2019/.

36 Across Europe, authoritarian populist parties have secured around 11 per cent of the vote, and hence about 11 per cent of legislative seats since the 1980s. See Lee Drutman, *Breaking the Two-Party Doom Loop: The Case for Multiparty Democracy in America* (Oxford: Oxford University Press, 2020), 228–31.

37 This argument for proportional representation as more likely to foster a multiparty democracy draws on Drutman, *Breaking the Two-Party Doom Loop*.

38 "One Person, One Vote: But Are All Votes Equal?," Voter Power Index, accessed 10 August 2022, http://www.voterpower.org.uk/. For a discussion of the underlying methodology, see Nic Marks and Stephen Whitehead, *The Voter Power Index: The Effects of the Alternative Vote on the Distribution of Electoral Power in the UK* (London: New Economics Foundation, 2011).

39 Carl Cullinane, "Voter Power to the People?," *LSE British Politics and Policy Blog*, 3 May 2015, https://blogs.lse.ac.uk/politicsandpolicy /voter-power-to-the-people/.

40 Political control over district boundaries, or "gerrymandering," accounts for about one third of the increase in the number of safe congressional districts in the U.S.A. since the 1980s. See Page and Gilens, *Democracy in America?*, 161.

41 There are other hybrid systems which achieve a strong degree of proportionality in a slightly different way. The most promising is the Single Transferable Vote model, which is currently used for national legislative elections in Ireland and Malta, and for Senate elections in Australia. In this system, citizens vote in constituencies with multiple candidates, and whom they rank in order of preferences. Like the standard proportional representation system, this model has the effect of allocating seats in close proportion to votes cast, but with the added advantage that citizens vote for specific candidates. See Drutman, *Breaking the Two-Party Doom Loop*, 177–83.

42 OECD, *Society at a Glance, 2019: OECD Social Indicators* (Paris: OECD Publishing, 2019), 129.

43 OECD, "Civic Engagement," *OECD Better Life Index*, accessed 10 August 2022, https://www.oecdbetterlifeindex.org/topics/civic engagement/.

44 Bernard Grofman, "Perspectives on the Comparative Study of Electoral Systems," *Annual Review of Political Science* 19 (2016), 533.

45 See Page and Gilens, *Democracy in America?*, 203–9, and Toby S. James and Paul Bernal, "Is It Time for Automatic Voter Registration in the UK?" (York: Joseph Rowntree Reform Trust, 2020).

46 Page and Gilens, *Democracy in America?*, 62; and Toby S. James and Alistair Clark, "Electoral Integrity, Voter Fraud and Voter ID in Polling Stations: Lessons from English Local Elections," *Policy Studies* 41: 2–3 (2020), 190.

47 Page and Gilens, *Democracy in America?*, 61; Eric Guntermann et al., "Are Inequalities in Representation Lower under Compulsory Voting?," *Policy Studies* 41:2–3 (2020), 151–71.

48 Any system with compulsory voting should include the option to

reject the candidates and vote to "reopen nominations." For a more detailed argument for compulsory voting along similar ones to those discussed here, see Emilee Booth Chapman, "The Distinctive Value of Elections and the Case for Compulsory Voting," *American Journal of Political Science* 63:1 (2019), 101–12.

49 For an overview of donation and spending limits, see OECD, *Financing Democracy: Funding of Political Parties and Election Campaigns and the Risk of Policy Capture* (Paris: OECD Publishing, 2016), 46–59.

50 Julia Cagé, *The Price of Democracy: How Money Shapes Politics and What to Do about It*, trans. Patrick Camiller (Cambridge, MA: Harvard University Press, 2020), 7.

51 The total cost of the 2020 elections is stated in nominal (2020) terms (i.e. not adjusted for inflation), and comes from "Total Cost of Election (1990–2022)," Open Secrets, accessed 2 November 2022, https://www.opensecrets.org/elections-overview/cost-of-election. The cost of successful Senate and House races comes from Michael J. Malbin and Brendan Glavin, "CFI: Independent Spending in 2020 Equaled the Candidates' in Close Races, and Parties Dominated the IEs," Follow TheMoney.org, 22 December 2020, https://www.followthemoney.org/research/institute-reports/cfi-independent-spending-in-2020 equaled-the-candidates-in-close-races-and-parties-dominated-the -ies.

52 Page and Gilens, *Democracy in America?*, 7.

53 The following report looks specifically at American donors: Sean McElwee et al., "Whose Voice, Whose Choice? The Distorting Influence of the Political Donor Class in Our Big-Money Elections" (New York: Demos, 2016). A survey of American multimillionaires reached similar conclusions. See Page and Gilens, *Democracy in America?*, 117.

54 For the UK, see Peter Geoghegan et al., "Cabinet Office Urged to Investigate Fresh Tory 'Cash for Honours' Scandal," openDemocracy, 3 December 2019, https://www.opendemocracy.net/en/dark-money -investigations/cabinetofficeurgedtoinvestigatefreshtorycash-for -honours-scandal/, and Simon Radford et al., "'Lordy Me!' Can Donations Buy You a British Peerage? A Study in the Link between Party Political Funding and Peerage Nominations, 2005–2014," *British Politics* 15:2 (2020), 135–59. For the U.S., see Robbie Gramer, "Senior U.S. Lawmaker Wants to Scale Back Pay-for-Post Ambassadorships," *Foreign Policy*, 26 October 2020.

55 Yascha Mounk, *The People vs. Democracy: Why Our Freedom Is in*

Danger and How to Save It (Cambridge, MA: Harvard University Press, 2018), 88.

56 For an overview of the evidence, see Yasmin Dawood, "Campaign Finance and American Democracy," *Annual Review of Political Science* 18 (2015), 340–42.

57 John Rawls, *Political Liberalism*, expanded edition (New York: Columbia University Press, 2005), 356–63. As Rawls pointed out, there is "limited space" in the public political forum: as individuals we can absorb only so much information, and there are only so many pages in national newspapers, or slots on mainstream TV. Restrictions on political donations are necessary to make sure that the rich cannot dominate this finite space, and hence to secure the fair value of our rights to political speech (ibid., 328).

58 OECD, *Financing Democracy*, 38.

59 Cagé, *The Price of Democracy*, 135–61.

60 OECD, *Financing Democracy*, 40.

61 A number of countries have adopted an alternative—and in some ways more responsive—model, where the state offers tax deductions on political donations, but since the wealthy pay much more in taxes, these kinds of schemes disproportionately benefit the parties supported by the rich. See Cagé, *The Price of Democracy*, 74.

62 How generous should democracy vouchers be? There is no single "right" answer to this question. Julia Cagé proposes roughly €7 per person, which would roughly replicate existing levels of public funding in a number of European countries. Bruce Ackerman and Ian Ayres argue for $50 per person: see Bruce Ackerman and Ian Ayres, "'Democracy Dollars' Can Give Every Voter a Real Voice in American Politics," *Washington Post*, 5 November 2015.

63 Ackerman and Ayres, "'Democracy Dollars.'"

64 For a detailed proposal, see Cagé, *The Price of Democracy*, 253–75. Cagé addresses a whole range of important practical questions, including how to decide which parties are eligible for funding.

65 Alan Griffith and Thomas Noonen, "The Effects of Public Campaign Funding: Evidence from Seattle's Democracy Voucher Program," *Journal of Public Economics* 211 (2022), article 104676.

66 Mounk, *The People vs. Democracy*, 86. A similar picture emerges from studies looking at the lobbying of EU institutions in Brussels. As of 2017, corporations and their lobby groups had about 60 per cent more lobbyists with access passes to the European Parliament than those working for civil society groups and trade unions; and a 2014 study looking in detail at lobbying related to the financial sector

found that businesses spent thirty times more than NGOs and trade unions combined. See David Lundy, *Lobby Planet Brussels: The Corporate Europe Observatory Guide to the Murky World of Corporate EU Lobbying* (Brussels: Corporate Europe Observatory, 2017), 10.

67 OECD, *Lobbying in the 21st Century: Transparency, Integrity and Access* (Paris: OECD Publishing, 2021), 20.

68 While some countries have taken steps to improve transparency, much more needs to be done. In 2020, ten years after launching a major initiative to enhance transparency and integrity in lobbying, the OECD found that most countries had failed to introduce robust systems and that the "risks of undue influence and monopoly of influence are high." See OECD, *Lobbying in the 21st Century*, 3.

69 Lee Drutman, "Three Fixes for Our Lobbyist Problem," *The American Prospect*, 5 June 2008.

70 We could match small individual contributions using public funds, or even extend the democracy-voucher scheme to encompass advocacy groups. Drutman has proposed creating an "Office of Public Lobbying" to promote unrepresented points of view. See Lee Drutman, *The Business of America Is Lobbying: How Corporations Became Politicized and Politics Became More Corporate* (Oxford: Oxford University Press, 2015), 229–30.

71 This framework is similar to the one put forward by Timothy Garton Ash, who argues that the media should be uncensored, diverse and trustworthy. See Timothy Garton Ash, *Free Speech: Ten Principles for a Connected World* (New Haven: Yale University Press, 2017), 183.

72 Most of this was accounted for by a massive 57 per cent decline in the number of people employed in print media newsrooms, only partially offset by an increase in employment at online news outlets. Mason Walker, "U.S. Newsroom Employment Has Fallen 26% since 2008," Pew Research Center, 13 July 2021, https://www.pewresearch.org/fact-tank/2021/07/13/u-snewsroom-employment-has-fallen-26since-2008/.

73 For the UK, see Stigler Committee on Digital Platforms, *Final Report* (Chicago: Stigler Center for the Study of the Economy and the State, 2019), 148; for the U.S., see Müller, *Democracy Rules*, 125.

74 Müller, *Democracy Rules*, 125.

75 A study in Brazil found that 98 per cent of President Bolsonaro's supporters had been confronted with pieces of false information, and 90 per cent had believed them. Müller, *Democracy Rules*, 122.

76 A Pew Research Center study of thirteen advanced democracies found that disagreement over basic facts is more common in some

countries than in others. In France, as many as 61 per cent of the population thought there were fundamental disagreements not just about policy but about basic facts, followed by the U.S.A. at 59 per cent. At the other end of the spectrum, the figure was just 18 per cent in New Zealand. See Laura Silver et al., *Diversity and Division in Advanced Economies* (Washington, DC: Pew Research Center, 2021).

77 Ben Kamisar, "Two-Thirds of Republicans Don't Believe Biden Was Elected Legitimately," *NBC News*, 25 October 2022.

78 See, for example, Sahil Loomba et al., "Measuring the Impact of COVID-19 Vaccine Misinformation on Vaccination Intent in the UK and U.S.A.," *Nature Human Behaviour* 5:3 (2021), 337–48.

79 According to one study, the period since 2000 has seen "a dramatic and quantifiable shift toward subjective, abstract, directive, and argumentative language, with content based more on the expression of opinion than on the provision of facts" in U.S. cable news, and a similar trend is evident, albeit to a much lesser extent, in newspapers and conventional broadcast television. See Jennifer Kavanagh et al., "Facts versus Opinions: How the Style and Language of News Presentation Is Changing in the Digital Age," RAND Corporation, 2019, https://www.rand.org/pubs/research_briefs/RB10059.html.

80 For a detailed discussion of the drivers of media concentration, see Eli M. Noam, "Introduction," in Eli M. Noam (ed.), *Who Owns the World's Media?: Media Concentration and Ownership around the World* (Oxford: Oxford University Press, 2016), 3–15.

81 For an overview of where people get their news in the UK, see "How Brits Get Their News," YouGov, accessed 3 November 2022, https://yougov.co.uk/topics/politics/trackers/how-brits-get-their-news; for the U.S., see Naomi Forman-Katz and Katerina Eva Matsa, "News Platform Fact Sheet," Pew Research Center, 20 September 2022, https://www.pewresearch.org/journalism/factsheet/newsplatformfact-sheet/.

82 Media Reform Coalition, *Who Owns the UK Media?* (London: Media Reform Coalition, 2019), 2.

83 Ed Jones, "Five Reasons Why We Don't Have a Free and Independent Press in the UK and What We Can Do about It," openDemocracy, 18 April 2019, https://www.opendemocracy.net/en/opendemocracyuk/five-reasons-why-we-don-t-have-free-and-independent-press-in-uk-andwhat-we-can-do-about/.

84 Stigler Committee on Digital Platforms, *Final Report*, 26–7.

85 Most European countries, including the UK, provide indirect subsidies through VAT exemptions. Many European countries also

provide direct subsidies to newspapers, targeted in various different ways. In Norway, for example, the focus is on pluralism, with public funding for the second largest paper in each local market as well as for a national paper that offers dissident and controversial views. In France, there are subsidies covering delivery costs as well as to encourage pluralism and modernization. See Stigler Committee on Digital Platforms, *Final Report*, 34.

86 House of Lords Communications and Digital Committee, "Breaking News? The Future of UK Journalism," HL Paper 176 (November 2020), 22. One option for strengthening independent democratic oversight would be to draw on the model of random selection, say by using a citizens' jury to help adjudicate on disputes over impartiality. As we shall see later in this chapter, random selection is particularly useful in cases where policymakers face a conflict of interest, as they undoubtedly do in relation to regulating the news media.

87 For a detailed discussion of this kind of model, see Stigler Committee on Digital Platforms, *Final Report*, 34–42.

88 Given the danger that such standards could be used for political ends, these should not be too stringent, and would need to be independently monitored.

89 Timothy Garton Ash refers to this as "transparent partiality." See *Free Speech*, 204–5.

90 Lara Fielden, *Regulating for Trust in Journalism: Standards Regulation in the Age of Blended Media* (Oxford: Reuters Institute for the Study of Journalism, 2011), 117–24. While Fielden recommends a range of incentives to encourage companies to adopt these higher standards, she does not discuss media vouchers per se.

91 Julia Cagé, *Saving the Media: Capitalism, Crowdfunding, and Democracy*, trans. Arthur Goldhammer (Cambridge, MA: Harvard University Press, 2016).

92 Dahl describes the discretionary authority of elected representatives, and the associated process of bargaining among political elites, as the "dark side" of representative democracy. See *On Democracy*, 113–14.

93 Erik Olin Wright, *Envisioning Real Utopias* (London: Verso, 2010), 155–60.

94 See *Participatory Budgeting World Atlas*, accessed 11 August 2022, https://www.pbatlas.net/world.html. Of course, these numbers hide enormous variations in the amount of funding and the nature of citizen involvement, and some of these schemes are purely consultative in nature.

95 Hollie Russon Gilman, "Engaging Citizens: Participatory Budgeting

and the Inclusive Governance Movement within the United States," Ash Center Occasional Papers series (January 2016), 4.

96 Wright, *Envisioning Real Utopias*, 158.

97 Ibid., 111. Although women were initially under-represented, they now comprise slightly more than 50 per cent of participants. See Carole Pateman, "Participatory Democracy Revisited," *Perspectives on Politics* 10:1 (2012), 11–12.

98 Wright, *Envisioning Real Utopias*, 111.

99 For this reason, random selection is sometimes referred to as "deliberative opinion polling."

100 For an overview of recent experiments, see van Reybrouck, *Against Elections*, 115–31.

101 Dimitri Courant, "Citizens' Assemblies for Referendums and Constitutional Reforms: Is There an 'Irish Model' for Deliberative Democracy?," *Frontiers in Political Science* 2 (2021), article 591983.

102 While the abortion debate in the U.S.A. is often framed as a binary choice between being "pro-life" or "pro-choice," only 8 per cent believe abortion should be illegal in every case, while 19 per cent say it should be legal in all cases. The vast majority of people think that abortion should be legal in at least some cases, and recognize the need to balance a variety of considerations. See Pew Research Center, *America's Abortion Quandary* (Washington, DC: Pew Research Center, 2022).

103 The past thirty years have seen an explosion of practical experimentation in the design of small deliberative forums (often referred to as "mini-publics") pioneered in particular by the political scientist James Fishkin. For an overview, see Fishkin, *Democracy When the People Are Thinking*.

104 See ibid., 69–128, for a range of examples.

105 Citizens' Initiative Review panels on Oregon have considered issues ranging from taxing corporations to the use of marijuana for medical uses. Of course, people don't always side with the views of panels, but the evidence suggests that their reports have helped voters to understand the issues more fully, and in many cases to change their minds. See John Gastil et al., "Assessing the Electoral Impact of the 2010 Oregon Citizens' Initiative Review," *American Politics Research* 46:3 (2018), 534–63.

106 For detailed proposals which address many of these questions, see John Gastil and Erik Olin Wright, "Legislature by Lot: Envisioning Sortition within a Bicameral System," *Politics & Society* 46:3 (2018), 303–30, and Arash Abizadeh, "Representation, Bicameralism,

Political Equality, and Sortition: Reconstituting the Second Chamber as a Randomly Selected Assembly," *Perspectives on Politics* 19:3 (2021), 791–806.

107 We can think about the proposals in this chapter as insulating the political system form wider social and economic inequalities. This is vital, but as Rawls put it, we also have to "disperse the ownership of wealth and capital, and thus . . . prevent a small part of society from controlling the economy, and indirectly, political life as well": *Justice as Fairness*, 139.

6. EQUALITY OF OPPORTUNITY

1 This idea is typically attributed to Fredric Jameson's book, *The Seeds of Time* (New York: Columbia University Press, 1994). See Francesco Boldizzoni, *Foretelling the End of Capitalism: Intellectual Misadventures since Karl Marx* (Cambridge, MA: Harvard University Press, 2020), 149.

2 This has been driven to a significant degree by the economist Thomas Piketty, who has done more than any contemporary thinker to raise popular awareness of these issues. See Thomas Piketty, *Capital in the Twenty-First Century*, trans. Arthur Goldhammer (Cambridge, MA: Harvard University Press, 2014), and *Capital and Ideology*, trans. Arthur Goldhammer (Cambridge, MA: Harvard University Press, 2020).

3 For a discussion of the role of genetics in explaining intergenerational income mobility see Samuel Bowles and Herbert Gintis, "The Inheritance of Inequality," *Journal of Economic Perspectives* 16:3 (2002), 10–16.

4 Some economists have tried to measure equality of opportunity directly, by attempting to isolate the factors that shape people's incomes which are outside their control, like race, gender and parental income. In practice, these measures are closely correlated with income mobility, reinforcing the intuitive idea that low mobility is often due to a genuine lack of opportunity. See Miles Corak, "Income Inequality, Equality of Opportunity, and Intergenerational Mobility," *Journal of Economic Perspectives* 27:3 (2013), 84–5.

5 OECD, *A Broken Social Elevator? How to Promote Social Mobility* (Paris: OECD Publishing, 2018), 195. The correlation between parental and child income (or earnings) is known as the "intergenerational income (earnings) elasticity," and is one way of measuring "intergenerational mobility."

6 Corak, "Income Inequality, Equality of Opportunity, and Intergenerational Mobility," 87. See also Jo Blanden, "Cross-Country Rankings in Intergenerational Mobility: A Comparison of Approaches from Economics and Sociology," *Journal of Economic Surveys* 27:1 (2013), 38–73.

7 See OECD, *A Broken Social Elevator?*, 69–79.

8 For the UK, see Lee Elliot Major and Stephen Machin, *Social Mobility and Its Enemies* (London: Pelican, 2018), 7. For the U.S.A., see Richard V. Reeves, *Dream Hoarders: How the American Upper Middle Class Is Leaving Everyone Else in the Dust, Why That Is a Problem, and What to Do about It* (Washington, DC: Brookings Institution Press, 2018), 61.

9 Corak, "Income Inequality, Equality of Opportunity, and Intergenerational Mobility," 82.

10 According to Daniel Markovits, the extra spending on education by the richest 1 per cent in America compared to a typical middle-income household, from preschool through to graduate school, was equivalent to an inheritance of about $10 million. In other words, if rich parents invested this money in a trust fund instead of spending it on education, the fund would have been worth about $10 million when they died. See Daniel Markovits, *The Meritocracy Trap* (London: Allen Lane, 2019), 146.

11 Heather Boushey, *Unbound: How Inequality Constricts Our Economy and What We Can Do about It* (Cambridge, MA: Harvard University Press, 2019), 46.

12 Meeting basic needs and reducing inequality to a level that is consistent with the difference principle will ensure that children in the poorest households have the best possible start in life, and in doing so will help us to achieve fair equality of opportunity. At the same time, putting fair equality of opportunity into practice will itself tend to increase economic growth and reduce inequality, and hence contribute towards the aims of the difference principle. In this way, the two parts of Rawls's second principle work together, not conceptually, but in a very practical way.

13 The UK statistic is based on the fraction of young people who have completed a degree by the age of twenty-three, as reported in Major and Machin, *Social Mobility and Its Enemies*, 99. In France, this number corresponds with the fraction of eighteen to twenty-four-year-olds who are or have been in higher education, as reported in Cécile Bonneau and Sébastien Grobon, "Unequal Access to Higher Education Based on Parental Income: Evidence from France," World

Inequality Lab Working Paper 2022/01 (January 2022), 15. The figure for the U.S.A. is based on the fraction of people who had completed college by age twenty-five, based on analysis in Kathleen M. Ziol-Guest and Kenneth T. H. Lee, "Parent Income-Based Gaps in Schooling: Cross-Cohort Trends in the NLSYs and the PSID," *AERA Open* 2:2 (2016), 1–10. Other studies have found a similarly strong relationship between parental education and children's educational achievement. See, for example, OECD, *Education at a Glance, 2020: OECD Indicators* (Paris: OECD Publishing, 2020), 249–60.

14 For a recent review of this literature, see S. Cattan et al., *Early Childhood and Inequalities* (London: IFS Deaton Review of Inequalities, 2022). See also Bruce Bradbury et al., "Inequality in Early Childhood Outcomes," in John Ermisch et al. (eds.), *From Parents to Children: The Intergenerational Transmission of Advantage* (New York: Russell Sage Foundation, 2012), 87–119.

15 Bradbury et al., "Inequality in Early Childhood Outcomes." The cited numbers have been calculated by combining the estimated gap in vocabulary outcomes between rich and poor children at age five (0.95 standard deviations for UK and 1.09 standard deviations for the U.S.A.: see fig. 4.2), with the estimated average monthly increment in test scores (0.05 standard deviations for both the UK and U.S.A.: see table 4.4).

16 Cattan et al., "Early Childhood and Inequalities," 50.

17 Ibid., 7–17.

18 Ibid., 18. For a discussion of the benefits of home visits, see Reeves, *Dream Hoarders*, 128–31.

19 Boushey, *Unbound*, 37–9. For an overview of the Perry programme, see James Heckman and Ganesh Karapakula, "Intergenerational Benefits of High-Quality Early Childhood Education for Underprivileged Children: Evidence from the Iconic Perry Preschool Project," VoxEU.org, 23 August 2019, https://voxeu.org/article/intergenerationalbenefits-high-quality-early-childhood-education-underprivilegedchildren.

20 Boushey, *Unbound*, 37–9, and Elizabeth Cascio, "The Promises and Pitfalls of Universal Early Education," IZA World of Labor, January 2015, https://doi.org/10.15185/izawol.116. Subsidized early years education can also help to increase household income by doubling up as childcare. But as Cascio notes, when provision is focused on providing childcare this tends not to have the same benefits for children's development as when it is focused on early years education.

21 Tarjei Havnes and Magne Mogstad, "Is Universal Child Care Leveling

the Playing Field?," *Journal of Public Economics* 127 (2015), 100–14. For a study documenting the benefits of universal childcare in Germany, see Christina Felfe and Rafael Lalive, "The Levelling Effects of Good Quality Early Childcare," VoxEU.org, 20 May 2018, https:// voxeu.org/article/levelling-effects-good-quality-early-childcare; and for a discussion of how this has particularly benefited disadvantaged children, see Thomas Cornelissen et al., "Universal Childcare, Family Background, and School Readiness," VoxEU.org, 7 June, 2018, https://voxeu.org/article/universalchildcarefamilybackgroundand school-readiness.

22 According to the OECD, "across G20 countries, per child spending tends to increase progressively from the pre-primary to tertiary level. For example, in the United States, public spending per child (or student) is USD 6 803 in pre-primary education, USD 11 281 in primary education, USD 12 573 in secondary education and USD 14 630 in tertiary education." OECD, *Early Childhood Education: Equity, Quality and Transitions: Report for the G20 Education Working Group* (Paris: OECD Publishing, 2020), 20.

23 Unsurprisingly, the connection between income and enrolment in early years education tends to be strongest in countries like the UK, the Netherlands and Ireland, where services for the youngest children are privately run and public subsidies are relatively limited subsidies. See OECD, *Who Uses Childcare? Background Brief on Inequalities in the Use of Formal Early Childhood Education and Care (ECEC) among Very Young Children* (Paris: OECD Publishing, 2016), 5. Much of the gap in enrolment between high- and low-income households is accounted for by the fact that mothers in low-income households are less likely to work. But this is itself partly a result of the high cost of early years education, and reducing these costs is likely to lead to both higher maternal employment *and* increased enrolment in early years education.

24 For an overview of different early years education systems, see OECD, *Education at a Glance, 2020*, 161–80.

25 OECD, *Who Uses Childcare?*, 7.

26 For an illustration of the net benefits of early years education in the American context, see Katherine Magnuson and Greg J. Duncan, "Can Early Childhood Interventions Decrease Inequality of Economic Opportunity?," *Russell Sage Foundation Journal of the Social Sciences* 2:2 (2016), 123–41. The authors conclude that "The benefits of even a moderately effective [early childhood education] program are likely to be sufficient to offset the costs of program expansion."

27 OECD, *OECD Family Database*, "Chart PF3.1.A: Public Spending on Early Childhood Education and Care" (data for 2017), https://www.oecd.org/els/soc/PF3_1_Public_spending_on_childcare_and_early_education.pdf.

28 To be clear, the argument here is against *fee-paying* schools, rather than privately managed ones. In principle, schools could be privately managed but publicly funded and available to all on equal terms. Whether schools should be managed by the state, by charitable foundations or even by private, profit-making organizations depends on what kind of school system is most likely to deliver good results for students, rather than any deep point of principle.

29 Independent Schools Council, *ISC Census and Annual Report, 2022* (London: Independent Schools Council, 2022), 17; for Eton's fees in 2020/21, see "Eton College," *Tatler*, 16 October 2020; Office for National Statistics, "Average Household Income, UK: Financial Year Ending 2021," ONS Statistical Bulletin (March 2022), 2.

30 Francis Green, *Private Schools and Inequality* (London: IFS Deaton Review of Inequalities, 2022), 8.

31 Social Mobility Commission, *State of the Nation, 2018–19: Social Mobility in Great Britain* (London: Her Majesty's Stationery Office, 30 April 2019), 54.

32 Major and Machin, *Social Mobility and Its Enemies*, 129–50.

33 The focus here is on whether fee-paying schools should exist at all. For a brilliant discussion about whether it is ethical to send one's children to fee-paying schools in a society where they do exist, see Adam Swift, *How Not to Be a Hypocrite: School Choice for the Morally Perplexed Parent* (London: Routledge, 2003).

34 "Private Education Is Not Prohibited in Finland," AACRAO Edge, 11 March 2022, https://www.aacrao.org/edge/emergent-news/detail/private-education-is-not-prohibited-in-finland. The Finnish school reforms also saw a shift from a two-tiered system of grammar and "basic" schools to a single comprehensive education system.

35 "Finland: Slow and Steady Reform for Consistently High Results," in OECD, *Lessons from PISA for the United States* (Paris: OECD Publishing, 2011), 118. For a discussion of the Finnish education system, see Pasi Sahlberg, "A Model Lesson: Finland Shows Us What Equal Opportunity Looks Like," *American Educator* 36:1 (2012), 20–27 and 40.

36 Countries where students are more integrated in terms of socioeconomic status tend to perform better on average, and abolishing private schools would significantly enhance integration in this sense.

See OECD, *Public and Private Schools: How Management and Funding Relate to Their Socio-Economic Profile* (Paris: OECD Publishing, 2012), 27.

37 The discussion here draws on Harry Brighouse and Adam Swift, *Family Values: The Ethics of Parent-Child Relationships* (Princeton: Princeton University Press, 2014). Although not explicitly a development of Rawls's theory, their approach is broadly consistent with it. In particular, the freedom to develop healthy and loving parent–child relationships is protected by the basic liberties principle because raising children is such an important part of many people's lives, and because this is necessary for the survival of society from one generation to the next. While some parents might want to send their children to schools with a particular educational, cultural or even religious ethos, we can achieve this within a publicly funded system.

38 Boushey, *Unbound*, 48–9; Reeves, *Dream Hoarders*, 131. Studies of school-finance reforms have confirmed that differences in funding have a real impact on results. One study found that a 10 per cent increase in annual per pupil spending across twelve years of public school led to 0.3 more completed years of education on average, as well as 7.3 per cent higher wages and a 3 percentage point reduction in adult poverty, with these effects especially pronounced among children from low-income families. See Boushey, *Unbound*, 49.

39 Major and Machin, *Social Mobility and Its Enemies*, 89–90.

40 For an overview of school funding in England, see Luke Sibieta, "School Spending in England: Trends over Time and Future Outlook," Institute for Fiscal Studies Briefing Note BN334 (September 2021).

41 According to the OECD, a "weighted funding formula seems to be the best option of funding schools from an equity perspective." See OECD, *Equity and Quality in Education: Supporting Disadvantaged Students and Schools* (Paris: OECD Publishing, 2012), 90.

42 See Mark Dynarski and Kirsten Kainz, "Why Federal Spending on Disadvantaged Students (Title I) Doesn't Work," *Evidence Speaks* 1:7 (2015), 1–5. Of course, this cost depends on how large those gaps are in the first place, which in turn depends on wider social inequalities. If we reduce income inequality itself, then we won't need to spend so much on closing gaps through the education system.

43 Jack Britton et al., *2020 Annual Report on Education Spending in England* (London: Institute for Fiscal Studies, 2020), 64–76.

44 This discussion draws on OECD, *Equity and Quality in Education*. For an overview of the evidence about grammar schools in the UK,

see Luke Sibieta, "Can Grammar Schools Improve Social Mobility?," Institute for Fiscal Studies, 12 September 2016, https://ifs.org.uk /publications/8469.

45 See Major and Machin, *Social Mobility and Its Enemies*, 204–5.

46 Raj Chetty et al., "Measuring the Impacts of Teachers II: Teacher Value-Added and Student Outcomes in Adulthood," *American Economic Review* 104:9 (2014), 2672. The authors estimate that the "present value" of this increase in lifetime earnings is $14,500.

47 OECD, *A Broken Social Elevator?*, 300–301.

48 OECD, *Education at a Glance, 2020*, 88.

49 See, for example, Andrew E. Clark et al., "Beyond Income Inequality: Non-Monetary Rewards to Work," *CentrePiece* 26:2 (2021), 26–8, which finds that having a degree is associated with overall job satisfaction and better non-monetary "amenities" at work.

50 Major and Machin, *Social Mobility and Its Enemies*, 99.

51 Raj Chetty et al., "Income Segregation and Intergenerational Mobility across Colleges in the United States," *Quarterly Journal of Economics* 135:3 (2020), "Ivy League Plus" is defined as the eight Ivy League colleges plus Duke, MIT, Stanford and the University of Chicago. For Ivy League fees in 2022–23, see Christy Rakoczy, "How Much Does an Ivy League Education Cost?," *The Balance*, 27 September 2022, https://www.thebalancemoney.com/can-you-afford-an-ivy-league -educationfor-your-child-795012

52 As of 2021, 47 per cent of 25-to-34-year-olds have attained a tertiary qualification across the OECD as a whole. This figure includes some advanced professional and vocational qualifications. See "Population with Tertiary Education," OECD, accessed 22 November 2022, https://doi.org/10.1787/0b8f90e9-en.

53 Bonneau and Grobon, "Unequal Access to Higher Education," 20; Chetty et al., "Income Segregation and Intergenerational Mobility." In the UK, by contrast, gaps in prior attainment appear to explain most if not all of the difference in university access between the richest and poorest 20 per cent of state-school students (in other words, students with similar attainment at age sixteen or eighteen are just as likely to go to university irrespective of parental income). However, a small gap remains in access to the most "high status" universities, and would almost certainly be larger if we included private-school students. See Claire Crawford et al., "Raising GCSE Attainment Crucial to Get More Young People from Disadvantaged Backgrounds into University, but Work to Promote Social Mobility Cannot End When They Arrive on Campus," Institute for Fiscal Studies, 5 December

2016, https://ifs.org.uk/articles/raisinggcseattainmentcrucialget moreyoungpeople-disadvantaged-backgrounds-university.

54 One study of high-achieving American students from low-income families found that the majority did not apply to selective universities, even though their grades meant they would probably have been admitted, and they would have been eligible for significant financial support. See Boushey, *Unbound*, 52.

55 OECD, *Education at a Glance, 2020*, 316–26.

56 Melanie Hansen, "Student Loan Default Rate," Education Data Initiative, 19 December 2021, https://educationdata.org/student-loan-defaultrate.

57 Bruce Chapman and Lorraine Dearden, "Income Contingent Loans in Higher Education Financing," IZA World of Labor, October 2022, https://doi.org/10.15185/izawol.227.

58 A form of income-contingent loan, known as "income-driven repayment," already exists in America, but eligibility is severely restricted and coverage is low. See Nicholas Barr et al., "The U.S. College Loans System: Lessons from Australia and England," *Economics of Education Review* 71 (2019), 32–48. For the details of President Biden's plan, see "Fact Sheet: President Biden Announces Student Loan Relief for Borrowers Who Need It Most," White House, 24 August 2022, https://www.whitehouse.gov/briefingroom/statementsreleases/2022/08/24/factsheetpresidentbidenannouncesstudentloan-relief-for-borrowers-who-need-it-most/.

59 These figures incorporate the reforms to the student loan system in 2022 which, among other things, increased the period over which people are expected to repay their loans from thirty to forty years, and lowered the repayment threshold. See Ben Waltmann, "Student Loans Reform Is a Leap into the Unknown," Institute for Fiscal Studies Briefing Note BN341 (April 2022).

60 OECD, *Education at a Glance, 2020*, 317.

61 Richard Murphy et al., "The End of Free College in England: Implications for Enrolments, Equity, and Quality," *Economics of Education Review* 71 (2019), 7–22.

62 The latest OECD estimate found that public funding accounted for about 25 per cent of total spending on tertiary education in the UK, but this was before the reforms introduced in 2022 which significantly reduced the overall level of state subsidy, making the UK even more of an outlier. Waltmann, "Student Loans Reform Is a Leap into the Unknown," 5.

63 In Australia, repayment rates increase from 1 per cent for those

with income above AU$48,361 (about £27,000) to 10 per cent above AU$141,848 (about £80,000). See "Study and Training Loan Repayment Thresholds and Rates," Australian Tax Office, accessed 10 November 2022, https://www.ato.gov.au/Rates/HELP,-TSL-and SFSS-repayment-thresholds-and-rates/. These rates are applied to *total* income, rather than income above the relevant threshold (as is the case in the UK). This creates large jumps in tax liability, which encourages people to change their behaviour so as to avoid breaching the threshold.

64 "Enlightenment Liberalism Is Losing Ground in the Debate about How to Deal with Racism," *The Economist*, 9 July 2020. For examples from Hume, Kant and Mill, see Jonathan Wolff, "Race and Justice 2018," blog post, 9 March 2018, https://jonathanwolff.wordpress .com/reading-lists/race-and-justice-2018/.

65 Rawls's most prominent critic on this topic is Charles Mills. See Charles Mills, "A Critique of Tommie Shelby," *Critical Philosophy of Race* 1:1 (2013), 1–27. For a discussion of, and response to, these kinds of criticisms, see Tommie Shelby, "Race and Social Justice: Rawlsian Considerations," *Fordham Law Review* 72:5 (2004), 1697–714, and Tommie Shelby, "A Reply to Charles Mills," *Critical Philosophy of Race* 1:2 (2013), 145–62.

66 In contrast to some of his liberal predecessors, Rawls was explicit about this point. See John Rawls, *A Theory of Justice*, revised edition (Cambridge, MA: Harvard University Press, 1999), 442–3. Indeed, he argued that the belief that racial discrimination is unjust is one of our firmest moral convictions (or "considered judgements"), and one that any reasonable theory of justice must account for. As Shelby notes, this is reflected in the construction of the original position thought experiment: since the parties are ignorant of their personal character- istics, no one can argue that our rights should depend on the colour of our skin—hence explicitly racist principles are ruled out from the start. See Shelby, "Race and Social Justice: Rawlsian Considerations," 1698–9.

67 Lynne Peeples, "What the Data Say about Police Brutality and Racial Bias—and Which Reforms Might Work," *Nature*, 19 June 2020.

68 As we have seen, fair equality of opportunity does not require strictly equal outcomes between different groups. In a society with perfect fair equality of opportunity, inequalities would reflect differences in natural ability and the choices that people make. Since there is no genetic basis for differences in natural ability, inequalities between

racial or ethnic groups would persist only if their members consistently made different choices, say for cultural or religious reasons.

69 Moritz Kuhn et al., "Income and Wealth Inequality in America, 1949–2016," *Journal of Political Economy* 128:9 (2020), 3469–519. Persistent racial inequalities also exist for some other groups in the U.S.A., including Native American and Hispanic people; though others, such as Asian Americans, tend to have better outcomes than the white majority, at least on some measures.

70 Brigid Francis-Devine, "Which Ethnic Groups Are Most Affected by Income Inequality?," House of Commons Library, 10 August 2020, https://commonslibrary.parliament.uk/income-inequality-by-ethnicgroup/. Racial gaps in wealth are also large in the UK: Black households have between 10 per cent and 20 per cent of the wealth of white British ones on average, while Pakistani households have about 50 per cent as much as white British ones. Omar Khan, *The Colour of Money: How Racial Inequalities Obstruct a Fair and Resilient Economy* (London: Runnymede Trust, 2020), 12–13.

71 Lawrence D. Bobo et al., "The *Real* Record on Racial Attitudes," in Peter V. Marsden (ed.), *Social Trends in American Life: Findings from the General Social Survey since 1972* (Princeton: Princeton University Press, 2012), 38–83.

72 Marianne Bertrand and Sendhil Mullainathan, "Are Emily and Greg More Employable Than Lakisha and Jamal? A Field Experiment on Labor Market Discrimination," *American Economic Review* 94:4 (2004), 991–1013. A review of similar studies in America found a preference for white candidates over racial minorities ranging from 50 per cent to 500 per cent. See Devah Pager, "The Use of Field Experiments for Studies of Employment Discrimination: Contributions, Critiques, and Directions for the Future," *Annals of the American Academy of Political and Social Sciences* 609 (2007), 114. Worryingly, there is little evidence of improvement over time, at least not since the 1990s. Lincoln Quillian et al., "Meta-Analysis of Field Experiments Shows No Change in Racial Discrimination in Hiring over Time," *Proceedings of the National Academy of Sciences of the United States of America* 114:41 (2017), 10870–75.

73 For a UK example, see Martin Wood et al., "A Test for Racial Discrimination in Recruitment Practice in British Cities," Department for Work and Pensions Research Report no. 607 (2009).

74 "Segregation Still Blights the Lives of African-Americans," *The Economist*, 9 July 2020.

75 Marie-Anne Valfort, "Do Anti-Discrimination Policies Work?" IZA World of Labor, May 2018, https://doi.org/10.15185/izawol.450.

76 These kinds of interventions require careful design and evaluation. A recent study of "ban the box" policies in New York and New Jersey found that preventing employers from asking applicants whether they have a criminal record increased the racial gap in who was called for interview, because employers assumed that Black applicants were more likely to have a conviction. See Abhijit V. Banerjee and Esther Duflo, *Good Economics for Hard Times: Better Answers to Our Biggest Problems* (London: Penguin, 2019), 112–13.

77 Rawls did not address this matter, and there is some disagreement about the circumstances in which his theory provides a justification for positive discrimination. According to Thomas Nagel, Rawls privately supported affirmative action: see Thomas Nagel, "John Rawls and Affirmative Action," *Journal of Blacks in Higher Education* 39 (2003), 82–4. And Samuel Freeman noted that Rawls in his lectures indicated that affirmative action "may be a proper corrective for remedying the present effects of past discrimination": see Samuel Freeman, *Rawls* (Abingdon: Routledge, 2007), 90–91. Others have used Rawls's theory to argue against affirmative action. See, for example, Robert S. Taylor, "Rawlsian Affirmative Action," *Ethics* 119:3 (2009), 476–506. For a response to Taylor, defending affirmative action on Rawlsian grounds, see D. C. Matthew, "A Reply to Robert Taylor," *Critical Philosophy of Race* 3:2 (2015), 324–43.

78 The most familiar justification for positive discrimination is that it promotes "diversity," which benefits everyone. This has been the primary legal rationale for its application in American universities: a more diverse student population will lead to better educational and social outcomes overall. A similar justification is often given for policies to increase the representation of ethnic minorities (or women) on company boards. But from the perspective of Rawls's principle, the primary argument for positive discrimination is that it can help to promote equality of opportunity, which is important in its own right, rather than benefitting its economic growth. See Nagel, "John Rawls for Affirmative Action." In fact, the precedence of fair equality of opportunity over the difference principle would appear to prohibit positive discrimination when the intention is solely to promote economic growth.

79 For a discussion of these kinds of concerns, see Yascha Mounk, *The Great Experiment: How to Make Diverse Democracies Work* (London: Bloomsbury, 2022), 260–68.

80 Areeba Haider, "The Basic Facts About Children in Poverty" (Washington, DC: Center for American Progress, 2021), 5. It's not just that Black children are more likely to grow up in a poor family—residential segregation means they are much more likely to grow up in low-income neighbourhoods: in America, Black children are six and a half times more likely than white ones to live in areas where the poverty rate is higher than 30 per cent. See "Segregation Still Blights the Lives of African-Americans," *The Economist*, 9 July 2020.

81 Khan, *The Colour of Money*, 18.

82 As Shelby argues, we need to work out what an ideally just society would look like in order to identify past injustices that might require reparations. Tommie Shelby, "A Reply to Charles Mills," 154.

83 For a powerful argument for reparations in America, as well as an account of the history that justifies this, see William A. Darity Jr. and A. Kirsten Mullen, *From Here to Equality: Reparations for Black Americans in the Twenty-First Century* (Chapel Hill: University of North Carolina Press, 2020).

84 Other philosophers have developed answers to these questions within a liberal (though not strictly Rawlsian) tradition. Shelby highlights the work of Bernard Boxill and Howard McGary. See, for example, Bernard R. Boxill, "The Morality of Reparation," *Social Theory and Practice* 2:1 (1972), 113–23; Howard McGary, *Race and Social Justice* (Malden, MA: Blackwell, 1999); and Howard McGary, "Achieving Democratic Equality: Forgiveness, Reconciliation, and Reparations," *Journal of Ethics* 7:1 (2003), 93–113.

85 William Darity Jr., "Why Reparations Are Needed to Close the Racial Wealth Gap," *New York Times*, 24 September 2021.

86 This closely paraphrases Shelby, "A Reply to Charles Mills," 158.

87 In this chapter, we will focus on economic inequalities, but gender disparities also affect participation in public life: across the world's rich democracies, women hold fewer than 30 per cent of legislative seats. Addressing this is properly the preserve of Rawls's first principle, with its commitment to "political equality." See OECD, *The Pursuit of Gender Equality: An Uphill Battle* (Paris: OECD Publishing, 2017), 35.

88 The average employment rate for women across the OECD is 63 per cent compared to 74 per cent for men. OECD, *The Pursuit of Gender Equality*, 156.

89 Ibid., 177.

90 OECD, *Is the Last Mile the Longest? Economic Gains from Gender Equality in Nordic Countries* (Paris: OECD Publishing, 2018).

91 However, teenage girls still do worse than boys in numeracy. See OECD, *The Pursuit of Gender Equality*, 100–117.

92 OECD, *The Pursuit of Gender Equality*, 105–109.

93 Ibid., 109.

94 Claudia Goldin and Cecilia Rouse, "Orchestrating Impartiality: The Impact of Blind Auditions on Female Musicians," *American Economic Review* 90:4 (2000), 715–41.

95 See, for example, M. José González et al., "The Role of Gender Stereotypes in Hiring: A Field Experiment," *European Sociological Review* 35:2 (2019), 187–204. Men are also discriminated against in female-dominated occupations.

96 The reported prevalence of sexual harassment often varies enormously from one survey to the next. Some surveys are "subjective," in the sense that they directly ask women whether they have experienced sexual harassment at work; while others are "objective," in the sense that they ask women whether they have experienced behaviours that the researchers deem to constitute sexual harassment. Objective studies tend to find much higher rates of harassment. In the study cited, the reported incidence of sexual harassment in America was more than double when based on an objective or behavioural survey (58 per cent) compared to a subjective or direct-query survey (24 per cent). See R. Ilies et al., "Reported Incidence Rates of Work-Related Sexual Harassment in the United States: Using Meta-Analysis to Explain Reported Rate Disparities," *Personnel Psychology* 56:3 (2003), 607–31. For a general discussion, see Joni Hersch, "Sexual Harassment in the Workplace," IZA World of Labor, October 2015, https://doi.org/10.15185/izawol.188.

97 A 2017 law requiring large firms in the UK to publish data about the gender pay gap led to a decline in pay disparities between men and women in about a fifth of those companies. See Jack Blundell, "In Brief . . . UK Gender Pay Gap Reporting: A Crude but Effective Policy," LSE Centre for Economic Performance, 6 October 2021, https://cep.lse.ac.uk/_new/publications/abstract.asp?index=8550. Similar results for gender pay reporting have been observed in Denmark: Morten Bennedsen et al., "Do Firms Respond to Gender Pay Gap Transparency?," National Bureau of Economic Research Working Paper 25435 (January 2019).

98 "Gender (In)equality," OECD, accessed 11 August 2022, https://www.oecd.org/general/genderinequality.htm; OECD, *The Pursuit of Gender Equality*, 189–93.

99 Across the OECD, the gender gap in hourly wages between men and

women with at least one child is 21 per cent, almost double that for men and women without children. See OECD, *The Pursuit of Gender Equality*, 160. While looking after children has always been an important factor in explaining the gender pay gap, it has become more important in recent decades. A recent study in Denmark found that the fraction of the gap which could be accounted for by having children rose from about 40 per cent in 1980 to 80 per cent in 2013. See Henrik Kleven et al., "Children and Gender Inequality: Evidence from Denmark," *American Economic Journal: Applied Economics* 11:4 (2019), 181–209.

100 Monica Costa Dias et al., "The Gender Wage Gap," Institute for Fiscal Studies Briefing Note BN186 (August 2016), 14.

101 Rawls argued that the gendered division of labour should be "fully voluntary and [should] not result from or lead to injustice": John Rawls, *The Law of Peoples* (Cambridge, MA: Harvard University Press, 1999), 161. In other words, it should not result from unequal opportunities, nor should it lead to women being dependent on men, or under-represented in politics. While Rawls said relatively little about gender in *A Theory of Justice*, he did develop his ideas further in later work—though not in as much detail as the topic deserves, or as many had hoped—largely in response to a number of important critiques from feminist philosophers, especially Susan Okin's *Justice, Gender, and the Family* (New York: Basic Books, 1989). For a discussion of the debates between Rawls and his feminist critics and interlocutors, see Martha C. Nussbaum, "Rawls and Feminism," in Samuel Freeman (ed.), *The Cambridge Companion to Rawls* (Cambridge: Cambridge University Press, 2003), 488–520.

102 OECD, *The Pursuit of Gender Equality*, 201.

103 There is also a strong case for the state, rather than individual companies, to bear the cost of parental leave and other policies to support carers. If employers shoulder them, then as long as women are more likely than men to use these benefits, firms will have an incentive to discriminate against women in order to avoid the potential extra costs.

104 OECD, *The Pursuit of Gender Equality*, 200.

105 Alison Andrew et al., *Women and Men at Work* (London: Institute for Fiscal Studies, 2021), 21–4.

106 "Parental-Leave Policies," in *Gender Equality Index, 2019: Work–Life Balance* (Vilnius: European Institute for Gender Equality, 2019).

107 OECD, *The Pursuit of Gender Equality*, 203.

108 This argument draws on Lori Watson and Christie Hartley, *Equal*

Citizenship and Public Reason: A Feminist Political Liberalism (Oxford: Oxford University Press, 2018), 189–211.

109 Rawls, *The Law of Peoples*, 157.

110 Rawls's failure to address the question of care work has rightly been highlighted by feminist critics and commentators. See Nussbaum, "Rawls and Feminism," 511–14.

111 The economist Claudia Goldin has highlighted the part-time pay penalty as one of the most serious obstacles to gender equality. This penalty means that, in working couples, there are strong financial incentives for one partner (usually a man) to specialize in full-time paid work, while the other (usually a woman) focuses on care work, rather than working part-time. If we can encourage employers to reorganize work in a way that reduces the part-time penalty, this would make it much easier for families to divide paid and unpaid labour more equally. Of course, this is easier said than done, but it is possible: Goldin discusses the pharmaceutical sector, which has gone from being a sector where part-time workers suffered a significant pay penalty, to one in which hourly rates of pay are almost equal for those working part-time and full-time. See Claudia Goldin, "A Grand Gender Convergence: Its Last Chapter," *American Economic Review* 104:4 (2014), 1091–119.

7. SHARED PROSPERITY

1 *World Inequality Database*, accessed 16 January 2022, https://wid .world/. All figures are for post-tax national income in 2019 (the latest year with data for all the relevant countries).

2 Thomas Piketty, *Capital in the Twenty-First Century*, trans. Arthur Goldhammer (Cambridge, MA: Harvard University Press, 2014), 304–35. As Piketty notes, the increase in inequality, as measured by the share of income going to the top 10 per cent and 1 per cent, has been much more pronounced in Anglophone countries (the UK, U.S.A., Canada and Australia) compared to Europe and Japan.

3 As we saw in Chapter 1, in Western Europe and North America, the top 1 per cent captured 28 per cent of total growth in pretax incomes between 1980 and 2016, more than three times as much as the entire bottom half. See Facundo Alvaredo et al., *World Inequality Report, 2018* (Paris: World Inequality Lab, 2018), 48.

4 This crucial feature of the difference principle has not always been sufficiently recognized. Indeed, it has often been interpreted solely in terms of inequalities in income (see Chapter 1, n. 61, above). This in

turn helps to explain why Rawls's theory has so often been misunderstood as little more than a defence of redistribution: if our aim is simply to maximize the income of the least well off, then we can achieve this by taxing the rich and redistributing to the poor. Inasmuch as Rawls's ideas have been taken seriously by economists, this is usually how they have been interpreted: within economics (or at least within the branch of economics known as "optimal tax theory"), "Rawlsian" has become a shorthand for how to maximize tax revenues, since this will maximize the resources available to redistribute to the least well off. This is a seriously impoverished—and misleading—way to construe the difference principle.

5 There has been a lot of debate about why Rawls rejected "welfare state capitalism" and how exactly this would differ from his preferred regime, which he referred to as a "property owning democracy." See Samuel Freeman, "Property-Owning Democracy and the Difference Principle," *Analyse & Kritik* 35:1 (2013), 9–36, and Martin O'Neill, "Free (and Fair) Markets without Capitalism: Political Values, Principles of Justice, and Property-Owning Democracy," in Martin O'Neill and Thad Williamson (eds.), *Property-Owning Democracy: Rawls and Beyond* (Chichester: Blackwell, 2012), 75–100.

6 As Martin O'Neill has noted, Rawls himself appears to encourage this way of thinking, since he framed his discussion of economic institutions as a series of choices between a list of discrete economic "regimes" ("laissez-faire capitalism," "welfare state capitalism," "property owning democracy," "liberal socialism" and "state socialism"), arguing that only "property owning democracy" and "liberal socialism" were compatible with his principles. Martin O'Neill, "Social Justice and Economic Systems: On Rawls, Democratic Socialism, and Alternatives to Capitalism," *Philosophical Topics* 48:2 (2020), 159–202. But Rawls's approach is best understood as a heuristic device for drawing out certain important distinctions between different systems. He was clear that we face a more complex and nuanced set of choices in practice, and that these "regimes" can be combined in different ways. See, for example, John Rawls, *A Theory of Justice*, revised edition (Cambridge, MA: Harvard University Press, 1999), 242.

7 Rawls's most detailed discussions of these issues can be found in Rawls, *A Theory of Justice*, 228–50, and John Rawls, *Justice as Fairness: A Restatement*, ed. Erin Kelly (Cambridge, MA: Harvard University Press, 2001), 135–40, 157–80.

8 Estimates suggest that it would take 1.6 Earths to maintain humanity's current consumption of natural resources, a problem that will

only get worse as the world's population continues to grow. Partha Dasgupta, *The Economics of Biodiversity: The Dasgupta Review* (London: HM Treasury, 2021), 30–31. See also Anthony D. Barnosky et al., "Has the Earth's Sixth Mass Extinction Already Arrived?," *Nature*, 3 March 2011.

9 United Nations Environment Programme, *Emissions Gap Report, 2022: The Closing Window—Climate Crisis Calls for Rapid Transformation of Societies* (Nairobi: United Nations Environment Programme, 2022). According to this report, existing policies would likely lead to a 2.8°C temperature rise by the end of the century. Including further policies that countries have pledged but not yet acted upon would reduce this to around 2.4–2.6°C. For the most authoritative overview of the climate science, see the three reports of the Intergovernmental Panel on Climate Change's sixth assessment cycle, released over 2021 and 2022, which look at the physical science, impacts and adaptation, and mitigation respectively: https://www.ipcc.ch/report/sixth-assessment-report-cycle/.

10 According to the World Bank, on our current path more than 200 million people are likely to be displaced within their own countries due to water shortages, crop failure and sea level rises by 2050: Viviane Clement et al., *Groundswell, Part II: Acting on Internal Climate Migration* (Washington, DC: World Bank, 2021), 80–83. Other studies have indicated that the number could exceed 1 billion. See Gaia Vince, "The Century of Climate Migration: Why We Need to Plan for the Great Upheaval," *Guardian*, 18 August 2022.

11 Intergovernmental Panel on Climate Change, *Climate Change, 2022: Mitigation of Climate Change. Summary for Policymakers* (IPCC, 2022), 21–7. "Net zero" is defined as a situation in which human emissions of greenhouse gases are balanced by their removal from the atmosphere, so that the overall impact is close to zero.

12 This is the conclusion of the United Nations Environment Programme, *Emissions Gap Report, 2022.*

13 Since Rawls's two principles are specifically principles of "domestic" rather than "global" justice, they cannot help us to determine how the costs of climate mitigation and adaptation should be shared between countries. However, a number of other thinkers have sought to extend and apply Rawls's ideas to the global context of climate change. See, for example, Robert Huseby, "John Rawls and Climate Justice: An Amendment to the Law of Peoples," *Environmental Ethics* 35:2 (2013), 227–43; Sarah Kenehan, "In Defense of the Duty to

Assist: A Response to Critics on the Viability of a Rawlsian Approach to Climate Change," *Critical Review of International Social and Political Philosophy* 18:3 (2015), 308–27; and John Töns, *John Rawls and Environmental Justice: Implementing a Sustainable and Socially Just Future* (Abingdon: Routledge, 2022).

14 In principle, we may be able to decouple economic output and growth from carbon emissions and the unsustainable consumption of natural resources, through the development of renewable energy and a more circular economy. But the record so far isn't especially promising. Of course, even if GDP does decline in rich countries, this doesn't necessarily mean life will get worse. Above a certain level, more income and material consumption appear to have little bearing on well-being, and we shouldn't underestimate the capacity of our culture and societies to adapt to new circumstances. For an overview of this debate, see Xhulia Likaj, Michael Jacobs and Thomas Fricke, "Growth, Degrowth or Post-Growth? Towards a Synthetic Understanding of the Growth Debate," Forum for a New Economy Basic Paper 02–2022 (May 2022).

15 The following discussion draws heavily on the proposal for a "Sustainable Economy Act" made by the Institute for Public Policy Research (IPPR) think tank's "Commission on Economic Justice." See IPPR, *Prosperity and Justice: A Plan for the New Economy—The Final Report of the IPPR Commission on Economic Justice* (Cambridge: Polity Press, 2018), 217–27. I want to thank Michael Jacobs—who led the Commission's work and was one of the leading architects of the UK's Climate Change Act—for his comments on this section, and for highlighting the transformative potential of this idea.

16 According to independent scientific analysis conducted by Climate Action Tracker, the UK's current policies are "almost sufficient" to meet the globally agreed goal of the 2015 Paris Agreement of "holding warming well below 2°C, and pursuing efforts to limit warming to 1.5°C," while the EU's are deemed "insufficient": see https://climateactiontracker.org/countries/, accessed 12 August 2022. For a discussion of how the UK has made faster progress in reducing emissions than in areas outside the remit of the Climate Change Act, see IPPR, *Prosperity and Justice*, 223.

17 Ibid., 222–7. The choice of limits across these areas should be informed by science and experts, along the lines of the Climate Change Committee, but ultimately made by citizens through the democratic process.

18 In 2019, more than 3,500 American economists, including twenty-eight Nobel laureates, signed an "Economists' Statement on Carbon Dividends" in support of a carbon tax: "Economists' Statement," Climate Leadership Council, 16 January 2019, https://www.econstatement .org/. Under a "cap and trade" scheme, the government would cap the total amount of greenhouse gas emissions, and then sell permits to energy and other companies which would allow them to emit a certain amount. In principle, the effect could be very similar to a carbon tax, since allowing companies to trade permits would establish a market price for emissions. However, a cap and trade scheme has the advantage that it would set a clear limit on total emissions, whereas total emissions with a carbon tax would remain uncertain. For an overview of carbon pricing schemes around the world, see World Bank, *State and Trends of Carbon Pricing, 2022* (Washington, DC: World Bank, 2022).

19 "Launch of IMF Staff Climate Note: A Proposal for an International Carbon Price Floor Among Large Emitters," International Monetary Fund, 18 June 2021, https://www.imf.org/en/News /Articles/2021/06/18/sp061821-launch-of-imf-staff-climate-note. According to the OECD, current carbon prices are just 19 per cent of where they need to be. See OECD, *Effective Carbon Rates, 2021: Pricing Carbon Emissions through Taxes and Emissions Trading* (Paris: OECD Publishing, 2021), 4.

20 In North America, on average the richest 10 per cent emit about seven times as much carbon per person as the bottom 50 per cent. See Lucas Chancel et al., *World Inequality Report*, 2022 (Paris: World Inequality Lab, 2021), 121.

21 Martin Sandbu, *The Economics of Belonging: A Radical Plan to Win Back the Left Behind and Achieve Prosperity for All* (Princeton: Princeton University Press 2020), 183–7. A carbon tax which reflected the true cost of emissions would probably need to be significantly higher than $50 per ton.

22 Amartya Sen, *Development as Freedom* (Oxford: Oxford University Press, 2001), 6 (original italics).

23 In principle, a planned economy where the state uses financial incentives to encourage people to do different jobs is also consistent with this basic freedom. In fact, most planned economies, including the Soviet Union, have allowed fairly wide freedom of occupational choice. See Giacomo Corneo, *Is Capitalism Obsolete? A Journey through Alternative Economic Systems* (Cambridge, MA: Harvard University Press, 2017), 119.

24 Some goods and services, like healthcare and education, should be allocated (or "rationed") by the state, at least in part, since this is essential for achieving equality of opportunity.

25 C. I. Jones, "The Facts of Economic Growth," in John B. Taylor and Harald Uhlig (eds.), *Handbook of Macroeconomics*, vol. 2A (Amsterdam: Elsevier, 2016), 11; Deirdre Nansen McCloskey, "The Great Enrichment: A Humanistic and Social Scientific Account," *Scandinavian Economic History Review* 64:1 (2016), 6–18. This increase in incomes went alongside a massive improvement in worldwide life expectancy at birth, from about twenty-six years on average in 1820 to seventy-two years in 2020. See Thomas Piketty, *A Brief History of Equality*, trans. Steven Rendall (Cambridge, MA: Harvard University Press, 2022), 17.

26 For a detailed discussion of how planning would work, and the arguments for and against, see Corneo, *Is Capitalism Obsolete?*, 99–127.

27 As Corneo notes, while the conventional model of planning involves the state directly collecting information about production capacities and consumer demands, it could in principle use what is known as "iterative planning" to determine a set of prices that would, in effect, simulate a perfectly competitive market. A proposal along these lines was developed in the 1960s by two Nobel Prize–winning economists, Kenneth Arrow and Leonid Hurwicz; but, as Corneo argues, it's uncertain this could be put into practice, and no one has ever tried. See Corneo, *Is Capitalism Obsolete?*, 107–17.

28 This is the essence of Friedrich Hayek's famous critique of planning which, despite his controversial ideas about inequality and social justice, is widely accepted by economists on both left and right. See F. A. Hayek, "The Use of Knowledge in Society," *American Economic Review* 35:4 (1945), 519–30.

29 Studies of the Soviet Union found that firms routinely tried to game the system by overstating their needs and understating their capacity to produce; while chronic shortages of parts and labour led to a combination of hoarding in some places, and unused capacity elsewhere. Although aggregate growth in the Soviet Union was similar to that in leading market economies in the 1950s and 1960s, this was largely the result of a one-off shift from agriculture to industrial production, and a process of catching up with more advanced technologies used elsewhere. By the 1980s, the Soviet Union was visibly falling behind, unable to keep up with the rapid pace of technological innovation. The experiences of India and China in the late twentieth century further support the advantages of a market-based economy:

in both countries, the shift away from planning and towards markets unleashed an unprecedented wave of economic growth. See Corneo, *Is Capitalism Obsolete?*, 118–27; John Roemer, *A Future for Socialism* (London: Verso, 1994), 37–45; and Abhijit V. Banerjee and Esther Duflo, *Good Economics for Hard Times: Better Answers to Our Biggest Problems* (London: Penguin, 2019), 57–60.

30 The key advantage of market socialism, at least in principle, is that it provides a way to harness the efficiency of markets without the inequality that results from the unequal distribution of profits. For a discussion of different models of market socialism, see Corneo, *Is Capitalism Obsolete?*, 152–97.

31 Within economics, a lot of attention has been paid to the "Fundamental Theorems of Welfare Economics," which "prove" that, under certain stringent conditions, markets are "Pareto efficient," meaning they lead to a situation in which no one can be made better off without someone else being made worse off. But since the relevant conditions rarely, if ever, hold in the real world, these theorems also serve to elucidate the various ways in which real-life markets fail to be perfectly efficient, and how the state might be able to intervene in or shape markets to promote efficiency.

32 For a discussion of the problem of growing market concentration in the U.S.A., and a powerful argument for how to promote competition, see Thomas Philippon, *The Great Reversal: How America Gave Up on Free Markets* (Cambridge, MA: Harvard University Press, 2019).

33 As we saw in Chapter 5, "public goods" are typically defined as goods whose availability is not diminished through use, and from which it is difficult to exclude people. In technical terms, they are "non-rival" and "non-excludable."

34 For an overview of the literature on public sector outsourcing, and the circumstances under which it is most likely to yield benefits, see Panu Poutvaara and Henrik Jordahl, "Public-Sector Outsourcing," IZA World of Labor, November 2020, https://doi.org/10.15185/izawol.65. For a discussion of specific successes and failures in the UK context, see Tom Sasse et al., *Government Outsourcing: What Has Worked and What Needs Reform?* (London: Institute for Government, 2019).

35 We can also define poverty in "absolute" terms, as having less than a certain fixed level of income (adjusted to account for changes in prices). Rawls's basic needs principle, however, corresponds with the idea of relative rather than absolute poverty, since the aim is to make

sure that everyone can exercise their fundamental freedoms and participate in society with dignity and self-respect, and this clearly depends on the overall wealth of society. There is no simple formula for working out precisely how much income would be sufficient, and the answer to this question is the proper subject of democratic debate. While the 60 per cent threshold is somewhat arbitrary, it has the major advantage that internationally comparable data is widely available. Ive Marx et al., "The Welfare State and Anti-Poverty Policy in Rich Countries," in Anthony B. Atkinson and François Bourguignon (eds.), *Handbook of Income Distribution*, vol. 2B (Amsterdam: Elsevier, 2015), 2078; Timothy Smeeding, "Poor People in Rich Nations: The United States in Comparative Perspective," *Journal of Economic Perspectives* 20:1 (2006), 79.

36 For the most part, the aim of social insurance is to help people to smooth their income over time, rather than to address chronic poverty or to redistribute from rich to poor; and since social insurance benefits are tied to past contributions rather than current needs, the highest earners tend to get the largest payouts.

37 Smeeding, "Poor People in Rich Nations," 79.

38 Mike Brewer et al., *Social Insecurity: Assessing Trends in Social Security to Prepare for the Decade of Change Ahead* (London: Resolution Foundation, 2022), 21. While extra support is available to help with housing and child-related costs, an estimated 2.4 million people experienced destitution in the UK at some point during 2019, meaning they had to go without the basics of food, shelter, heating or clothing. See Suzanne Fitzpatrick et al., *Destitution in the UK, 2020* (York: Joseph Rowntree Foundation, 2020), 2. If we define poverty by asking people how much money they think different households actually need in order to have a minimally socially acceptable standard of living, the UK poverty rate rises to roughly three in ten, or nearly 20 million people. See Matt Padley and Juliet Stone, *Households below a Minimum Income Standard: 2008/09–2018/19* (York: Joseph Rowntree Foundation, 2021), 1.

39 OECD, *Society at a Glance, 2019: OECD Social Indicators* (Paris: OECD Publishing, 2019), 103.

40 Figures here are for 2017, and poverty is defined as having an income below 60 per cent of median equivalized household income (in other words, adjusted for household size and composition, according to OECD parameters). For EU data, see "At-Risk-of-Poverty Rate by Poverty Threshold, Age and Sex—EU-SILC and ECHP Surveys," *Eurostat*, accessed 31 May 2022, https://ec.europa.eu/eurostat/data

browser/product/view/ILC_LI02?lang=en; for the UK and U.S., see Robert Joyce and James P. Ziliak, "Relative Poverty in Great Britain and the United States, 1979–2017," *Fiscal Studies* 40:4 (2019), 494.

41 Jonathan Cribb et al., *Living Standards, Poverty and Inequality in the UK: 2022* (London: Institute for Fiscal Studies, 2022), 34.

42 For an excellent overview of the debate about a UBI, and a persuasive argument in its favour, see Philippe Van Parijs and Yannick Vanderborght, *Basic Income: A Radical Proposal for a Free Society and a Sane Economy* (Cambridge, MA: Harvard University Press, 2017). For a detailed discussion of the case for a UBI within a Rawlsian framework, see Simon Birnbaum, "Radical Liberalism, Rawls and the Welfare State: Justifying the Politics of Basic Income," *Critical Review of International Social and Political Philosophy* 13:4 (2010), 495–516, and Simon Birnbaum, *Basic Income Reconsidered: Social Justice, Liberalism, and the Demands of Equality* (New York: Palgrave, 2012).

43 It would also make sense to give parents an additional payment per child, albeit at a lower rate than for adults. For a detailed discussion of the key features of a basic income, see Van Parijs and Vanderborght, *Basic Income*, 4–23. They emphasize that, as well as being universal and unconditional, a basic income must be paid both in cash (rather than in kind) and on an individual basis. They also highlight that the "basic" in basic income "is meant to convey the idea of a floor on which one can stand because of its very unconditionality," rather than that it will be sufficient to meet everyone's "basic needs" (ibid., 10).

44 It's possible that if there was more widespread acceptance of income support as every citizen's right, then benefits recipients would be treated with more respect. But we have to be realistic about the chances that these distinctions will be exploited in political debate in ways that can seriously undermine the status and dignity of disadvantaged citizens.

45 See Jonathan Wolff's concept of "shameful revelation" in his "Fairness, Respect, and the Egalitarian Ethos," *Philosophy & Public Affairs* 27:2 (1998), 97–122.

46 Deborah Padfield, "Through the Eyes of a Benefits Adviser: A Plea for a Basic Income," openDemocracy, 5 October 2011, https://www.opendemocracy.net/en/shine-a-light/through-eyes-of-benefits-adviserplea-for-basic-income/.

47 Tania Raffass, "Demanding Activation," *Journal of Social Policy* 46:2 (2017), 349–65.

48 Padfield, "Through the Eyes of a Benefits Adviser."

49 Guy Standing, *Basic Income: And How We Can Make It Happen* (London: Pelican, 2017), 76–8.

50 Van Parijs and Vanderborght, *Basic Income*, 20.

51 The increased individual bargaining power of low-paid workers would be amplified at the collective level, with a UBI acting as a sort of a "permanent strike fund." See Erik Olin Wright, *Envisioning Real Utopias* (London: Verso, 2010), 155.

52 See, for example, Daniel Susskind, *A World without Work: Technology, Automation and How We Should Respond* (London: Allen Lane, 2020).

53 Rawls, *A Theory of Justice*, 301, and *Justice as Fairness*, 179. Rawls's own comments about a UBI are somewhat inconclusive. In *A Theory of Justice*, he endorsed a negative income tax (243), a close cousin of a UBI in which a minimum income is guaranteed to all, irrespective of whether they are working or looking for work. But in *Justice as Fairness* he appeared to reject this idea, arguing that people who decide to live a life of pure leisure "must somehow support themselves" (179). For a discussion of Rawls's comments on these issues, see Birnbaum, "Radical Liberalism, Rawls and the Welfare State."

54 As Stuart White has argued in the context of debates about a universal basic income, an objection can be valid without being decisive. In the following discussion, I have focused on what I think is the strongest response to the worry that some people will freeride (also known as the "exploitation objection," in the sense that those who choose not to work are exploiting those who do), but this is by no means the only one. For a more detailed discussion of the various ways in which we can counter this criticism of a UBI, see Stuart White, "Reconsidering the Exploitation Objection to Basic Income," *Basic Income Studies* 1:2 (2006), 485.

55 Rawls, *A Theory of Justice*, 247.

56 The idea of a fair contribution is itself somewhat ambiguous. For a discussion, and a compelling proposal for how we might define this, see Stuart White, *The Civic Minimum: On the Rights and Obligations of Economic Citizenship* (Oxford: Oxford University Press, 2003), 97–126.

57 Rutger Bregman, "The Bizarre Tale of President Nixon and His Basic Income Bill," *The Correspondent*, 17 May 2016.

58 For an overview of the results from these trials, see Karl Widerquist, "A Failure to Communicate: What (if Anything) Can We Learn from the Negative Income Tax Experiments?," *The Journal of SocioEconomics* 34:1 (2005), 49–81, and Ioana Marinescu, "No Strings Attached: The

Behavioral Effects of U.S. Unconditional Cash Transfer Programs," National Bureau of Economic Research Working Paper 24377 (February 2018).

59 Marinescu, "No Strings Attached," 3; Rebecca Hasdell, *What We Know about Universal Basic Income: A Cross-Synthesis of Reviews* (Stanford, CA: Basic Income Lab, 2020).

60 Anthony B. Atkinson, *Inequality: What Can Be Done?* (Cambridge, MA: Harvard University Press, 2015), 218–23.

61 Van Parijs and Vanderborght suggest 25 per cent of GDP as a rule of thumb for a moderate to generous UBI: *Basic Income*, 11. In the U.S.A., a UBI set at the official poverty line (around $12,000 per adult and $6,000 per child) would cost almost $3,500 billion ($3.5 trillion), or around 19 per cent of GDP. See Karl Widerquist, "The Cost of Basic Income: Back-of-the-Envelope Calculations," *Basic Income Studies* 12:2 (2017). A UBI pitched at 60 per cent of median income (around £7,700 per year for adults in couples and £3,800 for children) would have a gross cost of around £438 billion per year, or 22 per cent of GDP. See Karl Widerquist and Georg Arndt, "The Cost of Basic Income in the United Kingdom: A Microsimulation Analysis" (2020), https://works.bepress.com/widerquist/119/.

62 In the UK, total spending on all benefits, including pensions, comes to around £200 billion, or about half of the cost of a poverty-level UBI. If we exclude housing benefits, and a range of other benefits targeted at meeting special needs, the figure falls to around £130 billion. See Widerquist and Arndt, "The Cost of Basic Income in the United Kingdom," 13. In the U.S.A., the cost of existing transfers excluding those related to health, education and Indian Affairs is around $1.1 trillion, or about 30 per cent of the gross cost of a poverty-level UBI. See Widerquist, "The Cost of Basic Income: Back-of-the-Envelope Calculations," 9.

63 A different way to think about the cost of a UBI is to focus on the total extra money that net contributors would end up paying to net beneficiaries. This represents the overall increase in redistribution that would be brought about by introducing a UBI. While the details vary from one scheme to the next, a proposal for the UK found that the total increase in redistribution from introducing a poverty-level UBI was £67 billion, or 3.4 per cent of GDP—just one sixth of the back-of-the-envelope gross cost. See Widerquist and Arndt, "The Cost of Basic Income in the United Kingdom," 1–2.

64 In the UK, the government could introduce a weekly cash payment of £48 to every adult simply by abolishing the personal allowance for

income tax (the amount you can earn before you start paying tax), which mostly benefits the top 35 per cent of households. See Alfie Stirling and Sarah Arnold, "Nothing Personal: Replacing the Personal Tax Allowance with a Weekly National Allowance" (London: New Economics Foundation, 2019). An OECD study found that, in Finland and France, a UBI set at the level currently guaranteed by means-tested benefits could be introduced without increasing taxes, while in Italy a basic income at the current minimum income could be introduced at a *net saving* of around €41 billion. For the most part, the UBI in these countries could be paid for by scrapping existing social insurance or "contributory" benefits. In the UK, by contrast, where contributory benefits play little role, a similar UBI would have a net cost of around £44 billion, equivalent to a 25 per cent increase in income tax revenue. See OECD, "Basic Income as a Policy Option: Can It Add Up?," OECD Directorate for Employment, Labour and Social Affairs Policy Brief (May 2017).

65 This is similar to what is known as a "minimum income guarantee," or a "guaranteed basic income." For a discussion and comparison of these options, see Mark Bryan, "What Is a Minimum Income Guarantee? And How Does It Relate to UBI?," UBI Lab Network, 23 July 2021, https://www.ubilabnetwork.org/blog/what-is-a -minimum-incomeguarantee-and-how-does-it-relate-to-ubi.

66 Van Parijs and Vanderborght, *Basic Income*, 32–43; Philip L. Harvey, "The Relative Cost of a Universal Basic Income and a Negative Income Tax," *Basic Income Studies* 1:2 (2006).

67 Rawls, *Justice as Fairness*, 140. The intention, Rawls explained, "is not simply to assist those who lose out through accident or misfortune (although that must be done), but rather to put all citizens in a position to manage their own affairs on a footing of a suitable degree of social and economic equality." Rawls, *Justice as Fairness*, 139–40.

68 Prominent advocates include the former Labour Party leader Ed Miliband in the UK and Democratic Senator and American presidential hopeful Elizabeth Warren. For a brilliant discussion of how best to make sense of this idea, see Martin O'Neill, "Power, Predistribution, and Social Justice," *Philosophy* 95:1 (2020), 63–91. The term "predistribution" was coined in a 2011 paper delivered by the American political scientist Jacob Hacker, "The Institutional Foundations of Middle-Class Democracy," *Policy Network* 6 (2011), 33–7.

69 This is especially true for the period from the mid-1980s to mid-1990s, which saw the largest increases in inequality in most countries.

See OECD, *Divided We Stand: Why Inequality Keeps Rising* (Paris: OECD Publishing, 2011), 262–80.

70 According to one recent paper, it is the fact that market incomes are so much more unequal in America than in Europe which explains its higher overall inequality, rather than America's relatively pared-back welfare state: Thomas Blanchet et al., "Why Is Europe More Equal than the United States?," *American Economic Journal: Applied Economics* 14:4 (2022), 480–518. See also Antoine Bozio et al., "Pre-Distribution versus Redistribution," VoxEU.org, 18 November 2020, https://voxeu.org/article/pre-distribution-versusredistribution.

71 Pretax national income in 2021, *World Inequality Database*, accessed 13 August 2022, https://wid.world/. These differences in absolute pretax income correspond to differences in pretax income shares: just 14 per cent of pretax income goes to the bottom half of earners in America, compared to 21 per cent in Denmark; while the top 10 per cent receive 45 per cent of pretax income in America compared to 34 per cent in Denmark. Note that these *pretax* income shares differ from the shares of *total* national income that were cited at the start of this chapter (see p. 196), which incorporate the redistributive impact of taxes and benefits. Average disposable incomes for the bottom 50 per cent are just under $30,000 in America, compared to nearly $40,000 in Denmark.

72 In practice, Denmark also does more redistribution, meaning average disposable incomes for the bottom 50 percent is nearly $40,000, compared to just under $30,000 in America.

73 A number of economists have highlighted the advantages of "predistribution" for economic efficiency, including J. E. Meade, *Efficiency, Equality and the Ownership of Property* (Cambridge, MA: Harvard University Press, 1965), and, more recently, Branko Milanovic, *Capitalism, Alone: The Future of the System That Rules the World* (Cambridge, MA: Harvard University Press, 2019), 42–5, which also draws attention to the political difficulties associated with further increases in redistribution.

74 Rawls argued that a property-owning democracy would guard against the emergence of a "discouraged and depressed underclass, many of whose members are chronically dependent on welfare," and that if such a class did still exist, it would be small and "the result of social conditions we do not know how to change, or perhaps cannot even identify or understand." Rawls, *Justice as Fairness*, 139–40.

75 According to one recent study, support for these kinds of policies is stronger among less-educated Americans. Ilyana Kuziemko et al.,

"'Compensate the Losers?' Economy-Policy Preferences and Partisan Realignment in the U.S.," Working Paper (March 2022).

76 There is clearly a limit to how much we can change the distribution of skills, since this depends, at least in part, on natural or innate ability: some people are born with a gift for mathematics or for music, and there is little that we can (or indeed would want to) do to change this. But what matters when it comes to how much people can earn is their "realized abilities," which depend to a large extent on the opportunities available to them through the education system.

77 In thinking about the design of the education system, we cannot rely on the principle of fair equality of opportunity alone. As we have seen, equality of opportunity is concerned with making sure that whatever opportunities for education exist in society should be allocated on the basis of academic merit, rather than class, race, or gender. But this doesn't tell us what educational opportunities should be available in the first place. So, for example, should everyone be able to go to university, or only those with the greatest academic gifts? In theory, equality of opportunity is consistent with a society where there are very few places at university, but everyone has a fair chance to win one. If we want to work out what educational opportunities should be available in the first place, we need to look elsewhere. The basic liberties principle justifies a minimum level of education for all: everyone needs a certain level of education to exercise their basic freedoms and participate in social and political life. Beyond this minimum, the difference principle suggests that we should organize our education system in whatever way is best for the least well off.

78 Alison Wolf, "Heading for the Precipice: Can Further and Higher Education Funding Policies Be Sustained?" (London: The Policy Institute at King's College London, 2015), 15.

79 For a sceptical perspective, see Wolf, "Heading for the Precipice."

80 We should also guarantee that those who lack the basic skills that are necessary to participate in social and political life can obtain them for free at any time. For a discussion of gaps in and the importance of basic skills, see OECD, *Universal Basic Skills: What Countries Stand to Gain* (Paris: OECD Publishing, 2015).

81 Luke Sibieta et al., "Big Changes Ahead for Adult Education Funding? Definitely Maybe," Institute for Fiscal Studies Briefing Note BN325 (April 2021).

82 For a comprehensive overview of best practice, based on twenty detailed country studies, see OECD, *Skills beyond School: Synthesis Report* (Paris: OECD Publishing, 2014).

83 Employers tend to underinvest in training because employees can simply take their skills and move to a different company. Isabel Sawhill, *The Forgotten Americans: An Economic Agenda for a Divided Nation* (New Haven: Yale University Press, 2018), 154–9.

84 In textbook models of a perfectly competitive economy, wages are determined exclusively by workers' productivity. But markets are rarely if ever perfectly competitive, and the relationship between productivity and wages is not as tight as simplistic economic models might suggest. For any given job, there is typically a wage below which workers will not work, and above which firms will not hire. Where wages actually fall within this range depends on bargaining power. See Atkinson, *Inequality*, 89–92.

85 Arindrajit Dube, "Impacts of Minimum Wages: Review of the International Evidence" (London: HM Treasury, 2019), 4. Even in low-wage districts, where minimum wages are equivalent to up to 81 per cent of median earnings, there appears to be little impact on employment.

86 OECD, "Earnings: Minimum Wages Relative to Median Wages," OECD Employment and Labour Market Statistics, accessed 28 December 2021, https://doi.org/10.1787/data-00313-en.

87 John S. Ahlquist, "Labor Unions, Political Representation, and Economic Inequality," *Annual Review of Political Science* 20 (2017), 409–32.

88 OECD, *Negotiating Our Way Up: Collective Bargaining in a Changing World of Work* (Paris: OECD Publishing, 2019), 105–35.

89 Ibid., 16.

90 In New Zealand, the so-called "Fair Pay Agreement" system gives unions the power to initiate industry-level wage negotiations with employers if they can win the support of either 1,000 workers or 10 per cent of the workforce in a given sector. See Daniel Tomlinson, *More Than We Bargain For: Learning from New Debates on How Institutions Can Improve Worker Pay and Security in Anglo-Saxon Economies* (London: Resolution Foundation, 2019), 12–14.

91 In other words, firms that are facing economic difficulties can negotiate lower rates if their employees are willing to accept them, and conversely workers can push for higher wages in firms that are making large profits.

92 OECD, *Negotiating Our Way Up*, 17. Australia provides a closely related model, where instead of bargaining between unions and employer associations, industry wage standards are set by an independent body called the Fair Work Commission which consults

closely with experts and with worker and employer representatives, but ultimately makes its own decisions. See Tomlinson, *More Than We Bargain For*, 11–12.

93 For a powerful argument in favour of this model in an American context, see David Madland, *The Future of Worker Voice and Power* (Washington, DC: American Progress, 2016).

94 Rainer Winkelmann, "Unemployment and Happiness," IZA World of Labor, October 2014, https://doi.org/10.15185/izawol.94; Ronnie Schöb, "Labor Market Policies, Unemployment, and Identity," IZA World of Labor, November 2021, https://doi.org/10.15185/izawol.270.

95 John Rawls, *Political Liberalism*, expanded edition (New York: Columbia University Press, 2005), lvii.

96 For much of the post-war period, "full employment" was the guiding goal of macroeconomic policy, but in recent decades it has taken something of a back seat to controlling inflation. There is undoubtedly a balance to strike here, but the evidence suggests that low-income workers have typically been the greatest beneficiaries of full-employment policies, and it seems likely that if we took the difference principle as our guide we would shift the emphasis towards a more aggressive pursuit of full employment, even at some cost in terms of higher inflation. Gene Sperling, *Economic Dignity* (New York: Penguin Press, 2020), 267.

97 David T. Ellwood and Elisabeth D. Welty, "Public Service Employment and Mandatory Work: A Policy Whose Time Has Come and Gone and Come Again?," in David Card and Rebecca M. Blank (eds.), *Finding Jobs: Work and Welfare Reform* (New York: Russell Sage, 2000), 299–372. See also Atkinson, *Inequality*, 140–47.

98 As with the jobs guarantee, evidence about the effectiveness of job transition programmes is mixed, but the most successful ones tend to combine financial support with a decent amount of time for retraining and job search (all of which would be much easier with a UBI in place). See Banerjee and Duflo, *Good Economics for Hard Times*, 314.

99 Net personal wealth share in 2021, *World Inequality Database*, accessed 16 November 2022, https://wid.world/.

100 The proportion of income going to capital has been increasing across the rich world in recent decades: according to the OECD, the "capital income share" increased in twenty-six out of thirty advanced countries for which data were available over the period from 1990 to 2009, with the median rising from about 34 per cent to 38 per cent. Since capital income is much more unequal than labour income,

this has contributed to growing inequality over the same period. See OECD, *The Labour Share in G20 Economies* (Paris: OECD Publishing, 2015).

101 Atkinson, *Inequality*, 158–69. People can accumulate wealth only if they have some income that they can save or invest, and the fundamental reason why wealth is so unequal is that many simply don't earn enough to do this. The policies we have already discussed to increase earnings would probably have a knock-on effect on savings, and hence wealth.

102 Van Parijs and Vanderborght, *Basic Income*, 70.

103 Bruce Ackerman and Anne Alstott, *The Stakeholder Society* (New Haven: Yale University Press, 1999).

104 Thomas Piketty, *Capital and Ideology*, trans. Arthur Goldhammer (Cambridge, MA: Harvard University Press, 2020), 975–81. Piketty refers to this as a "universal capital endowment."

105 We can, of course, combine a minimum inheritance scheme with a UBI, or a version of it. Indeed, Piketty has argued that we should combine his minimum inheritance scheme with a basic income guarantee, whereby someone with no other resources would receive a payment worth 60 per cent of median post-tax income, and this amount would be reduced as other income increases. See Piketty, *Capital and Ideology*, 1000–1004.

106 J. E. Meade, *Liberty, Equality and Efficiency: Apologia pro Agathotopia Mea* (London: Palgrave Macmillan, 1993), 156.

107 Existing sovereign wealth funds have typically been established with the aim of preserving the value of natural assets for future generations, rather than bringing about a more equal distribution of wealth, and this difference in underlying objectives is reflected in the way they have been paid for, and how their revenue is spent. Most of them have been paid for by selling natural assets, especially oil revenues; and the income from them is typically used to pay for general government expenditure, though in a handful of cases revenue is earmarked for specific social goals, such as civil service pension liabilities in Norway.

108 "Market Value," Norges Bank, accessed 16 November 2022, https://www.nbim.no/en/the-fund/Market-Value/.

109 This is the average value of payments between 1982 and 2015, adjusted for inflation and expressed in $2016 terms: C. Roberts and M. Lawrence, "Our Common Wealth: A Citizens' Wealth Fund for the UK" (London: Institute for Public Policy Research, 2018), 14.

110 Karl Widerquist, "The Alaska Model: A Citizen's Income in Practice,"

openDemocracy, 24 April 2013, https://www.opendemocracy.net/en/opendemocracyuk/alaska-model-citizens-income-in-practice/.

111 We could also establish a separate fund tasked explicitly with buying, or even creating, businesses where the state owns a majority of the shares and hence exercises ultimate control. These would still be run for profit, which would then be paid out as part of the annual citizens' dividend. While the state would own 51 per cent or more of the shares, the remainder would be owned by private investors, which in turn would provide an independent mechanism for holding management to account, since the traded share price would reflect investors' assessment of the company's profitability and long-term prospects. In this way, rather than decide in advance whether firms should be privately or publicly managed, we could allow this to emerge depending on how they actually perform. For a detailed proposal, see Corneo, *Is Capitalism Obsolete?*, 278.

112 For a detailed discussion of how these kinds of funds could be designed and managed, see Angela Cummine, *Citizens' Wealth: Why (and How) Sovereign Funds Should Be Managed by the People for the People* (New Haven: Yale University Press, 2016).

113 Piketty estimates that we would need about 40 per cent of GDP to pay for general government activities including public services such as education and healthcare, 5 per cent to pay for a guaranteed minimum income set at 60 per cent of post-tax average income, as well as wealth taxes in the region of 5 per cent of GDP to pay for a universal minimum inheritance. If we were to adopt a full-blown UBI, the total level of taxes could be even higher. While these are very rough estimates, they give a sense of the order of magnitude we are talking about. See Piketty, *Capital and Ideology*, 982.

114 OECD, "Global Revenue Statistics Database," OECD.Stat, data for 2019, accessed 17 May 2021, https://stats.oecd.org/Index.aspx?DataSetCode=RS_GBL.

115 The seven countries are: Austria, Belgium, Denmark, Finland, France, Italy and Sweden. OECD, "Global Revenue Statistics Database," data for 2019, accessed 17 May 2021.

116 Piketty, *Capital in the Twenty-First Century*, 475. Despite the tax-cutting rhetoric of the 1980s, there has been no widespread decline in overall tax revenues; and, in fact, across the OECD as a whole, taxes have continued to increase gradually over time. For long-term (pre-1990) trends, see OECD, *Revenue Statistics, 2021: Initial Impact of COVID-19 on OECD Tax Revenues* (Paris: OECD Publishing, 2021), 2.

117 Michael Keen and Joel Slemrod, *Rebellion, Rascals, and Revenue: Tax Follies and Wisdom through the Ages* (Princeton: Princeton University Press, 2021), 249.

118 Peter H. Lindert, *Making Social Spending Work* (Cambridge: Cambridge University Press, 2021). This book confirms the same broad findings as Lindert's original study, *Growing Public: Social Spending and Economic Growth since the Eighteenth Century* (Cambridge: Cambridge University Press, 2004), but using an even wider range of countries and over a longer time period. While Lindert focuses on the relationship between social spending and GDP, Jon Bakija has shown that the same results hold for the relationship between the overall tax level and economic growth, concluding that "When looking at data on [advanced economies] from the past five or ten decades, there is no convincing evidence that the countries choosing larger government suffered any significant loss of GDP per person as a result." Jon Bakija, "Would a Bigger Government Hurt the Economy?," in Jon Bakija et al., *How Big Should Our Government Be?* (Berkeley: University of California Press, 2016), 68. Other studies have focused on the relationship between redistribution and economic growth. A 2018 article by economists at the International Monetary Fund, for example, concluded that, at moderate levels like those found in the U.S.A., redistribution appears to *increase* economic growth; and in countries like the UK, Germany, France and the Netherlands, where redistribution is higher, "there is little evidence of an overall adverse effect on growth." Andrew Berg et al., "Redistribution, Inequality, and Growth: New Evidence," *Journal of Economic Growth* 23:3 (2018), 276.

119 For a detailed description of this puzzle, and potential explanations, see Lindert, *Making Social Spending Work*, 153–207.

120 Costas Meghir and David Phillips, "Labour Supply and Taxes," in Stuart Adam et al. (eds.), *Dimensions of Tax Design: The Mirrlees Review* (Oxford: Oxford University Press, 2010), 252. See also the brief discussion in Keen and Slemrod, *Rebellion, Rascals, and Revenue*, 220.

121 Ibid., 252.

122 There are also other, less obvious ways in which higher taxes and lower inequality can promote economic prosperity. A growing number of economists think that rising levels of inequality and stagnant incomes for poor and middle-income households in America are holding back investment and, therefore, growth, because companies are reluctant to develop new products unless they are confident there are people able to buy them. Inequality can also undermine prosperity

by leading to more frequent and more severe recessions. In particular, high levels of inequality are often associated with increased borrowing and debt, and high levels of debt in turn tend to make countries more vulnerable to economic downturns. For an important, detailed and wide-ranging discussion of these ideas, see Heather Boushey, *Unbound: How Inequality Constricts Our Economy and What We Can Do about It* (Cambridge, MA: Harvard University Press, 2019), 139–90.

123 Lindert, *Making Social Spending Work*, 188–207. See also Shekhar Aiyar and Christian Ebeke, "The Threat of Inequality of Opportunity," IMF Blog, 7 November 2019, https://blogs.imf.org/2019/11/07/thethreat-of-inequality-of-opportunity/; and OECD, *In It Together: Why Less Inequality Benefits All* (Paris: OECD Publishing, 2015), 44, which argues that "the inability of individuals from poor socioeconomic background to access higher education and developing [sic] their human capital is at the heart of the transmission mechanism through which income inequality lowers economic growth."

124 As Jon Bakija notes, "*some* econometric studies . . . have found an association between higher taxes and slower economic growth when looking at shorter time frames and controlling for enough other possible influences on economic growth." These studies often have methodological difficulties, but "even if we take [them] at face value, what they are concluding is that, in the industrialized countries that chose to increase taxes more over time, any negative economic effects of higher taxes seem to have been offset by positive economic effects that are the result of productive government investments (e.g., education, infrastructure) paid for by those taxes and by the more economically efficient public policies that these countries (not coincidentally) tended to choose." Bakija, "Would a Bigger Government Hurt the Economy?," 68.

125 International Monetary Fund, *Fiscal Monitor: Tackling Inequality* (Washington, DC: International Monetary Fund, 2017), 11.

126 Boushey, *Unbound*, 18.

127 Bakija, "Would a Bigger Government Hurt the Economy?," 121–33, and Banerjee and Duflo, *Good Economics for Hard Times*, 243–8.

128 Paul Krugman, "UK Suffers a Full-Scale Policy Zombie Apocalypse," *Irish Times*, 26 September 2022.

129 Peter Diamond and Emmanuel Saez, "The Case for a Progressive Tax: From Basic Research to Policy Recommendations," *Journal of Economic Perspectives* 25:4 (2011), 173.

130 Emmanuel Saez, Joel Slemrod and Seth H. Giertz, "The Elasticity

of Taxable Income with Respect to Marginal Tax Rates: A Critical Review," *Journal of Economic Literature* 50:1 (2012), 35.

131 Emmanuel Saez and Gabriel Zucman, *The Triumph of Injustice: How the Rich Dodge Taxes and How to Make Them Pay* (New York: Norton, 2019), 134–43. Note that this tax rate takes into account *all* taxes levied on top-income individuals, including corporation and consumption taxes. The marginal tax rate applies to income above a given threshold, whereas the average tax rate is the proportion of total income that is paid in taxes.

132 Saez and Zucman, *The Triumph of Injustice*, 136. Data on the decline in audits for the top 1 per cent comes from "IRS Statement— Updated IRS Audit Numbers," IRS Statements and Announcements, 26 May 2022, https://www.irs.gov/pub/irs-utl/statement-for -updated-auditrates-ty-19.pdf.

133 Saez and Zucman, *The Triumph of Injustice*, 135–8.

134 Ibid.

135 International Monetary Fund, *Fiscal Monitor: Tackling Inequality*, 10.

136 Stuart Adam and Helen Miller, *Taxing Work and Investment across Legal Forms: Pathways to Well-Designed Taxes* (London: Institute for Fiscal Studies, 2021), 33.

137 In 2012, Buffett claimed to pay 17.4 per cent of his income in taxes, compared to 35.8 per cent for his secretary, in large part because so much of his income was in the form of low-taxed capital gains. Seniboye Tienabeso, "Warren Buffett and His Secretary on Their Tax Rates," *ABC News*, 25 January 2012.

138 If lower capital taxes were so good for investment, then we would expect to see lower rates of savings and investment in countries with high capital taxes, and vice versa. But this is not the case. Taking the U.S.A. as an example, Saez and Zucman find "no observable correlation between capital taxation and capital accumulation": Saez and Zucman, *The Triumph of Injustice*, 103. Indeed, over the past 100 years, the private savings rate—a key determinant of overall levels of savings and therefore investments—has fluctuated at around 10 per cent of national incomes despite considerable changes in capital-tax rates over time. This is not to say that taxes on capital income don't affect investment at all, just that these effects appear to be small. See ibid., 97–106.

139 See, for example, Saez and Zucman, *The Triumph of Injustice*, 138–9; Adam and Miller, *Taxing Work and Investment across Legal Forms*; Ruud de Mooij et al., "Tax Policy for Inclusive Growth after the Pandemic," IMF COVID-19 Special Notes (December 2020), 4–5. For

details about the discussion of taxing corporate profits in the footnote, see Saez and Zucman, *The Triumph of Injustice*, 110–27.

140 Esteban Ortiz-Ospina and Max Roser, "Taxation," *Our World in Data*, 2016, https://ourworldindata.org/taxation.

141 Lindert argues that consumption taxes like VAT play a critical role in explaining the "free lunch puzzle." See Lindert, *Making Social Spending Work*, 178–83.

142 "Inheritance, Estate and Gift Taxes Could Play a Stronger Role in Addressing Inequality and Improving Public Finances," OECD, 11 May 2021, https://www.oecd.org/tax/tax-policy/inheritance-estate and-gift-taxes-could-play-a-stronger-role-in-addressing-inequality and-improving-public-finances.htm.

143 The primary concern is that inheritance taxes might reduce savings, but most studies find small effects. For a discussion, see OECD, *Inheritance Taxation in OECD Countries* (Paris: OECD Publishing, 2021), 53–5.

144 Ibid., 76–7. In the UK, the top tax rate on inheritances has fallen from 75 per cent in the 1970s to 40 per cent. Adam Corlett, *Passing On: Options for Reforming Inheritance Taxation* (London: Resolution Foundation, 2018, 13). In America, a similar decline in inheritance-tax rates has gone hand in hand with a massive increase in the threshold at which people start paying, which under President Trump reached nearly $12 million for single individuals and more than $23 million for married couples, meaning that fewer than 0.1 per cent pay any inheritance tax at all. Florian Scheuer and Joel Slemrod, "Taxing Our Wealth," *Journal of Economic Perspectives* 35:1 (2021), 215–16.

145 Piketty, *Capital and Ideology*, 982.

146 Atkinson, *Inequality*, 194; Piketty, *Capital and Ideology*, 988. This policy has the added benefit of providing an incentive to spread one's inheritance among more people, which would further reduce wealth inequalities.

147 Dan Moskowitz, "The 10 Richest People in the World," Investopedia, 1 November 2022, https://www.investopedia.com/articles/investing /012715/5-richest-people-world.asp.

148 An annual wealth tax of 2 per cent on wealth that generates an annual income of 4 per cent would be the same as a 50 per cent tax on capital income (i.e. the 2 per cent tax is 50 per cent of the total return of 4 per cent). Suppose, for example, that a $100 million fortune generates a return of 4 per cent, or $4 million, and this income is taxed at a rate of 75 per cent under a progressive income tax, leaving just

$1 million. In this case, an annual wealth tax of just 1 per cent on the stock of wealth—a further $1 million—would wipe out any income gains.

149 "Ultra-Millionaire Tax," Warren Democrats, accessed 30 July 2022, https://elizabethwarren.com/plans/ultra-millionaire-tax.

150 Saez and Zucman propose a marginal tax rate of 10 per cent on fortunes above $1 billion: *The Triumph of Injustice*, 175. Piketty goes even further, proposing marginal tax rates as high as 60 per cent for the super-rich with 1,000 times the average wealth, or even 90 per cent for those with 10,000 times: *Capital and Ideology*, 982.

151 In theory, wealth taxes should have even less impact than income taxes on labour supply, because they only indirectly affect the return to work—and the evidence largely supports this. The impact on entrepreneurial risk-taking, however, is more uncertain. See Arun Advani and Hannah Tarrant, "Behavioural Responses to a Wealth Tax," Wealth Tax Commission Evidence Paper 5 (October 2020), 22–3, and Scheuer and Slemrod, "Taxing Our Wealth," 219–20.

152 Emmanuel Saez and Gabriel Zucman, "How Would a Progressive Wealth Tax Work? Evidence from the Economics Literature" (February 2019), http://gabriel-zucman.eu/files/saez-zucman-wealth taxobjections.pdf. The authors also argue that wealthy business owners often use their wealth to restrict competition and protect their position, activities that can prevent innovative competitors from having a fair chance.

153 Advani and Tarrant, "Behavioural Responses to a Wealth Tax," 21–2.

154 Most of the response to wealth taxes appears to come through various forms of evasion and avoidance, from under-reporting to offshore evasion and splitting up wealth within families to reduce tax liabilities. See Advani and Tarrant, "Behavioural Responses to a Wealth Tax," 13–21, and Scheuer and Slemrod, "Taxing Our Wealth," 217–23. Of course, it's possible that if we close off opportunities for avoidance, we might see larger reductions in savings or labour supply.

155 Emmanuel Saez and Gabriel Zucman, "Wealth Taxation: Lessons from History and Recent Developments," *AEA Papers and Proceedings* 112 (2022), 58–62.

156 Scheuer and Slemrod, "Taxing Our Wealth," 220; Advani and Tarrant, "Behavioural Responses to a Wealth Tax," 23–5.

157 Under the existing system, the exit tax is calculated as the capital gains tax you would owe if you had sold all your assets on leaving. Elizabeth Warren has proposed a 40 per cent exit tax on net worth above $50 million. See Scheuer and Slemrod, "Taxing Our Wealth," 220.

8. WORKPLACE DEMOCRACY

1 It is often claimed that directors have a legal obligation to maximize profits, or to pursue the interests of shareholders to the exclusion of all else. Strictly speaking, this isn't quite true: even in countries like the UK and U.S.A. that have adopted the shareholder primacy model in its purest form, directors are allowed to give some consideration to the interests of other "stakeholders," including employees. In the UK, for example, while directors' primary responsibility is to advance the interests of shareholders, they are required to do so with "regard" to the interests of employees, suppliers, communities and the environment. But interviews with directors find that most see their role as advancing the interests of shareholders, typically interpreted as maximizing the short-term share price of the firm. See David Collison et al., "Shareholder Primacy in UK Corporate Law: An Exploration of the Rationale and Evidence," Association of Certified Chartered Accountants Research Report no. 125 (September 2011), 5–6.

2 Elizabeth Anderson, *Private Government: How Employers Rule Our Lives (and Why We Don't Talk about It)* (Princeton: Princeton University Press, 2017), 71.

3 David Isaacs, "Perks of Working for Google: A Playground for Grownups," Candor, 4 April 2022, https://candor.co/articles/tech careers/perks-of-working-for-google-a-playground-for-grownups.

4 Eurofound and International Labour Organization, *Working Conditions in a Global Perspective* (Luxembourg: Publications Office of the European Union, 2019), 41.

5 For the UK, see Mathew Lawrence and Clare McNeil, *Fair Shares: Shifting the Balance of Power in the Workplace to Boost Productivity and Pay* (London: Institute for Public Policy Research, 2014), 11; for the U.S., see Kochan et al., "Worker Voice in America," 16.

6 Eurofound, *Sixth European Working Conditions Survey: Overview Report* (Luxembourg: Publications Office of the European Union, 2017), 82–3. In the UK, just 27 per cent of workers in the bottom quarter of earnings feel they have a say over decisions affecting their work, compared to almost 58 per cent of those in the top quarter of earnings. Krishan Shah and Daniel Tomlinson, *Work Experiences* (London: Resolution Foundation, 2021), 6.

7 Francis Green, "Health Effects of Job Insecurity," IZA World of Labor, December 2015, https://doi.org/10.15185/izawol.212; Pierre Bérastégui, "Exposure to Psychosocial Risk Factors in the Gig Economy: A

Systematic Review," European Trade Union Institute Research Paper 2021.01 (January 2021).

8 Zephyr Teachout, "The Boss Will See You Now," *New York Review of Books*, 18 August 2022. For a first-hand account of low-wage work in the UK, including claims of Amazon workers peeing in bottles, see James Bloodworth, *Hired: Six Months Undercover in Low-Wage Britain* (London: Atlantic Books, 2018). Note that Amazon have disputed this claim: see James Vincent, "Amazon Denies Stories of Workers Peeing in Bottles, Receives a Flood of Evidence in Return," *The Verge*, 25 March 2021, https://www.theverge.com/2021/3/25/22350337/amazon-peeingin-bottles-workers-exploitation-twitter-response-evidence.

9 For the UK, see Lawrence and McNeil, *Fair Shares*, 11; for the U.S., see Nicole Maestas et al., "How Americans Perceive the Workplace: Results from the American Working Conditions Survey," RAND Research Brief RB-9972 (August 2017), 30–32.

10 While these questions have been largely absent from "liberal" politics in recent decades, this wasn't always the case. As Stuart White has shown, in a period roughly from 1945 to 1990, the UK's Liberal Party looked at ways to disperse economic power and control as an alternative to the centralizing tendencies of the Labour Party's commitment to public ownership, and the Conservative Party's commitment to shareholder capitalism. One of the leading advocates for these ideas was the economist James Meade, whose work was a major influence on Rawls. See Stuart White, "'Revolutionary Liberalism'? The Philosophy and Politics of Ownership in the Post-War Liberal Party," *British Politics* 4:2 (2009), 164–87.

11 See, for example, Michael J. Sandel, *The Tyranny of Merit: What's Become of the Common Good?* (London: Penguin, 2020); Gene Sperling, *Economic Dignity* (New York: Penguin Press, 2020); Angus Deaton and Anne Case, *Deaths of Despair and the Future of Capitalism* (Princeton: Princeton University Press, 2020).

12 We can also appeal to Rawls's basic liberties principle to make the case for workplace democracy, on the basis that it will help to nurture citizens' moral capacities and foster greater democratic participation. See Martin O'Neill, "Three Rawlsian Routes towards Economic Democracy," *Revue de Philosophie Économique* 9:1 (2008), 29–55. For a discussion of various arguments for and against workplace democracy from a range of philosophical perspectives, see Roberto Frega et al., "Workplace Democracy: The Recent Debate," *Philosophy Compass* 14:4 (2019), e12574.

13 Laura Silver et al., *What Makes Life Meaningful? Views From 17 Advanced Economies* (Washington, DC: Pew Research Center, 2021), 7.

14 Richard Layard, *Can We Be Happier? Evidence and Ethics* (London: Pelican, 2020), 44. Other surveys consistently find that interest, variety and autonomy are among the most important aspects of job quality. See Andrew Clark, "What Makes a Good Job? Job Quality and Job Satisfaction," IZA World of Labor, December 2015, https://doi .org/10.15185/izawol.215, and Jo Ritzen, "Happiness as a Guide to Labor Market Policy," IZA World of Labor, January 2019, https://doi .org/10.15185/izawol.149.

15 How satisfied people are with their work today depends on how you measure it. In one 2017 survey, 34 per cent of Americans said their job gave them a great deal of meaning and fulfilment, and 36 per cent said it gave them some meaning and fulfilment, while 30 per cent found little or no meaning at all. On the other hand, a global survey conducted by Gallup found that just 20 per cent of employees were truly engaged by their jobs, in the sense of being actively committed to their work and workplace. See Sperling, *Dignity*, 225–8.

16 Eurofound, *Sixth European Working Conditions Survey*, 81. A recent study by economists at the LSE found that people who are paid more derive a greater sense of well-being from their work overall, and that once we take these non-monetary rewards into account, inequality is significantly higher than appears to be the case if we only look at earnings. Andrew E. Clark et al., "Beyond Income Inequality: Non-Monetary Rewards to Work," *CentrePiece* 26:2 (2021), 26–8.

17 Samuel Arnold, "The Difference Principle at Work," *Journal of Political Philosophy* 20:1 (2012), 116.

18 This distinction comes from the typology developed by the economist Albert Hirschman in his book *Exit, Voice, and Loyalty: Responses to Decline in Firms, Organizations, and States* (Cambridge, MA: Harvard University Press, 1970).

19 John Rawls, *A Theory of Justice*, revised edition (Cambridge, MA: Harvard University Press, 1999), 464.

20 John Rawls, *Justice as Fairness: A Restatement*, ed. Erin Kelly (Cambridge, MA: Harvard University Press, 2001), 178–9.

21 Employment rights are only as good as their enforcement, which should be the responsibility of public agencies; while individual workers should receive support with the legal costs of taking employers to court. The importance of adequate legal support is underscored by the recent experience in the UK, where the introduction of employment

tribunal fees in 2017 was followed by a 70 per cent decline in cases, leading the Supreme Court to rule that these fees represented an unlawful obstruction to justice. See Abi Adams and Jeremias Prassl, "Vexatious Claims: Challenging the Case for Employment Tribunal Fees," *Modern Law Review* 80:3 (2017), 412–42.

22 Anderson, *Private Government*, 38–40.

23 Trades Union Congress, *I'll Be Watching You: A Report on Workplace Monitoring* (London: Trades Union Congress, 2018).

24 There is a separate question about the extent to which individual employers should have to cover the costs of these entitlements. As we saw in Chapter 6, the state should generally pay for parental leave so as to prevent discrimination against potential parents (especially mothers), but it seems reasonable for employers to cover the cost of paid holiday as part of their wage bill. For a thoughtful discussion of these issues, see Cynthia Estlund, "What Should We Do after Work: Automation and Employment," *Yale Law Journal* 128:2 (2018), 301–24.

25 Ritzen, "Happiness as a Guide to Labor Market Policy." See also Clark, "What Makes a Good Job?"

26 Green, "Health Effects of Job Insecurity."

27 As we saw in Chapter 1, the right to "own" personal property—or more specifically, to have extensive and largely exclusive control rights over it—is a basic liberty, because having this control is essential for living a free and independent life. What counts as "personal property" in the relevant sense depends on what we consider to be necessary for developing and exercising the "moral powers" that we discussed in detail in Chapter 1.

28 This is really an argument for combining income and control rights in the *same* hands. They could be shareholders," but as we shall see, they could just as easily be those of workers in a cooperative.

29 For a detailed history of co-determination in Germany, see John T. Addison, *The Economics of Codetermination: Lessons from the German Experience* (New York: Palgrave Macmillan, 2009), 5–26.

30 Piketty, *Capital and Ideology*, 495–505.

31 A growing number of countries, mostly in Europe, either allow or require firms to adopt a two-tier board structure, combining a supervisory board responsible for long-term strategic choices with a management board responsible for operational decisions. For the purposes of this discussion, "board" refers to supervisory boards, since this is where worker representatives should generally sit, as they do in Germany.

32 In most companies in Germany with more than 2,000 workers, the chairperson is elected by shareholders and has an additional deciding vote in the case of a deadlock. But in the coal, iron and steel sectors, the deciding vote is in the hands of a neutral external chairperson approved by both workers and owners. For details of the German system, see Lionel Fulton, "Codetermination in Germany: A Beginner's Guide," Institute for Codetermination and Corporate Governance, Hans-Böckler-Stiftung, Mitbestimmungspraxis no. 32 (July 2020).

33 Three other countries—Slovenia, Slovakia and the Czech Republic— allow but do not require firms to reserve half of the seats on their board for worker representatives. See Aline Conchon, "Board-Level Employee Representation Rights in Europe," European Trade Union Institute Research Paper 121 (November 2011), 12–13.

34 For an overview, see ibid. These rights generally apply to all companies that exceed the relevant size threshold, though in a few countries they apply only to publicly listed companies (whose shares are traded freely on a public stock exchange).

35 The following description of the German works council model draws on Addison, *The Economics of Codetermination*, 14–23.

36 For a recent comprehensive review of the literature on co-management, including both board-level representation and works councils, see Simon Jäger et al., "What Does Codetermination Do?," *ILR Review* 75:4 (2022), 857–90. See also Werner Nienhüser, "Works Councils," in Adrian Wilkinson et al. (eds.), *Handbook of Research on Employee Voice* (Cheltenham: Edward Elgar Publishing, 2014), 247–63; Olaf Hübler, "Do Works Councils Raise or Lower Firm Productivity?," IZA World of Labor, March 2015, https://doi.org/10.15185 /izawol.137; and Conchon, "Board-Level Employee Representation Rights in Europe."

37 The study in Finland is Jarkko Harju et al., "Voice at Work," National Bureau of Economic Research Working Paper 28522 (November 2021); while the German study is Simon Jäger et al., "Labor in the Boardroom," *Quarterly Journal of Economics* 136:2 (2021), 669–725.

38 The limited effect on wages partly reflects the fact that, in most countries with co-management, works councils are not permitted to engage directly in wage bargaining, which tends to be the preserve of trade unions, and is organized at the sector rather than the firm level. See Jäger et al., "What Does Codetermination Do?," 865.

39 In an influential paper, the economists Michael Jensen and William Meckling argued that giving workers more power would lead to a process whereby they would "begin 'eating it [the firm] up,'" and that this

would make it hard for firms to raise new investment, causing "a significant reduction in the country's capital stock, increased unemployment, reduced labor income, and an overall reduction in output and welfare." See Michael C. Jensen and William H. Meckling, "Rights and Production Functions: An Application to Labor-Managed Firms and Codetermination," *The Journal of Business* 52:4 (1979), 504.

40 A comprehensive review conducted by economists at MIT and Berkeley in 2021 concluded that co-management "is a broadly benign institution from the perspective of firm performance," with "largely zero or small positive effects" across a variety of measures: Jäger et al., "What Does Codetermination Do?," 869, 884.

41 Jäger et al., "Labor in the Boardroom."

42 Jäger et al., "What Does Codetermination Do?," 868–9.

43 Addison, *The Economics of Codetermination*, 27–40.

44 In 2019, for example, the "Business Roundtable"—a group comprising the CEOs of America's largest and most powerful corporations—officially rejected its commitment to the shareholder model in favour of the so-called "stakeholder model," where firms would be encouraged to consider the interests not just of workers, but of customers, suppliers and local communities too: see Business Roundtable, "Statement on the Purpose of a Corporation," Business Roundtable, 19 August 2019, https://opportunity.businessroundtable.org/ourcommitment/. For a powerful academic critique of the shareholder model, and a proposal for how we can get companies to focus on "purpose" rather than profit, see Colin Mayer, *Prosperity: Better Business Makes the Greater Good* (Oxford: Oxford University Press, 2018). While there is increasing interest in "stakeholder capitalism" and in "purpose driven" companies, most practical proposals focus on changing the legal mandate of directors. This would be a step in the right direction, but if we really want directors to act on the interests of other stakeholders then we need to give the latter a meaningful mechanism for holding the former to account. At least for workers, this is best achieved by giving them the right to elect directors in the first place.

45 Marcus Lu, "Long-Term Investing: What Are the Reasons behind Its Decline?," World Economic Forum, 17 December 2021, https://www.weforum.org/agenda/2021/12/long-term-investing-decline/. In principle, shareholders have an incentive to take a long-term perspective even if they hold shares only for a short period of time, because the future benefits of investments should be reflected in higher share prices today. But this is often not the case in practice. For an overview

of the challenges of investors' short-termism in a UK context, see John Kay, *The Kay Review of UK Equity Markets and Long-Term Decision Making* (London: Her Majesty's Stationery Office, 2012).

46 Piketty calls for a similar model, with half of the seats on boards to be reserved for workers in all private firms, both big and small. See Piketty, *Capital and Ideology*, 973.

47 With an equal share of seats on the board, the question of who has the deciding vote in the case of deadlock takes on crucial importance. If we want true co-management, then the chair should be independent, or jointly agreed on by employee and shareholder representatives, as in the largest German firms in the coal, iron and steel industries (see n. 32 above).

48 As things stand, even in European countries with a degree of co-management workers' authority is actually quite limited. Surveys of both employee representatives and managers find that workers have only a moderate degree of influence over working conditions, more limited influence over job security or wages, and almost no influence whatsoever on wider questions of corporate strategy. Jäger et al., "What Does Codetermination Do?," 874–7. See also Michael Gold and Jeremy Waddington, "Introduction: Board-Level Employee Representation in Europe: State of Play," *European Journal of Industrial Relations* 25:3 (2019), 205–18.

49 Piketty, *Capital and Ideology*, 510.

50 Isabelle Ferreras, *Firms as Political Entities: Saving Democracy through Economic Bicameralism* (Cambridge: Cambridge University Press, 2017).

51 For a discussion of how co-management fits within the wider institutions and culture of industrial relations, see Jäger et al., "What Does Codetermination Do?," 877–9.

52 The difference between Anglophone countries and continental Europe has not always been so stark. In fact, a report commissioned by the Labour Prime Minister Harold Wilson in 1977 recommended giving workers half the seats on the boards of large companies in the UK. See Piketty, *Capital and Ideology*, 508–9.

53 The studies that do exist of companies with the most extensive forms of co-management are reassuring, but they are inevitably limited to large German firms and, in the case of full parity on boards (where the chair is neutral), to the coal, iron and steel sectors. See Kerstin Lopatta et al., "Parity Codetermination at the Board Level and Labor Investment Efficiency: Evidence on German Listed Firms," *Journal of Business Economics and Management* 90:1 (2020), 57–108, and

Kerstin Lopatta et al., "When Labor Representatives Join Supervisory Boards: Empirical Evidence of the Relationship between the Change to Parity Codetermination and Working Capital and Operating Cash Flows," *Journal of Business Economics and Management* 88:1 (2018), 1–39.

54 Employees typically have individual share accounts and can cash out their shares when they leave their firm or retire. Crucially, the law requires that all employees are included in the ESOP, with the value of individual share accounts typically based on wages or seniority. For an overview of the American experience with employee share ownership, see Joseph Blasi, "Broad-Based Employee Stock Ownership and Profit Sharing: History, Evidence, and Policy Implications," *Journal of Participation and Employee Ownership* 1:1 (2018), 38–60; and, for a book-length treatment, see Joseph R. Blasi et al., *The Citizen's Share: Reducing Inequality in the 21st Century* (New Haven: Yale University Press, 2014).

55 Douglas Kruse, "Does Employee Ownership Improve Performance?," IZA World of Labor, May 2022, https://doi.org/10.15185/izawol.311. For the latest European data, see Eurofound, *Sixth European Working Conditions Survey*, 99.

56 Cyprien Batut and Chakir Rachiq, "Employee Financial Participation Schemes in France and Europe," Ministry of Economy and Finance, Trésor-Economics no. 281 (June 2021), 2–3. Across Europe as a whole, around 13 per cent of employees participate in some kind of profit-sharing scheme: Eurofound, *Sixth European Working Conditions Survey*, 99.

57 Douglas Kruse, "Does Employee Ownership Improve Performance?" While they may increase total income, especially for the lowest-paid, the overall impact on inequality is likely to be modest. See Jared Bernstein, *Employee Ownership, ESOPs, Wealth, and Wages* (Washington, DC: Employee-Owned S Corporations of America, 2016).

58 Kruse, "Does Employee Ownership Improve Performance?" The positive effects of these kinds of schemes are "usually of the order of 2 per cent to 5 per cent," while "meaningful profit-sharing generally has larger effects on output than employee stock ownership": Joseph R. Blasi et al., "Evidence: What the U.S. Research Shows about Worker Ownership," in Jonathan Michie et al. (eds.), *The Oxford Handbook of Mutual, Co-Operative, and Co-Owned Business* (Oxford: Oxford University Press, 2017), 212. Hristos Doucouliagos et al., "Is Profit Sharing Productive? A Meta-Regression Analysis," *British Journal of Industrial Relations* 58:2 (2020), 364–95.

59 Blasi, "Broad-Based Employee Stock Ownership and Profit Sharing," 45–7.

60 Ibid., 46.

61 See Gregory K. Dow, *Governing the Firm: Workers' Control in Theory and Practice* (Cambridge: Cambridge University Press, 2003), 80.

62 The fact that most firms are controlled by investors rather than by workers is one of the most striking features of most market economies, and yet there is no settled explanation within economics about why this should be so. In fact, this question has been largely ignored by mainstream economists. See Dow, *Governing the Firm*, 1–2.

63 Strictly speaking, worker cooperatives are merely one kind of "labour-managed firm." The defining feature of a labour-managed firm is that control rights are allocated on the basis of who provides labour, in contrast to a "capital-managed firm," where control is allocated on the basis of who provides capital (as with conventional firms owned and controlled by shareholders). A cooperative is typically defined as a company in which each worker has an equal share of control: in other words, "one worker, one vote." But a labour-managed firm could, theoretically, allocate control rights in proportion to the value of someone's labour contribution, as measured by their salary. Note that the idea of a labour-managed firm is separate from the idea of employee ownership: in principle, all the owners of a firm could be employees, but if control is allocated in proportion to how much capital each has invested in the firm, this would count as a capital-managed rather than a labour-managed firm. For a discussion see Dow, *Governing the Firm*, 101–7.

64 Georgeanne M. Artz and Younjun Kim, "Business Ownership by Workers: Are Worker Cooperatives a Viable Option?," Iowa State University Working Paper no. 11020 (November 2011), 2.

65 This makes Suma the largest equal-pay worker co-op in Europe. See "Our Co-op," Suma, accessed 10 November 2022, https://www.suma .coop/about/our-co-op/.

66 Most research on worker cooperatives has focused on measures of company performance, and surprisingly little attention has been paid to the implications for workers. When researchers have looked at the latter, the emphasis has been on wages, job security and staff turnover, rather than on job quality or well-being. For a summary of the available evidence, see Gregory K. Dow, *The Labor-Managed Firm: Theoretical Foundations* (Cambridge: Cambridge University Press, 2018), 85–101; Virginie Pérotin, *What Do We Really Know about Workers' Co-Operatives?* (Manchester: Co-operatives UK, 2018),

19; and Artz and Kim, "Business Ownership by Workers," 21–2. There is, however, much more research looking at forms of partial employee ownership, such as ESOPs in the U.S.A., the key findings of which are summarized in Blasi et al., "Evidence: What the U.S. Research Shows about Worker Ownership." In the absence of studies which focus specifically on worker cooperatives, it seems reasonable to extrapolate the findings from this literature and apply them to co-ops.

67 For a detailed review of the evidence, see Dow, *The Labor-Managed Firm*, 85–115, and Pérotin, *What Do We Really Know about Workers' Co-Operatives?*

68 "About Us," Mondragon, accessed 2 August 2022, https://www .mondragon-corporation.com/en/about-us/.

69 At its height in the 1980s, the Lega accounted for 12.5 per cent of GDP in its home region, and was Italy's fourth largest exporter. Labour Party, *Alternative Models of Ownership* (London: Labour Party, 2017), 16.

70 Rawls asked the same question in relation to John Stuart Mill's prediction that worker cooperatives would come to dominate over conventional companies, but didn't hazard an answer: Rawls, *Justice as Fairness*, 178.

71 Labour Party, *Alternative Models of Ownership*, 12.

72 Democracy at Work Institute, "Press Kit, 2015" (December 2014), https://institute.coop/sites/default/files/PressKit_1.pdf.

73 Dow, *The Labor-Managed Firm*, 88; Pérotin, *What Do We Really Know about Workers' Co-Operatives?*, 5.

74 Dow, *The Labor-Managed Firm*, 102.

75 The following discussion draws heavily on Dow, *Governing the Firm*, 165–256.

76 Dow argues that the distinctive challenges faced by cooperatives compared to conventional firms can ultimately be traced back to the fact that labour is inalienable, while capital is not. See Dow, *Governing the Firm*, 234–59.

77 The following discussion draws on the proposals put forward in Dow, *The Labor-Managed Firm*, 372–88, and Dow, *Governing the Firm*, 260–90.

78 Pérotin, *What Do We Really Know about Workers' Co-Operatives?*, 18.

79 Dow, *Governing the Firm*, 65.

80 Ibid.

81 For a similar idea, see the proposal for a "Co-operative Development Agency" in Mathew Lawrence et al., *Co-Operatives Unleashed:*

Doubling the Size of the UK's Co-Operative Sector (London: New Economics Foundation, 2018), 37–9.

82 Certain other events could also automatically trigger an employee referendum on whether to initiate a buyout, including a proposed acquisition by another firm, being listed on a public stock exchange, or a significant plant closure.

83 For a more detailed proposal about how employee buyouts could work, including the process for financing them, see Dow, *Governing the Firm*, 260–90.

84 This is also essential so that entrepreneurs can secure "equity" investment by selling shares. We would also need to protect the interests of shareholders during the transition: for example, they could continue to have 50 per cent of the overall voting rights, or a veto over certain decisions even as the fraction of shares owned by workers increased beyond this point, otherwise they might reasonably worry that workers would stop taking their interests seriously. See Dow, *Governing the Firm*, 273–6.

CONCLUSION

1 Oscar Wilde, "The Soul of Man under Socialism," *Fortnightly Review*, 49:290 (1891), 303–4.

2 This paraphrases Rousseau's claim in the opening to his book *The Social Contract* to be "taking men as they are and laws as they might be." See John Rawls, *The Law of Peoples* (Cambridge, MA: Harvard University Press, 1999), 11–13.

3 Gramsci wrote his famous phrase in 1930 while in prison, having been arrested by the Italian Fascist regime. *Selections from the Prison Notebooks of Antonio Gramsci*, ed. and trans. Quintin Hoare and Geoffrey Nowell-Smith (London: Lawrence & Wishart, 1971), 276.

4 It's important not to understate the current threat to liberal democracy. But as we saw in Chapters 4 and 5, for all the debates about the "culture wars," in most countries attitudes towards questions about religion, race, gender and sexuality are more "liberal" than ever, and most people still want to live in a democracy. This isn't a given: if we continue to drift, more people will start to question or even abandon these values, and we may well pass a point of no return. But if we act now, we can at least draw hope from the fact that values such as fairness, freedom and equality, which are the basis for Rawls's theory, have deep roots in our public culture.

5 This closely paraphrases Sebastian Jobelius and Konstantin Voessing, "Social Democracy, Party of Values," *Renewal* 28:3 (2020), 55.

6 Jan-Werner Müller, *Democracy Rules* (London: Penguin, 2021), 98.

7 Jobelius and Voessing, "Social Democracy, Party of Values," 55–6.

AFTERWORD: FROM WHAT TO HOW

1 Across Western Europe as a whole, the vote share of "social democratic" parties fell from a high of just over 30 per cent in the mid-1990s to around 18 per cent in 2020. See Tarik Abou-Chadi et al., *Left behind by the Working Class? Social Democracy's Electoral Crisis and the Rise of the Radical Right* (Berlin: Friedrich-Ebert-Stiftung, 2021), 4–5. See also Giacomo Benedetto et al., "The Rise and Fall of Social Democracy, 1918–2017," *American Political Science Review* 114:3 (2020), 928–39. While the 2019 election was Labour's worst since 1935 in terms of seats, its share of the vote (32.2 per cent) was still higher than in the 2010 (29 per cent) and 2015 (30.4 per cent) general elections. "Share of Votes in General Elections in the United Kingdom from 1918 to 2019, by Political Party," *Statista*, 13 December 2019 (accessed 27 October 2023), https://www.statista.com /statistics/717004/general-elections-vote-share-byparty-uk/.

2 Amory Gethin et al., "Brahmin Left Versus Merchant Right: Changing Political Cleavages in 21 Western Democracies, 1948–2020," *Quarterly Journal of Economics* 137:1 (2021), 1–48.

3 Diego Garzia et al., "Partisan Dealignment and the Personalisation of Politics in West European Parliamentary Democracies, 1961–2018," *West European Politics* 45:2 (2022), 317–18; "Most Volatile British Electorate in Modern Times," British Election Study, 8 October 2019, https://www.britishelectionstudy.com/bes-resources /press-releasemost-volatile-british-electorate-in-modern-times/.

4 Claire Ainsley, *The New Working Class: How to Win Hearts, Minds and Votes* (Bristol: Policy Press, 2018), 31–49.

5 Abou-Chadi et al., *Left behind by the Working Class?*, 22–5; Johannes Karreth et al., "Catchall or Catch and Release? The Electoral Consequences of Social Democratic Parties' March to the Middle in Western Europe," *Comparative Political Studies* 46:7 (2013), 791–822.

6 Richard Wike et al., *Citizens in Advanced Economies Want Significant Changes to Their Political Systems* (Washington, DC: Pew Research Center, 2021), 3.

7 Other progressive thinkers have also argued for a pragmatic and experimental approach, including Roberto Mangabeira Unger, *What*

Should the Left Propose? (London: Verso, 2005); Axel Honneth, *The Idea of Socialism: Towards a Policy of Renewal*, trans. Joseph Ganahl (Cambridge: Polity Press, 2017); and Erik Olin Wright, *Envisioning Real Utopias* (London: Verso, 2010).

8 Mark Engler and Paul Engler, "André Gorz's Non-Reformist Reforms Show How We Can Transform the World Today," *Jacobin*, 22 July 2021.

9 R. S. Foa et al., *Youth and Satisfaction with Democracy* (Cambridge: Centre for the Future of Democracy, 2020), 23–4.

10 Bobby Duffy et al., "The 'Fault Lines' in the UK's Culture Wars (London: The Policy Institute at Kings College London, 2021), 8–9.

11 John Rawls, *Justice as Fairness: A Restatement*, ed. Erin Kelly (Cambridge, MA: Harvard University Press, 2001), 30.

12 The label "tribalism" is proposed by Susan Neiman, *Left Is Not Woke* (Cambridge: Polity Press, 2023), 20.

13 Kenan Malik, *Not So Black and White: A History of Race from White Supremacy to Identity Politics* (London: C. Hurst & Co., 2023).

14 Neiman, *Left Is Not Woke*, 11–56; and Malik, *Not So Black and White*, especially 235–93.

15 For a detailed discussion of the Haitian Revolution, see Malik, *Not So Black and White*, 141–70. For the transcript of King's "I have a dream" speech, see "Read Martin Luther King Jr.'s 'I Have a Dream' Speech in Its Entirety," *NPR*, 18 January 2010, https://www.npr .org/2010/01/18/122701268/i-have-a-dream-speech-in-its-entirety.

16 Malik, *Not So Black and White*, 260.

17 Neiman, *Left Is Not* Woke, 92–126; Malik, *Not So Black and White*, especially 243–6.

18 OECD, *Does Inequality Matter? How People Perceive Economic Disparities and Social Mobility* (Paris: OECD, 2021), 14.

19 Bandau describes this as the "neoliberal contamination hypothesis," in Frank Bandau, "The Electoral Crisis of Social Democracy," *Political Studies Review* 20:3 (2022), 493–503. For data on the decline in turnout among lower-income voters, see Thomas Piketty, *Capital and Ideology*, trans. Arthur Goldhammer (Cambridge, MA: Harvard University Press, 2020), 741.

20 Sheri Berman and Maria Snegovaya, "Populism and the Decline of Social Democracy," *Journal of Democracy* 30:3 (2019), 5–19.

21 According to Tarik Abou-Chadi and Markus Wagner, an "investment oriented" economic strategy focused on increasing economic participation and productivity is more likely to attract a cross-class coalition than a "consumption-oriented" one focused on redistribution, as long as trade unions are not opposed. See Tarik Abou-Chadi and Markus

Wagner, "The Electoral Appeal of Party Strategies in Postindustrial Societies: When Can the Mainstream Left Succeed?," *Journal of Politics* 81:4 (2019), 1405–19.

22 For a description and critique of this narrative, see Abou-Chadi et al., *Left behind by the Working Class?*

23 Ibid., 19–21.

24 A recent study of ten European nations found that workers in manufacturing and service industries were significantly more likely to believe that their country's culture has been enhanced rather than undermined by immigration, and that more than 75 per cent of them believed that gays and lesbians should be free to live as they wish. See Abou-Chadi et al., *Left behind by the Working Class?*, 11–15. On gender, taking the UK as an example, while those with lower incomes and education are more likely to endorse traditional gender roles, even among this group such views are in the minority. See "Gender: New Consensus or Continuing Battleground?," in D. Phillips et al., *British Social Attitudes 35* (London: National Centre for Social Research, 2018), 8. On race, see Nancy Kelley et al., *Racial Prejudice in Britain Today* (London: NatCen Social Research and Runnymede Trust, 2017).

25 Abou-Chadi et al., *Left behind by the Working Class?*, 22–5; Tarik Abou-Chadi and Markus Wagner, "Electoral Fortunes of Social Democratic Parties: Do Second Dimension Positions Matter?," *Journal of European Public Policy* 27:2 (2020), 246–72.

26 See, for example, Sunder Katwala, *Culture Clash: Bridging Our Divides* (London: Labour Together/British Future, 2023); Luke Tryl et al., *Dousing the Flames: How Leaders Can Better Navigate Cultural Change in 2020s Britain* (London: More in Common, 2021); Stephen Hawkins et al., *Hidden Tribes: A Study of America's Polarized Landscape* (New York: More in Common, 2018).

INDEX

A NOTE ABOUT THE AUTHOR

Daniel Chandler is an economist and philosopher based at the London School of Economics, where he is Research Director of the Programme on Cohesive Capitalism. He has degrees in economics, philosophy and history from Cambridge and the LSE, and was awarded a Henry Fellowship at Harvard, where he studied under Amartya Sen. He has worked in the British government as a policy advisor in the Prime Minister's Strategy Unit and Deputy Prime Minister's Office, and as a researcher at think tanks, including the Resolution Foundation and Institute for Fiscal Studies.

A NOTE ON THE TYPE

This book was set in Minion, a typeface produced by the Adobe Corporation specifically for the Macintosh personal computer and released in 1990. Designed by Robert Slimbach, Minion combines the classic characteristics of old-style faces with the full complement of weights required for modern typesetting.

Typeset by North Market Street Graphics,
Lancaster, Pennsylvania

Printed and bound by Lakeside Book Company,
Harrisonburg, Virginia